Open Wounds

A Native American Heritage

by

Aleksandra Ziolkowska-Boehm

December 2009,
Wilmington,
Delaware

For Lee
hoping you will enjoy
my newest book —
Aleksandra Ziolkowska-
Boehm

Nemsi Books - rev. 08/25/2009

Published in Pierpont, South Dakota

Acknowledgements

The publisher and author wish to acknowledge with thanks the support of Homer Flute - member of the Apache Tribe of Oklahoma, Chief Executive Officer/Trustee of the SCMD Trust, a Native American nonprofit organization.

Photographs by:
Aleksandra Ziolkowska-Boehm,
Norman Boehm,
Bill Groethe,
Michelle Bishop,
Andrzej Bernat (Author's back cover photo)

Special thanks to:
National Archives Collection, College Park, Maryland
Crazy Horse Memorial, South Dakota
Oklahoma Today
The Morning Star, Volume 46 Number 4 Fall 2008
AnthroNotes, Volume 25 Number 1 Spring 2004

Foreword

Aleksandra Ziolkowska-Boehm started her first travels in the United States and Canada in the 1980's. Later, since 1990, she has resided in the United States and continued to write. In her earlier books about America, she had presented her interest in old and new cultures of North American Indians. The result of many visits to Indian reservations is her book "Open Wounds - A Native American Heritage" totally dedicated to Native Americans.

The book is presented in literary reportage that was created from the author's confrontation with the reality of American Indians. The subject is broad, and time was not restrictive, since the book was written over a ten-year period. Old photographs of great value and modern pictures illustrate the book. "Open Wounds – the Native American Heritage" is not only the result of curiosity of the Indian world, but a try of deeper penetration to understand the problems that are facing modern Indians. What is more, the author does not stop with a critique of the current situation but tries to look for the recipe for resolution and salvation. Her attempts are shown particularly in the second part of the book, where interviews are recorded with authors who know about Indians, as well as with Indians themselves, such as Northern Cheyenne, Apache, Kiowa and Chickasaw. Giving voice to the Indians, the people the book is about, is for sure a great attribute of Ziolkowska-Boehm's book.

Concrete examples by the author show how the politics of the American government in the past have lead to sad social and economical situations under which many Indian tribes now exist. Pushing Indians onto barren reservations, pillaging their land, broken treaties, trying to make farmers from nomads and hunters, schools with dormitories where the Indian children were kept far away from parents and forbidden to use their own language, are only a few examples that the author gives in chapters, like "Sadness of reservations" and "Bitter recollections of Indian schools".

Not minimized is the negative involvement of the American government whom the author blames for the current situation. She not only blames American politics but also the often mistaken writing and reporting about Indians by American writers. The writer shows, with all due respect and good feelings for the Native people of the American continent, that blame for "stagnation and sadness of reservations" also rests in part with the Indians themselves due to their lack of willingness to decide on firm steps and action to resolve their crises. It, of course, pushes one to think about, and diminish the stereotype opinion that all the blame is on white people only.

It is not the only stereotype that the author alerts her readers of in her book. The writer shows many examples, and among them the Sioux Pine Ridge Reservation in South Dakota, where most of the homes do not have running water or a sewage system, and where everywhere there is great poverty. Ziolkowska-Boehm also describes the reservations in Texas and California, where some tribes use their potential that is given to them by American law, where they reach a substantial wealth by building casinos, that on the reservations are free from income taxes. Casinos are able to finance many ambitious things, such as building schools, hospitals, and culture centers. On one hand, she tells about speeding, alcoholism, crime and unemployment among Indians; on the other hand, she shows the people of Indian origin who are scientists, artists and businessmen.

Showing such contrasts is a great feature of the book, in which two faces of Indian America are shown. It is also an attempt to focus on different tribes, which are now over a few hundred, and which are different by customs, language and beliefs.

The writer also shows that Indians had a rational influence on the building of American society, and they are not only "a race disappearing into the past". For example, the American Constitution was based on some principles and laws of the Iroquois Confederacy. One of the chapters shows the subject popularized by the movie *Windtalkers*, the Indian code talkers, that in many ways greatly helped the Americans achieve victory in the Pacific during WWII. The Japanese never broke the code, which was mainly based on the Navajo and Comanche languages.

Indians, the writer seems to show, balance on the edge of two worlds, the world of old tradition and beliefs, customs and the world of modern works with all its good and bad. In such a context, the writer shows the problem of identity of Indians tribes based on, for example, of disappearing of tribal languages and even the description of Indians. Now, for political correctness in the United States, they are named as *Native Americans* or *American Indians*. The Indians themselves prefer to be called by the names of their tribes, as one who belongs to the Apache tribe, to be called simply Apache, not Native American. Now, the Indians feel and consider themselves as separate nations, not tribes.

In "Trouble with identity", the author calls attention to the greatly discussed subject of the return to American Indians of their artifacts, belongings and goods. The possessions were part of graves or did have a special meaning in traditional Indian customs, and they were taken from graves by archeologists and anthropologists of the nineteenth century. The issue creates a lot of emotion, but it has to be stressed that modern American law is on the Indians' side in their efforts to retrieve these possessions.

One of the first chapters tells the story of the sculptor, Korczak Ziolkowski, from the family of the writer. After WWII, he started to sculpt a mountain in South Dakota. Sioux chiefs had asked him to sculpt the great chief Crazy Horse who was one of the warriors in the Battle of the Little Big Horn in 1876, when the Indians defeated American cavalry commanded by General George A.

Custer. Crazy Horse is the largest sculpture in the world, after Korczak's death his family continues his work, and the project includes an Indian Cultural center.

Summarizing, it has to be emphasized that the writer with clear and picturesque language was able to show the reader the things that are difficult for the whole of American society, which is still existing, with an open wound of injustice done to the Indians. It also seems that Ziolkowska-Boehm does not want to "scratch the surface" of the wound, but she looks for solutions to make the situation better for modern Indians, but she does not forget about their history. The whites and Indians created what is now one country, and the book describes the coexistence of both worlds. It is up to both sides to determine which way they will choose to go.

Radoslaw Palonka,
Jagiellonian University, Krakow, Poland.
Fulbright visiting scholar at Arizona State University,
participant at the archeological works in Mesa Verde, Colorado.

Content

I dedicate this book to my husband Norman who always encouraged me, kept the passion and faith that I could do it. I would like to thank him for his help, patience, generosity and heart shown to me and to American Indians.

Motto

There is a story of the Cherokee Indians, about an elderly Indian who speaks to his grandson about the good and the bad. The elder says that in each person there are two wolves fighting with each other.
One is characterized by anger, jealousy, arrogance, materialism, pride and other negative feelings.
The second wolf represents joy, piece, love, hope, calm, modesty, cordiality, generosity, and other positive feelings.
The grandson thought for a while, and then asked:
Grandpa, which wolf is going to win?
The one you will feed, answered the grandfather.

Introduction

"You write about Indians?...And with such a passion you talk about them?... You know, when I was growing up, Indians were considered as 'something worse'. Even as children, we didn't have contacts with the same age group as our peers", Clint Hern told me.

Clint was born and reared on a farm in South Dakota. He graduated from the South Dakota School of Mines with a degree in chemical engineering. In his house in Texas, a map of the world hangs upon a wall, studded with markers that indicate all the places he had visited. There were many of them. Clint and Norman both worked for Aramco (Arabian American Oil Company) in Saudi Arabia. Did the world give him a broad perspective?

Norman was born in the State of New Jersey, traveling to North Dakota to study chemical engineering at the University of North Dakota in Grand Forks. He told me that, after crossing the bridge over the Red River between Grand Forks in North Dakota and East Grand Forks in Minnesota, he passed taverns...one after the other. There were many of them, but could just anyone stop there and drink a refreshing beer and enjoy a meal? There were signs posted in every window that stated "No Mexicans, No Indians".

African-Americans were rarely seen in the Dakotas. The occasional one that the inhabitants of the Dakotas might see was a "porter" on a train of the Great Northern Railroad.

For Norman, reared on the East Coast, such sights and words were not known. When he was a young boy, he remembers playing "Cowboys and Indians", and he always wanted to be an Indian. He held a special esteem for them. He does not know if he would have such feelings had he been born and grown up not far from a reservation in Montana or in one of the Dakotas. We both believe, fervently, that his parents raised him in such a manner that he would still have his respect for Indians.

I did not have an occasion to ask the people reared in Montana or the Dakotas, if they wanted to be an Indian when they were young children playing "Cowboys and Indians". I think that Clint Hern would have wanted to be a cowboy.

Norman's other friend, Clarence "Casey" Emerson, who also studied at the University of North Dakota and in later years achieved the respectful position of state representative, told me that the closer people lived to the reservation, the more contempt they had for the Indians.

A friend of ours from Montana, of the Northern Cheyenne tribe, who grew up in the mid 1970's told us, that as a young boy, he remembers listening to white peoples' stories about "stupid and dirty

Indians". Usually these stories were about the Crow Indians whose reservation was close by. He recalls coming back home humiliated and crying and saying to his grandfather: - "But we are Cheyenne, we are not Crow...I am happy we are not Crow"...

It was like that in the mid 1970's, but in 2006 Ann Coulter, a well-known Republican whose statements are almost scandalous, has not once spoken publicly about Indians with any respect or regard. At times, I have thought that the lobby of the American Indians (the first Americans) is not big, since there were few, if any, publicized media reports of organized demonstrations or protests, as usually happens in the cases of a few organized and influential ethnic groups in the United States. Indians penned the only written protests one might read in obscure magazines or newspapers, hence those who listen to Ann Coulter's remarks do not hear or know of Indian reactions to her words.

I am aware that the farther away someone is from another culture, the easier it is to be influenced by the romantic ideas of that culture. In 1985, I was talking to a young American couple I met in Rapid City, South Dakota. They had moved there from the South because they had "such a special feeling towards American Indians". After ten years, they wanted to move away, because, as they said, they were disillusioned.

On the other hand, Dave Charpentier from Minnesota, a teacher at the St. Labre Indian School on the Northern Cheyenne Reservation in eastern Montana, feels accomplished and happy that he can work for the Indians (my conversation with him is included later in this book).

Two of our close neighbors in Delaware told us they were of Indian origin, but they did not tell us so when we first met. Instead they revealed this only when they heard us talking with such passion about the Native Americans.

Many of my American friends know about Indians the same as, for example, my Polish friends. They do not know much. They remember or have some recollection of a few movies, or some notes in the daily press. For many years, this was also true for me. I noticed that my photographs of dancing Indians in their native attire at a "pow-wow" are the most convincing proof that I am involved with such a subject matter. Such evidence does not evoke a discussion, because the majority thinks that it is "a dead culture".

My first awareness of the American Indians was most likely due to books and movies, as is the case with most people. My father, Henryk Ziolkowski, always gave me books to read, which he considered: "according to my age group". Thanks to him, I read the beautiful books of James Fenimore Cooper or the popular "story teller" Karl May. That German writer formulated his books while in prison and made the characters so popular, that a good part of the world loved the precious Apache chief, Winnetou, or his white friend, Old Shatterhand.

Kora, Unkas, Chingachgook were dear friends in my home. My father gave us – my two brothers, Henryk and Krzysztof - and I special passes to the cinema. Every week, we went to see a new movie. Then, there was an epoch of westerns - westerns that symbolized America: "High Noon, "From Hell to Texas", "3:10 PM to Yuma", "Rio Bravo", "Duel in the Sun". In my early youth, I saw so many westerns, that now when I can see them again on Turner Classic Movies or American Movie Classics, Norman and our friends are surprised that I saw those movies a long time ago in Poland, and that I remember them so well.

For sure, these westerns influenced my feelings about Indians.

In my family, stories were repeatedly heard about my grandfather's nephew, Korczak Ziolkowski, the sculptor from South Dakota, whose parents, Anna and Józef Ziolkowski immigrated to the United States, and when he was a little boy they died tragically. America and Korczak were far away, and our everyday difficulties occupied our time. There were no plans to visit or to even go to America…nothing like this was even contemplated. In my house, everybody was interested in Polish history, and my father encouraged us to read historical books. The writers, like Henryk Sienkiewicz, Melchior Wankowicz, Aleksander Kaminski and the like were well read. We have contacts with Aleksander Kaminski, who after World War II, moved to Lodz. We all loved his book about the Warsaw Uprising in 1944. The young peoples' bravery and dedication touched our hearts and minds. It was more familiar and real than the far away American Indians.

I remember reading the book of Konrad Lorenz (1903-1989), the Austrian scientist and Nobel Prize winner, who wrote about the aggressiveness of the American Indians. I was moved by his description of the Ute tribe. Lorenz quoted the work of the psychiatrist from Denver, Colorado, Sidney Margolin. The scientist proved that American Indians living on the reservations suffer from a huge amount of aggressions. They live in regular surroundings and are suffering a neurosis not so common among other people. Earlier, the Utes lived freely and roamed the prairie fighting and hunting. Only the most aggressive and strong human beings of the tribe survived this selection process. Rape and murder of the people from different tribes was permitted, but inside the tribal community, there were all kinds of taboos and no-no's. Most important was – facing the battles with the whites and with neighboring tribes – and to keep peace among tribal members. It was apparent that if someone killed a member of his own tribe, he would be punished severely, even being forced to commit suicide. Margolin's work showed the neurosis among the Ute Indians was a result of the "non-relievable aggressiveness" kept within them for generations.

The above thought of the scientist Margolin's research gave me unrest and intrigued me so much, that then, a student of Polish languages and literature, I made a note of it. That note is still in my archives, and now I am happy to bring it to the reader's attention.

The immediate inspiration to write this book was my great uncle, sculptor Korczak Ziolkowski, mentioned above. On a Fulbright stipend in 1985, I went to Rapid City, South Dakota. Korczak had died three years earlier, and his wife Ruth welcomed and took care of me. She gave me some books and gifts from the Crazy Horse Museum souvenir shop for my little boy Thomas. When for the first time I was invited to a reservation in Canada, and told my son about the place and the Indian's "pow-wow", he painted a drawing of dancing Indians. His painting is framed and hangs in our Warsaw apartment. After a few years had passed, Thomas Tomczyk graduated in architecture from the University of Arkansas in Fayetteville. Later, while studying for his masters' degree in journalism at the University of Missouri in Columbia, he took photographs for my essay about Indians published in the eminent Polish weekly "Polityka".

For many years, I prepared myself for writing this book, by reading literature about Native Americans and following their current affairs. Since 1990, I have subscribed to two Indian journals "Lakota Country Times" and "Indian Country Today". Three times I visited the Pine Ridge Reservation in South Dakota, and I have visited other reservations in South Dakota, Texas, Montana and Wisconsin. I also visited an Indian Territory in Oklahoma.

The more I read the stranger and more remote the subject became.

I was not only expecting more and more from myself, but most of all, I became very critical of my knowledge and understanding of the subject. My husband and I went to a number of "pow-wows", and I became afraid that I would show that subject lackadaisically. I was afraid of being non-objective, over-protective, indifferent or looking at Indians as exotic humans. For a long time, I thought I was not able to describe a subject that is very complicated, that I would show it one-sidedly. I was afraid I would write another "white image" of American Indians. I did not push myself, and the time was passing. I was not in a hurry. I took my time deliberately.

Gradually, I understood that to write about the current situation of American Indians, I have to free myself of the myths that have existed since Columbus came to America. There were many of them, and they were divided into the kind redskins and the savage redskins. Those stories gave imagination to many eminent Europeans, like Monteskius, Locke, Hobbes or Rousseau. There were terms like "the child of nature", "the victim of white men". Then there came a time when a new version appeared of the images of Indians – those the historian Robert F. Berkhofer Jr. described as "white man's Indian". A more favorable image of Indians was shown thanks to the movies like "The Last of the Mohicans" or "Dancing with Wolves".

I remember reading the book of the Polish Nobel Prize winner Czesław Miłosz "The Year of a Hunter"[1] where he wrote:

"Reading the diary of Father Pedro Font from his 1776 expedition to California. What it looked like before the white man arrived. I trust this monk more than I do romantic fantasies about noble savages. The life of the Indians: filth, stench, constant fear of death because of the unending war of all against all, and most important, the virtually constant malnutrition that will draw them to the Spanish missions, because they were given breakfast, dinner and supper in exchange for agreeing to baptism. Of the entire various characteristics, Father Font sees in them only the physical shape of man, otherwise, they are animals. This drives him to contemplate theological problems. Such poverty for millennia, and what about after death?"

Well, I did have a different opinion than Milosz who quoted father Pedro Fonta. And I did not agree with Miłosz. I read different books about Indians. Some of those books, I have written about here and quoted. For me, the words of Professor Bruce E. Johansen from the University of Nebraska, author of many books dedicated to the subject of Indians (my interview with him is later in my book) are more appealing. He stresses how big the role played by the Iroquois was in the development of the American Constitution. Americans are more accustomed to the belief that their culture has European roots, and thus superior to the rest of the world. Johansen asks for a redefinition of the concept what does it mean to be American. He writes:

"For those who are attached to the notion that our intellectual history is exclusively European -- and that European culture is superior to that of the rest of the world, the introduction of Native America into this discourse poses some fundamental problems of historical interpretation and even -- or especially -- self-definition concerning who we believe ourselves to be as Americans."[2]

---

[1] See: Czeslaw Milosz, *A Year of the Hunter*, translated by Madeline G. Levine, Farrar, Strauss and Giroux, New York 1994, pg. 204-205.
[2] See: Bruce E. Johansen, *Debating Democracy: Native American Legacy of Freedom,* Clear Light Books, 1998.

I started to write articles, essays about American Indians. I have published them in Polish in "Polityka", "America", "Odra", "Przeglad Powszechny", "Borussia", "Arkusz", "Przeglad Polski-Nowy Dziennik" and in English in "New Horizon". And finally, I decided to write this book. It has happened since I can truthfully say "I have friends who are American Indians". Living in the United States since 1990, I can say that Northern Cheyenne and Chickasaw number among my husband's and my own close friends. I can write to them, I can always ask them for help and guidance and I can talk to them.

There are so many unknown things, so many intrigues; I would like to know so much more. For example – more about Korczak Ziolkowski. I don't know much about his first wife, pianist Dorothy.

Too late I learned of Korczak's Polish friend Franciszek Liszka from Connecticut (who died in 1996) to learn more about Korczak's youth. He told me, later confirmed by Lottie Powozniak from Hartford, that Dorothy belonged to Boston's high society, was very elegant and organized concerts in her house. She invited many Polish people to attend. She was fond of her husband's Polish roots.

I would like to learn more about Crazy Horse, not in the guise of an Indian hero but as a human being. How interesting he was! Surrounded by the jealousy of his fellow Indians, his aloofness, his sudden death, the description of which always gives my heart a twinge ...those three wives of chiefs ... his involvement with them. I would like to know more. How really did he kidnap the wife of No Water, his beloved Black Buffalo Woman?

Norman's encouragement was the most helpful for me. As a university student, he chose as an elective a course entitled "History of the Trans-Mississippi West" (about the Plains Indians) taught by Professor Elwyn B. Robinson who instilled in Norman a great interest in the Native American people. Twice Norman went with me to the Pine Ridge Reservation. On our latest trip we traveled for two and a half months to Wisconsin, both Dakotas, Montana, Wyoming, Kansas, Utah and Oklahoma. We sponsor (within our means) three Indian schools, three foundations helping the Indians, as well as the Crazy Horse mountain sculpting project.

Norman knew I started this book, and that I put it aside a number of times. He patiently waited until I finished a few Polish history books and was very happy knowing that I returned to this subject. That passion made us even closer.

A great help for me was the friendship of Rod Trahan whom we first met at the St. Labre Indian School in Montana. Well educated and with excellent manners, he patiently explained to me many difficult subjects (such as ownership of Indian land). James Humes, a gentleman from Oklahoma, was very cordial and helpful. We met in Texas, then again in Oklahoma where he introduced us to new friends, Billy Evans Horse and Homer Flute.

Korczak Ziolkowski said it most eloquently, "What a privilege for a Polish orphan from Boston, that the Lakota Sioux Indian Chief Henry Standing Bear asked me to tell their story in stone that the Red Man had great heroes also". What a privilege! Only in America can a person sculpt a mountain.

One year before I was born, Korczak Ziolkowski decided to sculpt the Sioux Chief Crazy Horse from a mountain in the Black Hills of South Dakota. After visiting the place the second time, I decided to write this book. First it was a thought, almost a dream, but slowly I was shaping my thoughts into words and paragraphs. And now, as this book is completed, I can say, that a great opportunity was also given to me. I can say that my living in the United States gave extra meaning to my life. Like my childhood had returned with its books and movies. Imagination! The exotic and fanciful faced with reality. For me to be able to write about American Indians is a great privilege.

Aleksandra Ziolkowska-Boehm

Dinosaurs or the biggest wound?

I remember very well the morning in Rapid City, South Dakota. While eating my breakfast, I was looking through the window of the hotel's coffee shop, watching two Indians – a father and son - waiting for the school bus. The boy was straight as an arrow and very handsome. I looked at the father: I saw a haggard, tired face and an emaciated body. Is the boy going to have a similar look in the future? ... The thought scared me.

From the beginning, the Indians did not have a chance. They had to rely upon their arrows, knives, spears and traps. The white settlers had firearms, sophisticated tools and accessories that fascinated the Indians. These were things they started to need and like. Just imagine: guns, metal pots, needles, cloth, axes, beads and ... whisky. Some traded furs and animal skins for these newfound needs, while others traded the land that belonged to the creator. It belonged to all and everyone could use it. For this the Indians received 'firewater' from the whites, which they neither comprehended nor handled well.

Thus they were in the end forced onto reservations to eke out their existence by farming rather than hunting. Naturally this induced discontent. The Great Sioux Uprising of 1862 and early 1863 under Chief Little Crow resulted in over four hundred white settlers from Minnesota being killed. Three hundred and three Sioux were condemned for war crimes, but President Lincoln remanded the sentence for two hundred and eighty five. On December 29, 1862, thirty-eight Sioux warriors were hung in the largest mass hanging in United States history that took place at Mankato, Minnesota. Further rebellion was suppressed by promises to provide the things Indians needed. In 1887, Congress annulled collective ownership, but gave each Indian man or family eighty or one hundred and sixty acres respectively. The rest of the Indian land was, however, opened to white settlement. Then came the speculators and cheaters including bankers who, without any scruples, made non-meaningful promises for credit or benefits with terms they knew the Indians could not fulfill. They cheated the Indians to obtain their land. When this procedure was stopped in 1934, the Indian territories had diminished to a total of forty eight million acres. Two-thirds of the Indian population did not have enough land to live on.

Many Indian families have existed on financial support from the Federal Government. Such support has been ongoing for over one hundred and fifty years. What kinds of people are born into and depend on government "handouts" during their adult lives? What kind of attitude can they have when facing the reality of life?

I remember reading an interview with an Indian who had grown up in the 1940's, when the only work he could find was hard labor as a helper for white cowboys. Then by 1960, most of the work disappeared and almost every Indian family turned to the government for help. They needed that help, but it created a miasma, as it put the Indian down completely. People who must do nothing to finance their basic needs will stagnate and lose all ambition to achieve something in life or to better themselves.

An attempt was made to turn the Indians into farmers. In the late 1870's, the "giving away" of the land for reservations on the Dakota territories and other western parts of the country, was pledged with the promise "the land will be used forever and belong to" the Indians. During the ensuing years, almost everywhere such promises to the Indian tribes were withdrawn. Such withdrawals happened after brief consultations with the tribes, or more often, even without them.

From the year 1880 until late 1930, the concept representing the political attitude of the American government towards the Indian nations was a program known as *allotment* – giving them land, that is, land that already belonged to them. In the government's judgment, it seemed to be the best solution to solve the conflict between the white setters, always looking for the land and Indians, whose dependence upon the government was growing. In 1887, Senator Henry L. Dawes of Massachusetts, who developed the idea of "allotment", gave the following explanation:

"Indians should be one of us by the giving of their culture base as a strength and shining light for all Americans and for all the country".

For such an understanding, the solution for Indian problems was turning them into farmers. Each Indian family received the ownership of one hundred and sixty acres from the already existing reservation land, also money for crop seeds, tools and farm animals. This allotment came with the strict requirement that the head of family be able to prove that he had at least a fifty percent Indian blood lineage, and this level was never allowed to slip below twenty five percent. The Dawes Act had the effect of substantially diminishing Indian ownership of land, although this being reservation land, it strictly belonged to the Indians already. The rest of the territories (non-reservation land) were thus made available to the white settlers to purchase. The settlers were mostly interested in the rich lands of Nebraska, the Dakotas, Oklahoma, and Montana rather than the desert like and empty territories of Arizona or New Mexico.

The reservation laws did not govern the white settlers, and they could vote for their own representatives. A slow adaptation of the Indians into the white neighboring society was hoped for.

By 1920, it was concluded that the allotment system had not worked and that it was wrong, and in the 1930's, the legislation was repealed. During the years, the Indians who had proved their ownership of land had either sold it or were about to lose it. For example, ninety five percent of the Indians on the Cheyenne River Reservation had either sold their land or had a lien on their property. Indians did not farm the land; it was alien to their culture and way of life. On the other hand, the white settlers were interested in farming, and they wanted to acquire and use the land. In 1910, the government began "leasing" the land for farming, and this "leasing" also initiated the search for oil.

The Indian parcels became smaller and smaller. When an Indian passed away, he did not have a legal written will, so his land (in accordance with tribal custom) was divided amongst his family, and therefore, the parcels of land became smaller and smaller.

In the beginning of the twentieth century, besides selling land to the white settlers, the government without any consultation with the tribes created national parks. They took away the land that belonged to the reservations, like the terrain around Blue Lake in New Mexico – which the Indians considered sacred land. In 1909, two days before his presidency was over, President Theodore Roosevelt gave 2.5 million acres of reservation lands for national parks.

The distribution of land created by Senator Dawes did not include the lands of the Five Civilized Tribes (so named not with irony but for respect of their work and culture) for the territory that belonged to those Indian tribes based on their treaties with the American government. The Five Civilized Tribes: Cherokee, Chickasaw, Choctaw, Creek and Seminole– in the first half of the nineteenth century were forced to leave the southeastern territory and were settled on territory that later became part of the state of Oklahoma. After much misery, pain, illness and death connected with their physical movement and transplantation (the famous "Trail of Tears"), these Indian tribes adapted to the new circumstances, they started farming, built their own houses, schools and created their own organizations. The life of those tribes in the beginning of the twentieth century was much more advanced, partly because they were settled and were no longer nomads that lived by hunting. Like the many white established families, many Indians of the Five Civilized Tribes owned their own slaves. During the Civil War in 1863, those Indians took the side of the Confederacy. They agreed to build a railway system on their territory and to let Indians from other tribes, like Comanche, Cheyenne, Arapaho, Kiowa and Kiowa-Apache settle on their land.

A very interesting case is that of the Osage nation. In 1870, based on a separate treaty with the government, the Osage sold their reservation land in Kansas and moved to the northeast territory of Oklahoma. In 1896, oil and gas were found there. A turmoil was created. The Federal Government, after many debates and negotiations, agreed to the expectations of the Osage Indians, and in 1906, Congress approved a treaty with two thousand two hundred and twenty-nine tribal members awarding them with oil and gas rights (production royalties). During the years of the twentieth century, the Osage received large profits from the production of the oil and gas, and until the big crisis was over, they were the most prosperous of all Indian tribes.

The result of partitioning the land, according to the treaty of Senator Dawes, along with other states, has resulted in the state of Oklahoma not having any reservations. In Oklahoma, the largest number of Indians live – over two hundred and sixty thousand, of which one hundred and twenty thousand are Cherokee, the most populous Indian tribe not only in the United States but in the whole world.

Americans were taught for generations that their national history is the apogee of success, and that defeating the Indians was the triumph of civilization over barbarity. At the end of 1990, several literary works were published[3], that desire to prove that almost any aspect of present current life America owes to the Indians, even its democracy, constitution or products such as corn, potatoes, etc.

The complexity of relations between whites and Indians is shown as difficult and impossible to be solved, a conflict between an achiever and a victim, corruption and innocence, Euro-American "materialism" and "spirituality" of the natives. The real history, as happens many times, is denial of contradictions and others myths. I remember that the daily newspaper in Colorado "The Denver Post" attacked the University of Arizona for its plan to build an observatory on a mountain considered sacred by the Apache Indians. The possibility of even revering such a

---

[3] See: Kirkpatrick Sale, *The Conquest of Paradise. Christopher Columbus and the Columbian Legacy*, Plume 1991; Richard Drinnon, *Facing West, The Metaphysics of Indian-Hating and Empire Building*, University of Oklahoma Press, 1997, that show the settling of North America as a ribbon of tragedies, and bigger and smaller defeats. The treating of Indians is an example of victory by the cruelty of American civilization. Such understanding has moved into America's popular culture and given such movies, as "Dancing With Wolves" or books See: Jack Weatherford, *Indian Givers: How the Indians of the Americas Transformed the World*, Ballantine Books, 1989.

place was taken away from the Indians. The article was also published by others dailies as well and created severe reactions. Such a concept was akin to bestowing rights upon Indians, who lived there before Christopher Columbus arrived, which the author of the article considered to be the only "true Indians". There are many Christian Indians, and they do not practice the "sacred dispensation of the ancestor". The author fell into the trap of sentimentalism and myths.

To generalize that Indians were always innocent victims cannot be supported. For example, there are documents available from business negotiations in the Black Hills of South Dakota that were taking place at the end of the 1970's. The chiefs of the Sioux had access to money and wanted to make the best business deal they could. They followed the saying "Black Hills were the gold source for Indians". Chief Little Bear said: "If a person has something valuable that is normal and if he wants to make it bigger that is normal also". The other chief – Spotted Tail – said it more clearly: "I would like to live from the percentage of the sum of money that has to be big enough so the percentage for me will be enough"[4]. These negotiating postures of the Sioux are in contrast to the prevailing belief that the government of the United States wanted to destroy and ruin the Indians. Such laws never existed. Senator Henry L. Dawes, the idea creator of 'allotment' (mentioned earlier); described the history of the United States as one of "corruption, wars and degradation". He stated that Indians should be treated as "single human beings".

The current Indian Territories epitomize poverty, sadness and neglected landscapes. More than in the rest of the country, the inhabitants of the reservations are likely to be murdered or to commit suicide. Three times more often, they are killed in car accidents. Five times more than in other nations, Indians die from liver disease. In some of the reservations, the unemployment rate exceeds eighty percent of its population. Fifty percent of the young people do not complete a high school education despite the fact that access to an education is growing.

"For people live hanging in a culture that is not wholly Indian, and it is not wholly for the white people", writes Dennis Hastings[5], of the Omaha Indians, the tribe that occupies the northeast territory of the State of Nebraska. Hastings stresses the need for restoration of Indian culture and recapitulation showing the history of tribes as steps before their growing into an Indian society." In another example – he writes – it is like living in a house without a foundation. But we cannot return to the

---

[4] See: Fergus M. Bordewich, *Killing the White Man's Indian*, New York 1996.
[5] See: Fergus M. Bordewich, *Revolution in Indian Country*, "American Heritage", July/August 1996, pg. 44.

old days of hunting for bison, stop talking English and use only our language, ignore the whites and all that is their culture. If we do it, we will be stuck in history. We will be dinosaurs".

In the latter years of 1970, the government of the United States showed the concept of tribal independence to more than three hundred tribes (even five hundred, if Alaska were included). The government wanted to convince Indians that they can organize their own lives. As President Richard Nixon said, the federal politics towards the Indians should be created and planned by Indians themselves.

The following years brought more acts of good will (I write more about it later) as in 1986 when the beautiful gesture of the Museum of History at the Smithsonian Institution returned the remains of Indian chiefs, so they could, in accordance with Indian traditions, be properly buried. Four years later, Congress approved the bill for care of Indian graves including the return of items, now presented in museums, that were dug from the cemetery graves, to the various tribes.

Statistics (from the 2006 "Time Almanac") show that the population of Indians is growing constantly. In 1920, their population was around three hundred and fifty thousand, whereas, now there are four million[6]. Between 1960 and 2000, the number of Americans who claim an *American Indian* ancestry has grown rapidly. I am not writing about the increasing number of people hanging *"dreamcatchers"* in the windows of their houses. I am thinking more of those "would be Indians", who by deception or stratagem claim an Indian ancestry to achieve a business advantage or benefit.

There are, for example, problems with the producers of Indian cultural artifacts, particularly those popular among the people who love jewelry. The products are sold as made by Indians, but Indians did not produce them, they probably never even touched them. The "deceivers" make a lot of money from such products, they even hand out false certificates of authenticity.

According to the press, such a faux Indian is Ward Churchill, the professor from the University of Colorado who appears in public on behalf of the "harmed minority". He says that he is three sixteenth Cherokee and one sixteenth Cree, but he cannot prove it. When Churchill was in Vietnam as a soldier, he gave his ancestry as *Caucasian* (white). In 1978, in his application documents for a professorship at the University of Colorado, he wrote *American Indian* (knowing that the university gave preference to members of minority groups).

---

[6] Of the four million, 2,5 million are those who have only Indian ancestry and not mixed ethnic groups created because of weddings and the like.

I have visited the reservations of the Tigua tribe near El Paso, Texas, the Alabama-Coushatta north of Houston in Texas, in Montana: the Northern Cheyenne, in South Dakota: the Sioux (Oglala, Lakota, Lower Brule), in New Mexico: the Navajo, Isleta, Pueblo, and a few tribes of Apache (Mescalero, Jicarilla). Together with Norman, we have been in contact with the Indian schools that we sponsor (two in South Dakota and one in Montana). We spent a few weeks in South Dakota, where life is like in the song "There's nothing much to do except walk up and down". During several trips into the Indian territories since my first visit there in 1985, I often had the feeling that my curiosity, as well as the curiosity of white people, in general, is a form of exploitation. I also felt that no whites could write honestly and objectively about the Indian people or their plight. I talked with many people who wanted to show their point of accepting and understanding "the Indian case". James A. Humes, the Chickasaw Indian businessman from Oklahoma City, said: "Before you are caught in sentimentalism and myths, come to visit us, I will show you my friends".

I am aware that I have to be particularly careful of the traps of sentimentalism, a peculiar point of view when seeing through "rose colored glasses" when we talk about people who are dear to us. As Thomas Berger, author of the *Little Big Man's Man,* 1964, stated[7]: "If one genuinely respects and admires Indians, one must recognize them as being quite as human as people of any other color, which means no more and no less than that some of them will at times exhibit the same failings than can be found in mortals of other races".

I was thinking how one might best portray the recuperation of a culture, the appearance of aggressive tribal politics, ethnic chauvinism, and indifference to isolation from independence. Fergus M. Bordewich has asked similar questions.[8] How to show an interpretation of present problems through the past, as something that is gone? I am thinking of many things, and some of them make me uneasy. I would like to answer the questions that bother me:

Are the Indians fundamentally different from the other people of the United States, so they need a special category of law that has not much to do with the average American system of values?

Are they one of a group that creates the ghetto and ethnic enclave that shows American balkanization?

---

[7] See: Interview by Andrew Ward, "American Heritage", May-June 1999, pg. 95.
[8] See: Fergus M. Bordewich, *Revolution in Indian Country*, "American Heritage", July/August 1996, pg. 34-36, 40-46, 60.

Aleksandra Ziolkowska-Boehm

Is the lack of a plan to integrate the Indian into American society a form of discrimination? Or, are the Indians so nationalistic that they do not feel the need to think about such a subject?

Does the idea of having their own representation create a new form of segregation that will freeze the Indian culture?

Who are the Indians of the twenty-first century going to be?

Who are the Indians in respect to other Americans, and who are the other Americans in respect to the Indians?

I was looking for answers to these questions during my journeys and also in literature. Norman and I have a nice collection of books about the American Indian. Most of them are concerned with Indian history, their beliefs and their way of life. I like, for example, *Through Indian Eyes*[9]. I admire the more personal book, mentioned above *Killing the White Man's Indian*[10] by Fergus M. Bordewich, who writes, that in the 1950's and 1960's as a young man, he often accompanied his mother, who was a director of Indian Affairs and traveled far and wide on the reservations. The federal government wanted to improve the education system, health care, order and respect of the law. Wherever they went, there was tremendous poverty. They slept in broken beds, they listened to the stories. It seemed that everyone had his own story, but all of them were somehow similar and created one big loud lament. Bordewich remembered Indians as a people fighting poverty. They did not live in the past, nor did they tell the stories of the generations past to the youngsters, as is shown in books or in the films. They lived through the sadness of the present day.

Indians, as it seems to the outsider, protest a lot. Most of them do not work and have federal financial aid, so they can protest over the years, as it happens.

For many white people, it seems that Indians play their own game and by the rules only they understand. If anyone follows controversial events, they know, for example, that the Connecticut Indians built casinos that take a lot of money from the nearby region. The inhabitants of New Mexico stand in front of the dilemma of what to do with the decision of the Mescalero Apache tribe to build a nuclear waste system on their reservation.

In the states of Wisconsin and Washington, many arguments have been generated by Indian expectations that they have the right – according to a treaty from the nineteenth century - for fishing. None of the fishing rights decisions exclude whites. As Bruce E. Johansen

---

[9] "Readers Digest", 1996.
[10] Doubleday, 1996.

16

pointed out: "the best known one, United States vs. Washington (1974), the Boldt decision, holds that the Indians have a right to half the salmon. Indians have never caught anything close to even half. The decision is based on the treaties' use of the phrase "in common with"[11]. In Nevada, the farmers were on the edge of bankruptcy when the Paiute Indians, from their reservation near Lake Pyramid, took control over the Truckee River, that winds around the town of Reno and escapes into Lake Tahoe. Now, every year there is a kayak competition on the river, and thousands of people gather there to view it (and to spend money).

These conflicts are known because of publicity in the press that stimulates emotions on both sides. But most Americans do not know about any of this. For them, the indigenous people are the people of myths and who inspire a lot of imagination. Many times, they think about them with envy or disdain. The picture of the American Indians is many times crooked, built from dreams, idealism, expectations and fear.

It is something like that in my imagination too. Indians were of interest to me through the legend and pride of my family member, the sculptor Korczak Ziolkowski who, from a mountain in the Black Hills of South Dakota, started to sculpt the monument of the Indian Chief Crazy Horse. But that is another story.

---

[11] See: letter, February 13, 2008.

Aleksandra and Norman at Crazy Horse, 1999

American Sphinx
Crazy Horse and the Sculptor of the Mountain

When I came to South Dakota the first time, it was a bright early afternoon. Humid, the dust moved around with every step. There were no trees that could give me a relief from the sun. In the distance were the Black Hills that looked down upon the prairie. To the west, the clouds started to gather making the surroundings darker. The rains came and went, and then the sunshine came out. The only sign of rain that remained was the smell of ozone.

During the night, I was surprised by the noise of the wind – in the territory surrounding the Black Hills the wind utters peculiar sounds – sobs, groans, and then whimpers like a baby. South Dakota is a truly lonesome place where there are no signs of civilization for miles around. Years earlier, many animals populated the area, now their numbers have declined, but still one can glimpse a regal elk, fast and graceful antelopes, and even, but seldom, prowling wolves and grizzly bears. The dawning of a day or the deep shadows of twilight are the most beautiful times in this region as the natural forms of the terrain are enhanced. Canyons and hills in the shape of pyramids were formed by the wind and by the flow of water. It is very picturesque. "The land touches the sun", I caught myself on such a strange metaphor.

There is a subtle beauty to this land, with its' never ending open space. It gives the feeling of freedom. The prairie (or rather what remains of it) – is a rich cover of grasses and wild flowers. Mostly it is a grass that has a deep roots system that helps it to survive the time of dryness.

The Sioux Indians called this land *maco sica* – not good land, mainly because of the difficulties encountered in travel through such uneven terrain. The first white men that came into this area were the French trappers looking for furs. They called the land *mauvaises terres à traverser* (bad land to travel).

The Black Hills attracted the hearts of many settlers. In 1883, the young politician from New York, Theodore Roosevelt came to the area to hunt for bison. In a short time, he fell in love with the land around the Little Missouri River. He bought four hundred cattle, shares in a ranch, and returned the next year. The land was wild; the only people who lived there were cowboys (taking care of cattle). The newcomer was a source of mirth: he did not drink and wore funny glasses. They called him "Four Eyes". Slowly he gained the respect of the locals, mainly for his courage and determination. Now, after the years passed by, a national park bears his name.

The north prairies went through dramatic changes. In 1803, the United States bought the land from France as part of the Louisiana Purchase. Until the mid-1800's, not many white settlers lived here. Trappers who came because of the fur traversed the land then. They were able to live in harmony with the Indians. In 1862, the Congress of the United States opened the way for an ingress of white setters by signing a bill that each person over 21 years could receive 160 acres of land – provided they established a homestead of 20 acres and lived there at least 5 years. Settlers from elsewhere in the United States were coming, as did the immigrants from Sweden, Norway, Germany and Eastern Europe. All were attracted by the offer of free land. Villages and small towns were built, churches were constructed, and also a train line laid its steel rails into this region. In the years of 1870-1920, the population of South Dakota increased ten-fold.

At the end of the nineteenth century, gold seekers came. The first noted discovery of gold in the Black Hills was on July 27, 1874. A young man named Horatio Nelson Ross, a member of the Custer expedition stopped with his mules by a stream. A bright yellow glint of color in the water caught his attention. One year later the Black Hills, that belonged to the Lakota Sioux Indians and not to the Federal Government, unofficially became a territory for gold seekers.

The original gold mining company in Rapid City – and its' Homestake Mine, are the source of Landstrom's Original Black Hills Gold Creations – they are the most peculiar in the world and an attraction for many tourists. I visited Landstrom's in September 1985. The characteristic of this gold is its distinctive three shades of yellow, that is one pinkish, one greenish and one copperish. According to the law, Black Hills Gold Jewelry can only be produced here. Each item goes through over 20 phases of handwork. The 24 karat gold is reduced to 14 karat. Traditionally all items have the same design – delicate leaves and clusters of grapes. The design was created during the gold rush in California in 1849. A man named LeBeau, who in 1876 opened his own store, brought the design to the Black Hills. Since 1919, this characteristic design is repeated in rings, signets, and necklaces. Most Americans often recognize my small rings of tri-colored gold, which I purchased in Rapid City, as coming from the Black Hills of South Dakota.

Every summer in South Dakota there are Indian pow-wows. Also, often there are rodeos. It is a common saying that young people who live on a ranch learn how to ride a horse at the same time they learn to walk.

The South Dakota prairies once belonged to the Indian. Now they live on reservations. For example, the home of the Oglala Sioux is the

Pine Ridge Reservation. South Dakota has nearly sixty thousand Indians, mostly Sioux. Still in 1940, the teaching of the native language by the Oglala Sioux and other Sioux tribes was forbidden. Now the situation has changed, the young people at schools are learning their own language and history. There are excellent primary schools, high schools and colleges on the reservations, however, attendance is limited due to a lack of facilities and the inordinate commuting distances for students. Such distances can amount up to fifty miles each way. Dance-music groups are now organized whose performances are based upon traditional music and dances. The cities in South Dakota do not attract people as they did years earlier. The young people that live on the land tend to move to the big cities in search of employment opportunities. Unemployment on the Pine Ridge Reservation is dramatically high. I wonder why the Federal and State Governments do not encourage United States industrial companies to "out source" their low cost labor to Native Americans such as the Oglala Sioux? Why do we support offshore countries instead?

***

One of the settlers who came to the Black Hills - on the invitation of the Sioux Indian Chief Henry Standing Bear - was the Polish origin sculptor Korczak Ziolkowski. He came to South Dakota in 1948 and stayed for the remaining thirty-three years of his life.

Korczak Ziolkowski was born September 6, 1908 in Boston as the son of Polish parents Anna and Józef Ziolkowski. The name Korczak (that he took by himself) is a name of the family crest of the Ziolkowski family (that I belong to as well). His parents died tragically, and he was orphaned in his second year. He was sent to a Catholic children's home, from which he was rescued in storybook fashion by an Irish prizefighter and his wife. But unfortunately, this chapter wasn't from a storybook. He was abused, beaten and used for every menial chore. "I never slept in a bed until I was sixteen", he recalled, "I was treated as a slave, and my bunk was a couple of old coats in the attic".

He was raised by people who put him down, pushed him to do hard work. He always talked about them with disdain. When he was 16, he left the house of his tormentors. He took many jobs, among others he worked in a tailor's shop and in a store. He even found himself in a Boston shipyard, where for the first time he tried to do a sculpture in wood. As a teenager then, he discovered a talent for woodcarving.

By the time he was twenty-two, his abilities as a carver were such that he was doing figureheads for yachts, an occupation that brought him to the attention of Judge Frederick P. Cabot who took him under his wing

21

and encouraged him to develop his self-taught skills, which he did, originally in wood, then in granite. The other kind person to him was Jan Kirchmayer, who was seeking works of sculpture for a New York cathedral. Both men helped Korczak financially. When in 1932 Judge Cabot died, twenty-four year old Korczak sculpted his benefactor from a marble block. The death of Cabot was a shock to Korczak but an inspiration too. Soon he was sculpting busts of pianist Arthur Schnabel, Henry MacCracken, Romanian composer and flute player George Enesco, the Governor of Connecticut Wilbur Cross and singer Olga Alverino. He sculpted the hands of Leopold Stokowski and Katherine Cornell.

His first work in stone, a bust of his mentor the judge, was so well received that he switched almost completely to granite, turning out a succession of critically acclaimed pieces, one of which, a bust of a world famous Polish pianist and statesman Ignacy Paderewski, won the first prize at the 1939 World's Fair in New York. "That work is moving and impressive" – wrote Marian Murray, a then known and respected critic, about the Paderewski sculpture. Korczak Ziolkowski became a known and recognized sculptor.

By that time the sculptor Gutzon Borglum, who was sculpting the carvings of the presidential faces at Mt. Rushmore in the Black Hills, had heard of him and invited him to work on the project. Korczak accepted the proposition of Gutson Borglum to help him sculpt the heads of four presidents: George Washington, Thomas Jefferson, Abraham Lincoln and Theodore Roosevelt. The cooperation with Borglum went well and the work progressed, but a conflict with Borglum's son forced Korczak to leave the mountain carving project.

After that, Korczak went back to West Hartford, Connecticut, and accomplished a granite statue of Noah Webster for the town hall lawn. The proposal for him to make a sculpture of Noah Webster, American lexicographer and textbook author came from the inhabitants of West Hartford, where Webster was born and where supposedly his monument was to be placed. Initially, the inhabitants of West Hartford showed much enthusiasm for the project. However, they never imagined how big the work would be to achieve the project, that is, to build the monument from a marble block. When the work was prolonged longer and longer, their interest waned and their support became smaller and smaller. They started to be impatient and critical. Korczak completed the work, however, and it gave him more recognition all over the country.

Earlier, in November 1939, he received a letter from Sioux Chief Henry Standing Bear, which said that not only had the white man taken away the sacred Black Hills of the Sioux - which under the Treaty of

1868 were to be theirs, but, in fact, the sacred land only remained theirs until the whites under the same Gen. George Armstrong Custer found gold - and later carved their heroes on Mt. Rushmore right in the middle of what was to be Sioux land.

"My fellow chiefs and I would like the white man to know the Red Man had great heroes, also", said the letter from Henry Standing Bear[12], proposing that Korczak come to South Dakota and carve a statue of Crazy Horse, a Lakota chief and a war leader of the Sioux, in those same Black Hills.

Korczak, who had never heard of Crazy Horse and knew little more about the Sioux or any other Indians, became intrigued and traveled west to meet the chief and make a small model of the kind of statue he might do. And he had learned enough about the ordeal of the Indians - betrayed, cheated, dispossessed, slaughtered and despised - and about Crazy Horse to instill in him a lifelong cause.

"They were a magnificent people, intelligent, fearless, honest to their word", said Korczak. "Their only fault was they occupied land we wanted". As a symbol, Crazy Horse was a good choice, Korczak believed.

For several years, Korczak did not give an answer to Chief Henry Standing Bear. After he completed the Webster monument, at thirty-four years of age – he volunteered into the United States Army wanting to help Europe fight the war with the Germans. Korczak headed to World War II in Europe serving for three years with American forces. He was twice wounded and earned a sergeant's rank. After the war, he completed the wooden sculpture of General Charles De Gaulle that is now in the museum in Rouen. After returning to the United States, he accepted the offer of the Sioux Indian chief and moved to the Black Hills. He was almost forty years old.

"What an honor for a Polish orphan from Boston that the Indian chiefs asked him to tell their story in stone that the Red Man had great heroes also. What a great honor! Only in America can a person carve a mountain" – Korczak repeated those words many times. Korczak also said, "The treatment of the Americans Indian is the blackest mark on the escutcheon of the American nation's history", and that if by carving Crazy Horse he could give back to the Indian some of his pride and create the means to keep alive his culture and heritage, his life would have been worthwhile.

So, in 1946 Korczak and Standing Bear tramped the Black Hills seeking a mountain, the mountain, and a year later the Boston orphaned

---

[12] See: "The Progress", May 1999, pg. 5.

sculptor of Polish ancestry came back for good with a hundred and seventy-four dollars in his pocket and a head full of dreams, put up a tent and started building a log cabin that would be his studio home.

The next year, on June 3, 1948, the Crazy Horse Memorial was dedicated and five of nine survivors of the Battle of the Little Big Horn were honored visitors. Their names were: Pemmican (aged ninety), High Eagle (aged ninety-one), Iron Hawk (aged ninety-one), Comes Again (aged eighty-eight) and Callous Leg (aged ninety-three)[13]. The Crazy Horse Memorial Foundation was set up to handle all funds, and Korczak built a seven hundred and forty-one step staircase to the rounded top of the mountain and started work. Later, he constructed his own cable car system to carry himself and supplies to the top of the mountain and to avoid the arduous staircase route. The work was tough and dangerous, he says, but no worse than he experienced later running a seventy-five ton bulldozer on the mountain's edge at his age and his health. In those days, he ran a dairy herd and sawmill to finance the work, labored with inadequate equipment in a hostile environment and faced active local hostility. But nothing stopped the work. Not even his death.

For the project, Korczak was accompanied by Ruth, the young woman from West Hartford, who earlier helped Korczak when he worked on the sculpture of Webster. In 1948, she came to the Black Hills to work and share her life with him (he divorced his first wife, pianist Dorothy). Korczak and Ruth have ten children. They received the names that show Korczak's love and pride of his Polish roots: Marina, Monika, Joel, Marek, Anna, Kazimierz, Jadwiga, Adam, Dawn and Jasiu.

The family lived on the edge of poverty for many years. Their children collected bottles so later they could obtain the deposit for them in town. In a shack near the house, they kept a goat for its milk. Whatever savings the family were able to accumulate were dedicated to moving the project ahead. Ziolkowski was determined and stubborn, and he expected the same from his wife and children. He was heard to state that the most important elements in his life were his mountain to sculpt, followed by his wife, and then his children[14]. To his family he always emphasized perseverance and dedication.

Some say that in the beginning, many white people of Rapid City looked with suspicion at the newcomer from the East Coast. They were skeptics of his vision and for a long time could not understand what was so special in the mountain. All the controversies and animosities stopped

---

[13] See: "The Progress", May 1998, pg. 5.
[14] See: Jessica Seigel, *A Head above the Others*, "Chicago Tribune Magazine", 5 October 1997, pgs.12–14.

when the Crazy Horse Center became a great tourist attraction. The whole surrounding area started to live on tourism. Every year, the Crazy Horse project, that is twenty miles from Mount Rushmore, attracts huge numbers of tourists.

***

The Black Hills were the sacred lands of the Dakota tribes from a great nation of Sioux for more than a hundred years. The expedition under General George Custer (rather, as mentioned above Horatio Nelson Ross) discovered the gold and in a very short time, the gold seekers came. In 1876, Indians battled with white cavalry under Custer and won the Battle of the Little Big Horn. Beside Chief Sitting Bull, extreme bravery was shown by the young Crazy Horse known as *Tashunca-Wico* ("his horse is crazy") became one of the most known of Indian chiefs.

In the biography of Crazy Horse, there are many unknown events. There is not an actual date and place of his birth. Some sources give the year as 1840, others 1842 or 1844. It is known that he was born in South Dakota. Some believe it was in Bear Butte near Sturgis. In an article that appeared September 14, 1877 in the "New York Sun" after the death of Crazy Horse, his place of birth was stated as South Cheyenne River, whereas, most sources give Rapid Creek, not far from Rapid City. To the east from Rapid City are the Black Hills or *Paha Sapa* that are considered as sacred hills of the Lakota Sioux, who say about the relations between the human being and the land in such words: "It is not the land that belongs to the people; it is the people who belong to the land".

After his birth, he was given the name Curly Hair or Light-Haired Boy, since he did have a brighter complexion and lighter hair. His father's name was Crazy Horse, he was an *Oglala medicine man*, and his mother belonged to the Brule Sioux tribe. The brother of Crazy Horse's mother was Spotted Tail (*Sinte Galeska*), the famous warrior, who in 1870 with Chief Red Cloud went to Washington DC. Spotted Tail became an Indian spokesman, he battled the idea of the Federal Government that his people were to become farmers. The mother of Crazy Horse died when he was a little boy. According to Robert H. Lowie, among the Cheyenne, and among all the Plains Indians, there was a custom that after the wife of an Indian passed away, he was to marry her sister or cousin, so that the family remained a unit. The father of Crazy Horse married the sister of his first wife, and she helped him to raise the boy.

Crazy Horse as a youngster hunted bison. He had his own horse and spent a lot of time among the Oglala and Brule Sioux tribes. It was a time

25

when the bison were counted in millions. When he was growing up, he saw how the white people slaughtered them, and how the number of bison were becoming smaller and smaller so that only a few were left. At a young age, he witnessed the murder of a Sioux Indian woman and damage of her household by the soldiers of General William S. Harney.

He was called "Curly" until age ten, when he was named "His Horse on Sight". According to the Lakota Sioux, an Indian's true name is given later in life, when the warrior shows some ability, bravery or unique act of achievement. After Crazy Horse turned 18 years, he was with other tribal members catching wild horses in Sandhills, Nebraska, and he stole horses from the Crow Indians. Around 1858, the chief to be was attacked by two enemy warriors and he killed both of them. Then he was given his father's name: Crazy Horse. His father, after passing his name to his son, took the name Worm.

The author of the book *Crazy Horse*[15] Larry McMurtry writes that Crazy Horse as a young Indian never let the conventional interfere in his plans. He was somehow aloof, distant, a loner, he preferred the loneliness. In his youth apparently he had many visions whose interpretations helped him in life. On one occurrence, after fasting two days and wandering around, he had a dream – he saw a man on a horse wearing simple clothes that were carried away over the land. The interpretation of his vision was that when he, Crazy Horse, made or won anything he should not keep it for himself. During a war, he should only wear simple clothes without a head-dress, only a simple single feather. Before a battle, Crazy Horse would rub soil on his face and hair. He dressed always in a modest way and by doing so, gave that inspiration to others.

But apparently the envy of his fellowmen was always around him.

What was he like? It is known that many tragedies accompanied him in his life. He lost his brother Little Hawk, his daughter They-Are-Afraid-of-Her, and his friends Hump and Lone Bear. His most beloved woman Black Buffalo Woman married another man.

An interesting theme of his life involves women. It is known that his beloved woman was a Northern Cheyenne. Larry McMurtry writes that Crazy Horse fell in love with the young beautiful woman Black Buffalo Woman, and he liked to be around her. But they never married. One day as Crazy Horse and other warriors left for hunting, one of them, called No Water, complained of a tooth pain, left the group and returned to camp. When the whole group returned, Crazy Horse discovered with consternation that during his absence Black Buffalo Woman married No

---

[15] See. Larry McMurtry, *Crazy Horse*, Viking Press, 1999.

Water. A few authors think that it was an arranged marriage involving the girl's uncle, Chief Red Cloud. Black Buffalo Woman made a choice, and it should be the end of the story. But it is not. Crazy Horse was then twenty-one or twenty-two years old, and certainly deeply hurt. His feelings did not stop, and he still managed to remain around his beloved woman. Even when Black Buffalo Woman gave birth to a child, and then to two more, No Water, as a jealous husband, was irritated by Crazy Horse hanging around.

Around 1865, near the end of the Civil War, Crazy Horse accepted a prestigious function of "shirt-wearer". Four brave men with high morals were given an honorary task to think not about themselves but about the people. They were supposed to set a good example for others. The four chosen men were: Young Man Afraid of His Horses, American Horse, Sword and as a fourth Crazy Horse. He was known for his skills as a warrior, his compassion for others, one without greed and that he was unselfish. The only problem was that he was still not married, and he still "hung around" the beloved but married woman.

The Lakota Sioux let a woman divorce her first husband. Then, according to custom, she was to move to another man or return to her family. She could remove her first husband's belongings from their tent. But Black Buffalo Woman chose none of these. Also, by custom, Crazy Horse could try to give a horse to No Water in exchange for his woman. Probably Crazy Horse anticipated that No Water would refuse such an offer, so he did not extend it. Crazy Horse chose to live by his own rules and guidelines. One day, No Water left the camp for hunting, and Crazy Horse who was in the camp took off with Black Buffalo Woman.

When No Water returned and saw what had happened, he borrowed a pistol and went to look for the lovers. He broke the custom of the Cheyenne as well. As I mentioned above, a Cheyenne woman could make a choice and leave her husband for another man. The lovers did not travel too far; they spent the whole day together.

There are several versions of what happened next, one being a near fulfillment of an earlier Crazy Horse interpreted vision that he would die restrained by a fellow Indian.

No-one knows what really happened. One version says that Little Big Man had pinned the arms of Crazy Horse, No Water shot him and that he was wounded. The other version did not mention Little Big Man (the Indian chief, not a hero of Thomas Berger's book), who later will become a hero after Crazy Horse's death.

In all probability what happened was when No Water found the lovers, he shot Crazy Horse, and Black Buffalo Woman ran away. Luckily, Crazy Horse was not killed. He had a broken jaw, but he survived the shot. No Water gave a horse to Crazy Horse as a peace offering (because by shooting, he broke another rule too), but apparently, Crazy Horse rejected the gift. Black Buffalo Woman returned to her husband. It was said she gave birth to their fourth baby, and it was a girl. Presumably, the girl was said to have a light complexion (like Crazy Horse), and she was still alive in the 1940's.

For the blame and the shame of his deeds, the privilege and honor of being a *shirt-wearer* was taken away from Crazy Horse. He placed his own good over that of others. No one knows what happened later to Black Buffalo Woman.

Not long after that incident, around the year of 1871, Crazy Horse married Black Shawl from the Oglala Sioux tribe. He accepted her and later even loved her. Their baby girl was born, and they named her They-Are-Afraid-of-Her. Black Shawl became ill with tuberculosis. Because of her illness, Crazy Horse befriended Doctor Valentine McGillycuddy, who treated his wife's condition.

I also found information that ten or twelve years later, when Crazy Horse was at Fort Robinson, he took as a wife Nellie Laravie (sometimes her name is written as Laverie), a young half Cheyenne Indian and half French woman. Her photograph is placed in Ian Frazier's book *Great Plains*. I could not find more information about Nellie. Evan S. Connell, author of the book *Son of the Morning Star*, wrote[16] that Nellie Laravie came of her own volition to Crazy Horse as his *second mate,* and she received the approval for this act from Black Shawl.

There is no positive information on the life of Crazy Horse, because the Oglala Sioux, as with all Indian tribes, did not leave written documents in a European sense. As Bruce E. Johansen pointed out "many had records. Plains Indians had Winter Counts, Iroquois had wampum belts, Aztec, Maya, and Inca, among others in Mesoamerica, had languages and books with enough detail to work as writing"[17]. Many stories about him were passed on from one person to another. All the stories are about his death, not his life. There were a few witnesses to his death, and a few versions have been handed down.

A number of American leaders have been murdered: President John F. Kennedy, his brother Robert, Martin Luther King, Malcolm X. All of the deaths are presented in books with different interpretations of what did happen. With passing years, many books have been published about the death of Crazy Horse. For example, Maria Sandoz published *Crazy*

---

[16] See: Evan S.Connell, *Son of the Morning Star*, Promontory Press, New York 1993, pg. 71.
[17] See: Letter, February 12, 2008.

Horse. The Strange Man of the Oglala (New York 1942), in which she included the talks with Sioux Indians who remembered Crazy Horse. The conversations were documented in the years of 1930–31.

It is known that Crazy Horse lived as a warrior, hunted, and fought tribal enemies, but only when the whites started their aggressive assaults was the real chief in him born: the brave chief who took command and won a few battles.

When Crazy Horse became a chief of the Oglala Sioux, many Brule Sioux followed him. He also had friends among the Northern Cheyenne. All sources say that he expected and received the respect shown him, and that he always showed an equal respect to others as well. He was well composed, reserved and quiet. In a battle, he showed a great intelligence. Before he engaged in battle, he studied the enemy, looked for his weaknesses. Crazy Horse was interested in his people; he took good care of them. After a battle, he always stopped by the tipis asking the poor and lonely how they managed.

Crazy Horse fought with Sitting Bull of the Hunkpapa Sioux in 1860 battles in North Montana and North Dakota. As a warrior, he became known in the war years of 1866–69 fighting with Chief Red Cloud along the Bozeman Trail. Also earlier, during 1865–68, he took part in a battle under Chief Red Cloud against American settlers in Wyoming. He took the main role in destroying the brigade of William J. Fetterman at Fort Phil Kearny in 1867.

According to the treaty at Fort Laramie in 1868, the American army left their spoils along the Bozeman Trail, and the Chiefs Red Cloud and Spotted Trail with their people settled on reservations. The Treaty of 1868 signed by the President of the United States, said, "As long as rivers run and grass grows and trees bear leaves, Paha Sapa -- the Black Hills -- will forever be the sacred lands of the Lakota Indians."

The discovery of gold in the Black Hills brought many white people. Although the treaty of 1868 stated that the government considered the Black Hills and the surrounding land as an Indian Territory to be protected by the American army, the gold rush created conflicts between the Indians and the whites. Between the newcomers and the Natives, constant outbreaks, misunderstandings and fits of anger occurred with occasional skirmishes. After the battle of Rosebud, June 17, 1876, the Indians moved their camps onto the Big Horn (sometimes also called the Bighorn) River.

At the end of June 1876, the American army chiefs, including then General George A. Custer, who was known as a brave and talented soldier during the Civil War, decided to attack the Indians. He made the mistake of underestimating the number and the potential of the Indians camped along the Little Big Horn numbering not hundreds but thousands of braves from the united tribes of Sioux, Cheyenne and Arapaho. One of the stories of this engagement was that Custer ignored the intelligence given him by Indian army scouts who advised him not to go down to the river as there were too many enemies encamped there. In that famous battle on the Little Big Horn, one of the Indian chiefs was Crazy Horse. He and the other chiefs defeated George Armstrong Custer decisively, the career soldier who was considered as one of the most aggressive generals in the American army. In this encounter, Custer let his search for glory outweigh his military judgment. The chiefs: Crazy Horse, Sitting Bull and Two Moon survived, General George Armstrong Custer died. Custer had expected that the Indians' alliance would splinter, and they would withdraw when the time to attack came. What had happened - as later one of the Cheyenne Indians Two Moon said – to defeat the Custer soldiers took only as much time, as to "finish the eating by hungry man". General George Armstrong Custer and others under his command numbered 225 officers and soldiers (sometimes this number is stated as 263 or 267) all of whom were killed. The balance of Custer's command numbering 350 soldiers saved their lives by fleeing the battle area. (I write about it later.)

The name of Crazy Horse became known as a respected winner, and for many young warriors he became a living legend. The Battle of the Little Big Horn, June 25–26, 1876 is one of the most famous battles in American history; it creates also a lot of controversy. The books about the famous battles, like Alamo and Gettysburg do not have so many different versions as does the Battle of the Little Big Horn.

***

After visiting the Mission and St. Labre Indian School in eastern Montana, Norman and I drove to the little town of Colstrip where we stayed over night. The following morning, we first drove on Route 39 towards the town of Lame Deer, and then the main road Route 212 along the reservation of the Northern Cheyenne. Very soon we saw the stretched open fields, low rolling hills, and gentile valleys along the Little Big Horn River. We stopped to visit and explore the famous battleground, the place that everyone has heard something about: the Little Big Horn. We looked at the monument in stone dedicated to those killed, the burial grounds, we looked at the panorama of field and hills where the event took place. I could imagine them with difficulties. Another field and another hill.

Earlier in Rapid City, we bought photographs that we already knew much about. In September 1948, the photographer Bill Groethe took pictures of the Indian chiefs who survived the Battle of the Little Big

Horn. There were: Little Warrior, Pemmican, Little Soldier, Dewey Beard, John Sitting Bull, High Eagle, Iron Hawk, and Comes Again. On a separate picture is Black Elk, who was blind and (according to information given to Norman by photographer Bill Groethe) did not want to be in the group photograph. When photographed, the surviving warriors were in their late 80's to 90's. Those photographs are framed, prominently displayed in our home in Delaware and are more moving than the real look of the battleground we saw the day of our trip. Even the short description is more touching than the place itself. This is not the first time it has happened to me. Against opinion, I think that many times the words are more moving, more imaginative than the real thing. Maybe some things or places should be left to our imagination without confrontation with a real thing or place?

The defeat at the Battle of the Little Big Horn creates speculation and debate by historians that have not ended yet. It is said that the information about the defeat of General Custer came to Washington in time to spoil the national celebration of the centennial of America's independence in 1776.

What had happened later, is also a subject of many publications. The same year of victory on the Little Big Horn for Indians was only a memory. A difficult time came and a heavy strong winter. Too many bison had been killed and there was hunger. Crazy Horse did not want to follow in the steps of Sitting Bull who traveled to Canada. He considered the land he was born and reared in as his, and he did not want to leave it. Crazy Horse was not a chief literally, but he was considered as a leader of a few hundred (some sources give four hundred, others nine hundred) Indian people who came to him cold, hungry and suffering seeking help and protection. They were his responsibility. He could not escape with a small group and wait to the end of winter. There were people who waited for his support. He could not disappoint them or deceive them. He took them to Fort Robinson in northwest Nebraska. Everywhere there was respect for him, the atmosphere of the leader and the winner. He was a source of jealousy of the older chiefs; among others, Spotted Tail, who had been given the run of Fort Robinson on the orders of General Crook, was jealous. It is said that Chiefs Red Cloud and Spotted Tail were not happy when they saw Crazy Horse. As his fame grew, they and others conspired against him and related untrue stories about him.

The Indians were more and more tired of the heavy long winter. From time to time, a delegation of white people would meet with Crazy Horse trying to convince him to settle with his people on his own reservation in Powder River country. The whites also wanted to convince him to go to Washington to meet with President Rutherford B. Hayes. He rejected this invitation and countered it by giving his rifle and his horse to the white officers.

Crazy Horse always kept himself as far away as possible from the white people, and he also avoided all the meetings with them. He did not know them as well as, for example, Red Cloud, Spotted Tail and Sitting Bull. He did not understand their behavior. Apparently Chief Spotted Tail was aware that whites had large numbers of guns against which the Indians could never compete. After two years spent in prison at Fort Laramie, Spotted Tail was probably the first Sioux chief who realized that they could not win against the whites.

The promise of their own reservation for the people with Crazy Horse was not kept, so they remained next to the Red Cloud Agency at Fort Robinson. The presence of Crazy Horse created unrest amongst the whites, annoyed old Indian chiefs who knew that the young warriors respected and liked him. Someone started the rumor that Crazy Horse wanted to create a rebellion. One of the repeated rumors was that Crazy Horse planned to murder General Crook during a meeting. General Crook became very nervous and did not attend the meeting (after the death of Crazy Horse he regretted it); he sent one of his officers to represent him. The general decided the most "safe thing" would be to send Crazy Horse to prison in Florida.

At the same time, the friends of Crazy Horse found out about the rumored murder and told him about it. Crazy Horse is said to have answered the "supposed murder of General Crook" by saying "only cowards are murderers".

Then came the day of September 5, 1877.

Crazy Horse went to Fort Robinson to meet with its leader. His cousin Touch-the-Cloud warned him, there are plans for arrest and imprisonment. When Crazy Horse realized that they were taking him to a secluded place, he started to resist. Presumably, the only weapon that he had with him was a knife. He brandished it and shouted: "Another treachery of the white man ... let me fight.. let me die... let me die fighting ...". He tried to free himself, but a Sioux Indian policeman pinned his arms. Then the other policeman stabbed Crazy Horse with a bayonet.

What really had happened at Red Cloud Agency is not known, because there are different versions. For sure there was violence, and Crazy Horse was critically stabbed. The description of that scene regardless of the version does not matter, as I wrote in the introduction; the scene always gives my heart a twinge.

All the sources agreed that Crazy Horse, in the beginning, did not resist until he realized that he was being taken to the secluded guarding place. Then he started to rebel forcefully. His arms were immobilized by the Indian policeman, and then a regular army soldier came and stabbed Crazy Horse in the stomach.

All the versions say that one of the guards wanted to overpower him. It was his old friend, Little Big Man, now an Indian policeman, who pinned his arms (like in the prediction). At the same time, one of the soldiers stabbed him. That version is similar to the vision Crazy Horse had in his youth: to be critically wounded when one of his warriors would pin his arms.

He died the same night.

The other version, a broader one:

Crazy Horse never believed the white people. During his whole life, he never signed any agreement with them. He understood that even if the Battle of the Little Big Horn was won, Indians were not going to win against white people. Even though defeated, he was still independent by spirit. He did want to be put on a reservation. He was attacked and stabbed from the back by soldiers in Fort Robinson in Nebraska.

Another version:

The wife of Crazy Horse, Black Shawl, was ill. In September 1877, without a parole, he left the reservation to take her to her parents, and General George Crook gave the order to arrest him, being afraid that Crazy Horse had concocted some secret plan. There were rumors. One was that the translator, Frank Grouard, who personally hated Crazy Horse, deliberately gave a false translation between the Chief and General Crook, saying, that Crazy Horse stated "he is not going to rest while one white person remains alive". (General Philip Sheridan, who heard this statement repeated, asked General Crook to check its credence).

And yet another version:

The chiefs Spotted Tail and Red Cloud made a conspiracy plot against Crazy Horse by giving false reports to General Crook. They presumably told Crook that Crazy Horse planned to kill him. Crazy Horse decided to take his wife to her parents at the Spotted Tail Agency, and his enemies were saying he plans to leave Fort Robinson. Crazy Horse went to Captain Luke Lea, who counseled him to return to Fort Robinson and thereby end the speculations.

When on September 5, he returned to Fort Robinson, the guards were waiting to arrest him. He resisted, and then a twenty year old soldier William Gebtiles, who never was promoted over the rank of private, stabbed him close to his left kidney. Crazy Horse died the same night in the room where Doctor McGillycuddy had bandaged his wound. His father was singing songs over him.

Doctor Valentine McGillycuddy, who was with the dying Crazy Horse, wrote later, that the chief died "around midnight". Oglala Sioux say, he died "after midnight", September 6, 1877. The military reports say, he died "before midnight", so September 5.

He was around 34 years old.

The body was given to his parents who buried him somewhere in The Badlands. The other sources say, his father and stepmother, as their son wished, buried his body not far from Wounded Knee.

To this day, no one knows where Crazy Horse is buried. And to this day, no one truly knows what he looked like. Crazy Horse never had a photograph taken so the mountain carving will represent the spirit not the actual man, though the pose is true to life.

***

Korczak Ziolkowski shaped the Sioux leader's face based on descriptions given him by several Sioux veterans of the Little Big Horn. One of them, confirmed one of the many idiosyncrasies attributed to Crazy Horse - the wearing of a stone in his ear. Once when asked why, North Black Elk said Crazy Horse responded, "Because I will return in the stone". The sculpture shows him pointing over his horse's head as he did once when asked by a contemptuous white "where are you lands now?" Pointing out across the Black Hills, he answered: "My lands are where my dead lie buried".

Now, in the place where he was murdered, there is a plate with the words: "Here the Chief Crazy Horse was killed September 5, 1877".

He was supposed to have said to his warriors that he "would return in stone".

"My land is where the remains of my ancestor are", says a legend that Crazy Horse proudly answered the white man who asked him "Where is your land now?"

Those words will be at the foot of the monument. The monument shows the chief on a horse with outstretched arm pointing towards his ancestors. Korczak Ziolkowski in his project sculpted a characteristic of the Lakota Sioux ...: high forehead and pronounced nose.

September 5 (6) of 1877 Crazy Horse died, and thirty-one years later, September 6, Korczak was born. Some see it as an omen.

The mountain being sculpted is loved by many. People come to find its' piece, spirit and relief. Mountains inspire, and they are given names. The mountain chosen by Korczak he named Thunderhead Mountain.

Ziolkowski worked on the sculpture till his death in 1982 at the age of seventy-four.

After his death, condolences from the whole world came to Ruth and her children, also from then President Ronald Reagan, who wrote among others: "The vision and dream of your husband are the inspiration for those who reach for one's soul".

Another letter kept in the family archives came form then President Lech Walesa of Poland, who wrote: "As a Polish person, I am proud that Korczak Ziolkowski started the project that is a symbol of greatness, not of a broken soul, the love of freedom".

Since Korczak death, the work has continued under the supervision of his wife, Ruth, based on the sculptor's 1/34th scale model, detailed calculations prepared by Korczak and an outline of Crazy Horse he painted on the mountain. The statue's eighty-seven foot head of Crazy Horse has slowly taken shape, and details of the eyes and nose were finally completed. Crazy Horse's face was finished in 2000, but there's no date set for the completion of the entire sculpture. No tax money or United States government support of any kind goes to fund this amazing project - it's paid for by contributions and admission fees from visitors.

Nothing seemed to stop him, not his age, nor illness (four back operations with the loss of six discs), nor the absence of government financing (he twice turned down ten million dollar offers from Washington because he didn't trust the government from over influencing and endeavoring to control the project), nor the lack of an experienced assistant (he worked alone for the first fifteen years and later got help from three of his five sons).

The whole project is not only a mountain monument of pink granite that will shine in the sun and be visible for miles – but as envisioned by Korczak, it will also include the Indian Museum of North America and a planned university, medical training center and hospital for Indians, all of which will be financed and sustained by revenue from tourists coming to see the carving. Leading into the project's area and to the foot of the mountain sculpture is the Avenue of the Chiefs.

"I promised the old Indians who asked me to create the memorial that it would never be a tourist gimmick", said Korczak. "That all the revenue produced here, after the carving is finished, will be used for the benefit of the Indian people. And I think I've proven my good faith by working hard everyday and never taking a salary or submitting expense accounts".

Some of the income has gone for scholarships for Indian students and some for living expenses, but the bulk has gone directly into the mountain project, for machines, equipment, gasoline, and explosives, whatever. And income will continue to be so used until the project is finished.

"Each person has his own monument to sculpt... I have my own", he said.

As Korczak planned, work on the five hundred and sixty-three-foot high sculpture in the round now in progress in the southern Black Hills is being carried on by his family under the direction of his wife, Ruth. Korczak realized at the outset that the Crazy Horse monument was larger than any one man's lifetime. Years ago, he prepared three books of detailed plans and measurements for the mountain carving. His wife, Ruth, and seven of their ten children are dedicated to carrying on his work. (Three of the Ziolkowski siblings left their family roots). The work is periodically documented with photos in their publication "The Progress".

Mrs. Ruth Ziolkowski explains: "Our work was made so much easier by all the advance planning Korczak did to help us. And we took his advice to "go slowly - so you do it right". As the work progressed, we all realized the great wisdom of those words. It was emotionally difficult moving ahead without him, but at the end of the first year, I think we all felt more comfortable up there on the mountain".

Also carried out has been the expansion and painting of the huge outline on the mountain. It serves as a point of reference for the on-going work while at the same time helping visitors visualize what will be carved. The outline, which took about six weeks to complete, also enables visitors to gauge the enormous progress made blocking out the colossal equestrian. The horse's outline is defined by a painted line from six-to-ten feet wide that required approximately eighty gallons of paint. Korczak originally painted it on the mountain in 1951. And, in 1982 - while recovering from a quadruple heart by-pass operation - he supervised the painting of much of the present outline of the horse's head. Crazy Horse is being carved by the point-system - a centuries-old technique used on Mt. Rushmore. Computers calculate the thousands of measurements from a scale-model made by Korczak, thirty-four times smaller than the real sculpture. The Ziolkowski family's precise measurement of the entire mountain and all aspects of the carving progressed with the design and construction of a sixty-six foot boom. It was placed atop the Indian's head on a huge swivel. A plumb line is suspended from the boom, and it serves as a giant "yardstick" for the measurements utilized in granite removal.

Stories about him are legend. He worked alone, using just dynamite and a small jackhammer. Tunneling under Crazy Horse's arm took two years. Approximately two hundred thousand tons of granite was blasted from sculptor Korczak Ziolkowski's Crazy Horse Mountain carving the first year. At the time of the sculptor's death, total rock removed from Crazy Horse was estimated at approximately seven million six hundred thousand tons by his family.

According to press articles, there were some misunderstandings and even fights. One of the Ziolkowski son-in-laws took a hammer and devasted the Korczak sculptures in their home. Among others, the head of Paderewski was damaged. The press said Korczak did not want to walk where he would view the damage. I have wondered several times why he did not repair the damaged sculptures. Now, after Korczak's death, they are exposed in their mutilated condition.

In 1993, President Bill Clinton during a White House presentation accepted two of the bronze sculptures by Korczak. It was a large base relief of President John F. Kennedy and a Crazy Horse scale model mounted on a blast fragment from the mountain carving. President Clinton paid a visit to the Crazy Horse Memorial on June 6, 1999.

The Ziolkowski Family gave the Polish born Pope John Paul II a bronze replica of Korczak's award-winning Paderewski sculpture. The Pope called Paderewski "a great man, a very good man". John Paul II accepted the sculpture during a January 22, 1997 audience with Monique Ziolkowski in the Vatican.

The Crazy Horse Memorial also was visited by the famous Lakota Sioux Olympic athlete, winner at the 1964 Olympics in Tokyo, humanitarian Billy Mills, who praised the carving as an empowering, living symbol. (I write more about Billy Mills later).

"I believe the Lakota who invited Korczak sixty years ago would be very proud of how their vision is being realized", spoke Billy Mills[18].

"The world asks you one question: Did you do the job? And you say, you did not. You would have, if the people were friendlier towards you, if you had enough money, if you had not been injured... But your answer has to be: "Yes! I did the job!" (Korczak Ziolkowski).

The sculpture of Crazy Horse is going to be ten times bigger than the Presidents' heads on Mount Rushmore, bigger than the Great Pyramids at Giza. How big it is going to be is shown by the stretched arm of the chief that is one hundred meters long.

Tourist attractions now existing include the American Indian Museum, a natural pine museum located adjacent to the sculptor's studio-home where exhibitions are held. It will eventually be replaced by a *"hogan"* style Indian Museum of North America with a diameter of three hundred and fifty feet, located near the base of the mountain. There is a restaurant and a souvenir shop where memoirs of the visit can be bought – jewelry made in silver and turquoise by Indian craftsmen, replicas of the monument, and so on.

---

[18] See: "The Progress", December 1999, pg.8.

Korczak, called an impressive visionary and great romantic, did not speak Polish, but he collected Polish magazines. Almost each brochure about him clearly states: "He was American of Polish descent".

A quite peculiar testimony, subsequent to his visit to the Black Hills for the coming out sculpture of Crazy Horse, was written by the French journalist and philosopher Bernard-Henri Levy, who wrote and published the book *American Vertigo. Travelling America in the Footsteps of Tocqueville.* The book is supposed to be the continuation of a famous book written by Alexis de Tocqueville *American Democracy,* known for its very acute analysis of democratic society. In 1830, Tocqueville with his friend Gustave de Beaumont traveled all over America. Now, after the years have passed, in the beginning of the twenty-first century, Bernard-Henri Levy, started his journey similar to the famous Tocqueville journey. He reached South Dakota and saw Mount Rushmore and Crazy Horse. He wrote about the undertaking of sculpting an entire mountain of the Indian chief.

Quotation:

"Monumental indeed. Lyrical, standing up to the comparison in principle. But incomplete. Underfinanced."...On the one hand, Rushmore, a fully completed monument, a cathedral of stone. On the other, the rough draft, thus botched work, this incomplete relief carving whose very incompleteness, as the entire environment indicates, has already lasted for two decades and will last until the end of time"[19]. Bernard-Henri Levy published his book in France in the year of 2005. Not one word was mentioned about the completed head of the chief that is "awe inspiring" in the area. Perhaps his visit took place much earlier than the year 2000?

In contrast, I would like to mention the well-known and respected American writer Larry McMurtry who starts his beautiful book[20] with the sentence that Crazy Horse, Sioux chief, dead for almost a hundred and twenty years, not known is his place of burial, comes back in the sacred Sioux place Paha Sapa in the Black Hills of South Dakota. He writes that fifty years of efforts by the sculptor Korczak Ziolkowski and then his wife and children has made the great chief on horseback slowly come out from the Thunderhead Mountain. For half of a century, the Ziolkowski family has worked on this project, millions of tons of stone have had to be removed to create the Chief. It will be the biggest sculpture in the world. The human coming from stone will inspire travelers that will

---

[19] See. Bernard Henry Levy, *American Vertigo*, Random House Publishing Group, New York, 2006, pg. 65.
[20] See. Larry McMurtry, *Crazy Horse*, A Lipper/Viking Book, 1999.

come to the Custer town in South Dakota; the traveler will have the finest impression of Indians. There will be talk about Crazy Horse more and more. And he will come out from the stone mountain as an American Sphinx. Crazy Horse is an American Sphinx, and he will gaze over the Black Hills. Larry McMurtry writes that the Ziolkowski Family may finish the project in the next generation or in two. He states that if it is finished during his lifetime, he would like to come and see it.

In the end of his book, Larry McMurtry again writes about the monument. He writes that if the Ziolkowski family is going to stand by their dedication to continue, the Chief will come back and his soul will be dominant in the Black Hills. In such a case, the road started earlier by General Custer, and called by the Sioux "the thief road", will come back to the Indians.

I would like to quote the thought about Crazy Horse coming from the known journalist and reporter Judith H. Dobrzynski, who writes for "The New York Times" and "The Wall Street Journal". She visited Mount Rushmore and Crazy Horse Center in the summer of 2006[21]. Judith H. Dobrzynski wrote to me:

"In contrast to Rushmore, where the heads are more powerful alone, I think the beauty of CH will be the opposite -- seeing him in action. I think Crazy Horse also suffers because viewers can not get close up (...). Clearly, though, it's a labor of love and a wonderful story of dedication".

More than one million people visit the Crazy Horse sculpture each year to see the work. I am happy that I could visit such a special place several times. The first time I saw the project in 1985, Ruth Ziolkowski showed me the whole Center. The monument was still an enigma, an artist's idea, characterized by the need for extreme perseverance to believe it will come true some day.

When in 2000, Norman and I were driving on Route 89 through South Dakota, and we saw in the far distance the huge head of the Indian chief, we stopped the car. I was looking in awe. It was. Finally it was.

Now the family is working on the horse's head and the outstretched arm of the chief. I am proud I belong to the same family of Korczak Ziolkowski. He was the reason I decided to write this book.

---

[21] See: Judith H. Dobrzynski, *A Monumental Achievement. Mount Rushmore owes its power to Gutzon Borglum, timing and budgets*, "The Wall Street Journal", July 15, 2006, pg. 14.

Aleksandra Ziolkowska-Boehm

The Sadness of Reservations

The look of the reservations most often is disappointing. Imagination is not inspired. Most surprising is how ordinary they are. I remember when Norman and I went to the Pine Ridge Reservation in South Dakota. According to our map, we crossed the border of the reservation and were driving on an unpaved dirt road. Around us, there was nothing...only emptiness. Far away were small houses that were more like shacks. After half an hour, we approached a young man who was slowly walking along the road. He looked at us. We came closer, stopped the car, I opened the window.

"Can you tell me where the Pine Ridge Reservation is?"

With an amused look, he smiled warmly...a smile that exposed few teeth.

"Lady, just leave the car and look around".

Somehow it seemed that I had mistakenly or somehow wrongly come to the strange conviction that reservations will have – like so many things in America – a welcome sign or a special gate similar to the entrance to a Chinatown section in a big American city.

How different are the faces of Indian reservations in the United States! Being in Texas, we had formed a positive impression from the Tigua Reservation near El Paso. The reservation there was characterized by unpretentious but nice houses of southwestern style architecture, and in front of them, late model cars were parked. The Indian village of the Tigua Tribe on the Ysleta Del Sur Pueblo Reservation was located adjacent to their casino. The benefit to the Tigua people of the opportunity for gainful employment in their casino was evident. The neatness of these homes and their landscaping showed the pride of the owners.

I think it is easier to describe wealth and splendor than poverty; even so, poverty makes the most powerful impression. Poverty can be shown by pictures; the landscape does not need words. How does one show poverty and its associated surroundings by simple words? How can words best describe the views of penetrating poverty? How can I describe the sadness of reservations?

The Pine Ridge Reservation is located in Shannon County in the southwest corner of the State of South Dakota. Pine Ridge is the second biggest Indian reservation in the United States of America. The reservation area equals almost two million acres, and it is home for 41 thousand Sioux Indians. Many of them are the descendants of the brave warriors, like the famous Crazy Horse, Red Cloud and Sitting Bull.

41

There are no farms or ranches, there is no industry. None of the roads have a name; most of them do not have a hard pavement. There are no buses, trains, banks, theaters, clothing stores, pharmacies, restaurants, an auto repair garage and no postman brings home the mail.

There is no cinema, or a shoe store. I have not seen a barber or ladies beauty parlor. On the reservation, the Indians do not have an opportunity to buy men's trousers or the ladies a dress because no one sells them there. There is one big store open twenty-four hours day named Big Bat's, and a few smaller ones that look like fortresses because the owners are afraid of robbery. Transportation by car is possible, but not everyone has a car.

Not only does appearance show that it is the poorest region of America, but government statistics say so. Unemployment reaches eigthy-eight percent, one of every three houses does not have electricity or plumbing. There is an alcohol problem, even though by law, the reservation people cannot buy a can of beer. At the same time, the most frequent cause of deaths on Pine Ridge is car accidents because of drivers being under the influence of alcohol. A nearby town Whiteclay in Nebraska features alcoholic products stores where most Indians buy, because they cannot buy alcohol on the reservation. Some Indians ask for closure of the nearby alcohol stores in Nebraska, but their voices do not have any effect.

An October 2006 letter from Jesuit Father Peter Klink, head of the Red Cloud Indian School that is located on Pine Ridge, wrote to Norman and I[22]: "Only five miles from Red Cloud, four millions cans of beer are sold each year in a Nebraska border town that has a population of thirty-five people. This is the yearly equivalent of one hundred and thirty-three cans of beer for every man, woman, and child living on the Reservation".

One third of Indians live under the United States poverty level; half of the children live in misery. The yearly average income for one of the inhabitants of the reservation is four thousand five hundred dollars (for the rest of the country it is about eighteen thousand dollars). Of a thousand new born children, twenty-nine die, and many are born with alcoholic syndrome. Fifty percent of students "drop out" of school, and two thousand families wait for the government to help them obtain housing. But the homeless do not sleep on the streets; their families take them in, care for those in need and feed the hungry...usually in overcrowded living conditions.

---

[22] See: Fr. Peter Klink, SJ. Letter October 2006, Red Cloud Indian School, Pine Ridge, South Dakota 57770.

"Time" Magazine[23] described Anita Hollow Horn, Oglala Sioux Indian woman living on the Pine Ridge. In a one level three-room house she lives with four children, mother, stepfather and seven siblings. With her nine-year old daughter and a few adult people, she occupies the basement. Her cancer stricken brother with his two sons and the rest of the children occupy the main floor of the house. Most of them sleep on the floor. The worst situation occurs when the basement fills with water. Mold grows over the walls from the basement upward.

But Anita Hollow's house has a washroom, something that the other house owners on the Pine Ridge can only dream of. The secretary from the Red Cloud Indian School, a young woman named Luci Red Stone, told us, that in her house there is only a dirt floor. There is no running water, because no plumbing system is installed. She told us that sixteen people usually occupy her three-room house.

In front of the Gospel Fellowship Church is a sentence: *"Our Only Hope Services"*.

Before he came to the Sacred Heart Catholic Church that is on the reservation, Jesuit Joseph Daniel Sheehan worked for years in India. He said: "The poor Hindus were sort of a united society, their thinking was 'in poverty we are all'. The American Indians think 'everything that comes to us is left over'. They become angry with each other because the poverty breaks up their families. I do not know what I would do if I were an American Indian living on a reservation. I think I would become an alcoholic"[24].

This is not the first time I heard that poverty ruins Indian families.

The white people are usually moved by the poverty of others including the Indians. But most of the time, they do not have knowledge about it. The monthly "Biography" dedicated a long article[25] to the businessman from Seattle, who helps Indians on the Pine Ridge Reservation. His name is Rob Young. He has been very successful producing sports equipment and others things. His idea for helping the Indians was to ask the buyers of his products to leave some change in a can next to the cashier when they were paying their bill. Eventually, he took part in a program "Adopt a Grandparent". It is a program of volunteers who correspond with elderly people and help them. Some send them winter blankets or wood for burning during the winter. Rob

---

[23] December 16, 2002.

[24] See: *Poverty runs deepest on desolate Sioux reservation*, Peter T. Kilborn, "New York Times", republished by "Houston Chronicle", October 20, 1992, pg. 4A.

[25] See: *A Place to Call Home. One Man's Mission to help Native Americans*, Melissa Burdick Harmon, "Biography", April 2000, pgs. 92–112.

Young corresponded with the seventy-seven year old Katherine Red Feather living on the edge of poverty on the Pine Ridge. When Rob mentioned he would like to visit her, Red Feather responded that her house is "not so nice". He came anyway despite her reluctance to invite him. He was dismayed that his adopted grandmother lived in a one room trailer. She shared with another nearby family an outdoor toilet. "I met families of as many as twenty-eight people living under the same roof in a small house. I have never seen such poverty", said Rob Young.

After this visit, he came back to Seattle with the will and the ambition that he had to do something about it, at least for his adopted grandmother, Katherine Red Feather. He started to look around seeking assistance. After eighteen months, he had created a large network of help. The offers of help came from the local TV station and local magazines in Seattle. Volunteers came to him to offer their assistance. In his Sundance Film Festival catalog, Robert Redford ran an advertisement requesting volunteers to help and support the building of houses on the Pine Ridge Reservation. Architectural students from the University of Nebraska helped as well. They designed the houses specifying inexpensive but quality materials, and they themselves even participated in their construction. In June 1995, Katherine Red Feather moved to her new house. It was not big, but it has a small veranda and a plumbing system. For Red Feather, it was remarkable to have running water and toilet facilities.

Thirty houses were built, and some of them had "ramps" installed to allow the passage of wheel chairs. One man said he had not left his house for several years because he did not have a wheel chair ramp.

The Pine Ridge Reservation is so vast, one feels he is almost separated from the rest of the country. Living conditions on the reservation dramatically portray the differences between the dominant white culture and the repressed Indian culture. Indian people are neither fed properly nor do they live properly. They do not have habits that are accepted as civilized. In the Sioux culture, generosity is a virtue, and it is deceitful to be or to describe someone as greedy or cheap. Despite what was quoted earlier by Jesuit Daniel Sheehan, Indians share everything with each member of their family and close friends. They do not save money for a house, or to improve it, or for opening a business. The little capital they have usually is shared within their family. They do not have a motivation for saving money. Young people do not think about the future because they do not see any future. Not many Indians live until "a ripe old age". The average man on the Pine Ridge Reservation lives 55 years and a woman ten years longer.

Children do not think about what they would like to do in the future; no one asks them what they dream about doing with their life. What dreams can they have since their father and their grandfather did not work, but existed on a government subsidy? It is the fifth or sixth generation that takes on the effect of decades of unemployment. How can the stagnation of several generations that live without work be overcome?

The young people face an existence of no money and no possibility to work to earn money. Those with good intentions cannot find work on the reservation. Those who are fortunate often find employment in the state and federal Indian agencies. Some of them find employment outside of the reservation, but many return, because it is in their culture to take care of the elderly. Others return with regrets having experienced discrimination and isolation in the white environment. Sometimes those returning to the reservation have already turned to alcohol, and a significant percentage of young people commit suicide. According to statistics, in the United States, the suicide rate among the Native Americans is 6 times greater than that of the average in the country.

There are others, who after moving from the reservation, work but often for the minimum wage. They do not have money for health insurance, and they lose the free health care system entitlement of the reservation. The government does not pay for an Indian's health care outside of the reservation, deciding that it is up to Indian Agencies to use their budget for health.

The hugeness of the reservation, the isolation and the extreme poverty go hand in hand with the barrenness of the land and its harsh climate. A big part of the land is *The Badlands*. Just remind yourself of the landscape from western movies – the limestone sculptures standing in sand adjacent to the grass of the prairie. When I saw *The Badlands* for the first time, I was surprised. Not because it is so beautiful, but because it is such an awful monument to the poverty of soil – with no water and no green. It reminded me of sand roses that Norman brought from Saudi Arabia – pieces of sand formed into beautiful shapes like roses. They can be ornamental on a big bay window as in our house, but the Badlands terrain – they can scare and haunt one like the bad fairy tales and pictures from our childhood. How frightening it must be to spend the night in *The Badlands*.

That theory says: Indians are the nation to whom a capitalist system is strange, however a few facts indicate otherwise. According to anthropologists, Indians owned horses or teepees and had the traditional feelings of ownership – against "union" or community ownership. Meriwether Lewis ("Lewis and Clark") described the Chinook Indians as "wonderful bargainers in trading". The fur trading companies that exchanged goods for furs did very well and brought good income to the Indians. As Bruce E. Johansen pointed out: "The Northwest Coast peoples have strong traditions of ownership, unlike many Native peoples elsewhere in North America. Natives in most places had ownership traditions, but collectively, as groups. Ownership of land on the NW Coast was usually vested in families"[26].

During our travels, not far from Wounded Knee, Norman and I saw a group of Indians who had a few items for sale. On the reservation, I had not seen any stores with gifts for sale, so we stopped. I bought a "dream catcher" entitled: "American Indian Movement Wounded Knee". The seller helped me to select several others, and in very nice "soft sell", she also persuaded me to buy something else. After we finalized our small transaction, she shook our hands. – So Indians know how to sell – I thought. – What to do to encourage them to do so on a grand scale?

The land of the Pine Ridge Reservation is not blessed with natural resources. When in the 1980s coal was discovered on the Crow Indian Reservation, it was soon found out that there was not much recoverable coal, and it was emptied soon. The utility of the land of the reservations is thirty to ninety percent less than elsewhere in the United States. Corrupt courts and tribal governments tend to scare outside investors from the areas.

In many developing countries, government involvement is paramount to creating an atmosphere that will encourage investment by outsiders. A similar atmosphere is needed on the reservations. Institutions who govern the reservations do not have the capital (as they operate under restricted budgets) to invest and do not encourage people to do so. Indians cannot obtain credit since their land is h*eld in trust by the federal government*, such that it belongs to federal trusts and cannot be used as collateral for investment funds. The tribal system cannot help.

Travelling on the huge Pine Ridge territory we came west without seeing any hotel. There was only one small pension run by a white couple Larry and Betty Swick. It is located on the reservation and has a name Wakpamni. There are three small houses; one has a name "The Folks' House" that belonged to Larry's parents. Each house has three bedrooms and two washrooms. The Swick family has run the pension for over seventy years. The younger Larry and Betty moved there from San Francisco, when his parents started to have health problems. Each room is separately decorated and has its own name. For example, there is a room named Settlers, another named Lakota. There is also a nice library.

---

[26] See: Letter, February 13, 2008.

We gave up our earlier reservation at the pension when we learned that our fellow-traveler, the female cat named Suzy, was not allowed with us in the room. She was with us on the road from the East Coast to the Pine Ridge, and we did not want to leave her closed up in the car. So we drove for another three hours to Rapid City to a hotel where its guests were welcome with their travelling pets. The receptionist rightfully thought that if someone travels with animals, they are civilized and the animals are well trained and housebroken.

In a local paper, I read about an Indian woman named Alma Brewer who bought a ruined hotel and converted it into a pension using all her savings for the business. After a year of not much activity and endless renovations, she realized that she would be unable to pay off ten thousand dollars of government credit. She had to close the pension. Being fifty years old, she was left with no work and no security for her old age.

Some Indians try their luck in a sales business. Emma "Pinky" Clifford runs the only store thirty miles north of the Pine Ridge Reservation. She bought it eight years earlier. In the beginning, Clifford lived in a trailer and sold gasoline after installing a gasoline storage tank. Receiving bank credit for building a store, the entrepreneur also sells groceries while still running her gasoline station.

I have read about others initiatives. For example, Rosalie and Bob Benson were co-owners of an artist society. An Indian woman Leatrice "Chick" Big Crow opened a recreation center where Indian children and youth have the possibility to spend their free time in a productive way while not exposed to drinking alcohol or using drugs.

In April 2006, a press release gave the disturbing information that Indians from the Pine Ridge Reservation proposed to use their land to build a medical clinic for abortion. Women from all over the country could come there for the procedure. The Indian land would give the doctors security since no one can cross it and impose their outside laws.

For the last twenty years, the Federal Government has increased its budget in all fields, but has not increased the funding to solve the problems of the Native Americans. Some time ago, the government promised that each Indian child was going to have at least a grammar school education and would be assured of a house and basic health care. Like all the many other government promises, those were not kept.

Two hours driving from Pine Ridge, near Rapid City, there is a gold mine that should belong to the Indians since it is on their land.

The Sioux Indians are asking the government for compensation for the land taken away from them in 1877. "All the hills around are for us sacred" - says Sam Loudhawk.

Aleksandra Ziolkowska-Boehm

According to the treaty of 1868 signed at Fort Laramie, the great Sioux Nation received the right to land west of the Missouri River that is now part of South Dakota. The treaty was broken six years later when gold was discovered.

In July 1999, Pine Ridge was visited by President Bill Clinton. He was the first president to visit an Indian reservation since Franklin D. Roosevelt had stopped for a short time in 1936 at the Cherokee Reservation in North Carolina. Clinton's visit created considerable interest by the press and TV. There were many articles published. On TV, Clinton was shown holding discussions with an Indian group. One woman, forty-four years old Geraldine Blue Bird, told Clinton that she lives in a house that has five rooms. With her live twenty-seven people. She does not have money to warm the house during the winter. Sometimes she makes *tacos* and sells them in a small store. The other possibilities to make money are none. "It would mean so much for all of us if we would have work," Blue Bird said with tears in her eyes.

President Clinton subsequently organized a special committee to help in creating one thousand work places and to encourage business people to invest by creating appropriate circumstances for investment.

There was a government promise to build inexpensive housing, where in future years ninety percent of people from Pine Ridge were to live. But the two million dollars to be donated yearly by the government to that project is not enough for realization of such an ambitious endeavor. To start with and to create business interest, transportation is needed, and to create transportation good roads are needed. As I wrote earlier, on Pine Ridge that is part of the United States of America, a country so proud of its road system and highways, the roads are not paved.

In South Dakota, winters are long and bitter. When it rains, it becomes muddy everywhere. When it is dry; the roads are covered by dust. Each passing car raises its trail of dust. In the summer because of lack of sanitation, there are flies.

Pine Ridge is a unique reservation. It does not compare to the reservations where a few tribes make tremendous income thanks to the gambling casinos. The majority of Indian reservations are examples of unimaginable poverty and stagnation.

As reporter John J. Miller wrote: "It came time to close the Indian reservations"[27]. For sure, the concept of reservations should be thought all over again. Of course, there are many explanations (perhaps excuses)

[27] See: *Off the Rez*, "National Review", December 31, 2002.

48

of the situation that now exists. Most of all, it is said that the Indian suffering is because of the land that was taken from them. Pine Ridge is the location of the last huge massacre of Indians that took place at Wounded Knee in 1890. Three hundred Indians were killed including women and children. When Norman and I stopped there, only a simple sign identified the name as Wounded Knee. There is nothing else, only the name and the empty plains.

As stated by Rex Alan Smith (my conversation with him is included in this book), instead of thinking about the present, there is a tendency to open and stir up old wounds. He also said that the biggest current problem on the reservations is not the stolen land that the Federal Government took away form the Indians back a few generations. It is an unclear understanding of land ownership. Indians are not given credit so they can start a business, because the banks cannot take land as collateral. If the Indians cannot repay a loan, their land cannot be taken from them. For the same reason, the credit to buy or build a house cannot be obtained, as is so popular all over the United States. It cannot be done on the reservations. The only possibility, for the Indians is to receive credit for a trailer home. The banks will give credit for a trailer home because they can be taken away.

The independence of tribes is an illusion, Rex Alan Smith explained to me. Reservations are not like separate countries, their inhabitants are American citizens, even if they have their own jurisdiction and police.

Problems abound. The Indian issues are so complicated and complex that it is easier to give them forty million dollars every year in relief funds rather than endeavoring to correct the situation.

The solution is apparently a new *commercial code,* one that would allow the Indian to use his land as collateral, but for example, Pine Ridge does not agree to it. Also, the strong rivalry between tribes does not solve anything and does not create anything constructive. Furthermore, some full-blooded Indians are against those who are not full-blooded.

An elected president heads the tribe, but his term in office only lasts two years. The term is too short to provide time to enact any legislation that can bring about reforms. The jurisdiction of the president includes the judicial, legislative and executive functions.

The best minds in the country, experts in economy, say that only reforms in law on the reservation, to be enacted by Indians themselves, can change the existing rules and create an environment conducive to starting of business. So far, almost every business plan is criticized by the Indians themselves as a w*hite-man thing.* The result is such that for other than simple shopping, one has to drive far away, even outside of the reservations.

It is said that the basic ethics of the workplace and business environment, such as being on time for work and proper attire are not known among the majority of Lakota Indians. They do not understand the ethic – to be on time to start a day's work. This sounds like a feeble excuse to avoid provision of proper training and to instill inspiration in achieving success in the workplace. The achievements of the Indian people in the military are evidence of their ability to be on time, obey orders, live by rules, along with their outstanding bravery (that I write about later).

"If anyone would like to open a factory and needs fifty people for work, we will have a problem to find them", says Elsie Meeks[28] who lives on Pine Ridge and whom Senator Tom Daschle nominated in 1999 to the Washington Committee on Human Rights.

Indians have to grow into the changes, so their land instead of in *trust* will be their private ownership. Not the tribe's ownership. It will end the existence of reservations.

One of the trips to South Dakota that Norman and I made was in May 1995. How distinguished and beautiful are the Black Hills. How beautiful is Custer State Park with bison, antelope, sheep and goats. A big attraction was Bear Country near Rapid City where we drove with closed windows as instructed on the appointed roads amongst bears by the tens, twenties and more. We stopped and looked at them walking slowly or sleeping by the roads. There were bear cubs "roughhousing" with each other and young bears hanging from the trees or carousing on the playgrounds.

We visited Mount Rushmore National Park and saw the presidents' heads popularized in the movies. It is said, Washington was put there for his efforts giving birth to the republic, Jefferson for creating the government, Lincoln for symbolizing the uniqueness of every human being, and Teddy Roosevelt for his leadership in the impact of the United States on the world in the twentieth century. The sculptor John Gutzon Borglum dedicated the last fourteen years of life to this project.

---

[28] See: John Miller, *Off the Rez*, "National Review", December 31 2002, pg. 31.

Happy Feast Day in New Mexico

A heavy wind was blowing when the young Indian boy pulled the rope connected to the church bell. The ringing bell was the signal asking people to come to mass. Couples and entire families – women in bright colored dresses – men in loose dressy traditional clothing were making their way to the church. The dust rose from their steps. Then for about one hour everything was quiet. Sunshine warmed the *adobe* building, and nothing moved. And then the wooden doors of the church opened, and people were leaving...couple by couple, family by family. Excited dogs barked loudly at the exiting worshippers. Women were hurrying home to prepare the family dinners. Men stopped, some leaning back against the sunny side of the church. They talked and laughed together. Everywhere voices were heard saying. *Happy feast day*!

I was in Pueblo Tesque. It was November 12, the celebration day of the yearly holiday Feast Day. On this day, it is the occasion to perform traditional Indian dances. Even the old Spanish laws allowed Indians to celebrate the holiday.

On one hand, it is only fun, play, pleasure. Children do not go to schools, old friends meet and talk. On the other hand, it is a time for reflection and bonding, time for letting the mind be free and connecting to the spiritual side. People finish summer works and confirm their union with Mother-Earth. The main attraction of the Feast Day ceremony is dance, a chance to hug, to ring the bells and to take pleasure in appearing in colorful attire. Hundreds of people – men and women – move slowly in a dance, boys and men beat five drums and sing: "Give us life, bless us".

When autumn arrives it is time for hunting. Before leaving Pueblo Tesque for the areas rich in wild game, the hunters take part in the ceremony honoring the change in seasons, the Day of Thanksgiving, or rather Feast Day. They consider it the right occasion and take part in the ceremony. The Comanche people are dressed with bright feathers, and they dance an old ritual war dance. Years earlier the dance encouraged the warriors to confront the enemy and to enter into battle. Now in ritual dance, men thank God for the harvest and confirm their being together in the old natural ways and in the old rhythm of life. The Comanche people divide themselves into "people of winter" and "people of summer". Every autumn and spring, the leaders change. In the fall, the hunters, who are "people of winter" became the leaders.

All of this, I have heard from the deputy chief of the pueblo who was guiding me into a village. Pueblo Tesque lands are located north of Santa Fe, the capitol of the State of New Mexico. Only three hundred and fifty people live in Pueblo Tesque. They have similar problems as most of the Indian reservations: unemployment, poverty, and alcoholism. Bingo play was opened in the hope that it would generate some income. This activity is welcomed by Indians and by whites as well. "The whites are accustomed to a better way of life, and they prefer to keep us in a glass ball as poor people, full of tradition and not fashionable" was the opinion I heard talking to an Indian who repairs and restores adobe characteristics for area houses. These area houses built from unburned brick characteristically have flat roofs, are large, durable, cool in summer and warm in winter. Money for restoration of the old adobe homes is most often not available, and work goes slowly for my acquaintance.

I was invited into a newly renovated *adobe* home and was offered local Comanche specialties: chili, plum cake, bread baked in an outside oven, also coffee and candies ... I listened to their stories – another occasion to gather together and to dance ritual dances. For example, when a hunter kills a deer, there is a special ceremony to thank the deer for its "use". For four days, the Comanche smoke tobacco, pray and appreciate the spirit of the deer. The deer is cut into pieces, portioned out and given to family and friends. Similar procedures accompany the killing of a rabbit. The men kill rabbits and give them to women in the pueblo. Four days later, the chosen woman prepares the food and gives it to the hunters. Besides meat from the rabbit, the prepared food includes cornflower. Earlier there are gatherings needed for ceremonial herbs and leaves from one uncut tree that is "mediator" for the other already cut trees. Thanks to God for use of the herbs and tree leaves is always given. According to Indian beliefs, everything that lives in nature has a soul.

The Comanche told me that in far away regions, those never shown to newcomers or people visiting as tourists, in the autumn the elders of the tribe follow the sun to the south and pray for the return of the sun. They affirm their own sacred ties with the earth and compliance with its rules. The elders believe God should be thanked even for the rules and they do thank him. In December, in a special part of the eastern Rocky Mountains, the elder who is "leader of winter" prepares the people for the Days of Sun. For four days, the people pray for a change of the seasons. When spring comes, the "leader of winter" is changed, and another elder becomes the "leader of summer". The prayers are for sunshine to bring warmth and life.

Pueblo life has a different rhythm. The people work on the land, the earth, the soil and then await the crop. On artificially watered terraces, corn, wheat, sorgum and vegetables are grown.

When I arrived at the biggest city in New Mexico, Albuquerque, the guide, 85-year old Bill Cramp, was waiting for me at the airport. Bill had a reputation for a love of the land and a gift for talking about it. He told me that he was happy I was born in Poland because he had special esteem for my native country. In 1939, he worked in the American Consulate in Warsaw. Living with his wife in the Old City, the beautiful and most historical section of the Polish capitol, they had to leave the country after a few weeks due to the German invasion of Poland and the start of World War II.

Bill Crump (a volunteer guide for Fulbright scholars coming to the USA) accompanied me as we drove to pueblos. Near Tesque, I saw Santo Domingo, a very traditional area known for its turquoise mining. Also, I saw Isleta Pueblo, located not far from the Rio Grande River. In Isleta, I talked to Agnes Dill, a beautiful middle aged Indian woman. She was of regal bearing and exuded good warm feelings towards me. She told me of the faith of Indians, and that for ages they were native to New Mexico land. The Comanche legends say that they were "always" there.

In 1539, the Spanish conquistadors came to the New Mexico area, and seventy years later Spanish settlers began arriving and started the silver mining operations. In the seventeenth century, there were a number of Indian uprisings against the Spanish governing the land. New Mexico became part of Mexico and later became part of the United States. In those days, what is now New Mexico territory was also part of the states of Arizona, Colorado and Nevada. There were several Comanche uprisings against incoming settlers in 1863, 1882 and 1886. In 1912, New Mexico received the status of a "separate state".

On a road from the pueblos to Albuquerque, Bill stopped several times in *ghost towns*, left over from the silver mining days. He stood in the front of the remains of one house and asked me to take his photograph. –"You can say to your friends in Poland that this is your rich American friend in front of his residence" – he joked.

In Albuquerque, where the past and present mix together with every step you take, I saw old *adobe* houses and modern buildings with galleries and restaurants located in them. On the streets, Indian women sell silver jewelry made with turquoise. Bill explained to me, that Albuquerque was a good example of how cooperation, relationships and rights between whites, Mexicans and Indians are working well. All who are not of Spanish/Indians heritage are called *anglos*.

He invited me to the annual Balloon Fiesta attraction, an international competition of balloon enthusiasts. I told him that I was aware of being too late for the middle of October balloon competition, and had my visit been earlier, perhaps I could have attended the Fiesta and seen the extraordinary colors of balloons. Bill Cramp suggested

Aleksandra Ziolkowska-Boehm

coming to Albuquerque again in December for the traditional Christmas holiday.

Legend says that many years ago, an inhabitant living in New Mexico started a fire to warm himself and to brighten the road to church on Christmas Eve. Later, others lighted fires – to show the roads going to all the churches on Christmas Eve. Now, every year, tourists are treated to a spectacular attraction of these illuminations during Christmas Eve. Candles placed into the ground border the roads, and the churches are literally covered in light by hundreds and thousands of candles.

The light in New Mexico is very special - during the day – it is bright and clean, high, it creates a very beautiful radiance. Sunbeams touch everything – the flat terrain, the hills, the forests, the desert.

Its Native Americans of New Mexico call it the *Land of Enchantment* - delightful ground and soul. It became the state motto and appears on automobile license plates.

Bitter Recollections of Indian Schools

"School is for me a bitter recollection" said the elderly Sioux Indian Phil. He was five years old when he was sent to Wakpale in South Dakota, to a school for American Indians named Saint Elizabeth. She was a patron of Christian mercy that dedicated her life to serving the ill and poor.

Phil remembers how he and his colleagues were crying, their bodies hunched from being tightly bound and on their knees. In this subjugated posture, they were publicly flogged. Such punishment was over when he rejected Indian tradition and became more like his white peers. "It is like someone put a knife into your heart and slowly twisted", says Phil, when asked about the memories from those years. "Now, when I am old man, I look at it more sharply and see punishment of small children like punishment of plants that are coming from the soil."

A similar opinion about her Indian school was told to me by Madonna, Cheyenne, who works in a local hospital in Rapid City, South Dakota. She showed me poems, her writing for herself, as she says – to express her pain. Madonna went for a walk with me. As we walked, holding back her tears, she said, "I will never forget the nuns, who frightened us of the devil. For each bad thing I was accused of, I was taught to expect punishment by the devil that instilled in me a fear like the fear of fire. I will never forget my scare and my pain."

The story is like from Dickens, but it is not fiction, only a fragment of American history.

Since the second half of the nineteenth century, Indian children were separated from their parents and sent to schools that were financed by the American government. Some children visited their parents during vacation and holidays, but the majority was sent to schools far away from their parents and homes, such that they were unable to see their beloved family for years.

Indian schools were built as the result of an agreement between the government and the Indians. In exchange for Indian land, the government promised to give Indian children a basic education. The schools were financed by Congress and administrated by a special office of the Bureau of Indian Affairs, and sometimes by Christian groups. By the end of the 1880's, there were twenty-seven schools built on the Indian reservations. They were spread over a huge territory from along the East Coast to the West Coast. One of the most known was the Carlisle Indian Industrial School in Pennsylvania, which opened in 1879. It was the school attended by the Olympic hero, athlete Jim Thorpe. Other schools were the Haskell Indian School in Lawrence, Kansas and the Phoenix Indian School in Arizona.

Official historic sources agree that the schools intended to take children away from the "damaging and harmful" influence of parents and Indian culture. The schools were supposed to assimilate Indian children by cutting them away from their parents, tribe and culture.

As it happened, particularly during the beginning of the existence of these schools, parents who refused to permit their children to attend the schools, literally lost them by the virtual kidnapping and blackmail practiced by government officials.

"Government agents were coming even with pistols that were used to scare parents. If you do not give me your child, you will be in hunger", wrote the author of books Arlene Hirschfelder describing how Indian parents were threatened. For over twenty years, the writer was a member of the Association on American Indian Affairs.

The living accommodations at the schools were Spartan with no facilities even for medical care. Many times there were cases of long illnesses suffered by the students, often tuberculosis. The student's time was fully utilized, and a full schedule was enforced that included the learning of writing, reading, arithmetic and extra curricular activities such as work in school kitchens, laundry rooms etc. This practice was done so the children had little time together to share common interests of their tribal society, traditions and the past. The schools stressed disciplinary practices. Children were punished even for talking in their native language.

The schools did allow students to participate in sports as evident from the accomplishments of Jim Thorpe when he attended the school at Carlisle, Pennsylvania.

In 1928, a report prepared by the Brookings Institute for Government in Washington, DC stressed that Indians educated outside home "have to suffer heavily in contacts with their own people and that none of the official courses offered in the schools would heal it".

The highest number of children attending Indian schools was in the 1930's when economic circumstances favored expenditures by the federal agreement. Over twenty-four thousand Indian children were then attending the schools. Now, almost every Indian family has at least one relative who attended the infamous Indian public schools.

Sioux Tim Giago and his six cousins attended Holy Rosary Indian Mission on Pine Ridge Reservation in the 1940's, when as he stated: "the time was very difficult". "There was a choice between keeping us home, where there was no food, or sending us to school, where we had three meals a day and a roof over our head. I am one of those who never liked school", Giago was quoted as saying to the reporter of "The Dakota Times", a weekly in Rapid City.

Not all have such difficult recollections. Many remember interesting times spent outside home. "I think my experience was good", says Robert Bennett, who attended school in Kansas during the depression years, "for some of us, it was the only house we had".

Phil Lane, a well-known leader, is Sioux and Chickasaw origin. He was born at the Haskell Indian Residential School, where his parents met. He thinks being raised at school far away from home and the influence of his parents hardens the feelings. He stresses that the schools damaged the base of Indian families. Lane, in his later boyhood years, grew up in the town of Walla Walla in the state of Washington. Later he moved to Canada, to Lethbridge in Alberta. Lane became a professor at the Canadian Center for Management Development.

He emphasizes that the problem of a negative influence on children in Indian schools came to the public's attention only a few years ago. Lane thinks that Indians living in the United States and Canada have not the technique, the basic ability to be good parents. They did not have any model to influence them, homes in which rules and customs had to be followed, the way of dealing with differences, and how to build relationships. A high percentage of suicides, alcoholism, use of drugs, divorces – those are the result of sending five generations of Indian children to schools located far away from homes. Also, it is a result of the treatment that Indian children at schools were exposed to and the atmosphere in which they were raised in.

Some think that Lane exaggerates by stressing the difficulties he had in childhood and how they formed his adult life. Spero Manson, professor of psychiatry at the University of Denver, president of the American Indian and Alaska Native Programs, agrees that the schools damaged pride and dignity, and they took away the feeling of belonging to an Indian community. Manson also thinks that Phil Lane uses schools as a metaphor to show the injustices that came upon Indians throughout their whole life, not only during their school years.

Phil Lane is hopeful that he can help those who came through similar experiences by creation of a special program, of "listening and talking about their own pain", that he runs in workshops in Canada and the United States. He says that these programs should help the Indians to understand and to forgive. Most of the people in the United States do not have any knowledge about Indian children and their harmful experiences. Lane says the fact that his mother and father were regularly punished physically left an impact not only on them, but also on him. That punishment was and still is a source of pain to him. He remembers that he was flogged by his father, who likewise remembered that, in much the same way, he and other Indian school children who did something wrong were punished

Lane said that he understood that if the Indian community is to be healthy, they should remember all of this, talk about it, not to hide it. They learned how to save themselves by hiding their pain. They should reject pain, shame, feelings of being demeaned that are inside them.

A similar situation was evident in Indian schools all over the United States and Canada. In 1998, Jane Stewart, the Canadian Minister of the Ministry of Indian Affairs and Northern Development, during the ceremony in Parliament in Ottawa attended by Indians leaders, said: "It is sad, that our history to show respect to Native people is not something we can be proud of. We have to be sure not to repeat in the future our mistakes from the past. Those people, who came through physical and sexual abuse, we want to say that it should not have happened, and for all those tragedies at schools, we are deeply sorry."[29] Worthy of mention is the 2008 apology of Australia's Parliament to its Aborigine citizens. Along with Canada's apology to its native people, South Africa's 1992 expression of regret for apartheid and the United States Congress' 1988 law apologizing to Japanese-Americans for their internment during World War II, Australia joined a small group of nations apologizing for oppressing minorities. Prime Minister Kevin Rudd's motion in Parliament on behalf of all Australians was approved unanimously: "We apologize for the laws and policies of successive governments that have inflicted profound grief, suffering and loss on these our fellow Australians"[30].

How is the situation now? It depends. In many Indian schools the tribal languages are part of the school's curricula. Some of the schools are well equipped, almost as well as universities with attractive campuses. Mary Kihega, social worker in New Mexico, sends her fifteen-year old son to Indian school. The school is located seventy miles north of Santa Fe. "It is not just an average school", says Kihega proudly. "It has smaller classes than in public schools. My son is very happy there."

Many years have passed by since Marlon Brando used his Oscar award ceremony to call public attention to how Hollywood created and used its Indian image. Not much has been done during the ensuing years. The public institutions, like the Bureau of Indian Affairs and the Indian

---

[29] See: David Crary, *Canada apologizes to native peoples for injustices*, "Houston Chronicle", August 1, 1998.
[30] See: "Wilmington News Journal", February 13, 2008 quoting the Associated Press.

Health Service do not have enough funds. The Oscar award to Kevin Costner for his movie *Dances With Wolves,* based on Michael Blake's book, again put attention on Indian affairs. The movie is an artistic phenomena and shows nineteenth century Indians and government politics towards them. It shows the values that were important to Indians. It would be a tragedy if the following years created indifferences towards their complex situation.

Aleksandra Ziolkowska-Boehm

Indian School of Saint Labre in Montana

"This probably is my last check for you. I have supported the Saint Labre Indian School for many years, and I do not see changes. When will your condition start to be improved? For thirty years now, I have heard how difficult it is. Is anything better? I am tired of such a hopeless situation."

The staff of St. Labre, who are involved in seeking funds, like Rod Trahan who did it for many years and like others, often heard such remarks. Sponsors, people understanding the need and importance of help, most often cannot contribute large amounts, but donate smaller amounts regularly and consequently support the school. The whole system of support is based on those small regular donations and not on rare, large, one-time donations. Without such help, St. Labre, and other Indian schools, like St. Joseph's in South Dakota or Red Cloud on the Pine Ridge Reservation and many others could not survive and remain open.

Rod Trahan, whom we met in Montana, who was also a guest later in our home in Delaware, is a boyish looking Northern Cheyenne (my interview with him is included in a second part of this book.) He married a teacher, Nicole who also works for St. Labre. They have two sons: Hunter and Decker and in 2008 adopted a baby girl named Sawyer. When I asked Rod what arguments he uses to explain to those skeptical people, who want to know that their money is being used for good purposes, Rod says:

"The answer that would convince the doubtful is not easy. It is difficult to say something that would console everybody, and I cannot convince those who are impatient or irritated. It is true, help is essential to the survival of St. Labre and for the hopes of its Indian students to effect changes and for Indians to emerge from the poverty which is huge. Alcoholism is common, as are diabetes and kidney problems. I can only stress these facts to those who question the use of their contributions".

Statistics are sad too: poverty is ever present with a per capita annual income barely five thousand dollars on the Northern Cheyenne and Crow Reservations. (The average in the country is – as I stated earlier – eighteen thousand dollars). The average life span for men living on both reservations is sixty years of age. Suicides among young people on the reservations are three times higher than the average in America. Young people who finish high school is below the country's average. Also, the percentage of Indian youth that complete a higher education is only four percent compared to twenty-five percent the average in America. In Montana, where Indians are six percent of the state's population, fifteen percent of men in prisons and thirty percent of women in prisons are Native Americans. In the same state, twenty-five percent of children in foster homes are of Indian origin (of 1830, four hundred and forty-three are Indian children).

Why are there such statistics? For many years, the history of American Indians was falsely reported in books and in the media. By and large, this history was distorted. In the eighteenth, nineteenth and twentieth centuries, broken and not upheld treaties, genocide, wiping away of culture and language took place, thus creating despair and eliminating hope. Into Indian life, resignation and apathy were introduced. The wise Crow Indian Chief Plenty Coups projected that shattered Indian lives would prevent them from waking up for many years from this tragedy. He said it in a very sad way: "But when the buffalo went away, the hearts of my people fell to the ground and they could not pick them up again."[31]

How sad were those past years after the whites took over; the same sad years exist now. The billions of dollars that the American government has invested in Indian *welfare* have not produced any concrete positive results, nor were the investments big enough. On most of the reservations, the whole infrastructure is in ruin, the schools are in need of renovations and apparently the medical facilities and services are a disaster as well.

To all of these are added the accusations that the Bureau of Indian Affairs for over a hundred years has mismanaged Indian trust funds. For sure, this fiasco has contributed to the enlargement of poverty on reservations. The Federal Government that signed treaties and promised to abide and uphold them now is guilty of using the Indians' funds. There are many such cases. Elouise Cobell, a Blackfeet tribal member, an alumnus of Great Falls Business College and a lecturer at Montana State University, living on a farm near the town of Browning in Montana, started an independent investigation of why all the land use fees collected since about 1887 have disappeared. As Larry Cunnigham writes, she discovered ... "egregious misconduct by the federal government."[32] How did all the funds disappear? Where did more than 40 billion trust fund dollars disappear? Cobell revealed that, among other acts of mismanagement, Indian trust fund money was used for the New York City financial bailout in 1975, was spent to keep Chrysler Corporation afloat in the 1980's, and has been "borrowed" from to

---

[31] See: Rich Pittsley, *Chief Plenty Coups*, "The Morning Star", Volume 40, NR 3, 2002, pg. 2.
[32] See: Larry Cunnigham, *Keeping The Faith & Running The Race,* "The Morning Star", Vol. 40, NR 4, 2002, pg. 1, 7.

reduce the national debt. Everything was taken from funds belonging to destitute western plains tribes (like the Sioux, Cheyenne and Crow).[33]

Therefore, any example of positive action needs to be stressed. Positive action is exemplified by the St. Labre Indian School located in Ashland in the southeast section of Montana, on the eastside of the Northern Cheyenne Reservation. At the school, over seven hundred children aged five to eighteen years of age are schooled and exist thanks to donations from private sponsors. It is a place that gives hope. When one looks at the pictures of the St. Labre children (where you see bright, cheerful, clean-cut, and intelligent looking youth), it can be visualized, that after their schooling, they will become leaders of and the basic foundation of a future Indian society, one that is elite.

Looking from a historical point of view, the American government, from the beginning of the bill enacted under the presidency of Ulysses S. Grant in 1870, intended for government sponsored schools to change Indian culture into white culture. Schools for Indian children had only one goal: to push Indian children into Catholicism or another Christian belief, and of second importance – to give the children an education. The children were provided lodging, food and medical care.

The worst consequences came from another bill enacted in 1900 that was intended to force Indians to blend into white society. The Indians had to give away their children to schools, where the children learned they were prohibited from using their Native language. The students were forced to blend in with whites. The children were never taught about the importance of pride in their own culture and background. In the years 1885–1947, children could only see and visit briefly with their parents after Sunday mass. They were permitted to visit their homes only during the Christmas holiday. When families protested these indecencies, they were cut off from food rations.

There were cases of escapes. In 1934, eleven girls escaped from the St. Labre Center and wandered around until they were found. Father Marion Roessler was moved by the girls' escape and acted to improve the well being of the Indian students. First of all, he organized an increased financial support for the St. Labre mission. Many white people, living in far away states, learned about the mission, the condition it was in, and sent financial support.

The Federal Government's policy of forcing Native Americans into white society finally ended in 1934 when Indians were encouraged to organize into tribal groups. The forbiddance of celebrating cultural events was terminated, and Indians were even encouraged to organize

---

[33] See: *The Broken Promise*, "Parade Magazine", September 9, 2001.

pow-wows. Officials began coming to the *pow-wows* and taking part in them. But still, the Secretary of the Interior and his staff checked up on all decisions taken by tribes. They themselves did not guide the Indians tribes but obviously had a large involvement. The description of "Race of Sorrows" disappeared, and the Cheyenne called themselves "Morning Star People".

The opening of St. Labre Indian School in 1884 was one of the first effective steps on behalf of American Indians. Because of their separation and dispersal, they had a very difficult time. In the 1940's, the Northern Cheyenne were separated from the Cheyenne. The Northern Cheyenne were located on terrain - west from the Sioux reservation in South Dakota – to the Big Horn Mountains in Montana, and from the Yellowstone River of the north – to the southern ends of what is now Colorado state. Those were their hunting territories.

The spreading around of Indians into reservations started in March 1876, and it created considerable resistance by the Indians. On June 25, 1876, the Indians won the famous Battle of the Little Big Horn, but the action of moving them onto reservations had not finished.

In the early 1880's, Northern Cheyenne Indians were camping near Fort Keogh not far from Miles City in Montana. They did not have a place for themselves. General Nelson A. Miles of Fort Keogh took care of the group. He turned to former soldier George Yoakam, who was living not far from Miles City, and asked him to help the Northern Cheyenne get settled on land determined by the Indian Homestead Act of 1875. Yoakam helped the Indians, but he faced resistance from white people living on land near the Yellowstone River. At this time, Crow Indians had already moved onto territory given to the Cheyenne. The Cheyenne refused to join them, as they wanted to keep their separation.

George Yoakam, who was a Catholic, thought how much good the Catholic Sisters could do. He contacted the Bishop of Montana John Brondel and told him about the homeless Indians that had gathered around the Tongue River Valley.

The Bishop bought the land and decided to build a school there. He chose as its name St. Labre. The name was taken from a French saint, an educated beggar, Benedict Joseph Labre, who gave away all of his money to teach religion.

For years Yoakam helped the Indians to cultivate the land and defended them against accusations made by cattle owners. He wrote about "loving peace, honest Cheyenne, and about "drunk cowboys"[34].

---

[34] See: Orlan J. Svingen, *The Northern Cheyenne Reservation*, 1877–90, University of Colorado Press, 1993.

At the Bishop's request, priests and nuns who would work among the Northern Cheyenne, were sent from Toledo, Ohio. The group included four Ursuline Sisters: Mother Amadeus along with Sister Sacred Heart, Sister Ignatius, and Sister Angela. It was March 29, 1884. With the nuns came an educated chaplain, Father Joseph Eyler from Cleveland. The three-room cabin was established as the living quarters, school and chapel. At first, fourteen Northern Cheyenne students were enrolled. A small farm was created that helped to feed the group.

In a short time, Father Eyler became so ill, that a new priest had to be appointed. The difficult circumstances and the harsh winters did not help in keeping priests very long. In October 1885, the Bishop sent Jesuit priest Father Aloysius van der Velden who had come from Holland. With great enthusiasm for good work, he completely involved himself in the environment. He learned the Cheyenne language, and in 1895, he built the first church building that served as the St. Labre Church until 1971. Van der Velden also started the building of a boy's campus dormitory. Another separate building known as *white house* was built with help from the Indians. It became a place for nuns and female students to live, and there was a room for lessons too.

In 1897, Jesuit superiors withdrew their priests and since then (until 1914), diocesan priests were sent to the mission. There were two Capuchin priests among them as well who were especially dedicated, Brothers Francis Busalt and Gaul Neumann. Their dedication and work influenced many Indians to be attracted to the Catholic Church. Anther Capuchin, Brother Regis Neeser, compiled a dictionary of the Cheyenne language.

In 1954 sixty-four students were accepted. Thanks to the generosity of many helping people, the school slowly started to grow. Since 1956, a school bulletin "The Race of Sorrows" has been sent around with a request for financial support. The bulletin describes the history of the Northern Cheyenne and the situation at the St. Labre Mission. The children's pictures and photos of their activities are published and shown in the bulletin.

The public's response to the solicitation was bigger than anticipated and spread all over the whole of America. People sent money, clothes and books. In 1972, the bulletin changed its name to "The Morning Star People", and it has been published under this name until today (Norman and I receive it on a regular basis).

After completing high school at St. Labre, the graduate students are offered stipends to continue their education on a higher, university level. Such students who achieve university degrees in nursing, teaching, and administration – many times return to their place of birth. In Montana where unemployment reaches fifty percent, St. Labre provides work. Over half of the people working at the school and its administrative services, for example at printing, are Indians.

At the centennial of St. Labre Mission, Reverend Thomas J. Murphy from the Church of Eastern Montana sent the following letter[35]:

My Dear Friends:
The celebration of a 100th anniversary is a unique experience in the life of any community. Yet, the 100th anniversary of St.Labre has a unique importance. It is more than the accumulation of years, but rather the story of countless people who have shared their gifts and talents.

It is the story of Native American people and white people together involved on the journey of faith, understanding and respect; it is the story of selfless giving of countless others whose generosity and interest in the work of St. Labre has made the present St. Labre community a reality.

It is a privilege to be Bishop of the Diocese where St. Labre shares its ministry with people today. I pray that God will bless all and that time in the coming years may be filled with renewed hope and faith, and that the journey which people take at St. Labre may only bring new life to everyone.
Happy 100th Anniversary!
Sincerely yours in Christ,
Most Rev. Thomas J. Murphy
Bishop of Great Falls-Billings

Since the 1970's, Indians have been encouraged, even in a very clear and loud fashion, to maintain their traditions, cultures and their languages. A committee of forty-four tribal elders was organized to rebuild the lost heritage of the Cheyenne. In 1973, a reunion of nine chiefs was held. The chiefs came from the Northern and the Southern Cheyenne tribes. They decided that the Southern Cheyenne would have twenty-two chiefs as their representatives, and have responsibility of the so-called Keeper of the Sacred Arrows. The Northern Cheyenne would also have twenty-two chiefs and have responsibility of the so-called Keeper of the Sacred Hat.

Throughout the United States, interest in Native Americans' affairs is growing and growing. At schools, their history and traditions are taught, and many children voluntarily are taking lessons in Indian

---

[35] See: Sister Carlan Kraman, *A Portrait of St. Labre Indian Mission Through One Hundred Years*, Ashland, Montana 1984 pg. V.

languages. Every year in October, Heritage Day is celebrated, and every year *pow-wows* are organized. There are activities in music, sports and theatre groups.

James Spear, Cheyenne, wrote in 1972: "Despite many, many years of a systematic effort to absorb our People – we did not and are not disappearing. Our culture has been purposely eroded, but it still persists". He was quoted later in an article published in the St. Labre bulletin "The Morning Star People":

"A mechanized world can rob the unaware man his vision – of who he is and where he comes from. But the Indian has found a new self-awareness in the heritage he knows is his own. Today, the Indian speaks for himself, knowing that all America must listen, for all people in this country are bound in a common destiny.

We are striving for the same goal as other races of people – to strengthen our social and economic position. In order to do this we must become educated and encourage education for our children ...but this does not mean we have to discard our culture...We need only to follow the example of other Indians tribes and ethnic groups who are educating their children according to their own heritage and culture, while at the same time enabling their children to become educated for whatever role or profession they happen to choose in life"[36].

In 1972, as a result of meeting delegations of Northern and Southern Cheyenne, Chiefs John Woodenlegs and Joe Little Coyote stated the unity of tribes. As written about their unity statement, James Spear is quoted:

"Our world view and attitude toward nature is very different from that of the non-Indian. We see ourselves as a part of nature and we relate to it spiritually. Our People have always had deep reverence for land and nature. For them, it was the cultural core. They felt intimate with it. Our White brother, however, does just the opposite, he tries to master nature"[37].

In similar fashion, similar words were written by a young Indian woman, Lou Stops, then a senior at St. Labre High School during an All Indian Speech Meet[38]:

"Because of prejudice our ancestors suffered. They were pushed off their land and for this we still suffer. But we must accept this, for there is no hope to get back our loss. Yet the White Man has suffered a deeper loss, which people rarely talk about: the loss of good will to humankind,

---

[36] See: Sister Carlan Kraman, *St. Labre Indian Mission*, Ashland, Montana, 1984, pg. 26.
[37] See: Op. cit., pg. 27.
[38] See: Op. cit., pg. 27.

the loss of conscience. Perhaps it will be necessary for us to take the first step, if their loss does allow them to. We will have to accept them. We were born to love and live among each other. We are our brother's keeper. For someday we shall walk together in a sacred manner and become a nation, a nation of one people in friendship".

In 1965, St. Labre Indian School was asked to take under their jurisdiction the care of Indian children living on the Crow Reservation. The school agreed, and as a result, it was necessary to create two more campuses: the Pretty Eagle Catholic School in Saint Xavier and the Saint Charles Mission in Pryor.

In 1971, a new church building was finished on the Ashland school site. It is in the shape of a huge tipi constructed of stone. The symbols that were used are a combination of Indian tradition and Catholic religion. Huge wooden beams go through the high ceiling, and protrude through the smoke hole – the top opening of the tipi. On the other side, there are beautiful stained glass windows.

The important role of the school in the life of its Indian students is upheld by one of its superintendents - Larry Kostelecky. His statement from 1968 is interesting to quote:

"There is a very definite conflict between the values of the White Man and the Indian. In our education of the Indian we have thought only of conformity with our own ideals and values and have emphasized the same. In this process, the very rich Indian heritage is ignored and even destroyed. The end has been confusion and conflict by the time the Indian youth reaches the Junior High School level"[39].

In order to help the Indians preserve their culture and values, Kostelecky made an effort to add a course in Cheyenne history and culture to the school curriculum.

Curtis Yarlott, who is principal of St. Labre wrote:

"Here at St.Labre Indian School, we continue to do what we've always done: offer our students a superior education that will enable them to achieve anything they set out to do in life. We believe that this is the only way that long-term, positive change will come to the Indian reservations that we serve. It is interesting to note that the current Northern Cheyenne Tribal President and the executive directors of the other two most visible and viable nonprofit entities on the Northern Cheyenne Reservation are St. Labre graduates."[40]

The school owns three campuses located on terrain of the Northern Cheyenne and Crow Reservations. Children are taught in kindergarten,

---

[39] See: Op. cit., pg. 82.
[40] See: "The Morning Star", Vol. 42, NR 1, 2004, pg 1.

grammar school and high school, through grade twelve. There are also courses of business, economy, music, art, and many sport activities. Some children, whose homes are more than fifty miles from school, stay on the campus during the weekdays, and for weekends they are bussed to their homes. The children's education is not limited to only teaching them, but they participate in many programs and activities that, among other benefits, creates pride and teaches history. They also learn how devastating alcohol and drugs can be. The Director of the grammar school at St. Labre, Nicole Trahan, says that for learning, the children need a lot encouragement and a peaceful atmosphere They have to learn excellent English, so they can choose the right words. Nicole gave an example: A girl came and asked: "How much is a lock?" when she really wanted to ask what time it was, explained Nicole.

St. Labre is financed only on private donations, and it hires three hundred workers. School buses bring children from far away places on the reservations to the schools. They are offered hot meals every day. The Government supports this program of hot meals at schools, and St Labre provides over a thousand meals daily. The provision of these meals insures that the children receive substantial nourishment.

Beside the isolation created by the huge territory of the State of Montana, the weather does not help either. Winter is a season of great difficulty to go through and sometimes to survive. People are in need of basic things, for example fuel. The roads are icy, heavy snow and ice can hamper the ease of communications and bitterly cold weather prevails.

Geographically and socially, St. Labre is isolated, and it is a big problem also for children. When they finish school and are supposed to move to a new place, it is difficult for them to leave the friendly environment of St. Labre that they know and move to the unknown. This type of happenstance is experienced at St. Labre even before students finish their education. Occasionally, after a week or so, one, two or three students will leave the school and return to the reservation. St. Labre offers special programs run by teachers Carol Heath and Dave Charpentier. They help students to adapt. The children coming to school are often from alcoholic families or those using drugs. Many families on the reservations in Montana have alcohol and drug problems. Some children go to bed hungry, some do not go to bed at all. One child at St. Charles School slept during classes and was asked about it. His answer was straight and honest: at night he did not sleep, because he had to hide all the knives and forks, and other sharp tools, since the adults in his home argued and beat each other.

St. Labre is a center of education that also includes two other school centers.

Aleksandra Ziolkowska-Boehm

Pretty Eagle Catholic School – located on the Crow Indian Reservation in Montana - west from Saint Labre. It was established in 1887 and gathers children in the ages – from kindergarten through the 8th grade. Initially, the school operated independently, but it was not doing well until St. Labre took over its management. One hundred and forty students attend Pretty Eagle Catholic School.

St. Charles Mission School, similar to Pretty Eagle, for forty years has been under the umbrella care of St. Labre. It also gathers children from kindergarten age through the 8th grade of grammar school. It is located in Montana, on the west part of the Crow Reservation. A hundred students attend there.

***

Everything started in 1891, when Crow Chief Plenty Coups (1848–1932) asked the Government for permission for Jesuits to build a mission school. Chief Plenty Coups was a very interesting and impressive figure.

Plenty Coups was born the year when a smallpox epidemic killed many Crow Indians including his mother. Cheerful and energetic by nature, he was the favorite of many people. He became a spiritual man, and it is said, that as a teenager, he had a vision he would become a chief. He became a chief when twenty-five years old. He was raised during the years when Crow Indians were nomads, moving from one place to another, hunting for buffalo, living in teepees. And when the time came, like with other Plains Indians, he was forced to move onto a reservation, he recognized that the traditional life was shattered. Chief Plenty Coups knew that coming changes were irreversible and that he should prepare his people for its future.

In 1880, he was invited to Washington where he visited Mount Vernon, the place where President George Washington's house is located, and the museum. He wrote about it:

"I was one among many visitors at Mount Vernon that day, and yet there was no talking, no noise, because people were thinking of the great past and the unknown future. When people think deeply they are helped, and in the silence there, I sent my thoughts to the Great White Chief in that other life... Great Chief, when you came into power, the streams of your country's affairs were muddy. Your heart was strong, and your tongue spoke straight. Your people listened, and you led them through war to the peace you loved... As you helped your people, help me now, an Apsaloga (Crow) chief, to lead my people to peace. I, too have a little country to save for my children*"[41]*

---

[41] See: Rich Pittsley, *Chief Plenty Coups*, "The Morning Star", Vol. 40, NR 3, 2002, pg. 2.

Plenty Coups, like other Indians, missed and longed for the times that had passed away. But he knew the new time was important to face and to understand. He stressed how important education was as a key for the future, for success. His address about education is worth being quoted:

"Education is your most powerful weapon; with it you are the white man's equal; without it, you are his victim and so shall remain all your lives. Study, learn, and help one another always. Remember there is only poverty and misery in idleness and dreams, but in work there is self-respect and independence"[42].

On March 14, 1890, Plenty Coups sent a petition to the Secretary of the Interior asking that the Jesuits be permitted to build a church and school at the town of Pryor. As a result, one year later, in 1891, St. Charles Mission School and campus was built.

In his later years, Plenty Coups continued to stress the importance of education. In 1921, he was asked to take part in a ceremony at the Tomb of the Unknown Soldier in Arlington National Cemetery. President Warren G. Harding was a speaker. Chief Plenty Coups removed his war bonnet and put it on a sarcophagus. As writes Rich Pittsley, he lifted his arms to the sky and said a prayer that moved everybody who attended the ceremony (his war bonnet is still in the Tomb's visitor center).

When he was older, he told his biographer, Frank Linderman: "I am old, I am not graceful. My bones are heavy and my feet are large. But I know justice and have tried all my life to be just…I may be gone to my Father when you return here. I am very anxious to go where I may live again as men were intended to live".

When in March 1932 information about his death reached Washington, it was announced in Congress, and all present did pause to reflect on, as was said: *"this supreme representative of the Indian race"*. During the funeral, Baptist minister John Frost said:

"Many moons will pass and many snows will come and go, but we shall not see his like again."[43]

A big impression on the Crow Indians was made also by Chief Pretty Eagle (1846–1904). His name was taken from the Catholic School sponsored by St. Labre. Chief Pretty Eagle lived in similar times as Chief Plenty Coups (1848–1932). Both were warriors and members of the Crow Indians elders.

---

[42] See: Op cit pg.2.

[43] See: Frank Linderman, *Plenty Coups, Chief of The Crows – Savior of The Crows, Norman Wiltsey*, 1968, Gonzaga University Archives, Spokane, Washington.

The times were very difficult for Crow Indians: forced to move onto a reservation, slaughter of the buffalo, government efforts to change Indians, who were hunters and nomads, into farmers, and – also – in large numbers the coming of white people looking for gold.

Both chiefs were invited to Washington in 1880 (Pretty Eagle was thirty-four years old, Plenty Coups was thirty-one years of age) to discuss the sale of the western portion of the Crow Reservation, then located in the Stillwater Valley. In spite of government efforts and strategies to discomfort the Crow delegation (such as having the Indians wear non-traditional costumes, that is; white people's clothing), historian Frederick Hoxie described them as *"remarkably spunk"*[44]. Both chiefs signed a provisional treaty out of fear that if they did not agree they would be held as hostages. "Spunk" is not the best description of Pretty Eagle's behavior during the negotiations. A Government representative wrote that when he was seeing Pretty Eagle in his study, he always kept his pistol in his desk.[45]

Pretty Eagle had a big influence on the choice of the Indian school's location (who after a hundred years took his name as a patron), but also he made a considerable impact on the school's internal affairs and educational program. In 1883, he met on the reservation Italian Jesuit Father Pierpaolo Prando, who learned the Crow language. He achieved such competence that he could speak his sermon and teach in the Crow language. In February 1887, Prando with other Jesuits from the Spokane Diocese, walked through the terrain from Custer Station to the house of Pretty Eagle near Rotten Grass Creek and the Big Horn River. There they chose the location for the school.

According to the report sent regularly to the Spokane Diocese, Chief Pretty Eagle was involved personally in everything concerning the school. Later, he sent his own children and those of his relatives to the school.

In 1891, Pretty Eagle's friend Chief Plenty Coups, together with his delegation came to St. Xavier Mission expecting to have a similar school built in Pryor. One of the arguments for the location was that children would not have to be transported 60 miles to attend the government school at the Crow Agency. The request and its supporting argument resulted in St. Charles Mission being built along with its nearby school in 1892.

---

[44] See: *Parading Through History: The Making of the Crow Nation in America, 1805–1935*. Cambridge University Press, 1995.
[45] See: Lyndel Meikle, *No Paper Trail: Crooked Agents on the Crow Reservation, 1874–1878; Walter Dave, Speaking Ill of the Dead*, Helena, Montana 2000.

In the beginning of the 1970's, the school in St. Xavier took the name of Chief Pretty Eagle. When in 1983, it was taken under the management of St. Labre, its name remained intact, only the word Catholic was added: St. Francis Xavier Mission changed into Pretty Eagle Catholic School.

Chief Pretty Eagle died in 1904 and was buried close to his house near the Big Horn River. According to the Indian custom of *sky burial*, reserved only for chiefs, his body was wrapped in wet buckskin and put into a wagon, which - according to tradition - was elevated above the ground[46].

In the following fifteen to twenty years, his grave had been robbed, even his corpse was exhumed and then stolen. For the Crow people, this started a "sad time" that was not over until the remains of Chief Pretty Eagle were found in 1994.

"The only remedy for lonesomeness is to come back home"- Reverend Philip White, Chief Pretty Eagle's grandson said during the burial[47].

Robbery of Indian graves on the Crow Reservation was not a random event during the beginning of the twentieth century. In 1922, the "Hardin Tribune" reported, for example, that two seventeen-year old boys from Billings were arrested for grave robbery. They admitted their "crime" only after skulls and different Indian items were found in their houses.

The history of finding Pretty Eagle's corpse is fascinating. At the same time, it is also very sad. On November 16, 1990, President George H. W. Bush signed the Native American Graves Protection and Repatriation Act that required museums to review their collections and to notify the Indian tribes of their acquisitions. The tribal representatives were invited to see the museum collections.

In 1993, the Crow Indians were informed by the American Museum of Natural History in New York City, that the museum owned the remains of sixty-one Crow Indians and they should not be kept any longer. After receiving this information, a delegation of Crow Indians went to New York to see personally the remains themselves. One of the Indian representatives was John Pretty on Top, then Crow Cultural Director, later one of three commissioners in Big Horn County. What they learned from Ian Tattersall, the curator of the anthropology department, shocked the delegation greatly. Ian Tattersall was asked, if

---

[46] See: Art Pitts, *The Legacy of Pretty Eagle*, "The Morning Star", Vol. 41, NR 2, 2003, Pg. 1-3.
[47] See: Op. cit. Pg. 2.

among the collection, were there any items that could be linked to a wagon burial. He was shown a photograph of two men standing next to a burial wagon. This photograph had been sent to the museum in 1922, along with a skull described as belonging to "an important leader in the Crow tribe". The man who sent the skull, and received payment of three hundred and seventy-five dollars for it, was Dr. W. A. Russell. In those years, Russell was the Big Horn County Health Officer.

"According to our information", Tattersall said, "Russell was supplying material to a number of museums."[48]

From another museum in New York, the Crow Indians recovered the mummified body of a little girl named Brings Home Pretty Horses. For those remains, Russell was paid five hundred dollars.

At that time, John Pretty on Top did not know that the remains of an "important leader" were those of Chief Pretty Eagle. He viewed a photograph of the chief's burial place that he received from his great-grandson. He tried to match its topography with that of the photograph from 1922. A forensic scientist from the Smithsonian Institute agreed to identify the remains. After study of the skull, the scientist declared that it belonged to Chief Pretty Eagle.

A repeated burial of Chief Pretty Eagle took place in June 3, 1994. For his gravesite, a place was chosen where the chief had liked to fast and pray - not far from Fort Smith in Big Horn Canyon. The remains of other Indians were retrieved from museums and buried in the Crow Indian Cemetery.

Who was the plunderer Dr. W. A. Russell? In the papers "Hardin Tribune" and "Big Horn County News", some information about him can be found.

Dr. Russell was a physician who owned his own medical office and who advertised regular office hours in addition to his work as the Big Horn County Health Officer. He was a broadly respected member of a small local community. As a pillar of that community and as a doctor, he moved on the reservation without any difficulties. No one suspected anything, but one case evoked a surprise. In 1921, he and his wife hosted a dinner for the school board. His house was described as decorated with very strange items. Skulls were placed around the room to lend an "eerie" air to an otherwise festive evening. The nut bowls held plaster impressions of children's teeth. Apparently, none of the guests was suspicious, only people were surprised.

W. A. Russell is another example of Indian betrayal by a person supposedly a friend.

---

[48] See: Greg McCracken, "Billings Gazette", NR 5/27 and 5/4/1994

Northern Cheyenne – the Race of Sorrows

The Cheyenne called themselves Tse-tsehese-stahase, it means, "people like us". According to a legend, the Cheyenne lived in big forests near big lakes. Probably they were the Great Lakes amid the states of Michigan, Wisconsin and Illinois, as well as the wooded terrain area in Canada south of Hudson Bay and James Bay. The first mentioning record of them is noted on the Jolliet and Franquelin map made around 1673, based on information given by Dakota Sioux. On that map, they are called Chaiena and mentioned with seven other tribes that lived on the eastern side of the Mississippi River.

The early Cheyenne were mostly fish eaters, catching the fish with long willow nets that they put into shallow water. In the fifteenth century, using canoes, they moved into the area where Minnesota is located today and started to grow corn. They lived in villages surrounded by ditches, and it could be the evidence that they did have enemies whom they fought. In those times, they used dogs for transport. In the beginning of the eighteenth century, they moved from Minnesota into the Great Plains of North Dakota and started to hunt for buffalo. Their life style changed again. For hunting they used bows, arrows and lances. They learned to set traps for deer and buffalo, chasing them into huge holes dug earlier. In the winter, they chased the buffalo into snowdrifts or herded them over cliffs to be killed or injured.

They used the animal skins that they prepared with natural dye for their clothing. The buffalo skin was used inside a tipi for comfort. The dye was also to color the feathers used for the headbonnet and to beautify their clothes. They liked geometrical designs.

In the 1750's, by trading with different tribes from the southern plains, they obtained horses. Through encounters with the Assiniboin and Chippewa Indians, who were supplied by French settlers, they obtained guns. Having horses resulted in a big change in their lifestyle again. They could hunt in faraway places and move faster than earlier when they used dogs. They traveled from their villages into the southwest part of the Missouri River, into the area of the Black Hills. They met Arapaho Indians and became friendly with them, formed an alliance and maintained it ever since. Unlike the Sioux who were hunters only, the Cheyenne were also farmers. They lived on the rich soil around the Minnesota River and Cheyenne River in North Dakota, and they continued to plant crops.

The earliest description of the Cheyenne can be found in the 1806 journals of Lewis and Clark. They were described as stately with high cheeks, high noses and long legs. On their maps, Lewis and Clark show the Cheyenne as the largest tribe living in the area of the Black Hills.

The Lewis and Clark expedition took twenty-eight months – from May 1804 until October 1806. Their expedition was a great endeavor in a New World. It is worthy of remembrance.

In the aftermath of the 1803 purchase of the territory of Louisiana, President Thomas Jefferson decided to initiate the research and exploration of the West territory. Meriwether Lewis and William Clark determined one of the most interesting trails in the world. They covered the distance of over eight thousand miles moving in many ways – by foot, on horse and by boat. The expedition was full of many unusual circumstances and events that now, over two hundred years later, still appear as a great adventure. The trail, that began from the Mississippi River and ended at the Pacific Ocean, is beautifully documented. There is rich material concerning people, soil and its natural resources. Information was gathered on the following states: Illinois, Missouri, Kansas, Nebraska, Iowa, South and North Dakota, Montana, Idaho, Washington and Oregon. According to their journal of June 2, 1806, the travelers spent over one fourth of their time in Montana. Observations made by Lewis and Clark made it possible to gather rich sociological and geographical material concerning the people and terrain they traversed. They traveled with a small group of helpers. Included in the expedition team were translators knowing Indian languages, among them Toussaint Charbonneau and his wife Sacagawea (sometimes spelled as Sacajawea. I write about her later), that means *bird woman*. Sacagawea supposedly knew trails of the Shoshoni, and they were partly followed. Clark said that she was a pilot because she always could find the way to go into and out of mountains. The little son of Sacagawea and Charbonneau was named Jean Baptise, and Clark in his journeys called him by the nickname Pomp.

When the Sioux began moving across the Missouri River towards the Black Hills, the Cheyenne moved farther west. They entered the hunting territory of the Crow, and it became a reason of conflict between the two tribes. Together with the Oglala Sioux, the Cheyenne moved against the Crow. The fighting continued – with some interruptions – until 1862, when the Crow moved from their hunting areas south of the Yellowstone River and east of the Big Horn River. Part of this land became the Northern Cheyenne Reservation.

During their movements, the Cheyenne always went through a difficult adaptation process. They were united by faith and sacred ceremonies. They believe there is One Supreme Father of Everything – Maheo. The Earth was considered as Mother, and the Cheyenne hold great respect for her. Also, sacred for them were the Sun, the Thunder, the Moon, the Stars and the Whirlwind. Later in their hierarchy, animals and birds were held sacred.

For safety reasons, the Cheyenne were divided into ten bands. Each had three hundred to three hundred and fifty members; they lived by themselves but gathered together in the summer for ritual ceremonies, like the Sun Dance, the Sacred Arrows Dance and the Sacred Hats dance. The meeting usually ended when the bands joined together for buffalo hunting. The Cheyenne had a council of forty-four Peace Chiefs who gathered every summer and made decisions important for the whole tribe.

Why the Cheyenne did not gather together and make decisions and strategies on how to deal with white people is unknown. Since the signing of the first treaties between the Cheyenne and whites, there were "loopholes and inconsistencies" that could cause and result in misunderstanding.

In 1825, General Henry Atkinson moved his army up the Missouri River to sign treaties with the Indians living along the Missouri River and on the Northern Plains. One of General Atkinson's officers described these people as the most beautiful Indians he ever met.

The Cheyenne were living near the Black Hills, and on July 1825, a Treaty of Friendship was signed with the United States. Four Indian chiefs signed the Treaty in which the Cheyenne recognized the sovereignty of the United States and its right to regulate all trade. The problem was, that the Cheyenne who signed only represented one of ten Cheyenne bands. General Atkinson as the government representative, however, considered the treaty binding for the whole Cheyenne tribe.

Signing treaties with the Indians continued, and they were much needed. In 1851, in order to secure the plains east of the Rockies from Oklahoma to Montana and to make it safe for the white settlers coming west, the Government signed treaties with eleven different tribes at Fort Laramie in Wyoming.

In exchange for yearly annuities, the Indians supposedly agreed to:
1. recognize the rights of the United States government to maintain roads through the territories,
2. end intertribal warfare,
3. maintain peaceful relations with the Whites
4. comply with a defined territory for each tribe[49].

---

[49] See: Carlan Kraman, *Saint Labre Indian Mission*, Ashland, Montana 1984, pg. 18

The Cheyenne were considered as one tribe, not Northern and Southern, and their territory was mostly in Colorado. After the treaty, the Northern Cheyenne continued to live and hunt in the area west of the Black Hills.

When gold was discovered, many white settlers began to come west. Because the government had the right to build roads, the Plains became a terrain with many roads used by whites, and it was a source of many conflicts. Whites were hunting throughout the Indian hunting grounds, and whites brought with them their diseases that they exposed to the Indians. The American army started to build forts along the roads, but it was a very unwelcome presence for Indians. In the years 1857-1879, there were frequent fights between the Cheyenne and Arapaho Indians and the American army. In 1867, the Union Pacific Railroad was ready to expand into Western Nebraska and farther, so the government had to sign another treaty with Indians. By the treaty, in which the Indians' agreed to the passage of the railroad, the government agreed that the land north of the Platte River and the summit of the Big Horn Mountains eastward to the Missouri River and North of the Yellowstone River would be: "...non-ceded Indian Territory upon which no White person would be permitted to settle or pass through without the consent of the Indians."[50]

It meant that the land belonged to Indians and it was their hunting territory. The Black Hills belonged to this area. But around 1872, whites searching for gold came into those regions. In response to Indian protests to keep the territory intact, in 1874, the government sent the army under General George Armstrong Custer, hero from the Civil War. Regardless of the Army's presence, the Whites came anyway after the discovery of gold. In response, the Cheyenne, Sioux and Arapaho tribes entered the territory next to the railroads that did not belong to them. The treaties were broken all the time by both sides. Finally, the Government decided to keep Indians on the reservations only and under Army control.

On December 3, 1875, the Commissioner of Indian Affairs ordered all the Indians living off-reservation to report to their agencies by January 31, 1876, or military action would be used to force them. The Battle of the Little Big Horn was the result of the tension.

Earlier, before the Battle of the Little Big Horn, an event of March 17, 1876 gave Indians the certainty that if they would not listen, the army would start the war. On that cold morning, the Cavalry under General George Crook and Colonel Joseph J. Reynolds attacked the Indian camp on the Powder River. The Indians mobilized and forced back the

---

[50] See: Op. cit. pg.20.

attackers. Reynolds withdrew, and Crook and his soldiers returned for two months to Fort Fetterman. The Oglala, Miniconjou and Cheyenne moved to East Fork, not far from the Little Powder River, to unite themselves with the Oglala Sioux Chief Crazy Horse. They also decided to join with Hunkpapa Chief Sitting Bull, who was camped sixty miles north from the Powder River with his warriors.

When the Indians learned about the attack of the camp on the Powder River, they started to gather and join together. Nearing the end of June 1876, four hundred bands had joined together and there were around three thousand Indians, eight hundred of them being warriors. Afterwards, others joined them, and the warriors' number increased to two thousand as part of a total of seven thousand Indians. On June 25, 1876, Custer attacked the Indians presumably, according to one version, without any idea about how big the Indian gathering was. In another version of the tale, his mainly Crow Indian guides forewarned Custer not to attack the Indians because they far outnumbered his forces. He chose to ignore the warning!

The famous battle (as I wrote in the chapter "American Sphinx Crazy Horse and sculptor of the mountain") has many descriptions; many books are dedicated to it. The facts are the same. To engage the Indians, the army planned to employ three separate expeditions. The three were: General George Crook who was to bring his soldiers from Fort Fetterman in the Wyoming Territory (but after his defeat withdrew back to Fort Fetterman), General Alfred H. Terry who was to bring his troops from Fort Abraham Lincoln in North Dakota and Colonel John Gibbon who was to move his soldiers from Fort Ellis in Montana. They all were supposed to come from the Yellowstone River and arrive at the Little Big Horn. From the north, General George Custer with six hundred soldiers of the Seventh Cavalry was supposed to circumvent the Rosebud Valley and arrive at the Little Big Horn from the south.

On June 25, 1876 Custer decided to attack the Indians encamped along the riverside without waiting for Colonel John Gibbon who needed at least one more day of marching to arrive. General Custer assumed that the Indians would not fight, or that they would give up without resisting, or that they would just run away. He divided his regiment into three battalions. He himself led two hundred and sixty-seven men towards the north end of the Indian Camp. The two other battalions under the commands of Major Marcus A. Reno and Captain Fredrick W. Benteen were to attack from the south and southwest. The Indian gathering was probably the biggest ever. Some historians say there were not seven thousand Indians, as mentioned above, but ten to twenty thousand, the warriors being estimated around fifteen hundred men. Custer and his commands were almost immediately surrounded by the attacking Northern Cheyenne under Chief Lame White Man, by the Hunkpapa Sioux under Chief Sitting Bull, Oglala Sioux under Chief Crazy Horse and Hunkpapa Sioux under Chief Gall. The Indian victory was definite. Custer and his soldiers were killed; the Indian loss was not high.

The victory became a milestone in the history of Native Americans and their fight with white people.

Travelling through the huge state of Montana, Norman and I passed the Crow Indian Reservation, the biggest in that area. Every August, they organize a big *pow-wow* and rodeo. Enchanting is the landscape of the Big Horn Canyon. Driving, we passed the very well marked place of General Custer's encampment and the place of the famous battle on the Little Big Horn. A tourist center displays a large map showing how the battle progressed. Showcases display the army uniforms from the epoch and guns used by both sides – Indians and soldiers. The Little Big Horn Battlefield Memorial opened in 1879 just to honor the memory of General George A. Custer and his soldiers. The soldiers killed in the battle are buried in a large cemetery. The remains of General Custer, on October 10, 1877 one year after the lost battle, were moved from the Little Big Horn and buried at West Point, New York cemetery. The years had to pass until it was realized that Indians, who were fighting for their identity and were killed in the battle, should also be honored at the memorial with special plaques and maps illustrating the famous battle.

Even after its defeat at the Little Big Horn, the army still continued to pursue the Sioux and the Cheyenne. Some Sioux left for Canada, and a small number of Cheyenne under Chief Two Moon in April 1877 were forced to surrender at Fort Keogh. Those Cheyenne were separated from nine hundred and seventy two others staying at the Red Cloud Agency in Nebraska. As a punishment for their participation in the Little Big Horn victory, in June 1877, this group of Cheyenne were escorted to the south to Oklahoma to live together with the Southern Cheyenne. They did not adapt well to the hotter climate, and exhausted from the humidity and hot temperatures, the Northern Cheyenne were dying from malaria and other diseases. The food rations were minimal; they did not have game to hunt. Because of this situation, their leaders Dull Knife and Little Wolf asked the Indian agent to let them go back to their area in the mountains.

"This is not a good place for us", they said.[51] They were afraid that all of them would die. But agent John Miles, acting in accordance with government orders refused to grant them permission to leave Oklahoma. The Cheyenne leaders gathered in council; some of them decided to

---

[51] See: Op.cit. pg. 20.

remain, the rest secretly left the Oklahoma agency. In the early hours of September 9, 1878, a group of two hundred and ninety-seven Northern Cheyenne with Chiefs Dull Knife, Little Wolf, Wild Hog and Old Crow started to march to the north. In some miraculous way, they knew how to hide their trail and quietly passed the army. They had to separate a number of times, to divide into small groups and avoid detection, and then reunite again. Four times they had to fight, and they always won. Even after General Sheridan mobilized a full division to block their march, the Cheyenne managed to escape.

When in the middle of October, they appeared in Northwest Nebraska, two of the chiefs could not agree about their next move, so they separated. Little Wolf decided to wait until the winter was over and with his people camped along a stream. Chief Dull Knife with his group left to travel towards the Red Cloud Agency. During a big snowstorm, they were captured and taken to Fort Robinson. The army took their guns, but earlier the Cheyenne managed to bury most of them. A few Cheyenne escaped. Dull Knife and the rest were ordered to return to Oklahoma. When he refused, water and food was withheld from them. In retaliation, the Cheyenne retrieved their hidden guns and on January 9 broke out and escaped from the barracks. But they were weak, hungry and cold, so they were easy targets for the pursuing soldiers. The soldiers captured one hundred and forty-nine who were returned and imprisoned at Fort Robinson, while sixty-one were killed. Many of those captured were seriously wounded. Somehow Chief Dull Knife and his family escaped and a few weeks later they reached the Pine Ridge Agency.

It was the time when the Northern Cheyenne were called the Race of Sorrows; the name has stayed with them for years.

It is said that agent John Miles respected them and wanted to help. But good will was not enough. Little Wolf and his group, after the winter, in March, started to move into the Northwest. Lt. Clark from Fort Keogh was ordered to stop them and bring them back. They were surrounded and forced to do so. Once there, General Miles proposed that they become scouts for the army. Chief Little Wolf and many of his men accepted. Earlier Chief Two Moon and his group had joined the army.

I remember a moment when on the eastern end of the Northern Cheyenne Reservation, we stopped at a small Indian cemetery. The Indian cemeteries always make a strong impact on me – they are touching pictures of their faith, their poverty, their history. I saw many war veterans' graves. Those were the followers of Little Wolf and Two Moon.

Aleksandra Ziolkowska-Boehm

Settling of Delaware and the Lenape

The State of Delaware, called the "first state" (as the first to ratify the Constitution), where Norman and I have lived since 1990, has an interesting history. In 1631, the Dutch settled in Delaware, and then in 1638, the Swedes came and settled into the area where Wilmington is now located and established a village. Wilmington, the largest city in Delaware, earlier was known as Willingtown – the name taken after its founder Thomas Willing. Before the white settlers entered this region along the Brandywine River, the area was inhabited by Lenape Indians. They were on this terrain since the year 600. Lenape means "Original People".

Everything started in the area of the Brandywine River flowing through the state of Delaware and part of Southeast Pennsylvania, then into the Delaware River that flows into the Atlantic Ocean. That terrain is the land of Native Americans ancestors who named themselves Lenni Lenape, before the white man gave them new names. The white settlers called them Delawares after the river they lived along which was named after Sir Thomas West (Lord de la Warr).

The first Europeans who came into the American continent established relations with Indians, exchanged all kind of goods with them, bought their land and intended to leave the Native people in peace. As wrote Rick Mulrooney[52], "the Lenape's relationship with settlers at first was good. The Swedish adventurers established a trading post on the shore of Christina River in now Wilmington to collect furs to send back to Sweden. The Indians were trading beaver, bear and other pelts for steel knives, axes, scissors, cooking pots, warm woolen cloth and blankets, glass beads and other items that white people were introducing to them.

Not everyone was happy with the Indians. Johann Printz, governor of New Sweden, wrote that "it would be desirable to drown all the Lenape in the Delaware". Gary Mullinax, staff reporter for the Wilmington, Delaware "News Journal" and author of articles about Lenni Lenape, quoted Printz's words about Lenape: as "a lot of poor rogues... we have no beaver trade whatsoever with them". Printz was not harshly negative only towards Native Americans, and in his letters, he used such pejorative descriptions against many other nationalities.

The Lenape were hunters, not farmers. During the warm months, they also fished for fish, crabs and oysters. The wooded surroundings

---

[52] See: Rick Mulrooney, *Learn about those who gave us Appoquinimink, Naamans and others*, "The News Journal", July 18, 2005, pg. E4-5.

were full of deer. Unlike the Iroquois, for example, the Lenape were not of a "warrior character". They were peace loving people, and they even acted as negotiators between tribes fighting and arguing with each other. They visited the Swedish port of Christiana in need of trade. Also seeking trade with the Swedes were the Mingo Indians. The chief of the Lenape tried to avoid the Mingo, who were warlike, and many times attacked them. The Mingo had different features, looks and characteristics compared to the Lenape. The Mingo were taller than the Lenape and had longer faces. They used the Iroquois language and lived on terrain west of the Susquehanna River. The Mingo name was used in New Castle County, where the community of Minquadale is located.

The first English, after arriving in Delaware, dominated the Dutch and Swedes. They even did not bother to buy land from the Lenape. The English thought that all the land belonged to arriving settlers and not to the Native people. The situation improved when William Penn arrived and took control over the area. He paid the Indians money for using their land. He also is known for signing treaties with the Lenni Lenape. He published *A Letter to the Free Society of Traders* (1683), in which he defined a detailed description of Pennsylvania and commendatory remarks concerning Lenape Indians.

William Penn died in 1718. Settlers that came after Penn's death showed more and more dislike, indifference, and callous feelings towards the Native Americans. Of their own will, many Indians left the Delaware terrain. They wanted to live the way they were accustomed to, so they left behind their ancestral land and moved westward. Some historians say that the English settlers' cruelty forced the Indians to leave. The other misfortune that decimated Indians were illnesses from diseases brought by white people. After 1700, the Lenape left the East Coast and went to Kansas and Oklahoma.

They left behind forever the green forests around the Brandywine River, but in their memory it exists as a mythical Eden, and from one generation to another the memory is passed. The old people, now living on prairie land, keep as legend stories showing the picture of Indians who lived far away. Linda Poolaw, a grand chief of the Delaware Nation in Oklahoma, in the introduction to her book *"The Red Record"* writes stories about the land where *"the sun wakes up"*.

Not many Indians who stayed in the Delaware area became close to white settlers. One of the examples is Indian Hannah (also known as Hannah Freeman). She was born to Lenape parents in 1731 in Kennett Township (now Kennett Square) in Chester County. Her parents and brothers moved west, but she stayed close to the Christina River. She made a living by sewing and weaving baskets. She died in 1802 in Chester County as "the last Indian woman" in the area.

The Lenape slowly melted into Delaware and the surrounding area communities. Anthropologist Herbert C. Kraft, whose research threw light on the long reign of the Lenape, wrote that on the East Coast there are no full blooded Lenapes.

Presently, the biggest group (around ten thousand and four hundred Lenape), live in the area of Bartlesville, Oklahoma as part of the East Delaware tribe. In 1867, they bought their land from the Cherokee. It was a time when the Government considered the land as belonging to the Cherokee Nation. As I learned, the Lenape have now filed a petition to be recognized as a separate tribe. Around fifteen hundred of them live near Anadarko, Oklahoma and belong to the West Delaware tribe. That group is considered as an ethnic unit, meaning it can be supported by different aid from the Government. For example, they have a license for running a casino that provides a very substantial source of income. Around two thousand Lenape live in Canada, and they are part of the Munsie tribe that years ago lived mainly in northern New Jersey.

Michael Pace is an Assistant Chief of the East Delaware Tribe in Bartlesville, Oklahoma. Pace is a tribal elder with a great knowledge about dances and songs of the Delaware Indians. He was quoted as saying: "that during his infrequent visits on the East Coast, particularly in Delaware, he feels far away from home, but recognizes Indian names. Every time he finds more and more of them". For example, Hockessin, DE – the name has been translated as "good bark hill", Hackensack, NJ means in Delaware Indian language "place of hot land", and Conshohocken, PA – "elegant earth". As he says: "those names remind him of home and that the surroundings of the State of Delaware are his ancestor's land."

People living in Delaware are aware that many years earlier Indians lived there. The Delaware Nature Society presents a program of lectures in Ashland Nature Center dedicated to the Lenape culture. The program is quite popular, and many people attend it.

One of the parks, located close to the Pennsylvania border, is named Lenape Park. Another - Wawaset Park – lies along the Brandywine River. The Lenape called the river Wawaset. John Bierhorst, in his book *The White Deer,* collected many stories about the Lenape. The book has stories about the ocean, caves, deep forests and even the Delaware River.

The other publication *The Red Record*, a history of the Lenape and their journeys is full of stories mentioning the Brandywine River. There is also mention of the blue crab and the Dutch and Swedish settlers that first came and settled the area.

Much of the information about the Lenape has come from excavations, like Indian arrowheads found in the area of the Brandywine – quoting Jay F. Custer, an anthropologist from the University of Delaware.

Presumably, the Lenape Indians were not a populous tribe, although historians have different opinions. Historian C.A. Weslager says that at one time, when the first settlers came after the year 1600, there were around 10–12 thousand. But Marshall J. Becker, anthropologist from West Chester University, says, that before the year 1700, there were only three hundred and fifty to five hundred Lenape people.

It has never been positively decided exactly where the Lenape lived. Becker says that they lived in the area that is now north Delaware and southeast Pennsylvania, not far from the picturesque Delaware Water Gap.

Weslager considers that the group of Indians known as Sickoneysincks (there are different spellings) were the first that sold land to Europeans. In 1629, the bog area (where Lewes is now located) was bought by the Dutch to settle Zwaanendael, but the colony did not last long. On west Nunquam, the land was farmed on a large scale, and this was necessary since the village had thousands of people. Most historians agree that Lenape did not have steady campsites. Weslager and others divide Lenape into three groups: Munsie, Unami, (that lived near the Brandywine River) and Unalachtigo the "people who live not far from the ocean", an area that now belongs to south New Jersey and Delaware.

Herbert Kraft, anthropologist from Seton Hall University, considers that the Lenape terrain also covered Long Island and now New York. Others say that the Lenape occupied the East Coast – from New England – to Virginia. David McCutchen, publisher of "The Red Record" thinks a similar way. The Lenape were users of the group of Delaware languages called Algonquin.

Rick Mulrooney[53] gave a description of the Lenape, that among the Algonquins, they were respected as the grandfather tribe, in recognition of their long residence in the area and their role in settling disputes among the other tribes. He writes, that the Lenape ate from wooden bowls, using their fingers and spoons made from clamshells,

Henry Seidel Canby, the artist born in Wilmington, who was editor of the "Saturday Review of Literature", captured part of the life of the Lenape in his cycle "The Brandywine". He showed, among others, a

---

[53] See: Rick Mulrooney, *Learn abut those who gave us Appoquinimink, Naamans and others*, "The News Journal", July 18, 2005, pg. E4-5.

symbolic picture of two English settlers standing next to the Brandywine River with two Indian guides who came from the Delaware River.

The Nanticoke Tribe deserves to be mentioned when considering Indians of Delaware. They were close relatives of the Lenape and Munsie Indians, were farming people, and similarly, they spoke an Algonquin dialect. Like the other local tribes, they traded with other New England tribes, and they often fought with the powerful Iroquois Confederation. For war, the Nanticoke warriors often adopted a *"Mohawk hairstyle"* fighting with heavy wooden war clubs. They were known to have used poison on their enemies, so Nanticoke chiefs, like European monarchs, were very careful to safeguard and test their food before eating it.

The Nanticokes were known as *People of the Tide Water*, and logically, they carved dugout canoes from wood for transportation on water. On land, they used dogs as pack animals, as there were no horses in North America until the colonists brought them from Europe. The Nanticokes were not originally from the Delaware and Maryland area around the Chesapeake River, but traditionally, they claim to have come from the Plains region of the United States. By 1748, white encroachment caused the Nanticoke to move up the Susquehanna River to the Iroquois with whom they affiliated. Others joined the Lenape and Munsie groups. The remaining Nanticokes assimilated into the local populace mixing the blood.

There is no officially recognized Nanticoke Tribe in the United States, and they have no reservation or their own government. They do have an unofficial tribe that serves the cultural needs of the Nanticoke people.

Indian Princesses

Frances Slocum

This story - apparently passed from one generation to the next generation – was told to me by Marien Boehm, Norman's stepmother. By education and profession a teacher, she was from a Scottish family for several generations living in the town of Wyoming, Pennsylvania located in the Wyoming Valley. The State of Wyoming later took its name from that valley. Located nearby are the cities of Wilkes-Barre and Scranton and the towns of Forty-Fort and Kingston. The beautiful Susquehanna River runs through the picturesque Wyoming Valley that is known from many Indian legends and stories in the books of James Fenimore Cooper.

Not far from Dennison street, where Marien lived, stands a monument in memory of the Wyoming battle that took place on July 3, 1778. It is one of the most known battles in the history of the United States, and it is not known as a battle, but as a massacre. Seneca Indian warriors with an overwhelming proportion of three to one - defeated the whites killing two hundred and fifty of them. A few white survivors escaped by throwing themselves into the Susquehanna River. The fight took only half an hour. The white people who were captured were killed the same night. According to legend, fouteen captives were killed personally by the Seneca Chief Eghobund's wife Queen Esther by tomahawk blows to the head. Presumably, her vengeance was in retaliation for the loss of her only son Gencho, who had been murdered by whites a few days before the massacre. Esther (whose real name was Esther Montour) was the daughter of a white man and an Indian woman.

In October of the same year, Delaware Indians took from the family home of Quakers Jonathan and Ruth Slocum, in the town of Wilkes-Barre in Pennsylvania, their five-year-old daughter Frances Slocum. She was kidnapped during the daytime in her mother's presence. Ruth Slocum died soon afterwards never seeing her daughter again. Everybody believed she died from a broken heart. The Slocum Family did not lose their hopes and never stopped looking for the girl. There is not much known about the life of Frances, only that she was taken to Indiana and eventually married Miami Indian Chief Shepoconah.

Marien Boehm kept and presented to me an article from the 1961 local newspaper "Times Leader" titled "Will of woman snatched from city by Indians surfaces". I read that Slocum family members, after fifty-nine years of searching found her, and attempted to persuade her to return home to Wilkes-Barre. Frances could no longer speak English, so interpreters were needed to translate her response. According to the article she said:

"I have always lived with the Indians, they have always used me kindly, I am used to them. My husband and boys are buried here, and I cannot leave them. I have a house and large lands, two daughters, three grandchildren – why should I go and be like a fish out of water?"

She died ten years later, in 1847, after living with Indians for nearly seventy years. To the Indians she was known as Maca Mocanaquah or Little Bear Woman. The village in Conyngham Township, her family's birth area, was named Mocanaqua, and Frances Slocum State Park is located in Kingston Township, both townships located in Luzerne County, Pennsylvania. In the state of Indiana, a school has her name: Maconaquah High School, and also in Maconaquah Park is the Frances Slocum Trail.

The whole story came to light in the town of Kokomo in Indiana when the will of Frances Slocum was found. It was found in a box at a rummage sale in Per, Indiana. Also in the box, a document signed by President Zachary Taylor was found, dated in 1784 (??) granting six hundred and forty acres to Frances Slocum.

The owners of the box that was found are Jim and Laura Chadwell from Kokomo. They publicly presented Slocum's will, which leaves lands owned by Frances Slocum to her daughters and to Lora Siders, the Miami Indian tribal secretary. According to the article (that was presented to me without full bibliography) from the 1961 "Times Leader", Laura Chadwell was quoted explaining how she became owner of such documents. Her mother-in-law bought a box of books at a rummage sale in Kokomoaki, and "She didn't notice the abstracts were in there, but I did. I called the historical society in Miami County in 1985. A man asked me if they were bulky and bound in green paper. I said they were".

The Chadwells were asked to donate the papers to the museum. The documents were appraised for the approximate value of a thousand dollars. After the Chadwells had learned more about the Slocum story, they decided not to sell the document but to keep it with them. They knew the documents belong to the Indians.

Eunice Williams

A similar event took place in the state of Massachusetts.[54]

The story starts in Deerfield, when at the end of the eighteenth century, and for almost thirty years, the small village was subjected to attacks by the French allied with Indians. During the reign of King Philip, Deerfield was attacked seven times, and those years are the bloodiest in its history. When the war started between England and France in the fall of 1700, the village was in the midst of the ensuing events.

On February 29, 1704, Kanienkeha (Mohawk) Indians attacked Deerfield, killed fifty people and kidnapped many others, including Reverend John Williams and his wife and their five children. After a while, Reverend Williams, his wife and four children were released and returned home, but their seven-year old daughter Eunice was kept by the Indians. Consequently, the girl adapted to Indian life, was baptized as Catholic and was given a new name Marguerite. She eventually married an Indian and gave birth to a few children. Her father, Reverend John Williams (and after his death the oldest brother Stephen) never stopped looking for her. When Stephen finally found her, she did not speak English and despite the family insisting she return home, she chose to stay with Indian people who years earlier had kidnapped her.

It is said that Eunice visited her brothers four times, always taking her husband with her. Perhaps she worried that someone would make it difficult for her to return to the Indians. She died among the Indians at the age of eighty-nine.

Very touching is an epilog to the whole story. One summer day in 1837, a hundred an thirty-three years after the massacre, twenty-three Indians came out from the forest near Deerfield. They asked to be shown the grave of Reverend Williams and his wife. They were Eunice's descendents, and they had come to pay their respects to their ancestors, Eunice parents, and their great-grandparents. They stayed in Deerfield the whole week, and even took part in Sunday mass. Their visit aroused considerable curiosity. Everybody agreed they did have good manners, and they were well-composed young men.

It is said that of two Eunice's grandsons John and Eleazer were taken into the educational system in Massachusetts. For a while, they wore moccasins, wore blankets and had some feathers in their heads.

---

[54] See: *American Heritage: Of One Blood All Nations,* Geoffrey C. Ward, July/August 1994 and: *The Unredeemed Captive: A Family Story from Early America*, Alfred A.Knopf, New York 1994

Aleksandra Ziolkowska-Boehm

They did not speak English. Slowly they melted into the surroundings. After five years, John returned to Canada, but Eleazer spent the rest of his life among his white family members.

Eunice's life has inspired many. In October 2006 in the National Museum of American Indians, an opera opened, whose libretto was based on the events of Eunice William's life.[55]

Cynthia Ann Parker

The story of a little girl name Cynthia who was kidnapped by Comanche Indians in 1836 inspired a movie production and writers who wrote several books based on it. She was born in a Scottish – Irish family in Illinois, but soon the family moved to Texas. In May 1836, the Comanche attacked Fort Parker, took away five men, two women and three children. Among them was nine year old Cynthia Ann Parker, her brother John and cousin James Pratt Plummer. After a while, the boys were allowed to return home, but Cynthia was not and spent twenty-five years among the Comanche.

When she grew older, she married Comanche Indian Peta Nocona. She received her Indian name Naduah that means *she carries herself with dignity and grace*. She gave birth to three children: a son, Quanah Parker, who later became chief, a second son Pecos, and a daughter named Topsannah (Prairie flower). After twenty-five years had passed. Cynthia was kidnapped again in 1860 – now by Texas Rangers who were surprised that among the captured was a white woman with a girl, and they both had blue eyes. Her uncle, who had never given up hope for her return, quickly recognized Cynthia.

Cynthia did not adapt to life among the white society; a few times she tried to escape. She worried about what was going on with her sons. She learned that the younger son died of chicken pox and the daughter, who was with her in Texas, died of influenza.

Cynthia Ann Parker died in 1870 (some sources say in 1871) among white people who rescued her, but she never adapted to their life style. She was buried in Texas, and in 1910, her son Quanah brought her remains from Texas to a cemetery in Fort Sill, Oklahoma.

---

[55] See: *The Captivation of Eunice Williams*, music: Paul M. Kimper, libretto: Harley Erdman, producer Linda McInerney.

92

Miss Universum – Megan Kelley

Megan Kelley prefers her uncle would use her Comanche name Nive To-Tse-Yah, it means "Pretty Flower"[56].

Kelly was sixteen years old in 2002, lived in a house surrounded by pecan trees outside Fort Gibson. She is the only child. She owns beautiful tribal dresses that are from different tribes: Comanche, Osage and Cherokee. She goes to a school near Tahlequah that only Indian children attend. She likes singer Ricky Martin and is a fan of the University of Oklahoma, nicknamed "Sooners" (as pointed out by Bruce E. Johansen, for people who invaded Indian land before it was legal to do so). She would like to play basketball, but as she says, she is not tall enough.

She would like to study sport medicine or administration, but she is not really sure what she would like to do. Now she has only one dream – to become an "Indian Princess". Her uncle calls her "Miss Candidate".

I have learned about Indian pageantry from the magazine "Oklahoma Today"[57]. It was a long article that featured Megan Kelly, and I have used quotations from it.

In her family there were a few princesses. Her mother, Margrett, was once the Walters Pow wow Princess, her aunt Jackie was once the Comanche Tribal Princess. Her cousin, Georgia Oberly Vlaandra is a former Miss Indian USA, and a cousin Joyce Shield was once Miss Indian Oklahoma University, and another cousin, Faren Revard, was in the Miss Indian Oklahoma competition in 1999.

For reasons that many girls all over the World understand, not only Native Americans, Megan Kelley would like to become a princess too. How can an Indian girl think she could be a princess in her family? It sounds impossible, since within an Indian's family clan, not even a chief's daughter is considered a princess. The Indian pageantry started in the 1970's. It was, of course, a white man's idea and plan, but not really. There are earlier stories about Indian princesses. Clara Sue Kidwell, director of Native American Studies at the University of Oklahoma found the information about a girl who represented the University of Oklahoma's Sequoyah Indian Club in the 1930's. A well-known Oklahoma photographer Pierre Tartoue took pictures of, for example – Choctaw Marie Armstrong and Kiowa/Apache Vanette Mopope at the Anadarko Indian Exposition as early as 1948.

---

[56] See: Kelly Crow, *Princess and the pageantry. The serious and competitive world of Indian pageants*, "Oklahoma Today", May-June, Vol. 50, NR 3, 2000
[57] See: Kelly Crow, *Princess*, "Oklahoma Today", NR 3, 2000, pg. 39–45

The Miss America pageant began in 1921, but over time, Indian girls have willfully filtered it through their culture creating their own style of pageants. The first pageantry of Miss Indian of the State of Oklahoma was created in 1973, in 1983 there was the first Junior Miss Indian Oklahoma, and in 1986 Miss Indian USA. The first Miss Indian Tulsa received her award in 1985 and Miss Indian Oklahoma City in 1990. Margrett Kelley says that the pageantry ceremony has something to do with a change in lifestyle and that now well off Indians can sponsor the competition. In the past everybody was so poor.

As a little girl, Megan observed her cousins who took part in *pow-wows* and then in beauty competitions. She watched the people asking them for autographs. She liked the adulation very much, and at twelve years of age, she took part in Junior Miss Cherokee. She had to prepare a speech telling why she takes part in the competition, reading it aloud to the judges. She also had to answer various questions about her culture. She did not pass the judges' review. Her parents, as she recalls, told her that she had to prepare herself, but she was so sure of winning, she did little preparation.

The following year wearing moccasins and a Cherokee costume, she won the competition. Her mother said that it was the happiest day of her life. To enter the Junior Miss, Megan had to meet the requirements of the Oklahoma Federation of Indian Women, the organization that establishes rules of the pageant. Girls have to be good students and cannot live with a male other then a relative. For six months, they have to participate in a special school program. The swimsuit competition, so popular among white girls, is excluded, as are body size and physical perfection. Indians consider the beauty as all inside. More important is how friendly and nice the girls are, how they smile. Modesty is a more important attribute than sexuality. Contestants are seen as a future mother, how much they like and know tradition. The final title is not a single person award, but a tribal winning. These things explain why Indian girls are not part of the Miss America competition. Only two of them have ever made it to the finals of the Miss Indian America pageant: in 1941 Mifaunwy Shunatona from Oklahoma, and in 1971 Susan Supernaw from New Mexico.

There are not too many Indian candidates for Miss America. Encouragement for them to enter the competition has included such things as, for example, a university scholarship, an Arabian horse donated by Wayne Newton. All the privileges summed up equal a bonus of about one hundred and twenty thousand dollars, and such money opens many roads

The romantic idea of an Indian princess has more roots in myth than in reality. The myth can be credited to Captain John Smith and Walt Disney.

Pocahontas

Pocahontas is probably the most well known Indian female in the world, being particularly famous thanks to Walt Disney and the movie industry. Disney's animated movie came out in 1995. The movie tells the story of an Indian girl who became a part of American history. It was the time when the first settlers were coming to America. As an Indian friend told me, there are eleven versions of a princess' life. When I asked, how much he liked the movie, he said he liked it. It left positive feelings, and the color of skin does not matter.

Pocahontas was a daughter (apparently one of ten) of a Patawomeck Indian Chief Powhatan (his given name was Wahunsunacock). The Patawomeck tribe lived in an area of what is now Jamestown, Virginia, a region on the Chesapeake Bay. Jamestown was the first colony established by European setters, and that expedition should not be mixed with the first wave of white settler that landed in today's Plymouth Rock in Massachusetts. About the expedition for Virginia, Sir Francis Bacon apparently wrote that they represented the dregs of society, that among them were losers with titles, debtors with sentences, prisoners, merchants looking for a better chance and pastors with their people.

The first settlers came in April 1607. Four months later, their number was diminished in half due to illnesses, diseases and hunger.

Among the first settlers were seven Polish craftsmen producing tar, glass, soap ash and building material. Their skills exemplified the pioneering efforts that created the beginning of America's manufacturing industry. They all arrived on a ship called "Mary and Margaret". Captain John Smith, who later became administrator of Jamestown Colony, engaged the Polish craftsmen. Soon the Polish settlers built a glass works, which was to become the first factory in North America. They were asked to teach their trade and skills to emigrants from other European countries, for example German and Dutch settlers. The strength of the Polish settlers was recognized by the first American parliament in Jamestown, when in 1619, the Poles organized the first strike in America. They demanded equal rights and civil status.[58]

---

[58] See: Arthur L.Waldo, *True Heroes of Jamestown*, American Institute of Polish Culture, Miami, Florida, 1977.

Aleksandra Ziolkowska-Boehm

Nearly a hundred and ninety years later, the Polish-American Revolutionary War hero Tadeusz Kosciuszko was visited in Philadelphia by Miami Ohio Indian Chief Little Turtle seeking to stop whiskey traffickers from peddling alcohol to his people. According to the Kosciuszko biographer Alex Storozynski, from whose book ("The Peasant Prince", NY 2009) I learned about this story, the Chief had told his people: "Liquor is to be more feared than the gun and tomahawk." Kosciuszko's reputation as a supporter of human rights had reached Little Turtle, and he sought the hero's help to influence President Adams. Little Turtle presented his host with a ceremonial peace pipe-tomahawk that so pleased him that when he observed his guest admiring his sleeveless wool Tatar cloak, he gave it to the Chief. Noticing that Little Turtle squinted, Kosciuszko gave him his reading glasses. The Chief did not understand how the glasses worked, nor did he tire of the pleasure from looking at objects grown larger. As Storozynski writes, Little Turtle exclaimed, "You have given me new eyes!" The Polish hero was delighted by the Indian's visit and on departure gave him his favorite pair of pistols. "These pistols I have carried and used on many a hard-fought battlefield in defense of the oppressed, the weak, the wronged of my own race. I now present them to you with the injunction that with them you shoot dead the first man who ever comes to subjugate you or to despoil you of your country." Leaving the building on Pine Street, Little Turtle anxiously awaited the opportunity to tell his people of his new friend "Kotscho."

According to the legend, Princess Pocahontas saved the life of Captain John Smith, one of the first leaders of the colony. Among Indian people, she was known as Matoaka.

John Smith, in his memoirs, wrote in December 1607 how he was captured by Indians. During the ceremonial dances, they were supposed to portray his killing. According to his recollections, Pocahontas covered his head by her arms and by doing it saved him.

Anthropologists from William and Mary College in the State of Virginia analyzed oral Powhatan Indian customs and came to the conclusion that something else happened to Captain John Smith. Pocahontas was then ten or eleven years old. Probably, they were not ceremonial dances before the execution, but it was a ceremonial dance to fraternize with newcomers. None can prove now what is truth and what is a legend. But for sure, as agreed by all historians - Pocahontas was an extraordinary person and had an extraordinary but short life. Pocahontas was attractive and intelligent.

Captain Samuel Argall, the new administrator of the colony, one year after his coming, in 1613, arranged the kidnapping of Chief

Powhatan's daughter. He apparently did so to better negotiate with Indians the release of a few prisoners and some tools. One year later (because the negotiations lasted one year), the other administrator, Sir Thomas Dale, with a unit of a hundred and fifty people, went to the Indians and encouraged them to fight for Pocahontas. Then one of the colonists, a twenty-eight-year old widower John Rolfe announced to Dale that he wanted to marry Pocahontas. She spoke English and agreed to it, and the marriage took place. Two years later, Pocahontas with her new name Rebecca, that she received during the baptism of her son, Thomas, together with her husband left for England. She was welcomed there in the most cordial manner and became a sensation. The Royal family welcomed Pocahontas in England. When the family left to return to America, Pocahontas became ill aboard ship. The ship stopped, she was taken ashore and she was cared for in Gravesend. At the age of twenty-two, she died and was buried there.

Chief Wilma Mankiller

The first woman in modern times chosen as a Cherokee Chief was Wilma Mankiller. She held the position for ten years 1985–1995. Never in earlier history had a woman become an Indian Chief.

Her father Charles Mankiller attended an Indian grammar school, and kept strong ties with Indian culture. He says he had never experienced being put down as an Indian. Wilma's mother Clara Irene Sitton was Irish-Dutch origin and was born and raised in Oklahoma. She did not have any Indian blood. After marrying Charles, her life was totally involved with Cherokee affairs.

According to a program about the movement of Indian families, Mr. and Mrs. Mankiller with their family moved to San Francisco where they met other Indian families. Charles liked to take part in discussions about Indian affairs, and he always made sure his children knew their heritage. In 1969, Indian students, who insisted the island belonged to Indians, occupied Alcatraz. In such an atmosphere, Wilma was raised. She married a businessman from Ecuador and gave birth to two daughters – Gina and Felicia. The woman's liberation movement had just started. Wilma took an active role in it and in actions on behalf of the Cherokee Indians. She settled in Tahlequah, the Cherokee capitol and became a political agitator on environment, medical clinics, better schools etc. A few years later, she married again – to a full-blooded Cherokee Charlie Soap, an activist who helped her during the campaign for tribal Chief.

In 1985, Wilma Mankiller became a Chief of the Cherokee Nation, the biggest (according to population statistics) tribe in the United States.

(The second biggest Nation is Navajo. In 1990, the Cherokee were three hundred and eight thousand people, and in 2000, seven hundred and thirty thousand people).

The press has quoted Wilma Mankiller saying that her work is something between a social worker and president of a small country. Many times asked if it is difficult, as a woman, to be an Indian Chief, she answered – yes. But she reminded the questioners, that Indian women always held a very high status in the Indian social structure that was matriarchal. The women's voice was important in choosing or putting down a chief. She won, as she said, because she worked harder than her opponents. She was an optimist and realist. She often said even though Indian tribes' histories are different, all finish in the same way – defeat and a tearing apart politically, economically and socially. For some time now, Indians have tried to shed themselves of a hundred years of effort to inculcate in them that their culture does not exist, is archaic, and their religion is pagan. When the process of shedding is finished, they can trust their own thinking and vision of the future.

Wilma Mankiller overcame cancer; she went through seventeen medical procedures. She gives lectures and writes for Indian papers. Thanks to her efforts, a capsule for the future generations was closed in January 2000. In it other items were placed – the Cherokee alphabet. (the Indian who created the written Cherokee language was Sequoyah). In the capsule, Wilma Mankiller left a verbal message – the hope that in the future when the capsule is opened, her Cherokee people would still speak their language.

Wilma Mankiller has published her biography.[59] On its cover are words by Alice Walker, author of "The Color Purple" that are quoted: "Wilma Mankiller is someone I feel I've known in this lifetime and many lifetimes before. I recognize in her greatest beauty, dignity, and truthfulness".

Helen Maria Hunt Jackson

Another woman I would like to mention is Helen Maria Hunt Jackson (1830–1885), an American writer, a white woman, and one of the biggest fighters for Indian rights in the nineteenth century. She is the author of two books: *Ramona* (1884), a fictional story about how Indians were treated by white people and *Century of Dishonor* (1881) telling about the broken treaties and the broken human rights resulting from the

---

[59] See: Wilma Mankiller and Michael Wallis, *Mankiller. A Chief and Her People*, St. Martin Griffin, New York 1994

behavior towards Indians. Jackson's works were the first documented sources showing how white people treated and put down the Indians.

Helen Jackson, a well-known poet and a long time friend of poet Emily Dickinson, is usually mentioned many times during symposiums and quoted in many books. Her books on Indian issues are used by students and by Indian rights activists.

Mildred Imach Cleghorn

Mildred Imach Cleghorn (1910–1997) was compared to Jackie Kennedy because of her elegance and style. She was a tall woman of great personal charm. Her father of the Chiricahua-Warm Springs Apaches fought next to Chief Geronimo, and in 1886, was captured. Together with his wife Amy, he was put into prison in Fort Sill, Oklahoma. In prison, Mildred was born. The family was released in 1914. Mildred completed Apache High School and university at Haskell Institute in Lawrence, Kansas. Later she worked in the Bureau of Indian Affairs, where she met her future husband, a Mescalero Apache. They married on the Mescalero Apache Reservation in New Mexico, and adopted a daughter Penny.

Mildred's whole life was spent acting on behalf of American Indians, and for twenty years she was the chairperson of the Fort Sill-Chiricahua-Warm Springs Apache tribe. To popularize Indian tradition, she made Indian dolls dressed in tribal costumes. She discussed with elderly women every detail of the Indian costumes. Her dolls show the different tribal costumes worn by men and women. Six of the dolls are shown in the Future Homemakers Club of America in Washington, D.C.

By birth – as a prisoner of war - Mildred Imach Cleghorn was buried in the Apache Prisoner of War Cemetery at Fort Sill in Oklahoma, where the famous Chief Geronimo is also buried.

All who remembered Mildred called her "a great Indian Lady".

Sacagawea

Together they spent about one thousand days and nights, from rainy October, when they started in Ohio, until when traveling by canoe on the Mississippi River, they reached Saint Louis. They slept in different places, often in Indian teepees. They kept a journal that on publishing included thirteen volumes. They both came from Virginia, both were officers of the American army, both were tall and handsome men. They were twenty-two and twenty-nine years old when they started the famous expedition. Like President Thomas Jefferson, they were looking for knowledge: they were passionate about ethnology, zoology and botany. Their names were: Meriwether Lewis and William Clark. Their journey – not mentioning its planning and preparation - lasted three years (1804–1806). Their expeditionary force included thirty-two people and Lewis' dog, a New Foundland named Seaman.

Among the group was the translator Toussaint Charbonneau. Lewis and Clark had different opinions in judging his wife named Sacagawea who also accompanied the expedition. She was not even twenty years old, and she brought her two month little baby son along.

Lewis on his journey called Sacagawea "Indian woman" and wrote that if she would have enough food and drink and a few *trinkets to wear,* she would be happy anywhere.

The less formal Clark called her by the name Janey and treated her warmly. She responded to his kindness by giving him presents, for example, a half a dozen ferret tails. When the expedition was completed, Clark made the promise to help Sacagawea with the education of her boy Pomp, whom he described as a *"beautiful promising child".*

For Indians they might meet during the journey, they took presents. There were small mirrors, scissors, silk bows, pearl combs, handkerchiefs, knives, copper pots and many necklace beads.

Reading their journal, we learn about their feelings and moods. We learned that to survive, they had to eat horses and dogs. We meet the Indians that helped them such as Mandan. In the spring of 1806, without the aid of the Nez Perce Indians, Lewis and Clark would probably have died from hunger.

Clark toward the end of his life became governor of Louisiana. As a romantic fellow with aspirations, he became disappointed and fell into depression. Lewis had nothing to write besides his journal. According to historians, he committed suicide not far from Nashville in Tennessee. After his death, Clark wrote and published a letter starting with the words: "Dear brother…"

The journal published in two volumes in 1814 included maps of the West. They marked the maps to show tens of Indian tribes. All together they met fifty-eight tribes. The book did not sell well; the following editions were published with few copies in the years 1893 and in 1904–1905. Slowly, it seemed that Lewis and Clark were forgotten. Two hundred years later, "Time" magazine (July 8, 2002) dedicated their cover story to them and about the whole expedition, including the maps of the journey. The book about the expedition was published by historian and biographer Stephen Ambrose[60] and the Ken Burns documentary that followed.

Sacagawea died as a young woman before she turned thirty years of age, however, another version says she lived to an old age. She died of no recognized illness; there were many of them in the nineteenth century.

In 1838, William Clark, was in his son Meriwether Lewis Clark's (he gave him those names) house . He acted on behalf of Indians, became the so-called territorial governor – before Missouri became a state. He lost the campaign. As was written: *"he was too soft on Indians"*.

Sacagawea who was a Shoshone Indian was chosen for a new one dollar coin. The coin replaced the Susan B. Anthony coin that was minted from 1979 to 1981; supplies ran out in 1999. The coin was disliked because it looked almost like a quarter. President Clinton signed the legislation for a new dollar coin. The coin is different from others since it shows the Indian woman looking over her shoulder. Until then, coins used profiles. On her back, Sacagawea carries her small baby boy Jean Baptiste (called "Pomp"). It is the first portrait of a child on an American coin. The author of the project is Glenna Goodacre, a sculptor from Santa Fe, New Mexico. She is known as the sculptor of the monument standing in Washington DC of women soldiers who were in Vietnam.

Probably the best known coin is the five cents Indian Head Nickel. Its reverse side shows a buffalo. Seneca Chief John Big Tree posed for the Indian head nickel. In 1912, sculptor James Earle Fraser asked him to pose for the coin. He was paid one and a half dollars for one hour of posing. The same Chief took part in the movie with John Wayne *"She Wore a Yellow Ribbon"* (apparently he was paid two hundred and fifty dollars a week).

Lost Bird

At a place on the stream Wounded Knee in South Dakota, Lakota Sioux Indians were massacred in an act of ignorance, a lack of knowledge, a fear of white people who did not understand and were terrified by thousands of Indians spread over vast spaces chanting and dancing the *ghost dance*. Among the Indians who were shot was a woman with a child. The mother burrowed into a hollow, and snow came. Four days and four nights later when the bodies were collected for burial, the infant's cry was heard. The mother's body had sheltered and

---

[60] See: Stephen Ambrose, *In Undaunted Courage. Lewis and Clark and the American West*, A Simon and Schuster Press Release, 1996

shielded her daughter. The woman's body was dropped into a mass grave with some one hundred and fifty corpses. The baby lived. She had a bracelet on her wrist and she wore moccasins. An old Lakota woman named the little girl Zintkala Nuni, that means Lost Bird.

The press was full of the story. The little girl was named "little heroine", "little dusky maid", "Indian princess". Leonard Wright Colby, a brigadier general said that the baby could be " a most interesting Indian relic". He adopted her and told his wife Clara about it.

Clara Bewick Colby lived in Washington, D.C. where she was involved in a suffrage movement and ran the bimonthly periodical "The Woman's Tribune".

She went to Beatrice, Nebraska and took charge of her adopted daughter. She dressed the girl in white, the color of the suffrage movement. In her paper, she reported the growing up of her little daughter, saying "many mothers will watch with interest the mothering and education of this...child of the prairie. It is one of the most interesting cases of child study to be found in America"[61].

Everything was going well, but the adoptive mother could not isolate the girl from the world. When other children told the girl her mother was not a white woman but a *"dirty squaw"*, she attacked them with such a fury that older people agreed and said that she is not a "child of prairie", but "a savage girl".

Lost Bird did not know Indians, but she asked about them. She only knew of wooden statues imaging Indians. She liked to ride the circling painted carousel horses and liked to look at her bracelet and moccasins she was found with. She did not do well at school, and she had to change from several of them since she was expelled from one after another. When sixteen years of age, she made her way onto reservations. She did not know the language or customs. She behaved with different manners than Indian girls her same age. She looked straight into men's eyes, laughed too loud and was too sure of herself as compared to an Indian girl.

At seventeen, after learning she was pregnant, she was sent to a Nebraska reformatory, The baby was stillborn. She married and soon learned that her new husband had infected her with venereal disease. She left for California and played parts in silent movies including *The Round-Up, Battle of the Red Men, War on the Plains*. She married again, this time to a cowboy and actor who when drunk beat her. She stopped taking parts in movies and joined the *Buffalo Bill's Wild West Show*. During the

---

[61] See: Gene Smith, *Lost Bird*, "American Heritage", April 1996

season of 1914–15 with the show group, she traveled over the United States and Canada and visited reservations too.

She married the third time, a fellow actor who performed in the show. Lost Bird gave a birth to a baby boy and stopped performing with the show. To take care of the baby, she went to work in the saloons of San Francisco, dancing in Indian dresses. Her health was failing and she was weaker and weaker. Lost Bird, her baby and husband lived in one small room. She took all kind of jobs, finally giving the baby away to an Indian woman. She felt worse and worse, and died on Valentines Day of 1920. She was twenty-nine years old. She was buried in Hanford, California.

When seventy years later, in 1991, the historian Renee Sansom Flood, author of *Lost Bird of Wounded Knee*, wrote about her, the fellow Indians on Pine Ridge in South Dakota decided to bring her home and bury her at Wounded Knee on the Pine Ridge Reservation. They raised the money and buried her not far from the mass grave where her mother is buried. Like the others, she was killed during the Wounded Knee massacre. Now, near by her daughter is buried.

Lost Bird returned to the same place where she was taken from - the arms of her murdered mother.

Aleksandra Ziolkowska-Boehm

Listening to the Silence

Buying the house on Ridgewood Circle in Wilmington, Delaware, Norman and I spoke with its owner, Sherie. She had a degree in chemical engineering from the well-known Cornell University, had worked with big companies, the work requiring her to travel abroad. After thirteen years she changed her interest, and began dedicating herself to herb teaching and learning, therapy, and therapeutic massage. During the ensuing years, she studied in clinics that teach and give courses on herbs, therapy and therapeutic pressures. She opened her own clinic ten years later after moving from Delaware to the West Coast where she is now known in her field. We bought her red brick house with its beautiful wooden floors; the large garden took our attention with the pungent smell of good herbs. The smells gave a special atmosphere, and –as she described – were creating an atmosphere – letting people "listen to the silence" and look at the garden. The smells, the special atmosphere and the garden's beauty were important to our senses – Sherie said.

A few years later, on the same subject, I spoke to the Northern Cheyenne Indian, Linwood Tall Bull (my interview appears later in my book). Linwood calls me by the name *Ariel*, but never told me why and what does it mean? He travels around the United States frequently and is known as one who takes care of the elders of his tribe. He calls for his people to show the old people respect and patience. Linwood assured me that keeping our emotions inside is a source of many troubles, ailments, even illnesses. Those people who are "closed" and do not show emotions are the easiest target for illnesses. He says that everyone should free or release their anger. Otherwise, the anger acts as an organism of poison in our body. When a human being wants to change his life style, he thinks it over, realizes the good, but making the decision to change only leaves him half-cured. He must go "all the way" in changing to be fully cured. Very important are awareness and decisions. Linwood stresses the special connection between human and Nature…a basic belief of Indians. People should laugh more, rest more and be happy. The most important thing – a human being should use his senses: smell, hearing, taste and eyesight.

Sherie told me she believed in the Cherokee religion, that she adopted it as her own. Soon I realized that Sherie belonged to a bigger and bigger group of American women who look for inspiration and stimulus from outside the religion they were born into and raised. Such a phenomenon is connected with constantly searching for something new in life or looking for a deeper sense of life itself. Many people are looking for advice in *self-help books*, some in psychiatry and in all kinds of therapeutic courses. It is not only a woman's phenomenon. Many American men, as well, are looking for richness of meaning and sense to life. They discover and adopt other religions or beliefs. Found to be interesting to observe, such new religions or beliefs are sometimes eventually accepted as their own. These include Christian religions such as the *born again movement* and Jewish and Eastern beliefs.

The Indian culture is attractive also to those Native Americans who, for whatever reason, have never bothered with their own identity. Diamond Brown was born on a North Carolina reservation, but his family left the reservation, and he was raised outside of Indian culture. Now he lives near Atlanta, Georgia and travels to the East Coast and to Canada with lectures about Indian cultures. He is invited to schools to talk about myths and lies the white people have espoused for years about Indian culture and customs. He likes to meet with children, whom he tells that Indians are the same as others, and they have their own beliefs. They have respect for every creature alive: animals, reptiles, human beings, and also for trees and shrubs.

There is an American Indian anecdote[62] about the closeness of humans and dogs: When God created man and the animals, he placed them all on a large prairie. Then, God drew a line on the prairie and placed man on one side of the line and the animals on the other side of the line. Then, God widened the line between man and the animals, and the line continued to become wider. At the last minute, before the line became too expansive, the dogs jumped over the line to join man.

Horses led an important role in the life of Native Americans. They were used in battle, hunting and for transportation. Zenon Lipowicz, author of a book and articles about horses, wrote that warriors marked their horse's ears so at night by touch they could recognize them. Before battle, the warriors prayed for themselves and their horses. They painted them, they put a necklace made from bear claws (or other means) around the horses' neck. The Apache believed that a wounded warrior could be healed by his horse. The horses used in the battles were treated with great respect and tenderness. The modern Crow believe that God will punish one who is cruel to a horse

Diamond Brown remembers, when as a young boy, he saw Cherokee Indians like him for the first time. Brown was not proud of them, but fear and horror possessed him. As a boy, seeing so many western movies, a fear they would scalp him persisted. Brown does not like the name *Native American*: considering himself a Cherokee. He tells young people that the *peace pipe* was used in ritual prayers. A *tomahawk*

---

[62] I have been unable to attribute the anecdote to a specific tribe or Nation.

looks funny and odd when replicas of one are used by sport fans of the Atlanta Braves in their *tomahawk chop* –- it looks like they are pounding a nail into a board with a hammer.

The interest of spirituality of Indians is rather new, and it has resulted in the newest trend of interest in them and their culture. Such interest was not evident years ago in the attitude towards Indians. It came from a calling for respect for Indians and from feelings of guilt. Somehow, I found the guilt complex in many Americans, even though most of them had nothing to do with the old history, as their ancestors came to the United States much later than the time of mistreatment, cruelty and massacres of Indians.

Lisa Couturier, author of the book *The Hopes of Snakes*, writes about the connection between believers in Nature, and psychiatrist Joyce Mills, organizes courses for groups of Americans interested in Nature. Couturier and Mills both agree that the human's interest comes from wanting to belong to a group, or to identify with surroundings and the environment. Many people moved away from Nature and live in the cities that have and run by their own rhythm and rules. Now, people have started to move towards Indians as those who never rejected, never lost their relationship with Nature and have not denied their feelings of identity with their own people. Religion shows that Indians keep their relationship with Nature and search in it for wisdom and help.

There is a group of Americans who would also like to be present in that flowing stream of faith and show deep interest in understanding Indian faith. The publishers have picked up on this trend and they have published many books talking about, amongst other issues – Indian spirituality. There is a trend for the practice of "healing", particularly with the illness like Aids, so there is almost a need to heal by spiritual procedures and customs. The number of white people practicing "healing" using "Indian procedures", as a way to make money, is growing and growing.

Living in Houston, I have read the ad placed in the newspapers by a former Methodist pastor who every Saturday prays to dead Indians to give him more power and wisdom to brighten his brain. His practice is psychotherapy, and he heals patients using a *sweat lodge*, which is practiced by Indians to "clean" the mind and body. During that sort of sauna, people should be dressed lightly in cotton under shirts and take breaks, when it becomes too hot. They can drink water. The ceremony entails four phases of singing and praying. During the first, the ancestors' shadows are called, during the second, prayers call for not being scared, and other worries that disturb people. In the third phase – patients pray for themselves and for their families. The fourth phase is a thanksgiving

107

prayer. Each phase has symbols – colors, signs and instruments used during the ceremony of the *sweat lodge.*

"This place is like a mother's womb" – explains a white "healer"- "You are born, then die and come again as newborn. The people change a lot, after they come to us. It is not important who they are, if they are successful people or average. All of them want to know who they are and why they are on Earth".

According to an ad – taking part in such a "cleanser" costs an average of twenty dollars (however, genuine Indian sweat lodges do not charge an admission). Similar ads are shown in magazines, particularly in "New Age". Everything is for sale: - sacred rituals, healing herbs. Whites criticized for exploitation of the Native Americans' belief answer – that they have a respect for Native Americans and they do not harm anyone.

Indians think that white healer practices are somehow a sacrilege, and it shakes their Indian faith. They say that something that is special has now become approachable and common. White people close their eyes and say they have a vision. Indians say that the Creator punishes those who are doing such things. Exploitation of Indian culture and selling it for profit is bad enough, however, revealing everything that they learn about Indian's beliefs and rituals is worse.

Indians define white healers as *shake-'n'-bake medicine people* or *plastic medicine men.* They are aware that there are many cheaters who pretend they are "healers". They live in cities and ask big money for a spiritual ceremony connected with healing.

Meanwhile, the Indians leaders think, that even *medicine men* lose their healing power when they move away from their land. The power comes from the Earth, the terrain where the medicine men are born, that they belong to. To become a *medicine man*, the proper ancestry is needed and many years of practice. Indians who help others for financial reasons, who leave their place and move to the city, are traitors to their people. Their egoism and selfishness take their healing power from them, and they lose their healing abilities. *Medicine men* believe that ritual procedures can become a dangerous power in the hands of the evil.

Rick Two Dogs, respected Lakota Sioux Indian *medicine man* in Porcupine, Pine Ridge Reservation, South Dakota can trace his ancestry line two hundred and fifty years back. He recalls his vision that makes him realize that he cannot move out from the reservation. He is supposed to stay and help his own people. He says: "If you are an authentic *medicine man*, the power and strength you have takes energy from your land and your people. People you help also live on the same terrain. The gift of healing is like an inheritance".

Particularly after the movie "Dancing with Wolves" was released, many Indians (for profit reasons) started to act like they were "healers". "Indian Country Today", a newspaper published by the New York Oneidas, from time to time provides reportage about false *medicine men*. "Or is it like someone in Denver who wears the black cloth and priest's special clerical collar, says he is a Catholic priest, only because he "felt need of it", wrote Tim Giago, Oglala Lakota. Asking for payment in return for healing is considered fraud by real *medicine men*. Two Dogs words are quoted: "A traditional medicine man does not take money." If people want to give of themselves some gift as an appreciation, we can accept it. But not money. Gifts can be food, tobacco, clothes or other useful things. Tobacco is used for ritual. When anyone starts to take money, he loses his healing power.

Two Dogs sees an increasing trend. White people suffering from terminal illnesses, come to reservations to look for unconventional medicine. People with cancers, with Aids and other such life threatening diseases first of all ask about money saying: I will give you five to ten thousand dollars. Two Dogs answers them by saying that he cannot do anything only because it is not a way to ask for help.

Others come to Two Dogs who would like to learn about spirituality. Two Dogs says that it is not a thing to learn. Anyone can pray in different ways, but only Indians know the real tribal prayers.

Terry Knight, a Ute Indian from southwest Colorado, the son of a respected *medicine man* named Charley Knight says:

"The real *medicine man* stays like that all his life. It is a calling. It is difficult and responsible work. No one in a hurry can become a *medicine man*. I was asked by whites to make rituals to heal. They offered me big money…it was very tempting, but I refused".

When asked how a Ute Indian becomes a *medicine man* he answered:

"It depends upon the Creator and of your ancestors' souls. They should approve and confirm our calling in us".

Then come the others, hungry for knowledge, that later (without any consultation) publish all kinds of books, full of silly things. As writes "Indian Country Today" – "those books teach, give practical advice, but they are pitiful. They do not have much to do with healing and real Indian medicine".

Besides the negative opinions mentioned in newspapers, the interest in Indian medicine is big. When Norman and I lived in Texas, the press wrote about the late physician, full of mystique and vigor, that with passing years gained great respect. His name was Gideon Lincecum, and he was a "naturalist doctor". After many years, his advice and recommendations were quoted by such serious places as the Austin College (Presbyterian) in Sherman, Texas, where Professor Jerry Lincecum, Gideon's great-great-grandson is preparing to publish the Gideon memoirs. Jerry Lincecum recalled his ancestor as one of the first scientists of medicine, as a *medicine man* who lived in the years 1793–1874[63].

Gideon Lincecum, with passion and dedication, was an advocate of the effectiveness of Indian medicine. He was raised among Indians, then he left them to follow the trail of the first settlers from Georgia to Mississippi, where he lived a number of years. He moved from one place to another, and at seventy-six years of age, he joined former Confederate soldiers in Tuxpan, Mexico. He returned to Texas where he died. His practice was very popular, and as he was quoted: "the Indian herbs agree with white people". In his memoirs, he quoted an anecdote about his own discussions concerning medicine with a female Choctaw healer. They spent much time together in a woods learning about her and their powers. "How pitiful that you are white man", said Alikchi Chito, "You could be a good Indian".

Gideon Lincecum was considered a stranger among the "orthodox"- as he described the Indian – and also among his own associate doctors. His herbs made him a wealthy man, but he had many enemies. In his old age, he meditated a lot about human beings and ants. He particularly liked the Texas ants. He corresponded about it with Charles Darwin, the author of "On the Origin of Species" who read a letter from Lincecum in front of a forum of English scientists. Gideon was married and had ten children. Now, his great-great-grandson gives people advice based on his ancestor's remedies. He, for example, describes oil from rosemary for rheumatism. It is known that old women in Italy sleep on mattresses full of rosemary.

The Indians are now saying that after almost two centuries of white domination, when they see whites interested in their beliefs and rituals, the whites want to take away another part of their culture and existence, in the same way they took away their land. The Indians say that if whites are really searching for something deep in their life, but at the same time ignore the real problems in Indian life that the Indian communities face – high unemployment, illnesses, alcoholism and racism - those whites should start with thoughts. If they really have an interest in Indians, their

---

[63] See: *Adventures of a Frontier Naturalist: The life and Times of Dr. Gideon Lincecum.* Edited by Jerry Bryan Lincecum and Edward Hake Phillips. College Station, Texas A&M University Press, 1994

thoughts should be how to help them, how to bring economy to their lands and how to give Indian children the open gates to education.

According to Lakota Sioux beliefs, the Great Spirit lives in carved wooden traditional Indian flutes. Many years ago, the Lakota Indians heard the wind singing a beautiful melody coming from the flute. Since then, they believe that the Great Spirit is talking to them through music.

William Gutierrez says every time he plays on his own sacred flute, he feels the presence of the Great Spirit. Gutierrez is a Navajo and south Ute Indian. He was born in New Mexico. In 1993, Norman and I attended his concert when living in Dallas, Texas. He played on the fourth day of the annual American Indian Art Festival and Market. Over one hundred and fifty Indians from the whole American continent performed there. Indians displayed their hand made goods like jewelry, drawings, paintings and sculptures. There were Indian dishes offered to eat. William Gutierrez played the music and melodies of many tribes. He said, by travelling all over the country, he was able to learn them. He also learned many myths that he keeps to himself when he plays.

"I close my eyes and let my heart play...what is in me comes out through my music", says Gutierrez. His flutes are made from Red Cedar. Each of the instruments has a different sound; a different tone comes from every flute. Gutierrez considers the flute as a gift from the Great Spirit, and he adds, "I never forget to ask him about letting me play, and to thank him when I finish. I usually play one melody every day'.

In September 1995, Norman and I attended a Delaware *pow-wow*. The Nanticoke Indians were attending. Charlie Clark, a chief's son and organizer of the ceremony was quoted as saying, "I trust the Indian dances and customs shown are going to help people to understand the culture of Native Americans". In his prayer, he asked for work for everyone, regardless of the color of the skin. A three-year-old boy said that he wanted to be an Indian because he likes the colorful cloth that reminds him of roosters.

The *pow-wow* is organized not only so the people can learn about Indian culture, it is also the occasion for good times between Indians from different tribes. About forty-five tribes from all over the country send representatives to the *pow-wow*. They display their items for sale – including dream catchers and blankets.

I was looking at the painted white and red striped faces. First started the slow and rhythmic sounds of a drum. Then other drums joined in. Finally, the dancers came out, one after another, representing 50 tribes. I asked an elderly Indian who sat next to us to explain the basic dances of the *pow-wow*. He said that dances were always part of Indian tradition and that each dance had its own name: Fancy Dance, Jingle Dance, Grass

Dance, Women's Traditional Dance, Fancy Shawl Dance, Men's Traditional Dance, Warrior Dance, Flag Bearers Dance, Royalty Dance, Straight Dance. He told us also that the *pow-wow* is a way to meet each other in dance and renew old friendships, and it is the reason he looks so intently at the people around because he is looking for someone he knew in his youth.

According to Indian beliefs, life is a constant process of learning about oneself. The knowledge is gathered through facing problems, through efforts of inside peace and harmony with Nature around us. Nature gives us an example of how to live the honest way and in harmony with the life of others.

When an Indian woman would like to change her life and would not know which path to chose, she would go to the elderly for advice. He or she supposedly would tell her a story about one day of a hawk. Looking for food, the hawk would see a mouse. The hawk would start to fly lower to hunt for the mouse. A sudden strong wind would push back the hawk, and the hawk would forget about his daily prayer. When finally he would reach a place where he first saw the mouse, the mouse would be gone. The hawk would rise up again and for many hours would fly around in the sky. When the sun started to go down, the hawk was sure he would go to sleep hungry, and just then he would sight a rabbit, and would hunt for it (successfully).

The elder would not make a comment about his story leaving the woman to find its interpretation. He knew she would find similarities between her life and the hawk's life and that she would find out herself the lesson about not giving up and the need for persistence in life. The woman would think about perseverance and patience that would bring her unknown virtues. Indian women, through stories like this one, know that Nature is a guide in life and shows the face of God. The tribe's beliefs are different, but there are a few basic truths. I write about three.

Mitakuye Oyasin

Truth of Sioux beliefs. We are all related to each other. People are related with other people, and with everything on earth, with all life in a very broad sense. Be a part of the Universe: water, air, minerals and earth. It affects us every day. White people think that animals and plants are less valuable than human beings. Indians think that four legged animals, birds and trees are related to (and the same as) people. Everything – mountains, rivers, streams, valleys and land - are full of beauty. Birds, animals and insects have knowledge that is higher than human perception. Chief Standing Bear confirmed those similar thoughts.

The Cherokee Indian woman, Jamie Sams, author of many books, like M*edicine Cards, The Discovery of Power through the Ways of Animals* and *Other Council Fires Were Here Before Ours*, writes that people think that they only can communicate using the same language as a tool with other people. Indians believe in need for silence in life. Such time helps to keep in balance the brain, the body and the spirit. Indians believe that the whole of nature – trees, animals, stones speak the same language. If you come into a forest and you would be silent, you can hear Nature. Nature would use a language that you understand, and teach you how to live, to be honest and to be just.

Ed McGaa , a Sioux Indian and author of books like *Mother Earth Spirituality: Native American Paths to Healing Ourselves and Our World*, writes that people should work and live in harmony. If someone receives a gift from life, a gift should be returned. Everyone should live in inner harmony and know how to be appreciative of others and to Nature, for everything in life comes from Nature.

Cangleska Wakan

It is a concept of the Sacred Medicine Circle of Hope. The Sioux faith comes in a magical circle. Care for inner harmony and keeping in proportion to one's own feelings and emotions is a commandment in Indian beliefs. Courage has to be kept in balance with wisdom, obstinacy with flexibility, reticence with the will to adapt.

American culture shows human life as an even line or ladder, that we are going up. Indians see life as a process that has an end, as a circle. It is their symbol of life.

The Lakota Indian known from the book *Black Elk Speaks* says that Nature and human life are a closed circle – birth, adult life and old years. We should learn how feelings of friendship are coming and drift away, how big an influence on human life has love, how love can change loneliness into creative action. The old feelings and old habits can be taken off like old skin if there is a need for something new and better. Pain and sadness are periods in our life needed for our inside to change and grow.

According to Indians, symbols are letters and numbers. The tree is considered as sacred, a symbol of growth. It is good to pick out a tree, sit under it and meditate. A human being has to be strong, like a tree that has to face drought. When you start to think that way - using symbols from Nature - it makes us closer to Nature and able to better understand it.

The Cherokee Indian, Steven McFadden, in his book *Profiles in Wisdom; Native Elders Speak about the Earth* writes about the four cardinal points. East, or path of the sun, symbolizes spirituality, teaches respect for ones self and others. South or path of peace, symbolizes youth and innocence, teaches the need for play and trust. West or path of self-observance, symbolizes the role of physical strength and spiritual achievement, teaches the need for physical exercise and about the need to rest. North or path of silence, symbolizes rebirth, and teaches listening into one's own mind and soul. We learn about ourselves and world through listening, observation and acceptance.

Interesting are the Kickapoo Indian beliefs. They believe that they live in the last one of four worlds. The first three were damaged through air, decay and fire. The Kickapoo are supported by faith. As long as they keep tradition alive, live with dignity and peace, they would have eternity assured.

Icaga

The Sioux Indians believe in the power of growth. People who do not see themselves as part of Nature and the Universe reside in illusive and psychological isolation. To get rid of that, we have to develop in us compassion for others and for Nature itself. No one can achieve these virtues to a level of excellence, but pursuing itself is a path to freedom and a base for inner peace.

In the old days, Sioux Indians spent four days and nights in seclusion – without water or food. Indians encourage spending some time, at least one day and night in isolation and seclusion, in prayer and communication with the High Power in his biggest sanctuary, i.e. in Nature. Spending even one night on meditation near a mountain or hill, with only water, no food, will give us an awareness that we are a part of Nature. We should not interfere with talk to others or by eating. We should take with us a list of what we would like to do or achieve. When the day comes to an end, we should observe birds and animals, which with us share a place on Earth. Maybe we would see an owl or hear it? Maybe you will have luck and see a deer or rabbit? When we observe Nature, our "I" distracts and we are truly part of Nature. - says Eagle Man, Sioux Indian.

Seclusion gives us time to meditate why we are on the earth. Answers can be different, because every human being has his own purpose to fulfill, a destination determined by God, Nature and Destiny.

Indians also feel weak, sad and lost, like all people. But when they are in need – they turn to their brothers and sisters: ants, hawks, trees, also towards their inner self. And they listen in silence.

The Last of the Mohicans by James Fenimore Cooper is a wonderful American novel whose action takes place in 1757. The book relates the adventures of three Indians, who live along the Hudson River in the northern part of what is now the State of New York, as England and France fight for hegemony over the continent. It is a story about family, friends, love and hate, good and evil, life and death in America before its revolution. Based on the book, a movie was made with the scenario written by Philip Dunne in 1936. Starring in the movie were Madeleine Stowe and Daniel Day-Lewis. I like the opening scene when the camera shows a panorama of the Adirondack Mountains. Uncas, Chingachgook and Hawkeye run in a forest, they pass the trees, ferns and streams. Their faces seemed to be hungry, tense. Hawkeye with open breast runs, there is a shot, an elk falls down. Three of them surround the animal. There is respect in their eyes. Chingachgook prays with sadness "I am sorry that we had to kill you brother. We admire your courage and speed". Uncas shows respect to the animal by touching his right hand to the elk's eyebrow.

A friend of mine was telling me that one day she was taking a bus through Oklahoma. Suddenly in front of the bus a wolf ran across the road. Several passengers asked to stop the bus. Among them were Indians, and they asked to stop. She learned that – according to Navajo belief - the simple way to avoid bad luck, is asking for help from the "spiritual forces". The bus was stopped, and the Indian group went towards nearby bushes. The leader prayed, threw a flower into the bushes, into the wind. The Indians came back to the bus and the journey continued.

Indians believe they should start the day by sharing with loved ones their night's dreams. The elderly in the family can help interpret its meanings. Indians have respect for the elderly and love children. They have a beautiful lullaby for singing children to sleep.

I was once at a lecture where a Mohawk midwife's words were quoted during a presentation.

"Whenever I'm stressed, I close my eyes and conjure up the feeling of peace". I felt when she sang a traditional Native American song for the newborn; the translation was something like:

"May you always remember the warmth and safety you just left."
How nice.

Aleksandra Ziolkowska-Boehm

The White Buffalo

On our way West in the fall of 1999, Norman and I stopped in the village of Janesville in the State of Wisconsin. Norman's friends, whom he met in New York City after joining Arabian American Oil Company, who were now living in Kenosha: Dolores and Fritz Schneider were with us. We went to see the white buffalo.

The mythical white buffalo, a symbol of hope for Native Americans, was born on a farm in Janesville. The birth created an almost immediate sensation. Thousands of tourists from all over the United States were coming to see it. The same as we did. The white buffalo stood in a corral with its mother. They could be seen and photographs could be taken through the fence. I saw evidence of Indians who had made a pilgrimage to see the white buffalo; they left things attached to the fence, different kinds of amulets or ribbons. According to the Indian prophecy, the birth of the white buffalo was the herald of changes going to happen. The prophecy also foretold that the changes would be for the good, along with the rebirth of Indian culture.

If anyone thinks that such an event is not of significance, he should analyze this fact: the chance for birth of a white buffalo is smaller than the chance of winning the lottery, or one in six million. One earlier documented case of the birth of a white buffalo happened in 1959. The buffalo was named Big Medicine and lived thirty-six years.

The buffalo born on the farm of Dave and Valerie Heider was named Miracle. Before it was born, Mr. and Mrs. Heider did not know much about Indians and Indian culture. At 6:00 AM the morning of August 20, 1994, they saw the newborn buffalo – and instead of a red-brown calf, they saw a white calf. "We could not believe our eyes. It happened only in fairy tales, but now we know, that in Indian culture, fairy tales exist too".

They did not have an idea how important in Indian mythology is the appearance of a white buffalo. They called the local paper to tell that they had an interesting story to relate. The paper published it. The Associated Press agency published the story too, and soon the news was all over the country. People started to come to see Miracle. Many people phoned. The Heiders were a modest family and did not like the sudden gain of publicity. First of all, they refused an offer of selling Miracle. The Heiders wanted to keep the calf with the rest of their herd.

It has been reported that when Dave and Valerie Heider see a new group of people approaching their farm, they close themselves inside the house. They understand that Miracle will continue to draw attention and will be a sensation as long as alive, but they do not want to change their

117

life style. They are not interested in financial gain from the attraction that Miracle has aroused. The have requested donations from well-wishers to insure the safety of the white buffalo, such as for having to build strong fences and extra gates.

The news about the birth of the white buffalo reached the Indians from the national media or from a local newspaper. They began visiting the white buffalo in large numbers making pilgrimages to Wisconsin. It is not known if any Indian entrepreneurs have organized pilgrimages for large groups. "The arrival of a white buffalo is nearly as significant as the Second Coming of Christ", Floyd Hand was quoted as saying[64]. Hand, a Sioux medicine man from Pine Ridge in South Dakota was one of the first visitors to come and see Miracle. He prophesized that the buffalo would bring "purity of mind, body and spirit and unity of all nations, black, red, yellow and white".

There are a large number of Indian stories telling about the white buffalo. Each of them is a bit different, and the version depends on what tribe the version originated from.

Many years ago – say Sioux Indians – three hunters met the young white buffalo. In front of their eyes, it changed into a woman, and she said to the hunters, they should return to their village and be ready for her coming. When four days later she came, she carried a small medicine pouch and a peace pipe. With that pipe, she brought the right rules for Sioux to live by, and the good changes happened.

Those legends are interesting because according to them, a white buffalo is going to help many Indian tribes, to end fighting with themselves or arguing with each other. And, from an old story by the Fox Indians in Wisconsin, the shadow of a white buffalo appeared in front of an Indian hunter during his dream. The white buffalo had red eyes and horns, and as the Fox Indians say, it gave them strength and power, so they could successfully fight the Sioux.

Suzan Shown Harjo who runs the office of the "Morning Star" in Washington, whose purpose is to preserve Indian culture, cried when she heard about the birth of the white buffalo. She has roots of Cheyenne and Muskogee Indian. She was quoted: "My heart is full of great joy. According to the legend, the white buffalo is a symbol of awakening, the announcement of something important and extraordinary, also a wealth".

I was talking on this subject with a befriended Indian who asked me not to disclose his name. He did not want to be a prophet, but he wanted to share with me some stories he had heard from his tribal elders.

---

[64] See: Megan Garvey, *American Legend is made flesh*, "Houston Chronicle", Sept. 24-25, 1999.

One Indian story (over a hundred years old) related a prophecy that emerged from the Ghost Dances at the end of the 1880's. The Plains Indians said that when the buffalo would come back and take over the land, white people would start to leave it, and it would be the beginning of the end of the white civilization in Indian Territory.

The buffalo are coming back – my talker said, and there are more and more of them. The white population of the states of Oklahoma, Montana, Nebraska, North and South Dakota is decreasing, that is, becoming smaller and smaller. The transportation by train and buses has disappeared, hospitals and schools are closing, and farms and ranches are disappearing. Only the Indian population is growing – in South Dakota it is has doubled since 1960.

There are others, non-Indians, who see in the coming changes a more profound phenomenon. The press in Texas quoted an urbanist from Rutgers University, who prophesized that the prairie will be occupied by buffalo, like in bygone years. Buffalo are now in Yellowstone National Park; in the last twenty years, their number has doubled. There are also changes to views on the explanation for this phenomenon occurring in undeveloped territories. The return of the buffalo is a triumph of ecology. In 1999[65], Miracle had a fifth anniversary of its birth and its color had changed back into white. According to Indian legends, the white buffalo will change color four times before the prophecy about the Indian culture is fulfilled. Miracle was born white, remained white for three months, then changed color into brown, black and yellow, and then into light brown and finally returned to white.

Not so long after the birth of Miracle, another white buffalo was born in May 1996. It was named Medicine Wheel and was born on a farm in Merrivala on the north side of the Pine Ridge Reservation. Later it changed color into brown. A prophecy of the Lakota Sioux reveals that the birth of two white buffalo calves is for sure an event of major significance. Floyd Hand, the Sioux medicine man from Pine Ridge, South Dakota, was quoted as saying that Indians would rise up from their lethargic demeanor.

Four years later I read in the Indian press information titled: "The sacred buffalo shot on a road in the "Pine Ridge Reservation"[66]. As I learned on March 19, 2000, Medicine Wheel somehow wandered away from its pasture and was shot on a road. Officially, it was said that the buffalo had to be shot as it was a danger to public safety. Policeman Alec Morgan wrote in his report, that when he saw the buffalo on the road,

---

[65] See: According to the "Kenosha News", August 21, 1999.
[66] See: "Indian Country Today", April 5, 2000.

two cars almost had an accident trying to avoid the animal. The buffalo apparently was scared and panicked. Morgan and one of the drivers tried to follow the animal and remove it from the public road. The official report states that after the animal was shot, it was not sent to a slaughterhouse, because it was soon realized that Medicine Wheel was a "sacred buffalo".

"I fed that buffalo since it was weaned…it was almost like a pet and did not have any aggressive feelings", said its owner Poker Joe Merrival. He believed that the animal was stalked and ran away, that somebody scared it, because normally it was very peaceful.

There was no sense in shooting the buffalo because it was on a road. On many areas of the Pine Ridge Reservation, there are cows, horses etc. that wander onto the road, and no-one shoots them", the Indians protested. Merrival said that nothing excused the shooting.

The owners of the white buffalo Miracle that was born in Wisconsin said that many people called asking if Miracle had been shot.

Years ago they filled the space of the prairies. They adapted to the harsh climate. Their number in the past was estimated at thirty to fifty million, some even say sixty million. Amazingly, one generation of human beings, brought to the plains by the arrival of the railroad, managed to hunt and kill all the buffalo. The animals almost disappeared from existence. In the beginning of the twentieth century, the buffalo had disappeared, and according to Bruce E. Johansen, many buffalo were kept away from the white man's gaze.

In the 1990's, the National parks and private landowners started to implement care programs for the buffalo. Their number has grown since then. Now, according to the National Bison Association, in all of North America, their number is estimated at three-hundred and fifty thousand.[67]

During the winter, buffalo living in Yellowstone National Park looking for food leave their territory and approach ranches in Montana. The buffalo herds need a large area, and to keep them under control, some places have to be fenced in. It has to be a high fence, since the buffalo are able to jump over a low one. Warnings are posted for people not to be friendly to the buffalo, since although they appear docile and friendly, they can be unpredictable and dangerous. The press published

---

[67] According to the National Bison Association, two hundred and forty-four thousand buffalo are now in private hands in the United States. For example, Ted Turner has over seven thousand buffalo on his land, in Canada one hundred thousand. In public places in the USA, there are ten thousand, in Canada three thousand. Indians have seven thousand buffalo on their territories.

an article about a buffalo raised on a farm for five years, which suddenly attacked its owner and killed him.

In Montana in 1997, a judge refused to give a sentence forbidding the shooting of buffalo that wander out of Yellowstone National Park. Without special permission, a hundred buffalo a year can be shot. But farmers from Montana complain that buffalo spread the brucellosis, a disease that can be transmitted to cattle. A special commission stated that the threat of transmittal of such a disease is minimal, but if it would happen, the result would be catastrophic.

By the end of the 1990's, over a thousand buffalo had been killed by farmers. Indians protested as well as many white farmers. The protest took place in Montana and lasted twenty days. The protestors journeyed about five hundred miles over twenty days, some on foot and some on horseback, across the prairie and mountains from Rapid City in the Black Hills of South Dakota to Yellowstone in Wyoming. In a ceremonial Sun Dance, a Lakota Sioux activist Gary Silk, removed his shirt, while other protestors thrust sharp sticks through his skin. The sticks were left, a rope was attached to each. Many people, Indians and non-Indians, women and men, wept as they looked on[68].

Animal right's defenders think that the buffalo can be protected from brucellosis by shots, and the buffalo should not be killed. They want compensation, however, for the damages by the animals to fences and homes, but they want the animals to live. Not during the winter but in the spring, the buffalo return to Yellowstone remembering where they once grazed.

On their return, the buffalo herds take on a different look. The farm owners pay close attention to the buffalo that have adapted to life on the prairie, as they are cheaper and easier to raise than cows and bulls. The buffalo meat is lean, and it would serve as a good advertisement to a diet conscious public, being of "low fat" content. But even if all the buffalo alive were to be killed for meat, there would only be enough meat for two days of United States consumption. So, the buffalo have to be raised on special farms that specialize in breeding them.

In the State of Delaware where I live, there is a Greenwood Farm, where owner Bobby Collins raises buffalo. Collins says that young buffalo like to play, but they panic easily and then run fast with a tremendous burst of speed (confirming the opinion of Medicine Wheel's owner as related above). They do not mind bad weather, but they need strong fences for control. They can stand for hours and with big eyes

---

[68] See: Len Iwanski, *Indian ritual revived to stop bison killing*, "Sunday News Journal", February 28, 1999, pg. A12.

observe people. When they are unhappy, they raise their tails. Their meat is leaner than beef, and Indians buy their internal organs. Collins was quoted.[69]

Collins also said: "American Indians visit the farm from time to time to hold religious ceremonies. During the winter, we sell the hides. Then we bleach out the skulls and sell the skulls. And we sell the organs to Native Americans. They do some of their rituals with them".

Our Northern Cheyenne friend from Montana, Rod Trahan, is vehemently against such farms. He stated:

"People should not treat buffalo in such a way! Those animals should not be raised, and killed and sold. Buffalo are sacred animals, and they should be treated in a special way. For many Indians, the buffalo meat is like communion for Christians".

In Lakota Sioux language, buffalo or "Tatanka Oyate" means "who own us", and therefore, that means they are very important to Indians and their lives.

The prophecy says, the press quoting Lakota Sioux Chief Chasing Horse: "If the buffalo disappear, the Lakota will disappear".

Indians have many prophecies connected to the buffalo, and those stories give courage and pray on the imagination for years. The stories repeated during days of poverty and crisis helped them to survive. The Indians were able to recall the times when they lived in harmony in a natural world. The return of the buffalo means restoring of the old legends, old customs and a sense of Indian nationality and unity.

When we lived in Texas, we visited reservations there: the Tiguas in desert territory in far western Texas, the Alabama-Coushata not far from Livingstone and the Kickapoo along the Rio Grande River. I paid special interest to the Kickapoo Indians (knowing little about them), for whom buffalo were not special animals, as I learned. I also learned that the first white people they met were French. They battled for two hundred years with the French and with their enemy's tribal allies: the Iroquois that were coming from the east, and the Sioux coming from the west. Finally, they chose peace with the French and helped them fight the English. After the American Revolution, the Kickapoo fought the white settlers and American army soldiers. In 1819, they signed an agreement and were pushed to live on a reservation in the southeast part of Missouri. They did not like the place, they moved away, and some of them settled in Kansas and Oklahoma. The Kickapoo, as I learned, were different than Comanche, Kiowa or Cheyenne. First of all, they liked deer meat more

---

[69] See: Edward L. Kenney, *Bison are back in a big way*, "The News Journal", April 14, 2005, pg A5.

than buffalo meat. When Texas became independent, some of the Kickapoo moved to Mexico, where in 1852 they received land at the foothills of the Sierra Madre. Mexico gave them the land, but did not give them any official help, and they were left alone. The Kickapoo started to migrate elsewhere.

I remember when Norman and I drove on Route 89 in South Dakota; we passed Custer State Park, and saw a herd of buffalo. They stood motionless and looked very distinguished. We stopped the car and looked, holding our breath. As if we had waited for a long time for this scene, it seemed to us to be a good sign, the buffalo epitomizing the myth and ethos of the West and America. The buffalo herds bring tradition and somehow a longing for the past, for an old America, an America that brought hope and longing to so many people in the world and certainly hope and longing to its Native Americans.

They were called the *Code Talkers*

"Time" from September 2004[70] relayed the information, that in Tama, Arizona, Frank Sanache, eighty-six years old, passed away. Sanache was "the last of eight Meskwaki Indians who used elements of their native language to encrypt walkie-talkie communications between American officers during World War II". "Time" stated that the Meskwaki were among eighteen Native American tribes that served. At the same time, a short biography of the hero was presented. It was stated, that "five months after being sent overseas, Sanache was captured by the Germans in Tunisia and spent twenty-nine months in a Polish labor camp".

The American press had used such a description before, but this was the first time it was used in such a high profile context describing the Indian code talkers, who helped so much to achieve victory in World War II. Norman felt compelled to write a letter to "Time" describing that there were no Polish "labor camps" in Poland but that they were German prison camps. As an example, he cited how wrong and misleading it would be to learn that "Iraqi prisoners were being held in a Cuban prison camp in Guantanamo".

Norman wrote:

"At the time in question, Poland was totally occupied and under the control of the Germans. The Poles did not operate labor camps. Rather, to be historically correct, it should have been stated that the Germans operated such camps that were located in Poland. Your statement further tends to be misleading to readers not familiar with World War II history, and it is also disparaging to Polish Americans and Polish people as well. To give an example of what could be just as misleading and incorrect would be a statement that Iraqi prisoners were being held in a Cuban prison camp".

Norman soon received an answer from "Time", where it was stated:

Dear Mr. Boehm:

We have made note of your concern on reading that the late Frank Sanache, Meskwaki Indian and World War II code talker, was captured by the Germans in Tunisia and spent twenty-nine months in a "Polish labor camp"(Milestones, September 6). And we apologize for the error, on two counts really. When we said "Polish", we were referring to the geographical location, not to who ran the camp (in the rest of the

---

[70] See: "Time", September 6, 2004, pg.18.

sentence, it was clear that Sanache was a prisoner of the Germans). But not only is the ambiguity unacceptable, the location "Polish" was wrong too. The Germans ran the labor camp, at Hammerstein, – and it was also located in Germany, in Pomerania, which was German until 1945, when it became part of Poland.

Thank you for writing. Your letter wasn't selected for publication, but a letter similar in spirit appears in the September 27 column. Thank you for taking the time to let us hear from you, and best wishes.

Sincerely,
Gloria Hammond

"The other letter" from "Time" was to the Polish Ambassador in Washington, DC who reacted to the same news release. I noticed that the word "Nazi" was used three times and "German" once.

Przemyslaw Grudzinski, Ambassador of the Republic of Poland to the United States wrote to "Time" from Washington DC:

Prisoners of the Nazis
I was stunned to see the term "Polish labor camp" in the Milestone article on the death of Navajo code talker Frank Sanache (Sept. 6). The Nazis organized and ran the German concentration, labor and POW camps of World War II (including the one in what is now Poland where Sanache was imprisoned). We need to preserve the truth about atrocities committed by the Nazis instead of creating harmful stereotypes that involved Poland.

The Meskwaki are one of eighteen Indian tribes who participated actively in World War II, and as mentioned above, Frank Sanache was one of the legendary code talkers. The Meskwaki are not as well known as Navaho or Comanche, and their tribe is quite small. Frank Sanache was one of eight Meskwaki Indians taught to use their language as a code during World War II.

When we were in Montana, Curtis Yarlott, a Crow Indian and director of the Saint Labre Indian school, quoted the sentence of Chief Plenty Coups – Crow Indian tribe: "Whenever war comes between the country and another, you people will find my people pointing their guns with yours"[71].

Curtis Yarlott himself wrote in "The Morning Star"[72] that despite the history of broken treaties, American Indians achieved the highest

---

[71] See: "The Morning Star", Winter 2002, Volume 40, Nr. 1.
[72] See: Op. cit.

percentage – as an ethnic group – as volunteers into the American military forces. As volunteers, they fought in World War I and World War II. They fought for the Constitution and the rights it affords all Americans even though they did not even have the right to vote until 1924[73].

They were deprived, as well, of many other basic rights enjoyed by non-Indian Americans by virtue of their mistreatment by the Federal Government over decades. (The longest opposition to the Indians' right to vote occurred in the states of Arizona and New Mexico, where the right was granted in 1946. What a pity and so sad that such a right was not granted until after the Indians returned from the latter war where their involvement and achievements portray a beautiful chapter of Indian history. In World War I, at least six Indian tribes served in the American military forces, even though – as quoted above - they did not yet enjoy the right to vote until 1924 (except those from Arizona and New Mexico).

The United States did not immediately react to the start of World War II, when on September 1, 1939 the German Army crossed the border into Poland. The United States did not even react when Hitler took over France in May 1940. Until the Battle of England, when it became clear that the war was expanding, most Americans felt far removed from the war and that it was very distant from their everyday lives. Even more so, this feeling prevailed among the Indians living on the remote reservations or in small villages.

Everything changed, when on December 7, 1941, the Japanese bombed the military base in Pearl Harbor on Hawaii. The following day, the United States and Great Britain declared war on Japan, and on December 11, Germany declared war on the United States. Americans came into the war with eventually fifteen million in military forces and a huge financial and production potential. These determined the eventual victory.

Through the spring of 1941, thousands of American Indians enlisted as volunteers into the military. There were the Navajo, Hopi, Comanche, Choctaw, Cheyenne, Chippewa/Oneida, Menominee, Sac & Fox, Sioux, Crow, Mississauga and Creek. By the end of 1941, over two hundred and fifty thousand Indians wanted to go into the military, but not all of them were accepted. By the end of the war, about forty-four thousand Indians served in the various American military forces (some historians, like

---

[73] According to Bruce E. Johansen: "Many Indians received the right to vote after 1888 as their lands were allotted. Voting was a badge of assimilation, and many Indians refuse it to this day. Many Iroquis whom I know do not vote in U.S. elections". See: Letter, February 11, 2008.

Aleksandra Ziolkowska-Boehm

Kenneth William Townsend, stated the number as twenty-five thousand
with 40 thousand in Civil Defense forces).

Many Indians saw military service as a chance to leave their
depressed environment and to arouse their warrior soul (and the love of
battle). It was a case of honor, patriotism, and very often a chance for a
better payroll, because on the reservations, they lived as very poor
people. For some, it was also a step towards the assimilation with the rest
of Americans.

It is a fact, as quoted above by Yarlott – that looking at the ethnic
groups on a percentage wise basis, the Indians achieved the highest
percentage of volunteers. One of the first volunteers were Comanche,
and they were chosen first for a special group in the American Army.

During both World War I and II, hundreds of American Indians
served in the United State Army and Marines using their language to
send and to receive coded reports. Likewise, Indians served in the Navy
and Air Force as well.

Nothing was heard about the Indian code talkers for a long time
after World War II. Many years passed since the end of World War II
before Americans learned that Indians helped them to win the war. The
first time the Indian language was used as code occurred during World
War I, when an Army officer overheard a conversation between two
soldiers from the Choctaw tribe. Immediately he realized that the
language could be used as a code. Choctaw Indians were not widely
known for their involvement in the World War I victory, and historically,
they should be known as those who started to employ coded information
using their own language. It was a wonderful idea, since only Indians
living in the United States used the language. Other Indian code talkers
came from Navaho, Choctaw, Comanche, Creek, Ojibwa, Menomonee
and Hopi tribes. Hitler and his strategists knew that during World War I,
the Indian language was used, and before he embarked on World War II
preparations, he sent twenty German anthropologists to the United States
to learn the Indian languages. It was an impossible task, because among
other things, there were no dictionaries, the Indian language was not a
written language and the seclusion and remoteness of the Indian tribes
precluded sufficient contact with them.

The history of the Indian talkers is one of the most heroic stories
from World War II. When it was finally known, the press quoted the real
people and their recollections.

William Karty, thirty-year-old Comanche worked as director of the
Fort Cobb Indian Conservation Corps when the war started in Europe.
When the United States entered the fray, he was one of the first
volunteers of Comanche from the Lawton, Oklahoma area.

128

Karty decided to use it, knowing that the Comanche language can be used as a code. His idea was welcomed in the Army with enthusiasm. Twenty Comanche were chosen to be a part of the United States Army Signal Corps. Seventeen of them took part in the war. One of these was Charles Chibitty.

Chibitty was born near Medicine Park in Oklahoma. As a boy in Indian grammar school, he remembers being disciplined for using his language by flogging or pushed to clean the floors. In 1940, he started high school in the Haskell Indian School in Lawrence, Kansas. When he learned about the recruiting of Comanche, he did not hesitate and volunteered for the Army. He later recollected that his mother wanted him to finish high school, not to go to the Army and not to the war.

Twenty young Comanche, who in 1941 were qualified for admission to the Fourth Infantry Division in Fort Benning, Georgia, learned very soon, that their task would be using their language as a code. The years when people laughed at them for using their language were gone, now they even tried to learn their language. The Comanche language was very respected now. At the time, Lieutenant Hugh Foster (he retired as a general and resided in Virginia) was responsible for the Indian group, and after the war recalled that his soldiers, the Comanche, were laughing listening to his tries to use their language. So the situation turned around. The Comanche language, earlier oppressed, now helped the Allies to win the war.

Some English names were a problem for the Comanche, since they did not have them in their language. Chibitty and other members of the Fourth Signal Company decided to improvise. For example, *tugawee,* means gun, but can also be a gun or pistol of a different type, so the solution was to put numbers after "tugawee" to designate the caliber of the gun. The sound "rat-a-tat-tat" of a machine gun reminded one of the Comanche soldiers of the sound of a sewing machine. So they combined the Comanche words for gun and sewing machine to signify a machine gun.

The hard shell silhouette of the German tiger tank reminded them of turtles, so turtle in Comanche meant tank. The heavy bombers dropping bombs reminded them of a fish's belly being cut open and the eggs falling out, so bomber planes were called "pregnant airplanes". In Comanche language, the words *posah-tai-vo* meant Hitler, but translated exactly, it meant "crazy white man".[74]

---

[74] See: Robert Daily: *The Code Talkers*, A First Book Franklin Watts, New York/Chicago/London/Toronto/Sydney,1995. Page 50-52.
"Tanks were called 'turtles' (*wah-cah-tay*), because both have hard shells.

As Michael Michalak, the publisher from South Dakota who has studied the subject concluded[75], the Native American languages used by the many tribes have not been sufficiently studied by the uninitiated and thus these languages become an ideal medium for a coded message. Some writers have, however, fallen into the trap of romanticizing the Native American along with his language - making him into a "Noble Savage" rather than a human being who has his own unique experiences and customs.

The code talkers took part in many important war events. They were one of the first groups of soldiers to liberate Paris, and they took part in attacking Saint-Lo in July 1944. In September, they crossed the Siegfried line, and in November and December 1944, they took part in the battle of Hurtgen Forest. Many times, they were in the front, equipped only with helmet, radio and a .45 caliber pistol. The platoon of Chibitty landed on Utah beach in Normandy on D-Day. His platoon attacked the Germans, who were placed strategically on the cliffs overlooking the sea. "When I was asked later, what I was afraid of the most, I answered I was the most scared of drowning because we landed in deeper water than we expected."- His words were quoted in the press. Asked if he was afraid, Chibitty answered: "If anyone says that he was not afraid, he was either crazy or he lied".

The Comanches have only one word for gun. A machine gun, for example, was called a 'sewing machine gun', because both make a rat-a-tat sounds. They also have just one word for airplane, so they distinguished a bomber by calling it a 'pregnant airplane'!"
Kenneth William Townsend: *World War II and the American Indian*, University of New Mexico Press, Albuquerque 2000. Page 146-147
"Symbolic words and expressions represented military weapons and orders: 'bird' *(tsidi)* for airplane; 'hummingbird' for fighter plane; 'bird *shooter' (tsidi-be-wol-doni)* for anti-aircraft gun; 'tortoise-shooter' *(chayta-gahibe-wol-doni)* for anti-tank gun; 'cliff dwelling' *(annasozi)* for fortification, and 'horsemen' *(linyeanaldaihi)* for cavalry. A 'chicken hawk', or *gini*, referred to a dive bomber; 'whale' stood for battleship; a destroyer was termed 'shark'; 'Clan' *(din-heh-ih)* stood for Corps; and 'Frog' *(chal)* represented the word 'amphibious'.
Joe Haines, *Code Talker*, "Oklahoma Today", May-June 2000, page 57-59
(...) The hard shell of the German tiger tank reminded them of turtles; thus the Comanches word for turtle meant tanks. The heavy bombers dropping bombs resembled a fish's belly being cut open and the eggs falling out, so bombers came to be known as pregnant airplanes.
[75] See: http://www.defenselink.mil/specials/nativeamerican01/dictionary.html; http://www.snowwowl.com/histcodetalkers.html;

In 1945, when the war was over, Chibitty resided in Tulsa, Oklahoma, and he lived a quiet life. Forty years later, he was remembered and was granted government awards for his service. In 1989, the French consul in Oklahoma and Texas honored three code talkers who were still living. They were: Charles Chibitty, Roderick Red Elk and Forrest Kassanavoid. The chiefs of the Choctaw and Comanche tribes received the Chevalier de L'Ordre National du Merit in honor of the code talkers who took part in two world wars. In November 1999, the American Army bestowed a special award on Charles Chibitty, then the last living code talker of the Comanche tribe. During the ceremony in the Hall of Heroes, that took place in the Pentagon, Chibitty received the Knowlton Award for his service in World War II having accomplished the most unique and difficult tasks.

Chibitty said: "Now we could not repeat it. Everything is taken away by electronics and video". He also regretted that the other Comanche code talkers already passed away were not able to participate in the ceremony.

Charles Chibitty, the last *Comanche code talker died in* 2005 at eighty-three years of age.

The Comanche code talkers played an important role in the winning of World War II, but the most known were the Navajo Indians.

During the time the small group of Comanche, as code talkers took part in battles in Europe, the Navajo Indians were in battle in the Pacific. All together on the different fronts, around three thousand six hundred Navajo soldiers were in the war. Around three hundred and seventy-five to four hundred and twenty of them were code talkers.

The idea to use Navaho Indians belongs to one person named Philip Johnston, later the journalist, photographer, and author of two books. He was the son of Protestant missionaries and was raised on the Navajo Indian reservation, where he learned their language and culture. He was the only known non-Indian military who knew their language and English. When he was nine years old, he went to Washington to serve as a translator for President Theodore Roosevelt who met with the Navajo Indian chiefs. During the First World War, Johnston left the reservation and enlisted in the American Army and fought in France.

It was Philip Johnston's idea to use – as it was during World War I – the Navajo language as a code during World War II. In the beginning of 1942, he met with General Clayton B. Vogel and gave him the idea for the code. His project was welcomed with enthusiasm, and General Vogel asked him to recruit over two hundred Navajo Indians. Very soon the Army sent encouragement to the Navajos to join up. After some initial hesitation, encouraged by their Chief Chee Dodge, the Navajos began to enlist in large numbers.

In May 1942, a gathering of twenty-nine Navajo Indian recruits began the creation of the dictionary-code. The dictionary included many words that were not normally used by the Navajo. The words and code had to be memorized. The Navajo language was not simple; many words had more than one meaning. The recruits had to create the meaning for four hundred and fifty terms broadly used by the military that had not existed in the Navajo language. For example, the word *besh-lo* (iron fish) meant s*ubmarine, dah-he-tih-hi* (hummingbird) meant *fighter plane*, a *debeh-li-zine* (black street) meant *squad*.

Atsá – in Navajo means eagle. *Paaki* – in the language of the Hopi means houses on water. For Navajo and Hopi soldiers those words meant *transport plane and ships*. Commanding general: bih-keh-he, or "war chief"; dive bomber: gini, or "chicken hawk"; battleship: lo-tso, or "whale"; aircraft carrier: tsidi-moffa-ye-hi, or "bird carrier"; armor: besh-ye-ha-da-di-the, or "ïron protector"; communication: ha-neh-al-enji, or "making talk"; flamethrower: co-ah-ghil-tlid, or "that is all".

The secret Navajo Indian code was completed in September 1942. After schooling that required learning communications by radio, the Navajo were sent to the Pacific side of the war. They served in six divisions. All together, over three hundred and eighty Navajo Marines were located in the Pacific, where they were responsible to send and receive very secret information about the movements of the military and plans for the battles.

In the years of 1942–1945, the Navajo Indian code talkers took part in the action of all the important battles in the Pacific: Guadalcanal, Tarawa, Peleliu, Iwo Jima.

A small group of Hopi Indians were included in an artillery battalion. They created the code that was used in battles in the Philippines. As later said by the chief of the Japanese secret service, Generał Seizo Arisue, they were unable to decode the code used by the Marines, even though during World War II, they systematically were able to break the other American codes. Today it is common knowledge that thanks to the Indian code talkers, the battles in the Pacific were turned into Allies' victories.

An interesting story deals with an Indian Navajo man named Joe Kieyoomia, whom the Japanese captured in the fall of 1942 in the Philippines. In the beginning, they considered him as Japanese – American, therefore a traitor. He was tortured for months. When they finally realized he was a Navajo Indian, they tortured him even more to learn about the code. But Joe Kieyoomia was not a code talker and had no knowledge about the code. Tortures were very sophisticated. For example, they kept him naked standing for hours on ice, so his feet froze to the ice. When a guard pushed him, the frozen skin of the soles of his feet adhered to the ice and was torn off. Years later, he said he saw American soldiers who had to dig their own graves under the Japanese command. He also said that even had he had known the code, he would never have revealed such information to the Japanese.

Kieyoomia was released after three and a half years of imprisonment. He returned to the place he was born, Albuquerque in New Mexico. He died there in 1997.

Another Navajo Indian, Teddy Draper Sr., was raised in Canyon del Muerto, Arizona. He helped his family to graze cattle, sheep and raise turkeys. When he was fourteen, he entered the reservation school, but did not know the English language. At the school run by American officials, he was disciplined for talking in his own language on the campus. He had to kneel in a corner of the classroom. He revolted against it, and many times tried to escape. The situation changed when as a nineteen year old, thanks to his knowledge of his Native language, Teddy Draper Sr. ended up in an elite group of about four hundred code talkers recruited from the Navajo. Draper joined the Marines in San Diego. Years later, he recollected eating in the military cafeteria where he saw food he never tasted before. For example, never before had he eaten butter.

In February 1945, Draper was transported to Iwo Jima. There he had a guard assigned to him, a Marine soldier, Henry Hisey. When Hisey at the age of eighty years was shown on TV, he was asked if it was true, that if Draper were about to be captured, Hisey had the orders to shoot him (so Draper would not release the code). Kisey answered he did not remember. "Without the Indians, we would not win Iwo Jima". Such an opinion was almost unanimous. The island of Iwo Jima located near Japan was a very important strategic point and was heavily fortified. The battles for it stretched to thirty-six days in February and March 1945. The American victory, as is stated – was won thanks to the Indian code talkers. Twenty two thousand Japanese and six thousand eight hundred and twenty-one Americans died in the battle for Iwo Jima,. The Americans took control over the island, and at the same time they took control over the airfields. Well known is the famous picture of Americans raising the flag on top of Mount Suribachi. It was February 23, 1945. The America photographer, Joe Rosenthal, recipient of a Pulitzer Prize, took the picture. In 2006, the movie called *Flags of Our Fathers*, directed by Clint Eastwood (production of Steven Spielberg) was released. The movie tells a story of the destiny of those who raised the flag on Iwo Jima.

From the six soldiers in the photo, three did not survive the war: Franklin Sousley from Kentucky, Harlon Block from Texas, and Michael Strank from Pennsylvania. Franklin lost his life being only nineteen years old. Three of the soldiers survived: John Bradley, Rene Gagnon and Ira Hayes, a Pima Indian from Arizona.

Just after the war, Ira Hayes and the others were invited to the White House. President Truman called them the heroes. "How can I feel the hero, when from my forty-five man platoon, only five soldiers survived?" – said Ira Hayes. Indian Ira Hayes died at the age of thirty-two, an alcoholic.

Many years later, Johnny Cash, in his beautiful collection "Bitter Tears", sang "The Ballad of Ira Hayes".

After the war, the Indians returned to their reservations and returned to their poverty, but what the war did – their lives started to change. Children were eager to go to schools. Two of the former code talkers became chiefs. In 1970, Peter MacDonald and Wilson Skeet were part of the elders group among the Navajo Indians.

All of the code talkers had to swear to keep their secret. They returned home without fanfare. The code was released in 1968, but the involvement and the service of Indians – also from the Navajo tribe – was not made public for many decades.

In 1971, the Indians organized themselves into a reunion of code talkers, and it took place in Window Rock in Arizona. Also in 1971, President Richard Nixon officially acknowledged their patriotism and courage. But finally, President Ronald Reagan in 1981 revealed to his fellow Americans, the special missions and tasks of the Indian code talkers during World War II and their great heroic involvement in the victory. The day of August 14 was created as the national day of code talkers.

On October 17, 1992 at the Pentagon, the code talkers were recognized. Thirty-five Indians attended the ceremony. All of the veterans of the United States Marine Corps were invited for opening of the exhibition dedicated to the Navajo code talkers. The exhibition provides photographs, the actual equipment used and the original code, saying how some of the words were used. The Navajo Indians and their families came from the reservations in Arizona, New Mexico and Utah. Senator John McCain from Arizona and Navajo Indian Chief Peterson Zah gave the speeches.

More than sixty years have passed since World War II. In December 2000, President George W. Bush gave the highest award of the Congressional Medal of Honor to twenty-nine Navajo Indians – former code talkers. Only four came to Washington. The others were too ill for travel or were no longer living. In some cases, their families attended representing those unable to travel or those deceased. From the original twenty-nine, the four attending the ceremony were Allen Dale June from West Valley City in the State of Utah. He was only seventeen years of age when he joined the Marines. He lied that he was older.

Among those who came were eighty year old John Brown and Merril Sandoval from Tuba City in Arizona and eighty year old Chester Nez from Albuquerque, New Mexico. Ness said how much he regretted that the others were not alive to come. He remembered that in the 1920's, by his schoolteacher, he had been instructed: "Do not speak in Navajo language". He recalled that for using his language, they washed his mouth with soup.

The American press wrote about the passing away of the code talkers.

Carl Gorman from Chinle in Arizona, who was one of the first twenty-nine recruited, died in January 1998. When recruited and questioned, as many others did, he lied and claimed he was older. In 1998, seventy-nine year old Narciso "Ciso" Platero Abeyeta passed away. He was a code talker, artist, painter, his paintings are displayed in the National Gallery of Art in Washington DC, in museums in New York, Tulsa, Oklahoma, and in the Museum of New Mexico in Santa Fe. As a known painter, he specialized in showing the mythology of the Navajo. In 2004, Samuel Billison from Window Rock in Arizona passed away. He joined the Marines in 1943, just after finishing high school. After the war, he studied law and earned a doctorate from the University of Mexico in Albuquerque. He became a teacher, and in 1971, he created the Navajo Code Talkers Association.

Eighty-seven years old Ernest Childers died March 17, 2005 in Tulsa, Oklahoma. He was born in Broken Arrow, Oklahoma and raised on the farm, which was originally given to his father as an *allotment*. After his father passed away, Ernest took upon himself the duty of being the family provider by taking care of the rest of the family. He recalled, sometimes it was a better time, sometimes it was worse.

In the National Museum of the American Indian (Smithsonian Institution) /NMAI/ in Washington DC, there is a regular exhibition *American Indian Code Talkers*, that shows the extraordinary history of American Indians during World War II. According to the NMAI, the code could only be broken if the code talker and cryptologist cooperated together. It never happened. The same source states, that the early English used the language of the people from Wales as a code.

Aleksandra Ziolkowska-Boehm

The NMAI exhibition also presents the anthem of the Marines in Navajo language.

Navajo Jimmy King translated it.

(the last verse is sung like a prayer)
We are known to be tireless
The United States Marines
May we live in peace hereafter
We have conquered all our foes,
No force in the world we cannot conquer,
We know of no fear
If the Army and the Navy
Ever look on Heaven's scenes,
United States Marines will be there
Living in peace.

Do ni-din-da-hi ol-yeh
Washindon be Akalh-bi Khos
Hozo-go nay-yeltay to
A-na-oh bi-keh de-dlihn
Ni-hi-keh di-dlini ta-etin
Yeh-wol-ye hi-he a-din
Sila-go-tsoi do chah-lakai
Ya-ansh-go das dez e e
Washindon be Akalh-bi Kosi la
Hozo-g-kay-ha-tehn[76]

In June 2002, the movie industry presented the film *Windtalkers*. It was an occasion to relate again a story about the code talkers. Producer John Woo said that the movie keeps alive the extraordinary people and their mission. Before the movie began production, he said that Indians were going to by played by Indian actors. The time when Rock Hudson played an Indian chief in *Winchester 73* or Tony Curtis in *The Outsiders* was gone. In "Windtalkers", the leading role was played by the actor known from other Indian movies, Adam Beach, a Saulteaux Ojibwa Indian from the province of Manitoba in Canada. Also another actor, Navajo Indian Roger Willie, from New Mexico participated, and it was his first movie.

The movie created a big wave of sympathy and support. Some controversies occurred too. The well-known actor Nicolas Cage played a

---

[76] http://www.americanindians.com/CodeTalkers.htm

Marine sergeant who was chosen to help a Navajo Indian. According to the movie, the Marines were ordered and trained to kill the Indian, if the code talker faced imminent capture by the Japanese. It was feared that during Japanese torture, the code talker might reveal his code. Mentioned earlier (above), Teddy Draper Sr. was sure about it. "Taking care of us Marines was by saying to us, that if we were captured, we should kill ourselves".

Some veterans among the Navajo Indians were opposed to such an opinion. They said the non-commissioned officer assigned to the code talker was only to help, for example, to carry the radio.

About the same time, the press revealed that Clarence L. Tinker from the Osage tribe, a general in the American Air Force was lost in May 1942 (in the Battle of Midway). He was the first Indian to achieve the rank of general, and later was the first American general to die in World War II. His body was never found.

Pascal Cleatur Poolaw, Kiowa, was the most awarded soldier in the American Army. He received forty-two awards and medals. He served in the Army during World War II, later he served in the Korean War, and he fought in Vietnam, where he died November 7, 1967.

Ernest Childers, Creek, was the first Indian in the twentieth century to receive the highest American award: the Congressional Medal of Honor. For his involvement in World War II, he received five other medals. He retired as a lieutenant colonel in 1965.

The role of the American Indians during the wars is highlighted in the press rather frequently.

During Norman's and my stay in Texas, I read an interesting story. The daily "Houston Chronicle"[77] published an article about the Delaware and Cherokee Indian Lawrence Sampson. In 1988, he enlisted in the Army, eventually serving with the 82nd Airborne Division. He was sent to the Army base in Fort Bragg, North Carolina. He took part in arresting the leader of Panama, Manuel Noriega. He was wounded in a leg, and he witnessed the death of his colleague. He was awarded military medals for his action in Panama and in the Middle East operations Desert Shield and Desert Storm.

When he returned home, he did not want to have anything further to do with the military. He started to visit local schools - not as an American Army veteran - but as a Delaware and Cherokee Indian. He felt more Indian than a former soldier of the American Army.

---

[77] See: Marty Racine, *Not enough warriors*, "Houston Chronicle", April 28 1998.

When he came to the grammar school in Katy near Houston, Texas, he brought with him several boxes. The school administrator looked at their contents and joked that she did not want to have an "Indian on the war path" in her school. Sampson felt offended; he did not like such a remark.

In the boxes there were different things including the native attire that belonged to his father. He showed it to the school children. He told the children:

"It is not a costume like you wear on Halloween. We Indians do not pretend that we are somebody else".

"I have a question for you – he continued his dialogue. Tell me, what are the Indians like?"

Many children raised their hands.

"They wear special colorful costumes. They do not have real houses and they play with sticks", the children answered.

"How many Indian tribes existed before Christopher Columbus arrived?" – Simpson continued the questions.

"Two, maybe ten", was the answer.

"No," said Sampson. "it was six hundred. We have to remember that the Iroquois confederacy was a model for the American Constitution".

Sovereignty and its Consequences. Nation or Tribe?

An over fifty years old Chippewa Indian was stopped several times for speeding on the White Earth Indian Reservation in the state of Minnesota. He was always fined (and paid the ticket), and sometimes – because he was arguing and protested - was even taken to jail. The Indian insisted that the policemen who stopped him were not Indians, and they didn't have the right to stop him. He took his case to court, and the Minnesota Court agreed with him. The court ruled that the State troopers and police from the sheriff's office do not have the right to issue tickets on the Chippewa Indians' Reservation. Issuance of tickets can only be done by the Indian police because they have a very special status - they are officers of a "sovereign nation".

In 1787, an early political declaration (Northwest Ordinance) of the United States of America stated that Indians, the first indigenous people of the territory, were to have their own sovereign government and ownership of their land.

In the beginning of the nineteenth century, The Supreme Court under the leadership of John Marshall, defined the rights of the Indians and their legal relationship with the governments of the states and with the federal government.

These rights are known as the "Marshall Trilogy". The Supreme Court ruled Indians as having a fully recognized status of dependent separate government (sovereignty), and as being connected with a higher legal "country" that provides for protection of their freedom. "Sovereignty" is a legal status, but its meaning is "broad" and has had numerous interpretations. Therefore, many controversies, contradictions, and misunderstandings have resulted in legal battles because of different Indian rights or privileges.

The majority of five hundred and fifty-four tribes have their own rights, own constitutions and own police. The only departure from the Indian "sovereignty" occurs when an assault with weapons, murder or rape takes place on the territory of the reservation. Then the crime comes under the jurisdiction of the federal government.

Especially controversial are the rights for fishing, rights to hunt and rights concerning gambling legality.

In the State of Washington, two Tlingit Indian teenagers that were living in a small village assaulted with a baseball bat and robbed a pizza deliveryman working in the nearby town of Everett. As a result of the assault, the pizza man lost most of his hearing. The incident happened when both teenagers were 16 years old, but because the case was very brutal, they were treated as adults by the court for an assault in the first degree. The boys admitted the crime, and according to the State law, they were supposed to get three to five years in prison.

A very respected and over seventy years old tribal "elder", the grandfather of one of the teenagers, was very disturbed and in pain because of the deed of his grandson. He was also concerned, that being imprisoned the young man would be exposed to the brutal life of jail, homosexuals and even possibly catching Aids. He was looking for help and finally turned to another "elder" Rudy James, a tribal judge with considerable experience fighting for rights on the behalf of the Indians.

It was Rudy James who convinced the court in Washington that punishment for the crime should be based upon the right of banishment, that is, exile as a court order and sentence. He stated that the custom of the Tlingit tribes take into consideration rehabilitation, and not punishment, as a law of the white man.

"Can you take it into consideration?" James turned the question to the court.

It was the first such request in front of the State court. The judge agreed. He released the young men on bail and postponed the sentence for eighteen months.

"It is strange", protested prosecutor Jim Townsend whom the press quoted. "I understand that Indians were treated for years in an unfavorable manner. But now they should be under the same legal law as the rest of Americans".

In answering, the tribal judge told Townsend, "When Christopher Columbus came to America, he didn't find any prisons".

The judge stopped his own sentence and gave the tribal elders the chance to handle the rehabilitation of the Indian teenagers.

The Indians' rehabilitation judgment began with the sound of the sacred drum that continued for the whole afternoon. The Indians from the Tlingit tribe were beating the drum to scare the bad demons from the building where the judgment discussion was to take place. The thirteen tribal judges representing the Tlingit tribe, after feasting and certain rituals, were ready to hear the case of the two young men who were facing banishment into the forest for their brutal attack on the pizza deliveryman. For the Tinglit tribe, the act puts the blame and shame on the whole tribe. Now it was time to discuss the events. But it was not so simple.

They decided that according to the old law of the Tlingit tribe in Everett in the State of Washington, the teenagers were to be sentenced to banishment, meaning exile. During the sentence, the boys who were then seventeen years of age were supposed to live on the isolated islands of Alexandra Archipelago, each of them alone on a separate island, there to manage themselves for eighteen months. They would be allowed to take some food and basic tools with them needed for surviving. This – according to the elderly – should teach them responsibility, and it was better than putting them into jail, where the young men would be facing the brutal life and rules of imprisonment.

After the eighteen months, the young men were supposed to be brought before the judge and the sentence would be over.

For the victim of the attack, the pizza deliveryman, the Indians promised to give some money, reimburse his costs for medications and doctors, and to build him a small house.

The elders also promised to look in on them, from time to time to see how the young men were living, but not give them any help. The islands that they would live on were full of fish, the basic Tlingit Indian food.

What has happened, however, was an Indian society divided over the tribal sentence. The people could not agree that the banishment should occur. Many Indians were upset that the young men didn't face a regular sentence. They were upset with the whole case, including the sentence, considering it shameful for the Indians. Particularly shameful for them was the publicity given the case all over the country.

The judge, Rudy James, was nervous and didn't like the criticism. He even said that it was a small town jealousy. He was a leader, and he knew the tradition and the old rules. The case shows our Indian "sovereignty", he insisted.

After the boys were sent to the Alaskan islands, it was soon disclosed that their families were visiting them and providing them with food. One boy was even taken home for a dentist visit and to obtain his driving license. When he learned he didn't pass the driving exam, he showed a characteristically bad mood.

When the federal judge learned about this incident, he asked the Indian judge to come and explain what had happened. The tribal judge agreed that the banishment was broken and moved the young men to different surroundings. Subsequently, because he needed appendix surgery, the parents of the other boy removed him from the new location. Then, the first boy (of the dental/driving test incident) suffered an infected foot and with high fever was taken home by his parents. The federal court finally sent both young men to jail.

In 1934, the Senate accepted the Indian Reorganization Act stressing the definition of Indian Sovereignty as a structure of the federal government.

The rights of tribes for local legal constitutions were accepted. One hundred and sixty tribes created their own constitutions. Over the last decade and longer, there have been a series of legislation (throughout the country) stressing that local tribal governments have sovereignty over their own territory and tribal members. As an example of contention, when a tribe invokes taxes on the white settlers (non-Indians) living on its reservation, it is not known whether such a tax is legal or not.

The coffee shop run by Micky Hutchinson was in some way the symbol of the old look of the terrain. I have learned about that story from the author of the book "Killing the White Man's Indian", by Fergus M. Bordewich.[78]

Opening her coffee shop in the winter of 1991, Micky Hutchinson didn't anticipate any problems. The situation looked as straight as the streets in the village of Isabel, South Dakota that the government designed in 1910.

The streets were designed on empty terrain, where some time earlier, as it was said, was the Cheyenne River Reservation where the Sioux Indians were living. Now Isabel is a small town located to the west from the capitol Pierre.

Micky was sure that her coffee place had nothing to do with the nearby reservation, so when the local Indians' government of the Sioux tribe asked her to pay two hundred and fifty dollars for the license to sell alcohol, she ignored them.

"They don't have the right to charge me, I am not Indian and Isabel is not an Indian village", she stated.

Her neighbors' thinking was the same. They said, "These are our farms and that land was paid for to the Indians. If we don't have any right to decide what is going on within the reservation, why do the Indians want to tax us? It would be "taxation without representation".

As a result of the dispute – with loud siren signals - the tribal police came to the border of the town. It was so noisy and with as much unrest as if a tornado had come. Thirty-eight police cars belonging to the Sioux surrounded the building housing the coffee shop of Micky Hutchinson.

The chief police Marvin LeCompte announced that she was in conflict with the tribal law. And then he confiscated her alcohol license, saying that he had to also deal with the "contraband" alcohol and left to the nearby town of Eagle Butte, where the tribal buildings were located.

A young Sioux chief from the Cheyenne River Reservation, Gregg L. Bourland, is considered as one of the most efficient leaders in the whole region. He has a university diploma from the Black Hills State

---

[78] See: Fergus M. Bordewich, *Revolution in Indian Country*, "American Heritage", July-August 1996.

University in Spearfish. During the years that passed after the incident with Micky Hutchinson, he has described the rights of Indians, saying:

"The white people shouldn't talk about "taxation without representation". We are not one of the fifty States, we are a separate nation and the only way to be represented, is to be a member of the tribe. The white people cannot achieve it, because they are not Indians. But because they live on the land that is part of the reservation, they have to follow and respect the tribe's rules. Over a hundred years have passed during which the Indians did not have their own government, but now it is over".

The Indian and local white press quoted Bourland's words, and added what had happened in Isabel was more than local small town politics.

The taxes, the convoy of police, and the court case symbolize the new face of the American West.

Many of the fifty American States are displeased with the form of consequences of Indian tribal sovereignty. These states believe legal definitions are not clear enough and many times work against the interest of all the states' citizens (majority).

For example, in the State of Utah, the governor is unable to do anything to make Indians change their decisions to let nuclear radioactive waste be disposed of by storage under the terrain of the reservation. It is because the tribe, not the governor, has the right to decide what to do on its reservation.

For the disposal of nuclear waste under their reservation, the Tonkawa Indians living on the border of Kansas and Oklahoma say, that it will create five hundred and thirty work employment opportunities and twenty-five million dollars in yearly payments to their tribe.

It was announced that the Skull Valley Reservation in the State of Utah is going to be paid over three million dollars for "keeping for a while" nuclear waste, that is, exactly forty-four thousand tons of highly radioactive product.[79] The Goshute Tribe on the Skull Valley Reservation is going to be paid over a hundred million dollars over a forty-year period. For such money, they can build a health clinic, police stations and open businesses. As an independent tribe, they do not have to listen to the government critics from within Utah.

The Indian tribes in New Mexico see the storage of nuclear waste primarily as an opportunity. The Tonkawa tribe confirms they are being pushed to take nuclear waste and were also promised an extra two hundred thousand dollars – federal money – for the opportunity to study

---

[79] See: "Time", April 2006.

what the earth's reaction will be from the storage of the nuclear waste. The whole project of conducting the study will supposedly last twenty to forty years, and the Indians are hopeful it will offer opportunities for work.

Also, the Eastern Shawnee tribe judged the study project as an opportunity and would like to take part in it.

The two hundred Campo Indians of Mission, California not far from San Diego saw an opportunity for work and for income to the tribal government, and agreed to the building of a sewage treatment plant on their territory. For such a transaction, the reservation was paid between two to five million dollars and understood it would create work for them. The project would help the tribe to achieve financial independence, and the money would be spent for scholarships and building of new housing.

The decision to build the sewage treatment system aroused anger and protest among the thousands of white residents living in the small towns near the reservation. They hired geologists to prove that it would be a risk for their local water supply from near the reservation. They accused the Indians of not being careful and guilty of recklessness in treating the land. The writer quoted earlier Fergus M. Bordewich[80], who witnessed the discussion, related the Indians' words:

"It is our land, and we are independent", said the Indians.

"How can you say that the deal would improve the lives of over two hundred people on the reservation?" angrily asked a white farmer whose land was next to the reservation. "If our water is going to be infected, it would be a disaster for everyone. It is difficult to live here, much more difficult than in the rest of the country"...he said bitterly.

Four miles from the border of Kansas and Oklahoma, an old Indian Chilocco school with its buildings reminiscent of the old years gives a taste of the past years. Just to the south of the stream of Chilocco, a political battlefield has developed. The thirty-two leaders of the Tonkawa tribe have proposed to the federal government that a nuclear storage site be installed.

In the early 1800's, the three thousand people of the Tonkawa tribe were living on two million acres of land in Texas. Now they live in seventy-five houses on a hundred and fifty acres southeast of Tonkawa in Oklahoma. Among the locals, there is not one who is a full-blooded Indian.

One of the sources of income for the Tonkawa was a bingo hall, but in November 1993, the bingo hall was destroyed by fire and that source of work was over. The proposed tribal offer to store nuclear waste is not

---

[80] See: Op. cit.

approved by some of the Indians living in Tonkawa, while others talk hopefully about the possibility of work for five hundred and twenty people and a yearly income of twenty-five million dollars.

Presently, the reservation has an unemployment rate of twenty-eight percent.

The critics of the project say that the tribal leaders are too much involved in "economy". The protests came from everywhere, and delegations went to Washington to dispute the proposal. The majority of whites (non Indian) and some Indians are against a project to store the nuclear waste, but they learn that they do not have any right, because of sovereignty of Indian tribes.

There are other consequences of Indians' ignorance. Bordewich writes that he visited a white farmer who lived in a mobile home. In his kitchen, a poster was hanging called "Chief Seattle Speaks". It starts with the words reminiscent of the famous words of Lincoln (from his Gettysburg Address): "How can you buy or sell the sky, the warmth of the land?"

The farmer told Bordewich: "Before the conflict with the Indians about the nuclear leftovers ...I was idealistic about them. I believed that they have a special feeling and understanding concerning the land".

The quoted "testament of Chief Seattle" was translated into dozens of foreign languages, and in 1993, it was used in the beginning of the report of toxic left over. Those words were called "the most beautiful ever said and the most wise".

Who was Chief Seattle (Sea'th'l)? The chief of the Dwumish (Seattle was also part Suquamish) tribe is a historical figure. He converted to Catholicism and was a peacemaker. In his later years, he criticized the whites that he had trusted earlier. He was quoted as saying: "the Indians will die and only their ghosts will be a part of American land".

There is another truth about Chief Seattle. He owned slaves[81]. In 1850 he sold some land to the federal government in exchange for protection against his enemies. The "Testament of Chief Seattle", according to historians, was made from notes taken by a white doctor listening to the chief's speech. The beautiful form given Seattle's words was made by Texan Ted Perry.

I personally believe that the famous words of Chief Seattle, considered the most important document stating the tradition of Indians, are either a lie or at least twisted.

---

[81] As was common among Northwest Coast people. Later, he actually freed his slaves and campaigned for an end to slavery among his people.

My husband Norman shared with me another story.

Everybody was touched in the 1970s by the TV advertising concerning the ecology... not to contaminate the water and the land. The ad showed actor Iron Eyes Cody shedding tears, and the words were: "Keep America Beautiful". Iron Eyes Cody wore Indian attire and was crying artificial tears from glycerin. As was learned later, Iron Eyes Cody was not an Indian, as he said, but he was born as Espera DeCorti, son of Italian immigrants. His dark countenance was from his Sicilian mother. He acted in many Hollywood movies taking the part of an Indian. He stated his mother was Creek, and his father Cherokee. In his autobiography he lied. The truth came out after his death in 1999.

There are also court cases that Indians are taking against the states, or even the Federal Government, covering all kinds of different subjects. These cases are well publicized in the press.

In the state of New Mexico, the Isleta Pueblo tribe has asked the city of Albuquerque to spend three hundred million dollars on improvements to their sewage treatment system so that their water supply taken from the Rio Grande River is clean before it reaches the reservation.

In 1999, thirty-five tribes with four hundred and fifty thousand members started a case in Santa Fe, New Mexico against the big tobacco companies. They asked for billions of dollars as compensation for ruined health resulting from the effects of nicotine in cigarettes. Their case was based upon the misleading advertising of big tobacco companies that downplayed the harmful effects of smoking and cited the programs showing that the nicotine is bad for the health. They said that forty percent of Indians smoke, whereas less that twenty-seven percent of whites smoke, nineteen percent Hispanic and twenty-seven percent of African Americans.

Indians legally can have access to the feathers of eagles that they consider a sacred bird. The regulation was approved by the United States Fish and Wildlife Service.

Many controversies revolve around the use by Indians of peyote, a small cactus growing in Texas, New Mexico and Arizona. The peyote cactus takes thirty years to grow, and in the United States of America is listed as an "endangered species".

Indians say that in their rituals, peyote has been in use for over a hundred years. In the United States of America, the use of peyote as a heavy drug is illegal, however, in twenty-eight states the law allows the use of peyote to around seven hundred thousand members of the Native American Church of North America.

Most of the court cases, however, deal with ownership of the tribal land or compensation for it. In New Mexico, Indians are fighting to take back their land. They say that two hundred and fifty years ago the King of Spain wrote, that Indians can control Sandia Mountain. Now that land is known as a tourist attraction.

Indian farmers and ranchers are in court fighting for ten billion dollars against the USDA (US Department of Agriculture). They stated that the banks have rejected their applications for credit for twenty years.

The reason the banks refused them credit was presumably the lack of any assets to present as collateral for a loan.

The Lakota Sioux Indians of South Dakota for the last twenty years have refused compensation (totaling a hundred and six million dollars) for their sacred land in the territory of the Black Hills that belongs to them as per the terms of the 1869 treaty. In this treaty, it was said that the land would belong to them "as long as the water flows and the grass grows". When gold was discovered in the Black Hills, the Indians were pushed away. Now the Black Hills, where the Mount Rushmore memorial and Crazy Horse sculpture are located, are wanted by the Lakota Sioux.

Mohicans hope to recover six thousand acres in the western part of the state of New York. They refuse compensation; they want the land.

In 2003, various tribes on behalf of three hundred thousand tribal members asked the courts for one hundred and thirty-seven million dollars that they should have received from the usage of gas, oil and others natural resources taken from reservation territories.

Iroquois Indians sue for the return of land in the state of New York that amounts to a quarter of a million acres.

The Shinnecock tribe announced that they are ready to go to court to win back their land in Long Island, New York.

A Native American woman from the Blackfeet tribe, Elouise Cobell, went to court to fight in the name of three hundred thousand Indians. She works as an executive of the National Bank in southwest Montana. The Blackfeet Tribe owns the bank. The court case started officially in 1997, and I am one of many that receive regular information via the Internet on how the case is going. I must honestly say that I am confused in understanding it.

The case is an Indian fight for 2.4 billion dollars that the Federal Government has kept for years as tribal trust funds for the use of tribal land by the white settlers. According to the law, the Indians always can ask to have that money back and use it. When they asked about the money, they learned that the funds were badly mismanaged and wasted. It is difficult to follow how the money was used, says the Federal

Government. They didn't deal with payments by check. "If someone would do such a bad job he would be in jail", concludes Eluoise Cobell. Since 1980, Elouise Cobell and other Indians have been asking for an accounting of how the money was used when it should have been paying dividends to the Blackfeet Tribe.

The solving of Indian affairs led to 1887 legislature called the "Dawes Act-Allotment Act". According to it, Indians were given parcels of land. After twenty-five years, those parcels reverted to the Indian's ownership. The law was intended to assimilate Indians into white society and to encourage them to farm the land. The act was unsuccessful.

According to the early treaties, Indians should have one hundred and forty million acres of land. Now they have only fifty-six million acres. Another treaty gave them the opportunity to sell the land. They subsequently sold about ninety million acres. Most of the land was sold to white settlers. Now the Indians are seeking an amendment to the earlier treaty that would cancel the provision for selling.

The whites are upset – and there are furious protests - saying that their ancestors legally bought the land from Indians. The whites living on what were reservation lands say: "What do they want to do with us? Keep us on the reservation?" They also state, that Indians want to have the land back so they can build casinos.

Chief Leonard wrote: "My tribe does not wish to pay innocent landowners through pain and suffering ... but it appears I have no choice"[82]

The other characteristics of the court cases deal with factors where public opinion is involved. For example, Indian prisoners went to court so they can practice their religion in prison. Among the other things they ask for is to have with them their talismans with special herbs that give them strength. They want to have their sacred pipe and to be able to pray in private as they smoke and inhale the smoke. The prison executives say that the law for prisons prevents the use of drugs (herbs in talismans) as well as the tools used in taking drugs.

What happened is that the states of Texas and Montana let the Indian prisoners practice their religion by letting them own the needed items. The same has happened in the states of Nebraska, Minnesota, Iowa and South Dakota. The prisoners of other religions, like Christians, Jews, Muslims, etc. can practice their religion, so the Indians are treated the same. They can keep long hair that the other prisoners must cut for their safety (during work the long hair can go into machinery).

---

[82] See: Raad Cawhton, *Citing the old-treaties, Indian tribes stake a legal claim to land*, "Philadelphia Inquirer", August 7, 2000.

Comanche's don't cut their hair at all except when in mourning or as a sign of shame. The prisoners have to prove their Indian roots. According to their rituals, they have the right to the ceremony of the "sweat lodge".

On November 16, 1994, President Bill Clinton signed the right to practice their religion in a broad sense. The prison officials are afraid that the law will be twisted and abused and as a result the prisons will incur higher costs.

President Bill Clinton visited the Pine Ridge Reservation in April 1994 as the first American presidential visitor in over two hundred years. He also invited five hundred and forty-seven Indian leaders to the White House. Not all of them accepted the invitation. Only half of the invited came; some did not come for financial reasons. It was the first time in history that the president of the United States invited so many Indian elders to the White House. Beside Bill Clinton, Richard Nixon is considered as having been politically fair to the Indian nations.

In that special White House meeting President Clinton listened for over two hours to the complaints and problems of American Indians.

"Welcome to the White House", he said. He assured them that they have the right to practice their religions, that the sacred places for them will be protected (one such place is not broadly known: The Leon River Medicine Wheel in North Central Texas, the sacred place for Comanches).

The president was criticized for cutting the budget on Indian affairs, and he said that he would return one hundred and twenty million dollars in aid. He also signed an order that any federal decision concerning tribal natural resources has to be first subjected to consultation with and then approved by the elders of tribes. It was said that the sacred land of their ancestors has to be kept. The meeting was opened by presentation of the American flag and singing of the National Anthem to the sound of Indian drums. Some of the Indian leaders came wearing their native attire.

As a positive result of this White House meeting, Let me tell about some cases.

Some time ago, the Passamaquoddy tribe in the State of Maine was very poor. They are now prospering.[83] Years ago they were considered alcoholic without any prospects to better themselves. Now the Passamaquoddy Indians are a big conglomerate, one of the biggest in the state of Maine. They have money to invest. They create jobs and give the assurance for millions of credit by the banks. Now, with this different situation, the whites are looking for a connection with them. The Passamaquoddy Indian tribe has two thousand seven hundred people and

[83] See: "News Journal", Wilmington, Delaware, December 13, 1992.

live on the terrain of two reservations: Pleasant Point not far from the Canadian border and Indian Township.

A generation ago, the Passamaquoddy lived in shacks without electricity. They knew neighbors who died from the cold. The average life expectancy was forty-seven years. There was no opportunity to work, and no Indian students finished high school.

In 1972, the Passamaquoddy tribe and a small neighboring tribe of Penobscots, fought in the court against the State of Maine asking twenty-five billion dollars in compensation and return of twelve and a half million acres of land. Two-thirds of the state had belonged to the Indians and was taken away from them. It was an outrage in violation of a 1790 treaty. Now, after the intervention of President Carter, each tribe received forty million dollars compensation. What the Passamaquoddy did with such money is now a subject to study and analyze at Harvard business school.

"Our basic philosophy was to find things that work rather than taking the risk of starting up new businesses" said Tom Tureen, a non-Indian from Portland, who represents tribes who look after the investments of the Passamaquoddy[84]. One of the concepts was to cut the cycle of dependency and create something that gave them work on a big scale. They needed two things: the awareness of opportunities waiting for them and access to capital money. It meant establishing a basis of reliability with financial institutions that would help finance such enterprising.

The Passamaquoddy invested thirteen million in government trust-funds, and looked for possibilities in the State of Maine. The first step was buying a blueberry farm in Columbia Falls. In three years, they received back the invested 2.2 million. In 1983, they bought the biggest cement factory in New England that was not yielding a profit. They cut the number of employees, repaired everything, and the factory started to bring in a profit. Five years later, they sold it for sixty million dollars. In Calais, near the Canadian River St. Croix, the Passamaquoddy built a casino that employs over two hundred people, Indians and non-Indians.

"It is difficult to ask for love, but money that we own cut the discrimination", was quoted Ralph Dana, sixty-nine years old Indian, whose transit company is the biggest private business in the hands of Indians in the State of Maine. "I have the impression that those people who ignored us, now they are saying – maybe we should contact the Indians? They have work".

---

[84] See: David Lamb, *Once destitute Maine Indians now a financial power*, "Sunday News Journal", Dec 13, 1992, pg A17.

The big help is, of course, that Indian income on the reservations is not subject to federal taxation. Forty years ago Choctaw Indians in Mississippi were poor, over seventy-five percent were unemployed and their average age was forty-five to fifty years. When Philip Martin became the chief, the situation turned around. Martin contacted five hundred companies to invest on the reservation. In 1979, General Motors opened a big factory to put together automotive parts. They employ over a thousand people. Other big companies Ford, Chrysler, and McDonnel-Douglas opened manufacturing plants. It is said that on the reservation there are twelve big companies. The unemployment is under twenty percent, education has improved and housing has improved as well.

The Choctaws opened six grammar schools and two high schools that can teach over fourteen hundred students. A modern health clinic was opened and there are plans for more investments. The success of the Choctaw in Mississippi is translated into their high quality of work. Ford Company officials qualify Indians as the most efficient and reliable workers, more than in similar Ford companies located in Japan.

May I point out: the Federal government is out of any involvement in these changes, and maybe it is the reason for their success.

Aleksandra Ziolkowska-Boehm

Prosperity from Casinos

Casinos were intended to help all Indians...not just a small percentage of them. It has not turned out that way.

The casino saga began at the end of the 1980's when Washington began cutting the welfare for inhabitants of Indian reservations. To offset reduced welfare benefits, the government encouraged tribes to take the initiative and open their own businesses. In 1988, Congress established legislation, the so-called *Indian Gaming Regulatory Act*, that supposedly opened the way for American Indians leading to the possibility of economic progress. The Administration of President Ronald Reagan signed an agreement allowing for opening and running casinos on Indian reservations. The most important feature of the gaming act was that the newly opened casinos run by Indians were free from federal income tax.

The *Indian Gaming Regulatory Act* turned out to be imprecise, in that it has many "loopholes", is not clear and is not definite, that now lawyers still debate, for example, the subject of the definition of different games. It can be said, that instead of defining clearly rules, regulations and rights, its interpretations have become chaos. The chaos has created the opportunity for abuse.

It is unlikely that one "could even hazard a guess" at understanding the whole concept of the casinos: that they should help to overcome the poverty, help to heal the social problems of Native people and help to liquidate alcoholism and disease. Perhaps the writers of the legislation only "hazarded a guess" without a clear understanding of the Indian problems and how they could be remedied (like many poorly researched and poorly written bills in Congress). Very quickly it became evident that there were only a few Indian tribes who were winners and who benefited from casino ventures. Only a few tribes had access to capital to begin a venture. They have grown rich from casinos, whereas the majority of tribes, unable to invest in a casino project or located far from a population base that can support a casino, are still mired in poverty.

Casinos do not help to overcome the extreme poverty in which the majority of Native Americans live. Only half of the tribes, that all together have 1.8 million members, have casinos. Therefore, for around five hundred and fifty tribes recognized by the Federal Government, there are around two hundred and thirty tribes that operate casinos on their reservations. For about twenty tribes, the casinos have become a catalyst for economic prosperity. The remainder of the tribes can hardly manage. Poorer tribes, such as the Navajo and Hopi, rejected casinos as not the right source for acquiring an income, and they consider casinos a hazard from their religious point of view.

Casinos run by Indians operate in thirty states. In each of five states, in which the Native American people represent five to eight percent of the inhabitants, such as Montana, Nevada, Oklahoma, North and South Dakota, have on their terrain only three percent of the casinos. And the states where the Native Americans are only three percent of the population, like California, Connecticut and Florida, their casinos have the highest income.

In 2002, income from two hundred and ninety Indian run casinos in twenty-eight states brought in 12.7 billion dollars. From such an amount, the casinos kept for themselves over five billion dollars. These statistics confirm - according to "Fortune"- that Indian casinos for gambling are among the top twenty corporations who have earned the most income - with income higher than J.P. Morgan Chase & Co., Merrill Lynch or American Express. In California, its Indian casinos bring in an income greater than all the casinos in Las Vegas.

For a foreign viewpoint of the American casinos, I can again refer to my earlier recollection of the book by Bernard-Henri Levy *American Vertigo*. I talk about his book again, because for several reasons, it is very interesting and misleading. In the chapter entitled "An Indian Hero Stricken with Anti-Semitism" (which Norman thinks is ridiculous!), Levy writes about meeting with Russell Means, a well-known Indian and respected activist, a very colorful person and an earlier friend of Marlon Brando. Means apparently welcomed the French journalist with the greeting: "You here, Mr. Levy? Not in Israel yet? But I heard on the radio that Sharon wanted all the Jews in France to emigrate to Tel Aviv! Ha! Ha!"

Levy answered: "I have not come all this way to listen to this kind of bad joke, and I don't find this sort of thing particularly funny, that I'm a Jew who is sympathetic to the Indian cause and that I came expressly to ask you why on earth no one ever had the idea to create a kind of Yad Vashem of Indian suffering rather than the casinos that are a slow-working poison. I got this terrible reply, which is hammered out, word by word, in a restrained, affected tone of rage: I don't need advice from Zionists; can you understand? I don't need their advice; when I needed them, they weren't there; I went to see them, I went to see the Jews in Cleveland, and I waited, oh! I waited a long time and no one – you hear me? – No one answered my call; so don't try to give me advice! A little respect, no advice!"[85]

I wonder what kind of a picture of Indians the book *American Vertigo* reveals as it is translated into many languages.

---

[85] See: Random House, 2006, pg. 66.

A hazard to the proposal that casinos would possibly level up the standard of living for all Indian people was ill-conceived thinking that casinos could be opened even on a far away terrain of reservations where for generations the inhabitants lived very poorly. The problem was - as in many places of the world - location. Tens of casinos, because they are too small, are located far from populated areas, or whose potential patrons face inordinate distances to reach them, can hardly make ends meet. Casinos opened not far from cities, with a supportive population base and where there can be easy access to transportation, started to bring in a profit. As a result, Indians and their financial partners and advisors always looked for good locations.

Since tribes recognized by the Federal Government can open a casino, there are many cases of "dead for years" tribes who ask Congress to be recognized. There are even "dead for years" tribes, promoted by financial "god fathers" (non-Indians) who have come "back to life". Since 1979, there are about two hundred newly registered tribes (not to say they did not exist in the past) waiting for recognition – some for registration, some already approved but waiting for a license to be issued. The Press gives examples of tribes whose license application for a casino was rejected and who are now bitter about it (for example, the Chippewa in the state of Wisconsin). A petition for approval of a "lost tribe" comes with it a right to land. If the tribe does not have its reservation, it has to look for land and ask for its right, even if it is a place they never lived. There have been cases where non-Indian land was approved and then a casino was built on it. It is important that casinos be located close to the highways or close to big cities. It is not important if Indians live near by or not.

When casinos are opened, and their location is good, leaders of tribes and their partners have access to money that does not require reporting. For sure a few tribes prosper very well, and the rich are becoming richer. Twenty-five percent of tribes that benefit from gambling allocate some of the profit amongst their members. For one person, a few or tens of thousands of dollars may be given. For example, each member of the Seminole tribe in Florida receives a check for thirty five thousand dollars each year.

Of course, the best operating tribes are those who are lucky to have proficient leaders and who govern themselves. In California, the Pechanga Band of Mission Indians in Riverside County own "The Pechanga Resort & Casino", that makes a huge amount of money.

On Thanksgiving Day, each of a hundred members of the California Indian Table Mountain Rancheria is given a check for two hundred thousand dollars as a percentage from the income of the "Table

Mountain Casino". It is only a supplement (bonus) in addition to a monthly stipend of fifteen thousand dollars that all tribal members receive. These amounts are still not much compared to a few individuals who make hundreds of millions of dollars from casinos.

According to the bill from 1988 (Congress at the same time cut funds for reservations), tribes can distribute income from casinos to their tribal members as dividends after they finance the infrastructure on reservations, such as medical facilities, schools, etc. After years of living on welfare, thanks to the gambling casinos, Indians are able to improve their standard of living, afford sufficient and nutritious food and even enjoy some luxuries. The bill gives power to state representatives for issuing the license for opening casinos. Usually the governing representatives refuse to grant a license or seek a share from future income. Congress established the organization NIGC (National Indian Gaming Commission) to monitor the workings of the agencies for Indians. The Commission has sixty-three workers that oversee operations of over three hundred casinos. The Commission watches over the business affairs of casinos so that they are protected from the Mafia. The Indians make conscientious efforts to protect the gambling places from becoming potential places for misdemeanors such as drunkenness, drug peddling, sexual based activities and so on. In the casino of the Oneida Indians, for example, selling of alcohol is forbidden.

Despite the efforts of the Commission, it appears that the whole system of casinos may be slipping out of control. From most casinos, the biggest income reaches investors who are not Indians, who implement their own financial strategies and who have their own plans for expansion. Since they know the gambling business very well, these investors are able to execute such strategies. Presumably, around seventy-five percent of the employees working in casinos are Indians. However, it seems that the white man is again the top winner. Many white investors make hundreds of millions of dollars, many times using legal "loopholes" in a system that is within the law. It is said that elements of corruption, lack of honesty and even intimidation are "normal" everyday procedures in the operation of the gambling casinos.

Tribal elders may decide about what gambling rules to impose, without having concern for compliance with Indian interests, and the smaller the tribe, the bigger the involvement of its members in sharing the income. Enriched tribal leaders have a tremendous political power, and they are able to ignore other Indians or even ignore other Indians' rights, if keeping the status quo helps their system. As a result, Washington takes care of the rich Indians' interest but not the poor Indians who need help and support. In the past, Indians were not a visible or viable group, but since 1993, when they donated to the campaign funds 8.6 million dollars for the election, Washington has taken them seriously. Among others, the big money coming from Indians and their casinos in California helped finance the successful governership election campaign of Arnold Schwarzenegger.

The rich Indians tribes have money to support political parties and their campaigns, either on a state or federal level. The have money to support influential lobbies. In 2000, tribes contributed 9.5 million dollars to political parties in Washington. It was much more than the amount of money given by corporations such as General Motors, Boeing or even the now defunct Enron.

During the Bill Clinton presidency, the majority of Indian source money[86] was dedicated to the Democrats, but since there are Republicans in the Government, the Indians started to support Republicans as well. Much of the Indian money is spent on influencing Congress. In the years 2000–2001, they gave twenty million dollars on lobbying such things as tax exemption of gambling casinos and to keep the status quo of *Indian sovereign immunity*, helping to avoid outside control that usually comes with new ventures.

Millions of dollars are designated for promotion of the so-called *Proposition 5* – the legalization of gaming. One single casino in California gave over five million dollars lobbying for *Proposition 5*.

A big Indian lobby was created. The Choctaw tribe in Mississippi, starting from 1997, gave away eleven million dollars to support lobbyist Jack Abramoff, who was instrumental in seeking funds for the Republican Party. In 2005, together with Tom DeLay[87], they were accused of bribery in lobbying on Indian affairs and taking around eighty million dollars from the Indians. As quoted in the Press, Abramoff even showed no respect for Indians, using in his e-mails such descriptive terms as *monkeys, morons, idiots*.

Indians know they are manipulated and used, but when Norman and I spoke with a few of them about it, they were saying: "We know we are "fleeced", but sometimes it is better to have a pact with a devil than to do nothing. The other possibility – go back on welfare, and we do not want that for sure".

In "Time"[88], a letter signed by Tammy Miller of Onamia, Minnesota appeared, and it stated: "Not all Indians casinos deserve a bad rap. I'd like to point out the good that the casinos of Minnesota's Mille Lacs

---

[86] "Time" writes 86%.
[87] House of Representative majority leader.
[88] January 13, 2003.

Band of Ojibwa have done. Prior to our casinos, we had nothing. There was no source of clean water, we had tar-paper shacks for housing, and there were only dirt roads. Today, fourteen years after passage of the Indian Gaming Regulatory Act and the building of the Mille Lacs' casinos, we have all the amenities of a good community. We have safe drinking water, modern housing, good roads and, best of all, jobs for our people and also for members of the surrounding communities. We employ more than three thousand five hundred people, most of whom had few options before our casinos existed. Despite the bad news in your report, in the Mille Lacs Band's case, there is another side to the story".

In the same issue of "Time", a letter by Ernest L. Stevens from Washington, the president of the National Indian Gaming Association, titled *A different view* was published. He writes:

"Indian gaming is not a federal program. It's one tool that tribes use – like states use lotteries – to generate revenue for their communities. Indian gaming revenue is used directly for tribal government purposes, serving as tribal tax revenue. It is the step to self-reliance. Where tribes suffer high suicide rates among teens, Indian gaming builds schools, funds scholarships and gives children hope. Where Indians suffer diabetes and liver disease, gaming builds hospitals and fitness centers. Indian gaming has created more than three hundred thousand jobs nationwide and has lowered welfare rolls. Tribes are good neighbors and have numerous service agreements with State and local governments. They contribute emergency service equipment and donate more than $68 million annually to charities. Indian gaming is fully regulated. Tribes invest more than two hundred and twelve million dollars annually in federal, State and tribal regulation. Tribal gaming commissions, like State lottery bodies, serve as the daily regulators, and tribes employ more than two thousand eight hundred Indians. The tribal regulatory system ensures that Indian gaming is safe, fair and of the highest integrity".

Really, there is a lot of good going on. The Meskwaki Indians own the Meskwaki Bingo Casino Hotel. Around eight hundred and forty tribal members live on seven thousand acres of land along the Iowa River, west from the town of Tama in the State of Iowa. Thanks to money from gaming, it has built three hundred new houses, a hospital and the local schools are supported.

Ten years ago, the Prairie Band Potawatomi Nation, whose reservation is located not far from Topeka in Kansas, suffered from a seventy percent unemployment rate and eighty-five percent of the people were on all sorts of welfare. In 1998, everything changed, when Harrah's Prairie Band Casino was opened. It became a popular tourist attraction in the State of Kansas. Now it provides work for a thankful people, and the

158

over one hundred million dollars annual casino income location – according to the program – finances many needs on the reservations, such as care of children and education. From the income, investments are directed into the infrastructure, such as roads, bridges, fire departments, housing for the middle class, apartments and a center for elderly people. The Potawatomi tribe donates twenty-four percent of their income straight to their five thousand tribal members, even to those who do not live on the reservation. Annually, each member is due around two thousand dollars. The tribe also gives money for schools that are attended by other than Indian children.

In California, the Pechanga Band of Mission Indians owning The Pechanga Resort & Casino, that make a lot of money, in May 2006, gave four hundred thousand dollars to local high schools. It was only a part of the one million seven hundred thousand dollars in aid given to the educational system.

In 2003, the Oneida Indians of the State of New York gave Harvard University three million dollars to open a department of *Indian studies,* and its professor was paid too.

Those are all actions created by a feeling of pride. Earlier life on a reservation depended on federal "leftovers" and private gifts. Now everything has changed. The ability to share, as evident from such worthwhile donation of money, is inherent to the culture of Indians, and it has enhanced and promoted their feelings of pride. Everything has changed for better. The Choctaw Indians from Mississippi invest in building companies, in shopping malls, in paper manufacturing and products and computer services. The Oneida Indians of the State of New York, owners of the Turning Stone Resort & Casino, built a complete housing development for their people.

Another example – the Foxwoods Casino in the State of Connecticut is owned by a small Mashantucket Pequot tribe. From gambling income, their Indian leaders have built a recreational play center that attracts tourists from all over the world. Living in Dallas, Texas, I read about the tribe in the daily "The Dallas Morning News". In years past, Connecticut was the locale for Mohican, Narragansett and Pequot Indians. The Pequot Indians live on the Mashantucket Pequot Reservation. I remember how impressed I was learning that they live well. The reporter and author of books, Kim I. Eisler[89] wrote that on the reservation golf clubs, hotels, shopping malls and cinemas have been built. The income from the casino brings to tribal members five to twenty thousand dollars yearly. The Pequot Indians are buying land around their

---

[89] See: "Dallas Morning News", October 2, 1993.

reservation, and they have ambitious plans for use of the purchased land in the future.

The history leading up to such a successful venture is almost unbelievable. In earlier days, the population of the Pequot Indians reached over eight thousand. In 1978, only a small group of elderly people lived on the reservation, most of the young people having moved away. Elizabeth George, an almost eighty year old Indian woman saw her daughter with child move away from the reservation. Before her death, Elizabeth George asked her grandson, Richard "Skip" Hayward, to move back and live on the reservation. She asked him to sell the empty land to the government, otherwise, the government would it take over for free.

Richard Hayward, a man with fantasy and experience, called himself a leader of the "Pequot Tribal Council". He asked twenty-nine tribal members to come back and live again on the reservation. They all started to farm, produce and sell vegetables, also to harvest maple syrup and to log wood for fire. Their efforts became an income profitable for survival only, but it was not enough for "Skip". He went to Hollywood in Florida to visit the reservation of the Seminole Indians, about whose "economic boom" he had heard a lot.

A chief of the Seminole, James Billie, had a beautiful dream of a wonderful future for his people. In 1979, he received a license for the Seminoles to run their own bingo gaming business. Later, the Seminoles were licensed and expanded their gambling operations to include roulette, poker, blackjack, baccarat, pulltab machines and slot machines. Soon it brought them a huge income.

Mr. Hayward knew that he wanted the same for his people in Connecticut, but it was difficult to persuade them to support his vision. The majority of the Peguot tribe, who then counted fifty members, were Jehovah Witnesses, who do not allow their members to take part in gambling, as well as the other, who were Baptists. It was difficult, but he finally managed to convince his people to participate in a gambling venture.

Richard Hayward received a bank loan (from the Arab-American Bank in New York) and also received an agreement to build the casino where the bingo parlor would operate. In 1990, thanks to business magnate Lim Goh Tonga from Malaysia who knew everything about casinos and gambling, the casino was opened. The State of Connecticut tried to stop this venture, but the Indians won. The casino is now a giant, and members of the Mashantucket Pequot Indians rose to five hundred.

The "New York Times" published an article by Judith H. Dobrzynski titled "Casino profits help tribe reclaim its history"[90]. The journalist reminds readers that "the Pequots did not disappear in the seventeenth century when they were ravaged by the combination of war with the colonists and smallpox, measles and other European diseases". When they asked in the 1970's to be recognized as a tribe, and later for a license to operate casinos that was granted, life for them changed dramatically.

As Dobrzynski stated, profits from Foxwoods, the Peguots twenty-four-hour casino, are paying for a three hundred and fifteen million dollar museum and research center. Thanks to work by archeologists, artifacts were found such as fragments of wampum, tools, flints and a cooking pot the size of a pumpkin

On June 1, 1997, the first anniversary celebrating the massacre in Mystic[91], a museum was opened. The museum displays the items recovered from digging in the area and a collection of artifacts belonging to other tribes. A library and research center was opened as well. I keep in hand a book written by historian Laurence M. Hauptman "*The Pequots in Southern New England: The Fall and Rise of an American Indian Nation*".[92] I am happy that it relates the research of the history of the Pequot Indians and that the funds for research came from the Indians themselves.

When I visited Albuquerque in New Mexico in 1997, twelve years after my first visit, I went again to the Isleta Indian Reservation. I could not find in my memory a picture of the area when I now saw a new golf course, fifty new houses across from the casino, recreation homes for young people and good roads. All of it was built from casino income that also supports the local university.

Opponents of Indian casinos are known, people like Donald Trump, owner of the Taj Mahal Casino in Atlantic City in the State of New Jersey. Trump publicly complains and criticizes Indian run casinos, pointing out that they are privileged and not subject to the same laws that apply to other Americans. Indians, for example, are allowed to sell gasoline and cigarettes cheaper as they are exempt from state taxes. It creates a conflict between local businesses and state officials. The Indian tribes as "sovereign nations" do not pay income taxes (but individual Indians pay income taxes like any other American citizen). The income

---

[90] See: Judith H. Dobrzynski, "The New York Times", September 7, 1997.

[91] In May 1637, English colonizers murdered over five hundred Indians in a village near the Mystic River. The murders did not take longer than one hour. In the end, all Indian housing was burned.

[92] See: 1990 University of Oklahoma Press.

tax benefit provides their companies with a privileged position compared to its competition.

In Connecticut, a society of restaurant owners has complained that Indians are not subject to the same payments as the rest of the Americans. In restaurants belonging to the Indian casinos, alcohol is served that in non-Indian restaurants is more expensive, since restaurateurs have to pay high taxes and must buy an annual liquor license.

In August 1997, the Isleta tribe issued a report (I read about it in the local paper) that showed their Isleta Gaming Palace hires two thousand six hundred and fifty people. Other casinos have been opened in the area, and all together, they hire around four thousand people, twenty percent of them are Indians.

The State of New Mexico is one of the poorest in the United States. Critics say that casinos take money from poor people who are addicted to the hazard of gambling. The hazard of gambling was always synonymous with organized crime and earlier was legal only in the State of Nevada..

In spite of those arguments, public opinion is on the Indians' side. The success of the tribes who are doing well showed one way to break the bonds of poverty and dependence upon the Federal Government. Casinos are like a Godsend freeing them from an imprisonment of poverty, hopelessness and dependence on the Federal Government.

In November 1997, Norman and I took an automibile trip from Houston to El Paso. On the road, we stopped in Fort Stockton, the only town in this region where we could eat and replenish our gasoline supply. Finally, after eleven hours of a monotonous journey, on a road that from time to time revealed barren mountains and cactus, and after achieving seven hundred and seventy miles, we reached El Paso on the border with Mexico. On the Mexican side of the Rio Grande River in the State of Chihuahua is the town of Juarez that we also visited. Loud and dirty, Juarez did not remind us of the charming, though poor Mexican towns deeper in the country. In the afternoon, we returned to El Paso and drove to the Tigua Indian Reservation, which is also known as the Ysleta del Sur Pueblo. For dinner, we went to Speaking Rock Casino.

Crowds of people and dim lighting, it seemed weird to us that people can spend the evening and nights in such a way. As a whole, the local people went to the casino. The waiters were both white and Indians, and using trays, they served alcoholic drinks and other beverages. The dim lights and gaudy décor were similar to the Las Vegas casinos. Only here, the people seemed somehow more provincial than in the popular Tourist City in Nevada. The following day, we went again to the reservation of the Tigua Indians, this time to see the housing development. We were deeply impressed with the picture that we saw. The row of comfortable houses had garages and small gardens in the back. In front of each house, a car was parked. The surroundings were clean, tidy and showed that the people were doing very well. With pride in their homes, the Tigua maintained their property and cared for it. It was not a bit like the picture of houses we remembered from the Pine Ridge Reservation. During the trip to South Dakota in 1999, we saw rather small gambling casinos. In the northern plains of the West, it is difficult to attract people let alone a/crowd, as there are not many local inhabitants. For example, near the Oglala Sioux reservation casino, there were only three trailer homes on wheels. The South Dakota reservations are among the poorest in the United States.

Now, in El Paso, we started to appreciate the possibilities that were brought by casinos located on the outskirts of a big town. We learned that the Tigua Indians opened Speaking Rock Casino in 1993, that they support many useful projects and, they build houses (that we had occasioned to admire). We were told that the Tigua built two hundred and thirty-six houses for their people. They have also built and operate a well-coordinated health system and education center. The Indians have found work in the casino, and they receive subsistence from extra yearly bonuses. We learned that in 2000, income from the Speaking Rock Casino reached fifty million dollars[93].

What a positive example!

I had a thought ... perhaps the white buffalo born in Janesville, Wisconsin in 1994 has brought Indians a renewed hope for prosperity and rebirth. Maybe casinos and income from the gambling are the first omen?

Not a long time later, after returning home in 1999 to Delaware, I read that the Tigua Indians have two stalwart enemies: the Baptists and George W. Bush, the governor of Texas who has ambitions to become president. We learned that Governor Bush was against the casino and wanted to close it. Apparently a strong "power" in Texas was against the hazard of gambling in the State of Texas. The case was tried in court. The Tigua Indians defended themselves by bringing attention to the bill from 1988 *Indian Gaming Regulatory Act*, that allows casinos to be opened on reservations.

"It's the new buffalo", said Vince Munoz, executive gaming commissioner for El Paso's Tigua tribe[94].

---

[93] See: "Time", December 23, 2002, pg. 63.
[94] See: "The Dallas Morning News", May 29, 1994 pg. 45A.

As it was realized, the two sources of law – State and Federal - are in contradiction, and because of it, there are different interpretations and unpredictable difficulties. The problems began when the Supreme Court in 1832 gave to Indians the status of *sovereign immunity from state laws on their reservations*. The critical voices of this status were frequently supported in courts. It was shown that if Indians were treated as sovereign nations, they should not donate money to political parties because it is not legal for a foreign government or business to make donations to American political parties. The Press wrote that Indians want to have both privileges at the same time – to influence – campaigns and to keep sovereignty.

In Florida, as in Texas, there is a ban on gambling, but on Indian reservations casinos are doing very well. The Seminole and Miccousukee tribes run high-class casinos on their reservations, even so in the rest of the state, gaming is forbidden. In 1996, the Federal Court ruled that Seminole Indians do not have to obtain authorization from state officials to open casinos.

Texas did not fully respect the national Indians' right to own and run casinos. When asked about similarities to the Texas Lottery authorized by voters in 1991, the Tiguas' attorney was quoted as saying, "the lottery is the biggest slot machine in Texas and in the world with ten thousand terminals sucking up money all across Texas". Bush responded to the newspaper: "The state of Texas voted on a lottery, I did not vote on casino-style gambling"[95].

A war in the Texas court system soon started. The Texas general prosecutor, John Cornyn, Republican, was so eager and full of passion, that some citizens sported a bumper sticker on their cars saying *Last of the Indian Fighters.* The Press released articles stating that gambling casinos in El Paso were giving money to the Democratic Party, and that in the 1998 campaign Indians donated forty-six thousand dollars on behalf of Democrat Jim Mattox, opponent of prosecutor Cornyn, and also eighty-nine thousand dollars for Bush's opponent in the competition for the governor's office. Apparently Bush, having presidential aspirations in mind asked for support from the Baptists in exchange for dedicating himself to the Baptist Church. The Baptists were against the gambling and apparently Bush personally was involved in the conflict by promising to help in closing the Indian gaming places in Texas. In February 2002, a year after George W. Bush became president, the Texas

---

[95] See: *Bush may again fight Indian casinos*, "Houston Chronicle", May 18, 1998. pg. 12A.

court decided to end the operation of Speaking Rock Casino. Bush is quoted as saying: "It should not be a hazard in the State of Texas".

Seven hundred and eighty-five workers lost their jobs!

As was written in "Time"[96], soon on the other side of the Texas border, in Sunland Park in the State of New Mexico a new casino was opened. The owner was Stanley E. Fulton, a known entrepreneur from Las Vegas, who in 1998 donated a hundred thousand dollars to the Republican Party, and in 2001 donated eight hundred thousand dollars. John Cornyn was competing for a Senate seat, and he gained it in the fall of 2002.

Two years later, on September 30, 2004, the Congressman from Texas Silvestre Reyes wrote a letter to Ben Nighthorse Campbell, Senator from Colorado (I write about him later in the book), son of an immigrant from Portugal mother and a Northern Cheyenne Indian father, who was head of the Committee for Indians in the Senate[97].

Reyes wrote about Jack Abramoff asking for an investigaton of the money that was given to him by some Indian tribes, including the Tigua (to help reopen their casino). He reminded Campbell that the Speaking Rock Casino and other nearby companies helped to liquidate an unemployment issue in El Paso, that the real estate became more valuable, the Casino was bringing in fifty to sixty million dollars yearly and that the income was used also for building medical centers, a library, a senior center and a housing development for members of the Tigua tribe.

When in February 2002 the casino was closed, Texas Congressman Tom DeLay and lobbyists Jack Abramoff and Michael Scanlon " wheedled out" from the Tigua tribe alone four million two hundred thousand dollars for the promise to act on their behalf. It was an illegal and unethical action. Congressman Silvestre Reyes demanded that the knowledge be made public and to punish the guilty Congressman and the lobbyists.

The trial that was going on also showed the way that big money from casinos can foster acts of intimidation, greed, fraud, corruption, create evil and tempt weak people to cheat. Millions of dollars go into paying lobbyists, and the average Indian who doe not have anything to do with casinos has a yearly income of less than eight thousand dollars.

---

[96] December 23, 2002, pg. 63.

[97] Letter is on the Internet:
http://wwwc.house.gov/reyes/news_detail.asp?id=670

Indian Museums

It was 1990. W. Richard West had became a director of the newly opened National Museum of the American Indians in Washington (NMAI). He flew by plane and talked to the flight attendant. When he told her he was of Southern Cheyenne-Arapaho Indian ancestry, he heard the following remark: -"Really? I thought that all Indians died?"

This reaction West quoted when giving the press interviews at the museum's official opening. Thinking about Indians in the past tense is not a rare occurrence.

Indians I know have told me: "We are in history books, and we have our museums. But we would like that everyone knows we are still here and did not move anywhere".

When quoted earlier, the French journalist and philosopher Bernard Henri Levy asked Oglala Lakota Sioux Russell Means, why Indians did not build a museum something like Yad Vashem in remembrance of the Indian's sorrow and pain. Maybe he did not know (or cared to investigate) how many different museums are dedicated to Indians in a country Levy described in his book *American Vertigo*. He had not mentioned any of them, and I myself counted over two hundred in the United States[98], and there are also museums in Canada.

An interesting Indian museum is located in the State of Illinois near the town of Peoria, and situated on the Illinois River. Earlier its site had been an Indian cemetery. There were two hundred and thirty-seven graves of Native Americans buried in a special cave covered by soil. The gravesite real estate belonged to the Dickinson family who, seven years after discovering the graves[99], put them on public display. Indian organizations protested; they thought that showing graves of their ancestors and their skeletons, as a tourist attraction, is showing no respect to such a place as a graveyard. State authorities in Illinois took the protests under consideration, and dedicated four million dollars to modify the project. After a few years of work, the museum was again opened in 1994 to show the public the Indian artifacts buried in the graves. The big terrain was covered by cedar wood. At a central point is the museum, and there are artifacts belonging to Indians who lived there. Tourists can learn the history of the local Indians. There is a section for children, displaying Indian toys; a gift store offers items for sale having certificates of authenticity.

---

[98] See: Annex Number 2.
[99] As a result of digging in 1920.

The most impressive and biggest Indian museum is the Washington DC National Museum of the American Indian. It took fifteen years to build it following extensive planning and preparations. The museum is situated in a representative section of the American capitol at the corner of 3rd Street and Independence Avenue. It was opened in September 2004. The opening ceremony included a march of around twenty thousand Indians in colorful Native American regalia. The march proceeded from the Smithsonian Institution to the new museum building. The designer of the project that is based on an Indian motive is Canadian architect Douglas J. Cardinal who is of Indian origin.

At the opening, Northern Cheyenne United States Senator Ben Nighthorse Campbell from Colorado gave a speech, and a Congressman from Oklahoma, a member of the Chickasaw Nation read the letter from President George W. Bush. Exhibits displayed show the life of Indians in the past and now. Some of them refer to the pain, the suffering and the extermination of Indian tribes in the nineteenth century, but most of them are displays of current life. The museum shows the past, does not focus on the conflicts with arriving Europeans, but shows the history of Indian people for over a thousand years, from the time when white people first came to the American continent. As was said by W. Richard West, thinking about the year of 1492: "It was long and wonderful "before"". He reminded that Indians were the first artists that used symbols and abstraction – long before Europeans did.

The museum in Washington has three study sections: "Our Universes" that shows the spiritual bond between human beings and the universe, "Our People" that presents the tragic history of Native people after Europeans came onto their continent and "Our Lives" that answers the question of how Indians maintain their own community and culture in a modern world. Shown are ritual dresses worn during *pow-wows* and other ceremonies, along with changes in the manner of dress. Traditional moccasins have been changed to sneakers.

In our house amongst the different memorabilia, there is an Indian *tomahawk*. It was carved from dark green stone and with no doubt was used some time ago by American Indians. Norman told me, he received it from his father, who received it from his father. Norman's grandfather Carl Henry Adelbert Boehm emigrated from Germany to the United States before 1900[100]. Working in Chicago, one day during the lunch

---

[100] In the USA he met another emigrant Blenda Bergman from Sweden and they married. Blenda was the sister of Justus, father of the famous actress Ingrid Bergman. Blenda had emigrated to the United Sates from Sweden and settled in Chicago also before the year 1900.

period, Carl observed the excavation works for a new building. In a pile of removed soil, he saw a green stone partially covered with mud that intrigued him. He picked up the mud-covered stone. After cleaning, he discovered it was a beautifully carved *tomahawk*. The found item became a cherished family heirloom to be passed on from one generation to another. Having a United States map of Indian tribe locations in front of us, we contemplated to which tribe the *tomahawk* might be traced. We thought that perhaps it may belong to the Sauk and Fox, whose locale was near to the current location of the State of Illinois, or to the Kickapoo, or the Chippewa, both who also lived on the terrain. In the near future, we intend to donate the *tomahawk* to the Crazy Horse Memorial in South Dakota.

The objects that once belonged to Indians are under special protection. In 1990, legislation was passed by Congress entitled the *Native American Graves Protection and Repatriation Act* (NAGPRA). Based on this act, many art objects have to be returned to Indians. Generally, the act deals with items that are important to Indians and should be returned to them, such as those dealing with their culture and national identity. The bill was enacted to help in healing the wounds of the past. Based on the NAGPRA, museums at first returned the human skeletons and remains, returning around two hundred and sixty thousand human remains. According to Indian traditions, the remains should be buried in soil.

The Congressional bill calls for the return of the entire number of human bones found on federal land that were decided held remains belonging to tribes. If it became too difficult to decide, a tribe is still entitled to request the remains based on geographical location, traditions, or even historical verbal or written evidence of location.

The museum at Harvard University gave back to Indian tribes in New Mexico around two thousand human remains that were dug out in the years 1915–1929 by American archeologist Alfred V. Kidder. For over seventy years, Harvard scientists have examined those remains and many dissertations were written. Now they are buried in Sangre de Christo Mountains not far from Santa Fe. Over a thousand Jemez Pueblo Indians took part in the burial ceremony for those remains.

The Smithsonian Institute returned a famous totem pole to its rightful owners that measured forty-five feet long and was one of the longest on record.

The University of Nebraska Museum returned seventeen hundred items, and from other museums, nearly a thousand sacred items have been returned to the Indians.

169

On this subject, all agree on the principle of returning sacred items, however, there is considerable controversy on the judging of the objects and whether or not they actually belonged to the Indians. When the items previously mentioned were returned by the museums, many scientists protested, using arguments that those objects were respected, and most importantly, they were helping the future generations to learn of and to understand the history and cultures of the Native Americans.

The NAGPRA bill became the cause of many misunderstandings, arguments and even cases in courts.

A rather famous court case against Richard Corrow took place in Scottsdale in Arizona. Corrow bought from the widow of a Navajo medicine man Yei B'chei masks paying her ten thousand dollars. After a while, he wanted to sell them to a wealthy collector from Chicago. Then he was taken to court. The prosecutor explained neither the widow nor Corrow should have sold the masks, since they were part of Indian culture/art. According to the beliefs of the Navajo, the masks still have within them *living, active spirits*.

Lawyers argue that the NAGPRA legislation is too broad and not clear. International collectors of art, giving examples, explain that often Indians themselves sell all kind of items, and then later complain and want them back. The value of many sacred items are decided in different fashion and often dependent upon the time and place.

A sixteen-ton meteorite the size of a small car fell on terrain that is now the State of Oregon. The Clacthama Indians believe the meteorite is sacred. In the nineteenth century, by devious means the meteorite was taken from the Indians and sold. In 1905, it was bought by the Williams family, who donated it to a museum. Until 1935, the meteorite named Tomannoas was exhibited in a planetarium. Now, relying upon the NAGPRA bill, the Indians asked that the meteorite be returned to them. After many debates and arguments, it was decided that the ten thousand years old meteorite would stay in the Museum of Natural History in New York. It was also decided that Indians are allowed to visit the museum every year to celebrate and conduct their ceremonies.

The remains of Indian corpses have been returned to American soil also under different circumstances – having nothing to do with the NAGPRA bill. The remains of Sioux Chief Long Wolf and an Indian girl, daughter of Ghost Dog, known as White Star, after a hundred and five years were buried in a communal cemetery on the Great Plains.

According to a historical story, Long Wolf fought with Sitting Bull and Crazy Horse against George Armstrong Custer in the Battle of the Little Big Horn in 1876. He died in London at fifty-nine years of age due to pneumonia. In England, he was featured with the group performing "Buffalo Bill Cody's Wild West Show" at London Earls Court.

The girl named White Star, from the same Buffalo Bill's troupe, collapsed from her horse on the circus arena and died shortly after Long Wolf. Long Wolf and White Star were buried in the same cemetery in West London.

Apparently (it is said) that when Long Wolf was dying, he presumably had expressed a fear that his bodily remains would be placed on a ship and put to sea (as was done to some Sioux) where, according to Indian beliefs, his spirit would wander with no end (forever). He told his wife to request his remains be sent to the soil of his ancestors.

The long odyssey of the return home of Long Wolf ended thanks to Elizabeth Knight.

Her passion for history led her to read some old documents found in an antique store, and she was touched by the story. When she learned that the dying Long Wolf wanted to return home but instead was buried in England in 1892, she was overcome with the desire to remedy the situation.

Elizabeth found the grave, then she contacted Long Wolf's wife Black Feathers, who also wanted his remains from England to return to the old familiar family surroundings. Against that idea were other members of Long Wolf's family who believed that his remains should not be exhumed. They were of the belief that someone has to die to "to fill the empty grave". They were also saying, that after Long Wolf's burial in England, a special ceremony of "farewell" had been performed in which Sitting Bull and Black Cloud took part in.

His family confirmed the information that Long Wolf took part in the Battle of the Little Big Horn and later he joined *Buffalo Bill Cody's Wild West Show*, with whom he traveled to London where he died. Everything was true according to the story.

Exhumation of Long Wolf's remains evoked much discussion; there were different opinions about the matter. The local churches did not help either. The Sioux numbered at twenty-three thousand members belong to thirty different churches, some of them mix their Christianity with tribal songs and dances.

Finally, the exhumation took place. Jessie Black Feather, eight-two year old granddaughter of Long Wolf, flew to London to accompany her grandfather's remains on the journey across the ocean. The second burial took place in an Indian ceremony in Wolf Creek in South Dakota.

"It means, he is now free" – the press quoted the words of spiritual leader Wilmer Mesteth. He would be among his own people; his remains will stay with us[101].

The subject that is of interest to the scientists but many times arouses the ire of American Indians is the case of locating the place from where the first inhabitants of the American continent came from. The scientist Dennis Stanford, archeologist from the Smithsonian Institution, for over thirty years has tried to convince people that ancestors of modern Indians came not from Asia, but they traversed the Atlantic Ocean from Europe fifteen thousand years before.

The case came to life again when the weekly "Time"[102], described the case in its cover story. Time's story followed the discovery in the current State of Washington of a skeleton named the "Kennewick Man" that was eight thousand four hundred years old and had characteristics that some people thought might have been European. A hot debate continues over this. The "Kennewick Man" seems to challenge old academic beliefs that both continents – North and South America too – were populated for the first time around ten thousand years ago by Asiatic people moving into the continents by the land platform between Siberia and Alaska.

The "Kennewick Man" is not the first skeleton with Indo-European bone structure found in North America. In 1940, the "Mummy from Nevada", was found, but of real interest to scientists was the trick on how the mummy's age of nine thousand four hundred years was determined. The initial examination of the mummy showed many similarities in the shape of bones with those of the Indo-European race. Unfortunately, to continue the examinations was not possible since the Northern Paiute tribe asked for return of the remains (based on the bill to protect graves) and for the right to bury the mummy. In 1994, anthropologists returned the mummy to them.

Note: The bill protecting the graves also applies to bits of hair – it even has to be returned to Indians.

For years, paleontologists used a technique of genetic examination of human remains that refutes many scientific stereotypes. In 1997, German scientists using genetics in paleontology examined remains of a Neanderthal man. Their analysis proved small genetic similarity between him and the modern human. Most probably he was not our ancestor.

---

[101] See. Dan Balz, *Sioux warrior's remains begin long journey home*, "Washington Post". Republished: "Houston Chronicle", September 26, 1997.
[102] March 13, 2006.

Words often are used that say Indians were part of the American continent "from the beginning of time". Some Indians believe that their people migrated to America from a different continent. They do not believe anthropologists saying they are part of a conspiracy to take Indian rights, land and cultural heritage. But not only Indians are against the European theory. Also the scientists of the Solutrean theory (an upper Paleolithic culture of Europe), among others Professor Lawrence Guy Straus from New Mexico University think that there is not any proof to believe that Solutrean people could build boats that were capable of crossing the Atlantic.

A friend of mine, archeologist Janusz Paluch, put me in touch with archeologist Radoslaw Palonka from the Jagiellonian University in Krakow, Poland who wrote me:

"Concerning the settling of the Americas, there are now two main theories or schools of thought. Some archeologists and anthropologists believe that first human migration to America took place around 30 thousand years ago through the land bridge called Bering land bridge (Beringia) that connected northeast Asia (Chukotka) and Alaska in the Ice Age (today it is the Bering Sea). Those are the believers of the so-called "long chronology". They are proved by archeological and linguistic data as well as the examination of mitochondrial DNA.

The second theory (the so-called "short chronology") says that the migration took place later (around twelve thousand years ago) and was connected with people of the Clovis culture. Clovis is archaeologically well-known and documented culture.

About at least eighteen thousand years ago in northeast Asia there was the so-called Diuktai culture that is somehow connected to migration to America".

Aleksandra Ziolkowska-Boehm

Protests as a Fight with Stereotype

December 2000. We were in Manhattan in New York. In front of the company building of the well-known fashion designer Liz Claibourne, a group of American Indians were protesting. The Indians insisted that Liz Clairborne stop the series of clothing named Crazy Horse. The next day, the press was full of stories of the event. One of the demonstration organizers, Bill Means, a member of the Oglala Lakota Sioux, had given interviews to the press. He said that to his people the use of the name of Crazy Horse for advertising clothes or any other product was improper. The use of the names of known American heroes for a similar purpose, like Martin Luther King or John F. Kennedy was also improper. He reminded the interviewers that Crazy Horse for Indians was a great chief and spiritual leader.

The Indian activists have initiated protests against the use of Indian names for sport groups, different non-Indian teams, schools, mascots, etc. Indian groups have protested against Indian names being given to sport mascots, and for singing and chanting school songs using Indian rhythms, as they found it offending.

Now protests have become official and are stressed with demonstrations that instill press interest. The demonstrations by Indians are reminders that in the past and in a similar way, Black people demonstrated against the children's book character named Little Black Sambo or Mexicans, whose feelings were hurt by the name Frito Bandito.

The names connected to the Indians are plentiful throughout the United States. Tens of sport teams still use Indian names, such as the Braves, but many teams have already changed their names. For example, the team Scalping Braves from Alcorn University changed this name that was offensive to Indians.

The St. John's University Redmen have been renamed Red Storm, Stanford University teams are now the Cardinals instead of Indians (the red color remains). In Ohio, the Miami University teams named Redskins was changed to Red Hawks.

The Marquette Warriors have changed to Golden Eagles. The Washington's Redskins professional football team name remains unchanged. In Boston and Massachusetts, Indian names cannot be used. The Cleveland Indians professional baseball team name is unchanged as is the Atlanta Braves professional baseball team name. The former team's mascot Chief Wahoo now tends to go unmentioned, and the Tomahawk Chop used by sport fans of the Atlanta Braves to express their fervor is now virtually unused.

The sport teams of the University of Illinois are named the Illini, as is the Indian confederacy. Their mascot has the name Chief Illiniwek.

In Delaware, there is an Indian River, and one of the high school teams has an Indian name, but the whole area has the name Indian River.

One Wilmington high school's sport teams are named Warriors, but the press in Delaware wrote that the name is "broad", and taken not from the Indian warriors.

A Florida state university has its sport teams named after the Seminole Indian tribe living there. The heads officials of the university said they would consider a change, but they are not in a hurry to do so. The Seminole Indians officially cooperate with the university and its sport teams. The Seminoles actually helped the university in finding its mascot the Chief Osceola. For the Indians, the chosen mascot helped to remind them of the real Osceola, who in the years 1830–1840 successfully fought the American Army. The Seminole tribe, the Indians themselves and the members of the sport teams, said with pride, that Osceola never was defeated.

The members of The Spirit Lake Sioux tribe protested that the University of North Dakota named their sport teams the Fighting Sioux[103]. The university officials in Grand Forks, as an answer to the protests of some Indians, quoted the words of Chief Skip Longie, who said that he does not object. A specially created committee for correctness still fights, saying that the name is *disrespectful and offensive*, shows no respect and creates an unfriendly atmosphere particularly when there are Indian students. Norman and I observed in the newspaper "Indian Country Today", also the university "Alumni" (Norman is an alumnus of the University of North Dakota and regularly receives that magazine) – discussions on the use of the name Fighting

---

[103] The conflict between the Indian protestors and the University of North Dakota has reached the State courts. A judge has delayed making a decision on the case and postponed a decision for three years. The University is continuing its efforts to convince the Indian protestors that the Fighting Sioux name and the logo are not an affront to them, nor meant to be disrespectful or offensive, but a symbol of pride in, admiration of and respect for the Sioux Nation.

According to the media report, May 14, 2009, North Dakota's Board of Higher Education has agreed to drop the University of North Dakota's Fighting Sioux nickname and Indian head logo, a move intended to resolve a decades-long campus dispute about whether the name demeans American Indians. The name and logo, which is a profile of an American Indian man with feathers and streaks of paint on his face, could still be saved if North Dakota's Standing Rock and Spirit Lake Sioux tribes agree to give the university permission to use them for at least 30 years.

Sioux for university sport teams. There was voting, and it was decided not to change a name so well known and recognized. The university officials reminded the Indian committee that the Indian artist Bennett Brien created the "logo" symbol for the teams that shows a profile of an Indian's head and headdress. The specially created committee answered that people should be more interested in achieving a degree for education at the University of North Dakota rather than its logo or to be members of its sport teams. The university issued a special statement[104]. The statement proclaimed that the university was proud that many of its students were of Indian origin, and that Indian chiefs and leaders were invited to see for themselves how much the university does to help them to study, learn and achieve a useful and beneficial education.

There are good relations between the Arapaho Indians and the University of Colorado whose school teams use the name – Buffalo, and as well with the University of Arizona who use Apache. Taking into consideration the popularity of particularly American football, the use of Indian names is a good way to popularize those tribes all over the country.

The majority of Indian names used do not have a negative meaning, even to the contrary, they are the result of respect and liking of every American and sport lover. As pointed out by the university officials and directors of sport clubs, the names show respect for Indian warriors and their bravery. But the explanation that only names that are liked are chosen does not help. As in an average – the teams are given the names of people or places that are liked and respected, and that by these choices, Indians are symbolized as brave in fights and strong in spirit. Therefore, association with Indian names is very positive.

Cars like Jeep Cherokee and Dodge Dakota are another example; the American Army names their helicopters after the tribal names of Apache Longbow, Kiowa Warrior, the Comanche, and the Blackhawk.

Indians are also shown on American coins. Many American towns have names related to Indians: Chicago, Milwaukee, Miami, Manhattan, also rivers: Mississippi, Missouri, Potomac, and in the state of Delaware, for example, Hockessin. In the Annex following the book, I have presented the names of states that are taken from Indian words.

For eighty years, a school in Charleston, West Virginia used Indian tribal names for dividing students into different age groups during the summer vacations. But the Indians protested. Since 2005, a bill enacted by the State does not allow schools to use Indian names, some of the

---

[104] See: "Alumni", Grand Forks, North Dakota, January/February 2001.

names were changed, some not, but it seems as though the whole case has quieted down.

Not only Indian names are used in sports. Names of different nationalities are used. For example: Irish, as Fighting Irish of Notre Dame University, Swedish as Bethany College Swedes, Scottish as The Edinburg University Fighting Scots, Canadian, as the Montreal Canadians, Aztecs as the San Diego State University Aztecs, Vikings as the Minnesota Vikings, or the others: Sonoma State University Cossacks, the Idaho Vandals, Southern California Trojans, San Diego Padres, etc. Somehow the Irish, the Swedes, the Scots, and the Canadians have not asked to change such names.

Quite a problem occurred with the town of Devils Lake in North Dakota. There is also a lake with the same name. The local Indians think using such a name is almost blasphemy, and they asked its name be changed to Spirit Lake Dakota Nation, saying that some time ago the settlers wrongly interpreted the meaning of lake Min Wakan, that means "spiritual water". In a geography dictionary, the name Devil is listed one thousand six hundred and seventy-two times, and the name Spirit only two hundred and eighty-seven times. At the same time, the inhabitants of Devils Lake protested and explained that tourists are coming because of such a name. "Indian Country Today" gave a lot of attention (published many articles) on the subject, and the journal is still dedicated to changing the name Devil.

"Lake was for us is sacred, so it is like the Vatican having the name House of Devil", the non-Indian press wrote in response, pointing out that Catholic people do not react so critically to names. The same press reminded its readers that in the State of Colorado, there are many names with the word Devil: Devil's Slide, Devil's Point, Devil's Thumb, Devil's Nose and Devil's Backbone. Pope John Paul II even celebrated mass in the stadium named Sun Devil Stadium, where the Arizona State Sun Devils football team play their games. Thank God, it was stated, Catholics did not gather a "national movement" to change the name Devil to Spirit, as Indians in North Dakota want to do.

For sure, the context in which some Indian names are used is degrading and subversive to the American Indian. Some have an immoral context, and in such cases, the Indians' protests to change them are understandable and correct. Everything started from the word s*quaw*. First, names with such a word were changed all over the globe. In many places, the word meant Indian woman, but also it was the name for an intimate part of a woman's body (vagina). According to Indian culture, it is important who is talking, how he is talking, and whether or not it is subtle. Two students from Cass Lake High School that studied Indian culture, looked into the etymology of the word *squaw*. They found the link between a description of the French term and Iroquois – the intimate women's body part. Discussions on the word showed the first meaning of *squaw* was – woman or young woman. With time, the word was distorted to a vulgar meaning (whore). The word has been the basis for many heated and loud discussions, and as a result, names with *squaw* have quickly vanished.

Many names connected with Indian history were changed, such as Squaw Valley to Valley of Peace. When in 1995, the State of Minnesota first enacted a bill to eliminate from its entire geography the word *squaw*, it had to be changed in nineteen different places. For example, the town Squaw Lake became Nature's Lake.

Of ten counties in Minnesota, two of them did not want to be pressured. They explained that names are used with respect, and they are not a joke to their officials and citizens. The people who were against changes proposed to change Squaw Bay, near the Canadian border, to Politically Correct Bay, but the commission in charge rejected their suggestion and asked them to propose a less sarcastic name.

A similar confrontation occurred in the States of Montana and Maine, and later Oklahoma and Oregon. In 2000, ornithologists changed the name o*ldsquaw,* describing a type of duck to *long-tailed duck.* Some wanted to change it to *Indian woman*, but it was not approved.

A peculiar situation developed in California that has many more geographical names using the word *squaw* than any other state. There are over a hundred - from the not well known place Squaw Camp in Glenn County to the well known (all over the world) Squaw Valley not far from Lake Tahoe.

Processing of name changes does not go fast. As some say, it is very bothersome. Californians protest, write petitions to prove the names on Indian land should not be changed. The island of White Squaw in the state of Maine belongs to the Penobscot Indians.

Some Americans are skeptical of this wave of correctness. They say, Indians can disappear from everyday life if the Indian names are removed from sport teams. The remaining names would be names of cowboys, bison, animals, birds, etc. The lack of Indian names in the future could surprise Indians, they might consider it as discrimination and their opinions might change.

Popular colored pencils by Crayola have in their pallet several kinds of red color – red with reddish was called *Indian red*. The Crayola factory explains that the color was born from pigment of such colors, very popular in India. Children who use the pencils call the names straight: *Indian red,* as the color of American Indians. Now the teachers think that the word Indian should be used only in describing the country. The color was created in 1958, and since then, more than thirteen million pencils are produced each year. On a politically correct wave, the name was changed. In the past, it happened only twice – the color *prussian blue to midnight blue*, because teachers said children did not know the history of Prussia. In 1962, color *flesh* was changed to *peachy*, because not everyone has the same skin color, it was explained.

An interesting case of political sensitivity I read in "The Washington Post"[105]. The discussion confirmed that Indians still have to fight with stereotypes. Myrna Mooney (Sacred Beaver Woman), activist on behalf of Indians, was born on the Blackfeet Reservation in Montana. As a graduate of the University of Colorado, later she took part in action whose purpose was to have removed – or at least to cover – from one of the government buildings – a mural – the huge painting from 1930 titled *Dangers of the Mail*. The mural shows Indians murdering white half-naked women and with knives stabbing white men in the back. Myrna, with a group of Indians, organized a protest in which they stated that it was a false history of American Indians and proposed the painting – mural – be removed. In response, a new commission was established, and they stated that the painting – mural - was an integral part of the building. Indians responded by questioning – what if the mural was a public display painting showing the battle of Wounded Knee or Sand Creek, showing hundreds of Indians murdered by white people. Or – what if it was a public display painting showing African Americans murdering white women. "For sure, there would be protests, so we do it exactly the same" – was their explanation.

The agitators for leaving such paintings – not removing them - said that the building Ariel Rios is old and has a historic value, and the mural is done on thin canvas. Moving it from the wall would destroy it. (As far as I know, the mural was not removed, it was covered).

When we were living in Dallas, Texas, the newspaper "Dallas Morning News"[106] published an article that Navajo Indians in Arizona protested against the name for a virus that killed forty people, including Indians. The virus was named Muerto (Death) Canyon after a canyon on their reservation. Such a proposal was made according to the custom of giving the virus the name of the place where it was discovered. The elderly of the Navajo voted unanimously (fifty-two to zero), so the center for fighting the disease in Atlanta Centers for Disease Control and

[105] See: Fern Shen, *The Past and present collide on a Washington mural*, November 24, 2006, pg. A29.
[106] See: April. 23, 1994.

Prevention would not name the virus Muerto Canyon. As an answer to their petition, the Indians received the assuredness that the committee would take into consideration their request. When I checked over ten years later, the virus is listed under two names Sin Nombre (Without a name) virus (SNV), but mainly as Muerto Canyon virus.

In the State of Arizona, officials wanted to rename the super highway three hundred and forty-seven to John Wayne Parkway, in remembrance of the well-known actor who owned a ranch in that area. Indians protested. They did not want such an honor bestowed upon the actor who received his fame in movies portraying him as one who fought with Indians. Part of the road passed through the Gila River Indian Reservation. For that part of the highway, it was proposed to name it 'The American Indian Veterans Memorial Parkway', but it was decided to stay with the old name Arizona three hundred and forty-seven.

At the end of November a few years ago, Norman and I went to San Francisco, where my son, Thomas, was working as an architect. I remember the day quite well. It was the fourth Thursday of November, when all over the whole United States, Thanksgiving is celebrated as probably the most liked and popular holiday. On the island of Alcatraz, as I learned, around three thousand people came – white and Indians. They gathered to protest.

When all over the country people celebrated Thanksgiving, the day remembering the beginning of a difficult life for immigrants coming from Europe, the group of Indians, the natives of America – on the island of Alcatraz celebrated a day of anti-thanksgiving. For Indians, it was a day remembering their loss of land to the newcomers from Europe. Television showed these protesters and gave them voice.

"It is a sad day for us" – said Bear Lincoln who performed a ritual of cleaning the land and expelling away bad spirits – in a praying circle created by Indians. "Our big mistake was helping the newcomers to survive the first winter. They betrayed us when they received back their strength", Lincoln continued in his speech.

The tradition of eating turkey for Thanksgiving comes from the feast by the Pilgrims, the first immigrants in a New World. With thanks to God for a successful yield of crops in the year 1620, they ate the feast with the Wampanoag Indians.

Around fifty English settlers were taught by around a hundred Native Americans how to cultivate the land and how to hunt for the wild turkey and other game. At the same time, the Indians helped the newcomers to survive the first difficult winters.

Aleksandra Ziolkowska-Boehm

Historians say that the Puritans not the Pilgrims, who came ten years after the Pilgrims, changed the events and started the murders, first murdering Pequot Indians and later the other tribes.

Europe, between the sixteenth and seventeenth centuries, was a theater for reforms in the Roman Catholic Church. Puritans, called reformers, to avoid repercussions and to look for freedom of religion, moved to Holland in 1609. From Holland, they decided to go to North America. They called themselves Pilgrims, because they wanted to spread Jesus Christ's teaching into a different continent. During their first journey across the Atlantic, a hundred and two passengers consisting of families and single people were on board the sailing ship. Also on board the ship there were thirty-one children of various ages, including infants. The leader of the journey was William Bradford, later the first governor of the colony in Massachusetts, named Plymouth as a remembrance of the port from where they started the journey (Clint Eastwood says his roots trace back to William Bradford).

The passengers aboard the Mayflower were recorded by Bradford on a passenger's list, and he described their fortunes. Bradford was the governor for thirty-five years, and he made copious notes. Thanks to them, we now have a quiet knowledge of the Pilgrims. The descriptions of their lives can catch one's breath. The first 6 people died before the end of the year, during the following three months, thirty-eight died. Death touched mainly children and women. Four entire families died completely, four children were left without anyone to care for them.

Pilgrims were people from different backgrounds and a different class of society, including troublemakers. Among them was John Beelington who received a death sentence by hanging. He was the first human being on the American Continent who was put to death.

One of the women, Susanna White, during her first five months in America became a mother, a widow and a fiancée. It happened when she gave birth to her son, her husband soon died, and then she married Edward Winslow.

Probably the best known female Pilgrim was the attractive and intelligent Priscillla Mullins, who came with her brother and parents. Her sibling and parents died soon. Two men fell in love or were at least attracted to her. The ups and downs of those feelings were the basis for a poem by Henry Wadsworth Longfellow[107]. Priscilla chose the younger man, gave birth to ten children and lived a long life. She was the grandmother of sixty-one grandchildren and four hundred great-grandchildren.

---

[107] See: Henry W. Longfellow, *The Courtship of Miles Standish*, (1858).

182

The longest living Pilgrim was Elizabeth Hopkins, who during the journey was four years old.

In 1952, a movie was made about the unhappy love life, apparently between Dorothy May wife of William Bradford and Jones, Captain of the ship Mayflower. Dorothy fell overboard from the ship leaving her two year old son.

During the journey, a sad story happened to four children aged four to eight, who were members of the Royal family. Their father had taken them from their mother, was granted custody, and he brought them aboard the Mayflower. Only one child, the boy named Richard, survived the journey,

All the Pilgrims went through hunger, illnesses and poverty. They became a symbol of survival and fighting the obstacles brought on by life. The first person that came to welcome the Pilgrims was the Indian Squanto. He became a friend of white people until his death in 1622.

Winter of the first year 1620 was bitter and long. From hunger, lack of nutrition and from cold, forty-seven people died. They buried their dead at night so the surrounding Indians would not know how pitifully few they were. There were very careful in dealings with Indians.

It was after the arrival of many hundreds of Puritans some ten years later when incidents such as the Pequot slaughter happened.

Bradford wrote in his diary, that in the winter 1620/1621, Squanto taught the colonial people how to build houses, and in the spring, he showed them the secrets of the land – how to sow corn, where to fish, and how to make traps to catch wild game.

The first harvest was very poor, but the settlers were able to enjoy corn, oats and beans. The pilgrims enjoyed a holiday for three days. In Plymouth, there were seven private houses and four municipal buildings. A big parade was organized with soldiers showing their skills. Governor Bradford took part in the celebration as well as invited Indians – Massasoith, chief of the Qampanoag tribe with his ninety warriors. It was recorded, the Indians took part in sports competition and racing. The Indians brought with them game meat, ducks, goose, white corn bread, fish and vegetables, and for dessert prunes, dry berries and wine from wild grapes.

There is no mention of turkey or pumpkin pie that now is on every table during Thanksgiving dinner.

My observations in California were not mine alone. As I learned, for years the Thanksgiving holiday is interrupted by a group of Indians and other protestors. Frank B. (Wamsutta) James, from the Wampanoag tribe and a known musician who plays the trumpet, in 1970 described the holiday as "racist" and disgracing for Indians as the holiday honors the

Aleksandra Ziolkowska-Boehm

invasion of America and turning Native Americans into Christianity. He proposed naming Thanksgiving – National Day of Mourning for Native Americans.

A momentous discussion came after the movie *How the West Was Lost* was released. It reminded one of the beautiful movie *How the West Was Won* with James Stewart and Gregory Peck as heroes who were continually pushing West to the Pacific. It seemed like a fairy tale compared to a 6-part movie produced by Chris Wheeler showing another picture of how the Indian lands were taken over. Many Indian tribes think that the West was not won but lost, since during the many battles that took place over 50 years, the Indians lost their land and culture.

The movie *How the West Was Lost* shows fierce battles with the Navajo, Nez Perce, Apache, Cheyenne and Lakota Sioux Indians. They took place in locations like the Little Big Horn, Sand Creek and White Bird Canyon. The Indian heroes are Sitting Bull, Chief Joseph and Cochise.

One of the first episodes shows a young Indian woman, who says "No one discovered us, we were here. Similarly, if we were to go to Spain and say to the Spanish that we discovered Spain, the Spanish would be surprised and irritated. Americans should be taught the real history".

Jim Thorpe and Others

Sport heroes

Norman reminded me not to forget about the famous Indian sports heroes, such as Billy Mills or Jim Thorpe. America loves sport, boys from childhood play on different teams, learn to play as a group, learn to back out, to adjust, to resign and how to lose.

The committee that decided the itinerary of the Olympic torch in 1996 routed the fragment in Oklahoma in such a way, that it went through Jim Thorpe's birthplace. The local government of Prague (his birthplace) and Thorpe's family for years had tried to achieve this. They protested the choice of Yale as Thorpe's birthplace when first it was mistakenly chosen over Prague. Corrections were made, and Grace Thorpe, daughter of the sport hero (who died in 1953) met with Lori Stone, the president and organizer for the running of the Olympic torch. Grace officially stated how happy she was with her father's remembrance.

"From the beginning we wanted to underline Jim Thorpe's great achievements in the Olympics", said Ginger Watkins, the main manager.

Each of the citizens of Prague were supposed to get (as a Christmas present in 1995) the message that Grace Thorpe officially stated the route of the Olympic torch was going to go through the Sauk and Fox Nation and through Jim Thorpe's birthplace.

Thorpe was born in 1888 in a one room house in Keokuk Falls to Hiram Thorpe, a farmer and Mary James, a Potawatomi Indian and descendent of Black Hawk, a Sauk and Fox chief. Thorpe was born a twin, but he lost his twin brother Charles who died at age of nine. His Indian name, perhaps a premonition, was "Wa-Ho-Thuk" meaning "Bright Path" which was proven to be ahead of him. The Indian town Keokuk Falls does not exist any longer, but was located on the outskirts of today's town Prague. He was raised on the Sauk and Fox Reservation. From 1904 until perhaps 1910, he attended the Carlisle Industrial Indian School in Pennsylvania. While at Carlisle, his football talents were recognized by election to the third team All-America in 1908 and the first team in 1909 and 1910. Thorpe lived for awhile in Yale, but most of his adult years were spent in travel taking part in sports competition. When he won gold medals in the 1912 Olympics in Antwerp, Belgium for the pentathlon and decathlon events, the King of Sweden, Gustaw V, shook his hand and pronounced to him "Sir, you are the greatest athlete in the world". Thorpe replied, "Thanks, King". In the 1950's, a poll of

Associated Press sports writers affirmed what King Gustav said, naming Thorpe the greatest athlete of the first half of the twentieth century.

Another very well known Indian athlete is Billy Mills, the distance runner, who as a United States Marine, won a gold medal for the ten thousand meters race in the 1969 Olympics in Tokyo, Japan.

Billy Mills was born in 1939 on the Pine Ridge Reservation in South Dakota. His family was Oglala Lakota Sioux. He received the Lakota Sioux name "Makata Taka Hela", which means "love your country" or "respect the soil". Orphaned at twelve years of age, he was raised in severe poverty. With determination he dedicated himself to sports. He attended school on the reservation and later the Haskell Institute in Lawrence, Kansas. Then he received an athletic scholarship to the University of Kansas. Later, he joined the United States Marines. In 1983, based on his life story, a movie *Running Brave* was made. Billy Mills now lives with his family in Sacramento, California, and is in close touch with the Pine Ridge Reservation. He established the organization Running Strong for American Indian Youth, which supports Indian youth and their families on the Reservation[108]. Billy Mills wrote a book about his life entitled *Wokini*[109]. At the St. Labre Indian School in Montana, a glass display case is dedicated to Mills, and several thoughts from his book are presented there. I quote those that I wrote down, and I consider them a testament to his wisdom:

"God has given me the ability. The rest is up to me. Believe. Believe. Believe..."

"My life is a gift to me from my Creator.

What I do with my life is my gift back to the Creator."

"The ultimate is not to win, but to reach within the depths of your capabilities and to compete against yourself to the greatest extent possible. When you do that, you have dignity. You have the pride. You can walk about with character and pride no matter in what place you happen to finish."

"I was constantly told and challenged to live my life as a warrior. As a warrior, you assume responsibility for yourself. The warrior humbles himself. And the warrior learns the power of giving."

Another great athlete was Allie Pierce Reynolds, called "Superchief", and a Creek Indian by origin as well as a star of the New York Yankees professional baseball team. Reynolds is considered one of the *Yankees' greatest pitchers*, having performed the remarkable feat of

---

[108] Norman and I support this organization and regularly read their bulletin.

[109] *Wokini* - in Lakota it means – searching for a new beginning. Billy Mills, Wijubum Hay House Inc. 1999.

pitching two "no hit" games in the same season 1957. After his death in 1994, the state of Oklahoma established (in his name) a yearly scholarship award for the best student in Oklahoma high schools who had achieved scholastic and athletic excellence as well as excellence of character.

Senator

Senator Ben Nighthorse Campbell, of Northern Cheyenne ancestry from Colorado, was raised in poverty; he did not finish high school. He took part in the Korean War, and became an Olympic athlete. He was also a rancher, teacher, jewelry designer, and the first American Indian (since 1929) who was elected to the United States Senate. In his public appearances, many times he talked about his life experiences and how they shaped him:

"I know what it means to work hard and not to have money for a doctor, I know how to load a lorry, how tired children sleep during their school lessons, I know what it means to be hungry."

Born in 1933, Campbell's young years were spent in Auburn, California. Most of the time, his father was drunk. His mother, a daughter of Portuguese immigrants, suffered from family and health problems and spent much time in hospitals. Once, when she was in the hospital for an extended time, Ben and his sister were sent for 6 months to a foster home.

As a young boy he became interested in judo, and dropped out of high school. He enlisted in the Air Force, and was sent to Korea. After his return to the States, he completed high school and entered San Jose State University. He returned to his interest in judo, and was sent to Tokyo where he studied Japanese culture. In 1963, he won a gold medal in judo for the United States in the Pan American Games. During subsequent training, he injured his knee and was unable to compete. Even though he won no medal in 1964, he was the one who carried the American flag during the closing ceremony of the Pan American Games. He met his wife Linda while training for judo. They married in 1966 and have two children. He became the deputy sheriff in Sacramento, California, taught judo, coached Olympic teams and gave advice to Indian prisoners in the San Quentin Prison. He started a jewelry making business, and for his own designs of jewelry received many awards. When he started to have health problems, he moved to a ranch in Ignacio in Colorado, raising cattle and training horses.

Ben Nighthorse Campbell came into politics almost by accident. He took part in a meeting of the Democratic Party since his friend was running for the sheriff's office. He became a spokesman on his friend's behalf. His speeches made impressions on everybody, and he was asked if he would like to go into politics. Six months later, he gave his thirteen thousand dollars towards a campaign for the United States Senate. His supporters gave the rest of the money. He won the election, and in 1992, he became a senator.

While he was in Congress from which he resigned in 2005, he did a lot for the Northern Cheyenne Indians. He fought against Indians being stereotyped. He introduced the bill to build the Indian Museum near the Smithsonian Institution. In 1992, he was instrumental in having the name of Custer Battlefield National Museum in Montana changed to the Little Big Horn Battlefield National Monument.

In his speeches, when he talked to Indians, he tried to instill the thought to give their children a better life and not to forget about their past and traditional family values.

"We say a nice home and lots of money are symbols of success. But for Indians, it is the other way around: Success isn't what you have, it's what you've given away. The most revered member of the tribe may be the poorest, because giving away increases your stature. We should place greater value on what we contribute to society rather than what we accumulate. I want people to see American Indians as part of modern America. Too many people think we are a dead culture. But that's not true"[110].

Professor Bruce E. Johansen underlines the point that Ben Nighthorse Campbell is one of a few Indians, who achieved such a high position in American politics. The other was Charles Curtis, a Senator and the Vice President during the presidency of Herbert Hoover. Curtis was criticized as an idea maker as a result of the so-called Curtis Bill of 1898, that pushed Indians to assimilate with the whites by taking away their land[111].

Astronaut

John Herrington, when a child in the late 1960's, collected paper and dreamed that some day he would be sent to the Moon. He introduces himself as a Chickasaw Indian, even though some say he does not have Indian blood.

---

[110] See: Wallace Terry, *Success Isn't What You Have – It's What you've Given Away*, "Parade Magazine", June 2, 1996, pg. 17.
[111] See: Bruce E.Johansen, Ben Nighthorse Campbell. *The heritage of Cheyenne*, "Tawacin", Nr 3 (751) fall 2006.

"When I say I am an Indian, people ask how much Indian blood I have. I answer one eighth. My maternal grandmother was an Indian and spoke only in the Chickasaw language. I do not have much Indian blood, but what is most important, in my heart I feel Indian".

Born in Watemuka in Oklahoma, he was raised not far from the Chickasaw Indians. His family often moved from one place to another. They lived in Colorado Springs, Colorado, Riverton in Wyoming, and in Plano, Texas, where he finished high school. At the University of Colorado, he studied mathematics. In Colorado Springs he entered the Air Force Academy. He says that his favorite movie is A*n Officer and a Gentleman.*

When NASA was recruiting candidates for astronauts, he came forward. Of one hundred and twenty candidates, only forty-four qualified. John Herrington was one of them. He signed up for the astronaut program, and in 2002, he was sent into the cosmos. He had with him the flag of the Chickasaw Nation.

Polish accents

Capuchin Father Charles Joseph Chaput O.F.M.Cap, whom Pope John Paul II nominated as the bishop and deacon of the diocese in Rapid City, South Dakota, took part in the international Day of Youth on Jasna Gora, Czestochowa in Poland. Two years later, he took part in a similar youth gathering in Denver, Colorado. In 1997, the Pope from Poland nominated him as archbishop in Denver.

Charles Chaput is Indian-French ancestry. His grandmother was Potawatomi Indian. The diocese in Rapid City covers over half the State of South Dakota - East from close to the Missouri River. The diocese of Rapid City consists of thirty-six thousand Catholics of which forty percent are American Indians. The diocese has a hundred and ten parishes. On the terrene of South Dakota, there are eight reservations where Indians of the Dakota, Lakota, Nakota, Oglala, Brule, Hunkpapa, Teton, and Yankton Sioux live (they are called The Great Sioux Nation). Of seventy thousand Indians (representing ten percent of South Dakota's population), around thirty thousands are Roman Catholic and Episcopalian. The remainder are Indians who worship in accordance with their ancestral culture.

In the autumn of 1996, Bishop Charles Joseph Chaput, with the daughter of sculpture Korczak Ziolkowski, visited Rome. They presented a special gift to the Pope – a copy of Korczak's sculpture of Ignacy Paderewski.

Aleksandra Ziolkowska-Boehm

Actors and writers

Among the famous with American Indian roots are Elvis Presley, Kevin Costner and Brad Pitt. Claiming a Cherokee father are actors James Garner (born in 1928 in Norman, Oklahoma), Johnny Depp, and Burt Reynolds. Robert Mitchum (1917–1997) said in a TV interview with Dick Cavett, that his father was a full blooded Indian. The Encyclopedia Britannica says his father Robert James Thomas Mitchum was of Scottish Irish origin, and his mother Blackfeet Indian. Mitchum's father died in a accident when he was eighteen months old. He was then sent to live with his older sister and grandparents in Felton, Delaware (I always like to note facts/trivia concerning the state where Norman and I live).

Known Indian actors are Graham Greene and Wes Studi.

Graham Greene, an Oneida Indian, was born in 1952 on the Six Nations Reserve from Ontario in Canada. He performed major roles in two of my favorite movie *Thunderheart and Dances With Wolves*.

Wes Studi was born in 1947 in a small town in Oklahoma. He is a full blooded Cherokee Indian. He played in *Dances With Wolves, The Last of the Mohicans, Geronimo*. Before he became an actor, he took part in the Vietnam War and was a trainer of horses.

Will Sampson (1933–1987), a Creek Indian, took part in *White Buffalo* and *Orca*, but his most remembered role is thanks to the film *One Flew Over the Cuckoo's Nest,* where he played a Sioux Indian. Everybody remembers his erect posture, height and stoicism.

Popular singer Shania Twain presents herself as an Ojibwa Indian. She was born in Windsor, Ontario, Canada as Eileen Regina Edwards. Her mother, after divorcing Clarence Edwards remarried. Her new husband Jerry Twain, Ojibwa Indian adopted his then six years old stepdaughter Eileen, who according to Indian custom became fifty percent Indian. When Eileen was twenty-two yeas old, both parents died in an accident, and Eileen took care of her stepsiblings. In 1991 at twenty-seven years old, she changed her name to Shania that in Ojibwa language means *I am on my way.*

Among writers of Indian origin, a most known and respected writer of Sioux origin is Vine Deloria Jr. (1933–2005), author of over twenty books, the most known is *Custer Died for Your Sins*. He is an author of the saying *"We have brought the white man a long way"*. Deloria was born near the Pine Ridge Reservation, and on the reservation he attended grammar school.

Louise Erdrich, Ojibwa on her mother's side, spent her childhood in Wahpeton, N.D., where both parents taught at a Bureau of Indian Affairs

190

school. She writes the saga of the North Dakota Chippewa families. Erdrich is the author of the novels: *Love Medicine, The Beet Queen, Tracks, The Antelope Wife* and *The Bingo Palace*. As John *Skow*[112] wrote, her central theme comes through clearly: "reservation life does little to preserve the strengths of Native American culture and is a cruel hothouse"

Jamake Highwater (1930–2001), is the author of the books *Anpao: An American Indian Odyssey* or *The Sun, He Dies: A Novel About the End of the Aztec World* who changed his biography several times. Only when he became older did he admit that he was an Indian boy adopted by a white couple. None can check this disclosure because people who raised him have passed away.

In 1999 "Esquire" published an essay *The Blood Runs Like a River Through My Dreams*. The text caused considerable interest and was nominated for the National Magazine Award. The Press wrote about its author, a talented Native American born on an Indian reservation. Nasdijj was introduced as the son of a Navajo woman and white man. When over a million copies of his book were sold, it came out that Nasdijj was a different person. He was not Native American, and his real name is Timothy Patrick Barrus. When his fraud came out, he defended himself in an aggressive manner saying that people should not care who he is, that a real scandal is the poverty among Indians.

During the years 1981–1983, I lived in Canada and read the books by W.P. Kinsella. I brought them with me to Poland and proposed them to a Warsaw publishing house Czytelnik. There were titles *Shoeless Joe, Born Indian, Indiana Comes Home*. In 1993 living in Dallas, I read that Canadian Indians had started a campaign against Kinsella, even expecting libraries in Ontario to remove his books. The group called The Onkwehonwe Anti-Racism Alliance stated that Kinsella presented a false and damaging stereotype of Indians. The Orillia and District Public Library's board refused to remove Kinsella's books as demanded by the Indians and they kept the books in circulation.

Kinsella was quoted: "All of these characters exist in my head. This is all make-believe. And I have a right to do it".[113]

Are the Native Americans a New Age of warriors who survived a holocaust of the Wild West territory? The question was raised in the 1996 PBS documentary movie series "The West" by producer Ken Burns. The answer was left to the viewers.

---

[112] See: An Old Bear. Laughing, "Time", February 7, 1994.
[113] See: "Dallas Morning News", October 22, 1993.

The Cherokee, as I wrote earlier, are considered as one of the Five Civilized Tribes, along with the Choctaw, Chickasaw, Creek and Seminole. They had a standard of life higher than some Europeans. The name Five Civilized Tribes was given them since they practiced many European customs. The Cherokee are the only tribe to use an alphabet in their language. They were the first to develop a dictionary for their language. Their women wore dresses from cloth they wove themselves, men somehow fashioned trousers and kinds of turbans. (Even though carefully dressed, it did not save them from tragedies and murders). They befriended the first English settlers to live among them, and they helped each other. The Cherokee origin of the famous humorist Will Rogers was well known. He often said: "My ancestors didn't come over on the Mayflower, but they met them at the boat".

I became interested in Sherman Alexie born in 1966 on a Spokane reservation in Wellpinit, Washington. A Native American writer, he has received awards for his novels and stories showing current life on reservations. He is the author of such books as *Ten Little Indians*, *Reservation Blues*, *The Lone Ranger and Tonto Fistfight in Heaven*. Sherman Alexie is a Spokane Indian. He was born ill, and at six years of age underwent difficult surgery. In time, he regained his health and became a very bright man. He graduated from the University of Washington.

Sherman Alexie's novel titled *Indian Killer*[114] describes a man named John Smith, an Indian who was adopted by a white family. John does not know much about his ancestry; he only knows his mother's tribe and who at fourteen gave birth to him. He lives a lonely reclusive life working at a steel company in Seattle. After years of searching for his roots with no results, he starts to kill white people whom he met accidentally. In the end, he kills himself. It is a well-written very sad story. The anger and fury that is in the hero of this book is not explained. The white people he meets are shown as naive and good-natured. The end shows that even though John Smith dies, his "Indian revenge" does not die with him. It is going to last.

Interesting is Sherman Alexie's saying: *Indians call each other Indians. Native American is a guilty white liberal thing.*

Parker McKenzie (1897–1999), a Kiowa Indian linguist created a dictionary of the Kiowa language. He is supposed to have said that the Kiowa do not have a word for the English *hello*, because they do not see the need for it. He was born in a tipi not far from Rainy Mountain in Oklahoma. As a child, he spoke only in Kiowa and was punished for it.

---

[114] See: Atlantic Monthly Press, 1996.

He never was educated but was awarded an honorary doctorate degree from the University of Colorado.

When dying he was supposed to have said "Maybe next year I will go hunting for buffalo", because in Kiowa there is no word for good-bye".

Aleksandra Ziolkowska-Boehm

| Black Elk, survivor of Battle of Little Big Horn 1876. Photo by Bill Groethe, 1948 | Children at St. Joseph's Indian School Pow-Wow 1999. Photo by Aleksandra Ziolkowska-Boehm |

Children Dancers. St. Joseph's Indian School Pow-Wow. 1999.
Photo by Norman Boehm

Code Talkers Cpl. Henry Baker Jr. and
Pvt. George H. Kirk, Navajo's,
Courtesy of National Archives.

Grave of Red Cloud, Pine Ridge
Reservation Cemetery.
Photo by Aleksandra Ziolkowska-
Boehm.

Crazy Horse Sculpture in progress- South Dakota.
Courtesy of Crazy Horse Memorial.

Indian Girl. St. Joseph's Indian School Pow-Wow. 1999. Photo by Aleksandra Ziolkowska-Boehm.

Indian Dancer. St. Joseph's Indian School Pow-Wow 1999. Photo by Aleksandra Ziolkowska-Boehm.

Drummers, St. Joseph's Indian School Pow-Wow 1999. Photo by Norman Boehm.

197

Aleksandra Ziolkowska-Boehm

Entering Pine Ridge Reservation. Norman
Boehm at entrance. South Dakota, 1995.
Photo by Aleksandra Ziolkowska-Boehm.

Mildred Imach Cleghton.
Courtesy of "Oklahoma Today"

January 17, 2004, St. Labre Indian School Pow-Wow in Bel Air, Maryland.
Aleksandra 2nd from left. Rod Trahan at right.
Photo by Norman Boehm.

An Interview with Rex Alan Smith
A Writer[115] and Rancher

Will the real Indians please stand up?

Aleksandra Ziolkowska-Boehm (AZB) : Your book "Moon of Popping Trees" came from an interest in the story of the Wounded Knee tragedy of 1890. You were asked to write an article first. As you describe in "the preface", to be "accurate", you decided to write a whole book dedicated to that subject.

Rex Alan Smith (RAS) : *"Reader's Digest" that earlier published my article on flying, was looking for someone to do an in-depth study on: "What Do Americans Indians Really Want".*

In 1977, there was an occupation of the Bureau of Indian Affairs building in Washington DC by the American Indian Movement. All kinds of protests were going on. In 1973, there was a second occupation of Wounded Knee. "Reader's Digest" was interviewing a number of writers to do an in-depth study. They chose me to do an article on Indians.

I stayed on reservations, interviewed my way through the Bureau of Indian Affairs, and the Indian Health Service. I attended Indian political meetings and conventions. I did three months of academic research for reinforcement. The editors agreed with my idea that you can't understand the present if you can't understand the past. Out of that came the book "Moon of Popping Trees" as an assignment from "Reader's Digest" to help understand the past, "this knotty", ever present, often all too complicated situation.

AZB : The difficulties you met in "accuracy" were several. You mentioned that there was no written language for the Indians to record their stories of earlier time. Indian history was written by non-Indians and was based on oral accounts. How did you overcome that problem?

RAS : *It took a couple of years of my life to write the book. The difficulty was – like you said – primarily based on two reasons. One, No written language existed for Indians to record their stories and two,*

---

[115] REX ALAN SMITH – is the author of *Moon of Popping Trees* (referenced in the above interview), *The Carving of Mount Rushmore*, and *One Last Look*, a sentimental return to World War II bomber bases of the American Eight Air Force in England. He resides in Rapid City, South Dakota.

Aleksandra Ziolkowska-Boehm

Modern history was written by non-Indians based on oral accounts. It was based on accounts to the extent they had to be. The non-Indian and European invaders arrived and could start recording. My research was of written material, like diaries, letters, history and transcriptions of interviews.

I read the Army records, War Department records, State records, talked to descendants and survivors of Wounded Knee, or descendants of survivors of Wounded Knee. I was given a lot a good stuff, but if you work in the line of controversial history, you are dealing with people who have victims or who feel wronged. If that wrong has been passed down as a memory from generation to generation, much of those accounts are hardly reliable. People talking to you think what they tell you is reliable, of course. I know many people on the reservation, and family after family will know the truth about Wounded Knee (They got it from a grandfather or grandmother or a great grandparent, or somebody). Their accounts are lengthy but factual.

I availed myself of information from as many sources as I could find. I filtered it down, put together the incidents that held together and that made sense. I had to fight the battle of sorting out fact from fiction, especially on testy and controversial subjects. On controversial subjects, there was a lot of visiting of "revisionist history", people writing as they think it should have been. Cutting through "revisionist history" is a "whale" of a problem. In a given situation, if it doesn't seem to make sense, usually it doesn't.

Other difficulties were with Indian genealogy. Dewey Beard started life as Dewey Horned Cloud, and he was the Watamajah at the time of Wounded Knee. For the rest of his life, he was Dewey Beard. That's what drives you nuts when studying Indian genealogy.

On Indian history, a lot of it is written and taken as gospel by people who wrote the history to suit their attitudes rather than (as they should have) forming their attitudes to suit the history.

I overcame the problem to the extent I did, and according to the receptions the book still gets after twenty-five years, I did a good job of it.

AZB : A number of times you questioned the stories repeated for years. For example, the story about the wagon full of whisky, that in reality was just a keg.

RAS : *As I said, I got everything I could from wherever I could, especially the main and controversial points. I put together those things that seemed to fit and which made sense. For example you mentioned the wagonload of whiskey. Author after author has written that the soldiers at Wounded Knee were drunk. To get more drama out of it, phrases like*

"I'll bet you didn't know that" were used making it more biased like the soldiers were all drunk. The facts from research confirmed that a keg of whiskey was sent to the officers to celebrate the capture of Big Foot. Down through history, the keg became a bigger keg, became a barrel and ultimately a wagonload of whiskey. The keg was a half-gallon keg[116] or one drink for each of the officers. Second, soldiers have been known to drink but don't have a wagonload of whiskey with them out in the field, and if they did, every officer involved would have been fired out of the Army. Yet, a few years ago a lady doing an article on Wounded Knee, was referred to me as someone who knew what he was talking about. She asked about the whiskey, and I explained how it could not have been a wagon load of whiskey at Wounded Knee and that the soldiers could not have been drunk out there. She listened and thanked me. But, she liked the wagonload of whiskey better and that's how she wrote it.

AZB : Thanks to your perseverance and persistence you also find new circumstances of capturing Chief Big Foot.

RAS : *When dealing with problems around the time of the death of Sitting Bull, I was able to get into Army records. Around the time that Big Foot was going to Pine Ridge (Wounded Knee), I was able to read War Department records of reports from patrols going out daily on the reservation looking for Indians, or whatever they were doing. In due course, I was able to get records of the Agents on the reservations and into papers of the post traders. The recount tells you when Big Foot was apprehended in the wagon, drops of his blood from his nose were freezing in the wagon bed. Sure, it makes the story all the more pungent, and authors have been repeating this version for years. Once in a while, we get a story as "a little grain of sand on the hill of history". I was able to provide such an event a couple of places in my book.*

It was December 29th, South Dakota in winter is God's icebox, and people have seen pictures of the bodies in the snow. Naturally, it had to be frigid and everybody freezing their tails off. Stories were told that the Indians slept with their rifles in their blankets so that the oil would not congeal. Such a thing doesn't happen, but it's a good story. That author was a bit inconsistent because the next day, he maintained the Indians were unarmed.

My tip off was from a newspaper article that stated the soldiers had taken off their coats and all anyone could talk about was the weather. I went to the Government Weather Bureau records, and sure enough, in surrounding areas, the Signal Corp kept records. I checked records for the entire area, and it tuned out that a warm pattern had moved in,

---

[116] 2 quarts

Aleksandra Ziolkowska-Boehm

perhaps it was a Chinook situation for the whole area. In December, when Big Foot was apprehended and his blood was freezing in the wagon, the temperature was at least fifty degrees Fahrenheit. It was a beautiful rather warm day!

As the truth falls into the hands of those who are trying to make a wrong story, as wrong as possible, they exaggerate to make it a totally one-sided story.

AZB : As we know, in the past, Indian stories were written mostly as fictional romantic novels. How much in those written books did pathos and feelings of emotions overcome the truth?

RAS : *American Indian history really is, as most people know it, a morality play... a pure good versus pure evil. In the old days, the visitors tended to make all Indians evil, and the frontiersmen and the settlers coming in all good. Then, back at the time that "Popping Trees" was written, the coin had flipped over, and now it was the fashion to assume all the Indians had been good, and all the white people were all dishonest and out to rob the Indians.*

Writers, for whatever reason, tended to exaggerate the truth to make everything as grim and pathetic as possible. Certainly, it makes a better story for them if everyone is freezing to death at Wounded Knee on the infamous day rather then the day before, which was one of the nicest days of that winter.

I assume that these words I preach you are somehow for people who don't know how these things were. So many people don't realize how much fictional history we have.

You make the point and it is true. In the late 1800's, writers were pushing out novels about the frontiers, and people were taking them as fact. Before the twenty-first century, writers out on the frontiers could write whatever they wanted, and readers wouldn't know the difference. Today, writers can still write on a subject without too much concern for actual fact. Even with the average population today, the reader wouldn't know the difference.

There is a phrase given in speeches "Will the real Indians please stand up?" Hollywood type panel show contestants try to guess the occupation of a space walker, a plumber etc. and finally the moderator asks" Will the real space walker or plumber please stand up".

AZB : How much has the movie industry helped to create the image of the American Indians to the rest of the world?

RAS : *About American Indians even today and I feel very strongly about this, we have two sets of Indians. One set is the real Indians and the other set is the indented Indians as from films. Hollywood, the movie industry really helped this along. In the late 1800's, writers were* *pushing out novels about the frontiers and people were taking them as fact.*

Movies got into the act with cowboys and Indians, and it became very romantic. Writers could write these wonderful stories without worrying if readers would know the difference.

An example: maybe you can use this somewhere. As far as I know there is no incident of Indians attacking a circled wagon train. There were times when they did attack settlers going West in the wagons on the Overland Trail. Usually they would attack, because they were irritated about something or some injustice to them.

But they were no fools! Indians did not amass armies in those days. War parties went out from the various nomadic bands such as the Lakota. (There were many). Generally, these bands were fairly small, as they couldn't afford to lose men. So as portrayed by Hollywood, the large numbers attacking a wagon train as being shot out of their saddle, to attack again and lose large numbers is fictional. It would have been stupid for them to fight this way. They couldn't afford to lose so many men; same with the attacks on the forts that are seen in the movies. Some, there may have been some, but that too is mostly invented.

An example: Fort Laramie, the famous old fort on the Overland Trail. It was one of the most used, most prominent of the frontiers' forts, but it never had a wall. I "blew it" in "Popping Tree". At a mixed meeting of the Western History Association, made up of professors and authors and researchers from all over the country when I was writing this book, I sat down with these associates and asked them the question: "Did Ft. Laramie have walls"? They hadn't researched the subject either, and the consensus was the fort did have walls.

There is a restoration at one of the sites of Ft. Laramie. I didn't use it in the book. I learned about immigrants in Mormon records entering the adobe walled compound. Fort Laramie did not even have a fence around it. It sat out there naked on the open prairie. It was more of a garrison of a couple hundred cavalry and more often, not that many.

More people by far died by disease and accidents on the Overland Trial than were killed by Indians. There is no way to accurately determine how many, but researchers have indicated maybe three hundred were killed by Indians.

AZB : The same Hollywood, some time ago, started to change their pictures showing Indians as warm hearted, soft and kind people, whereas the settlers were greedy and racist. It seems that the Indians still can be the subject inspiration for the books and the movies. I find characters shown in your book very appealing and colorful. For example, I was intrigued by the white widow in her mid-forties. Catherine Weldon, who was from Brooklyn, was involved in the National Indian Defense Association, and as their representative had come West (with her furniture and fine china). This was in 1889, and she came to encourage the Indians to fight the Land Agreement. She acted as Chief Sitting Bull's secretary and was accused by the press as being in love with him. I think she is a woman worthy of a separate book or movie.

Do you think now, in this new phase where the Indians are shown in a fair way, as a possibility to show the real truth about those years?

RAS : *To Hollywood, the movies have been a good source of a low cost, high yield research… also many actors benefited from them, like Jane Fonda.*

Some twenty years ago, Marlon Brando was about to receive an Academy Award for acting. So, he sent a sassy little cupcake dressed in fringed buckskin and one thing and another to the Academy Award. She presumably was a White Mountain Apache named Sacheen Little Feather, and Brando sent her to decline the award on his behalf as a protest of what was being done to her people. That got a tremendous amount of press…a lot of press for Brando. Only one problem…Sacheen Little Feather had a German mother and got her beautiful golden complexion from a Filipino father (or is it vice versa). There was no Indian blood in her at all. Her name was Maria Cruz who had received a New Jersey award of Miss Vampire America.

And the modern movies don't help much. A little disaster came out here with the book called "Lakota Woman". An engaging woman, life and attitudes on the reservation are shown quite well. Then it all goes to pieces. In the end, because off in some secret corner of the reservation, the tribal council or the chairman tries to keep from the people's knowledge, a secret place developed for minerals (presumably uranium). They got out there and find this is a disastrous thing for the reservation. This is a place where people get killed when they know too much.

It has been written many times, as far as we know, there are no marketable minerals on the Pine Ridge Reservation than there is your average window box. Back at the time of occupying Wounded Knee in 1922, one of the big complaints by the Indians and pushed up by the press and played back without research, was that Dick Wilson, the tribal chairman was secretly trying to sell off a quarter of the reservations to uranium mineral mining interests. There is no way a tribal chairman can sell off any part of a reservation. He can in no manner make any secret agreements. There was no way that anyone could look for uranium on the Pine Ridge Reservation.

In "Lakota Woman", the Wounded Knee 1972 incident (which I know much about, as there is to know; I was allowed in as a member of the Sun Dance Camp after the occupation), we see armed government snipers on the roofs of building at the Pine Ridge Reservation ready to kill Indians. It wasn't that way! It wasn't that way!

AZB : How much have books like yours helped to show the history as it was, not as a romantic perception? How do you see your book as a contribution towards a better understanding of the Indian problem?

RAS : *How many of books like those by me have helped to tell history as it was? It must be helping some. It was a success with the "Reader's Digest" edition. And it is now, at the University of Nebraska press and has been for many years. It sells a few more copies each year than the year before. Less then a year ago, professors at Cornell and Princeton asked my permission to use parts of "Moon of Popping Trees" in their courses. Yes, I gave permission.*

AZB : As you mentioned, "Reader's Digest" first published the book, it was a success, had four printings (1975, 76, 76, 86, had wonderful reviews praising it as "the most definitive and unbiased book of all", and "one of the best books of Indian history to be published in this century"... those statements were made by historians of Western history, as well as Chief Eagle, Indian author and historian who stated: "I consider "Moon of the Popping Trees" triumphantly superb...history in its truest form and as an untarnished perspective".

Do you consider yourself as an expert on the Indian subject?

RAS : *At the time of Columbus' landing, over four hundred mutually unintelligible languages were being spoken on the American continent by Indians. Even today, there are four hundred different recognized tribes, and they have their own customs, traditions and language.*

For this reason, it is impossible for anyone to be an expert on American Indians in total. We get into specialization and because of my own upbringing, specialization etc., I am a specialist in Lakota and Teton Sioux. I would not claim to be a specialist on the American Indian generally. I am well informed on problems that affect them all, on their conditions and what they are trying to do about it. I'm all modesty; I can claim to be an authority on the Lakota and Teton Sioux.

AZB : What other authors' books do you recommend concerning American Indians?

RAS : *Books I recommend on Sioux: Dr. Robert Utley "Last Days of the Sioux Nation" (it is sold). For years, he has been a landmark in the field and I quote other historians for this recommendation. "Moon of Popping Trees" is joining it.*

Alvin R. Josephy Jr. is an overall authority on the American Indian. When the American Indians Movement occupied the Bureau of Indian

Aleksandra Ziolkowska-Boehm

Affairs in Washington DC in 1972, Alvin was the guy chosen by the Indians to be their go between and negotiate for them. He has been a long time friend, commented most favorably on my book and gave it a fine testimony. I agree with Dr. Elmo Scott Watson and Lewis Tate of Northwestern University as authorities on the subject.

AZB : Wounded Knee in South Dakota on December 29, 1890 was a significant battle in the American Indian Wars. Three hundred and fifty Indians were in that battle, eighty-four men were killed, sixty-two women and children, and of five hundred soldiers about thirty were dead, some from their own crossfire. It was not a battle; it was a massacre and a complex tragedy of errors. You showed in beautiful details how the tragic events happened. Part of the blame is on the press, who reported events as sensationalism, exaggeration to the extreme, lacking of knowledge and poor judgment by the government people. Do you think, the press even then was the same as now, easy to judge prematurely and sensationalize?

RAS : *Without the press, there would not have been a Wounded Knee. It was a newspaper war, and what you find in "Moon of Popping Trees" is absolutely accurate on that subject because I sure did research it. You have to go to Washington DC, even today as I speak, to find out the real lies that the media press announce. It is not always just the reporters but members of the event who are presenting their shaken attitudes to the reporters. Like the Ghost Dance, was there really ice, and certainly there was no danger in it. But, we have to judge this issue and the people in it as it appeared then. History is still being made; we still make our own mistakes, and sometimes more than one at a time. React to an occasion/situation as it appears to us now; that's all we know how to do.*

AZB : The Ghost Dance was purely a religious rite and no one, including the agents, had any business interfering with religion. You write the agent's concern was that it could easily produce highly emotional mobs whose purpose was to wage war or an uprising. They sang: "Father, give us back our arrows". The press distributed false stories about the Ghost Dance by more than four thousand Indians on the reservation. It wasn't true. What do you think would have happened if the agents had left the Indians on their land free of interference?

RAS : *I think had the Indians been left alone to dance the Ghost Dance out that would have been the end of it. Now the Ghost Dance... generally took place over the West at that particular time, among the Paiutes, the Shoshone, and the Arapaho... all were doing it. Agents and the Government were not sending in troops to put the Ghost Dance down among those tribes. And there was no trouble. But, as you know and as*

206

depicted in the book, the reason troops were sent to South Dakota was Kicking Bear, who as near as I could determine from research sources, came up with the idea of the bullet-proof shirt. None of the other Ghost Dancers had the concept of the bullet-proof shirt, but this would cause a good deal of concern among a lot of people, because, and of course as the sensationalism get hold of it, it came out and naturally would scare a lot of people and I'm surprised there were not more scared people.

In the book's last chapter, there were areas, one notably in Southern North Dakota where the settlers (and non-Indians) residents panicked. Around Pine Ridge, one can read the accounts of panic in the various newspapers. The citizens didn't take it seriously. But that idiot, the agent at Pine Ridge, ultimately, almost, single-handedly was responsible for bringing the troops on the reservation. And the rest is history.

AZB : You showed how many programs that the Government had for Indians failed. For example, the farming program (it was a failure), because Indian men still retained enough of their heritage and spirit to see farming as a demeaning thing beneath the dignity of a man. They were hunters, they could hunt and fish. The attitude of the Plains Indian toward agriculture was most pungently expressed by the Shoshone Chief, Washakie, whom you quote: "God damn a potato".

Is it the reason that the "allotment" program made by Senator Dawes failed? (Reminder: Each Indian family received one hundred and sixty acres which they would be expected to farm. It didn't work, the whites didn't give up. They rewrote the act and promised to loan fifty dollars to be paid to each family when it began farming). Is there the same attitude and lack of interest even now? Don't forget about the point you made in your book, that because of the harsh climate, not only unskilled Sioux couldn't cope; even for the farmers it was a climate impossible to farm in. What is the truth about farming in South Dakota?

RAS : *It has been difficult to get programs from the Government i.e. programs that work for the American Indians. In the early days, farming and like for the Lakota, that was women's work. But also this country was not suitable then for any kind of productive farming, with the farming machinery available at that time. But, of course, white men didn't know that.*

Nobody knew it till they tried it with people out there in a semi-arid country. Even today, nobody could make a living on a one hundred and sixty to three hundred and twenty acre parcel (size of Indians allotments tract). Plus the fact, Indians knew nothing about farming and they didn't want to. Yes, it was a failure.

207

AZB : Do you think in recent years, after a hundred and ten years that the attitude towards farming among American Indians in South Dakota is the same?

RAS : *The attitude toward farming among Indians in recent years is not the same as it was back in the 1800's. There are quite a few successful farmers. The problem out here for the young Indian is that land is getting expensive. Even young white people find it hard to get into farming or ranching unless it was through inherited land. That's the big problem.*

AZB : I would like to remind you about another program - rations. What had happened, as you write, - every two weeks the Indians loaded their tee-pees, blankets and journeyed to the agencies, then they stood in line to receive their rations. After that they feasted and partied in the camps, like the old days, when there was food after the hunting. The agents found it impossible to teach them to make the rations last. As a result most of the Indians ate well only at ration time and then starved. You presented in your book, the white determination to make the Indians over in the white man's image. Was that the main mistake? Was there another way?

RAS : *The problem here is a solution to the problem poverty has made it. The big problem is alcohol...there are human theories about it, and I subscribe to one theory about it by many including the people of the Indian Health Service.*

Our North American Indians like the Lakota never had fermented beverages till the white man gave them to the Indians. They couldn't handle it! There were times when some trapper would introduce whiskey into a village and destroy it overnight. Once introduced, all the problems arising out of drunkenness would destroy small villages that had been together over five hundred years.

At the Wind River Reservation in Wyoming (Shoshone and Ute tribes), Health Service there have records showing that eighty five percent of the adults (quite a few years ago) had an alcohol problem. I could go on, but I leave you with an Indian research project on alcohol problem, which I have been peripherally involved in.

AZB : In recent years many people go to the reservations and many want to do some good for their Indian brothers. A number of American sponsored Indian schools are run by the Catholic Church, and there are many other Indian programs. Do those efforts help go into the right directions?

RAS : *Even now, to a lot of people, American Indians are viewed as a great national resource. To the tourists, they are viewed as specimens of frontier wild life that drop out of the closets every spring to dance and* *make beads. And then they are put back till next year. The Indians also provide a good deal of high cost, low productivity work on the part of government employees who try to administer programs to help them without knowing what the problems are they're going to help. But first the bureaucrat (maybe the public at large) have to learn what and who the real Indians are before they try "to help" them.*

Among the treaties, those that did the most damage were those thought to be helping the Indians...the National Indian Defense Association, the Lake Mohawk Conference and all of those deciding how Indians should begin to farm.

Here is the problem – Aleksandra - that bothers the dust out of me: Not only, does it concern the Indians or the Black people (they don't want to be called Negroes, but that is a prettier name and is the anthropological name) and easier to speak than African Americans; same problem in Europe. Lots of people have made a living of this problem.

Under the veil of trying to solve the problem, actually they keep the sores open... first the American Indian Movement, then a lot of well-meaning humanitarians telling the American Indians in South Dakota how they have been abused. They just hammer on keeping the wounds open and the victim hurting. How you were abused in the past and how you are abused now and the problem is you have let the white people tell you what to do and how to do etc.

Vine Deloria Jr., if you haven't read any of his stuff, you should. I think his father is mentioned in "Moon of the Popping Trees". Young Vine is a lawyer, believe he studied for the ministry as well, he's written some wonderful stuff. To help and understand a lot of the attitudes and feelings on the reservations, you should get his book "Custer Died for Your Sins". In there, he will mention the people who descend on the reservations in the summers seeking to "research" and to do "good". They bring neither paper nor pencil, because they already know what they are going to find. We get an awful lot of that. People going onto the reservations seeking to find what they know they are going to find.

We've had too many young people trying to see to it that the Indians must not adapt to life and society as it is now, but rather adapt life and society as new to themselves.

But, one of our problems is and still is a big one, are the people who come onto the reservations and tell Indians how sorry they are for what their ancestors did to the Indian's ancestors, telling them they are abused, that they don't have a chance unless they do as we tell them. Keep that up, and you very often throw people into a victim paralysis, that is, we're Indians no matter what we do, we can't go anywhere and these people tell us so.

Whether there are people working with the American Black or with the Indians, whatever the system is, what we need are budgets. Melting people together in a society and keeping their traditions, all of their beliefs and religious can be accomplished... other people do it.

AZB : Your book shows the tragedy and helps to understand how it was almost impossible for two worlds to exist together – world of whites and world of Indians. What is your prediction on the near future for Indians in the United States?

RAS : *I think the biggest misunderstanding of the American Indians is the assumption that they are so different from us. Our similarities are so much greater than our differences. But when you cut through all that stuff, the print, the film, the misconception, the people who abuse them for whatever purpose, we are not so very apart.*

We could talk all day about making the Indians over into the white man's image, and I think the deliberate forced attempt to do that was counter productive. But at the same time, the American Indian (and you know me well enough now to know my heart is with them), I have to recognize that they too have to reach some understanding and some of them already do understand the changing of time and that this is a new world and a new time.

And you just can't sit back and wait for the buffalo to return because someone comes on the reservations and tells you that is what you ought to do.

But first there has to be recognition of the fact that this is the twenty first century, and things now are not quite what they were in the seventeenth century. We all have to make adjustments whether we like it or not. My old ranch where I was born...my gosh, urbanization is pushing out towards us. It's terrible, but I have to cope out here.

For American Indians, one of the answers is education and contrary to a lot of propaganda, it's working more and more. It is a difficult problem, but we are getting there. I'm seeing this more and more all the time. We have some good schools on the reservations, propaganda not withstanding. I myself observe the good changes. I was asked to give the hundredth anniversary Wounded Knee address at Little Room High School on the Pine Ridge Reservation. Afterwards, they took me on a tour of the school, and I was impressed. I was impressed with the computer laboratory, for example, the physics professor showed a model of a helicopter and the study of aerodynamics and later rocketry and the building of models and firing them off...with photos taken by the photography class.

Reservation schools are not just held out under a shady tree somewhere. They need more, but the opportunity is there.

We have a lot of people helping to build bridges. Through this gaming business, reservations are starting to get some money. We are finding more and more American Indians in responsible and leading positions. There are professionals in cities and all over.

Back then, in the big disturbance days of the early 1970's, Vernon Belacourt declared Rapid City as the most racist town in the US. At the time he said it, we had an Indian mayor. Now the town is ten percent Indian. Art LeCroix (an old friend) is the first person ever elected to three consecutive terms as mayor of Rapid City, and he actually wound up being elected to six terms. Which is not very racist... when you looked at Art LeCroix, you knew you were looking at an Indian.

One of my old classmates a young woman, and I'm from Class of '39, lived on Pine Ridge Reservation, was a class president, published the year book, and now is a retired vice president of the largest bank in South Dakota. These are among the real Indians, and on the reservations, some of those needing help are real Indians too.

Frank Ducein is an Indian friend of mine and a lawyer for the Indian Affairs Subcommittee of the United States Congress. I was talking to him in Washington, DC one time, and he said: "You know, all these people come around and tell us we ought to go back into the log cabin, and now I have a split level and I'm going to keep it".

An Interview with Dave Charpentier
A Teacher at St. Labre Indian School in Montana

The Boy Who Promised Me a Horse

Aleksandra Ziolkowska-Boehm (AZB) : How did the poetry loving person like you find the job as a teacher in the Indian school?

David Charpentier (DC) : *My father taught me as a child to have respect for other cultures. He did not tolerate any type of racism. I grew up in a small town in Minnesota, which was predominantly white. It was rare to see anyone of any different background. Since he was a history teacher, he introduced me to many books about Native American people. In the 8th grade, I did a research paper about the Sand Creek Massacre. While in college studying English, a friend asked me during my sophomore year what I was going to do after I graduated. Without taking time to contemplate the question, I told him I was going to teach on an Indian reservation in Montana. It just came out like that. I hadn't really thought of it before. However, by the time I finished college at St. John's in 1989, I had forgotten what I had told my friend. I applied to every job that was listed by the career services office, almost all of these being in Montana, but I did send a cover letter to St. Labre Indian School in Montana. I did not know at the time that St. Labre served the descendents of the Sand Creek Massacre. The director of schools called me one morning and asked if I planned on completing the application. I hadn't filled it out because I was so overwhelmed with applications, and to be honest, I felt a little defeated because I was receiving only rejection letters. I asked him if I could come out for an interview. He told me that I would need to complete the application before they invited me for an interview. Then I told him a little lie; I told him I was planning on taking a trip out west, and would it be ok if I just stopped by to visit the school? He said that would be fine. I packed up my truck that night and left in the morning. I stayed overnight in Rapid City, South Dakota (SD), and filled out the application and put on my tie at a rest stop in Sturgis, SD on my way to Ashland, Montana. I interviewed around midday, and two days later, while camping in the Black Hills, I called my parents and they told me St. Labre had offered me the job.*

AZB : Did you have a contact with Native Americans before?

Aleksandra Ziolkowska-Boehm

DC : *I did not see many Native Americans in Minnesota, especially in the area where I lived. The reservations in Minnesota are not as isolated as in Montana, so it is not obvious when you enter a reservation in Minnesota like it is in Montana. When you enter a reservation in Montana, you know you are on a reservation. It is almost like entering a separate country.*

AZB : What do you mean saying that being on a reservation in Montana - "it is almost like entering a separate country").

DC : *On the Northern Cheyenne Reservation and Crow Reservation, there are not convenience stores, fast food stores, car lots, etc. If you're looking for a latte and Starbucks, you're not going to find it. The houses are much different, too. No three-car garages. In fact, most houses do not have garages at all. Many people live in trailer homes, and around the homes are parked old cars that do not run. Nobody waters his or her lawn or landscapes at all for that matter. Most people I know drive through the reservation just to get through it. They pray they don't break down. To me, the separateness of the reservation is its chief appeal. The tribes truly maintain distinctness. They are not blended in with the rest of society like in the east. I try to imagine what it must feel like to be a Northern Cheyenne entering the reservation; it must truly really feel like coming home each time he/she crosses the reservation line. There are places where brothers live next to brothers, and near their parents, so that families live in close proximity and share a sweat lodge and ceremonial teepee. This type of community is unheard of in the suburban white world.*

AZB : You have been working since 1990 as a teacher in the St. Labre Indian School in Montana. What expectations did you have with such work?

DC : *Yes, I started teaching at St. Labre in Ashland, MT in 1990. The first year was full of many wonderful and exciting experiences as well as stress and anxiety. Teaching at an Indian school is difficult for almost all teachers, especially coming from the background I did. I had done my student teaching at a private, Catholic high school in St. Cloud, MN. (Nicknamed White Cloud because everyone is white). Right from the first day, I made friends with kids and adults in the village where I lived. After living in Ashland for four days, I was invited to a peyote meeting and sweat ceremony. I also began taking some of the young kids in the village fishing. I felt very welcomed by the Indian community, and they seemed to sense my genuine commitment. I had an awe and respect for their culture. I remember thinking that I would have liked to have enough money to buy more land and to greatly expand their reservation. I told a man this one night when he was asking me questions about what I*

214

thought about Indians. He seemed very pleased with my answer. I definitely had a romanticized view of Indians, though I did not have the delusion that I was going to save them. One of the big issue/concerns I had was that, since I was working for a Catholic School, I was going to continue the work of the dominant culture to force assimilation on them. I did not want to do that. I made an effort to distance myself from the church and to stress that I was there only to provide a quality education for their children, that I was not trying to make them Catholic or white.

I struggled more in the classroom than I did in the community. Even though the kids liked me and respected that I went to sweat lodges, I could not get them to keep up with their schoolwork. I was basically teaching like I had been taught, and it wasn't working. One of the first books I tried to teach was Steinbeck's Grapes of Wrath. The kids did not keep up with their reading at all, nor did they seem to have an interest in the content of the novel. When it came to writing, they did not have their drafts done on time, and when I collected the final drafts, only one or two students would have it finished. They did not seem to care if they passed or not. This was very frustrating. Also, the students seemed defensive and distant, and I was only 3 to 4 years older than them. There were times when my lessons failed and I had a half hour to kill and I thought I would lose control of my class. I never gave up and spent several hours every night after school ended preparing lessons for the next day. I also played basketball with the kids in the evenings or took them fishing or went swimming with them. There were several young kids who came to my house almost every day. They would hang around the house and play with my dog. We did all kinds of things, like hiking, horseback riding, chasing wild horses, rock climbing, bowling, baseball etc. I was exhausted much of the time, especially when I was going to sweats 2-4 times a week. If someone were to ask me during my first year if I liked living on the reservation, I would have said I loved it. If someone were to ask if I liked teaching, I would have had to have said I'm not sure.

My teaching improved only when I made the goal to have successful students, students who succeeded and learned. In the past, I had taught to better grades, and if students did not meet expectations, they failed. I was failing most of my students. I realized it wasn't working for them or me. I completely changed all of my strategies and began to implement student directed learning strategies in both reading and writing. I had students direct their own discussions and peer writing sessions. I worked my hardest to ensure that all students succeeded and learned, and soon I was giving mostly A's and B's. I did not lower my expectations at all. I just taught in a new way. After my fifth year of teaching, I was telling people that I loved teaching.

Aleksandra Ziolkowska-Boehm

AZB : Did I understand you correctly, that the new method you started and achieved such success, was that you gave the students more independence in choosing the program or method of teaching? Were they then able to start and participate in their lessons as they desired and at their own pace?

DC : *You know, that would be the ideal level to get to with the students, but I never got that far. I chose the texts, for the most part, and the pace at which we would read them. I let them organize, facilitate, and grade their own discussions. I also let them choose their own writing topics and facilitate their own writing workshops. The more choices I gave them, the more responsible they became and the higher their grades were. I guess if I truly were a master teacher, I would have been able to choose their own texts, pace, and assessment. Oh well, I've got something to strive for now.*

AZB : What is the biggest misconception about Native Americans?

DC : *I think misconceptions occur about Indians because the rest of the country continues to judge Indians by the values of the majority culture. If an Indian home has brown grass, then they are lazy, poor, and bad caretakers of their homes. This reflects the attitude that grass must be watered and mowed. However, it dismisses the value of not wasting water, or contaminating the soil and ground water with fertilizers, or wasting time while cutting the grass. Indian people are amused at how much time white people waste on their lawns. The contrast between how a white person and an Indian person spend a Saturday in the summer is startling. A white person might wash a car, trim the grass, cut the grass, spray poison on the weeds, etc. An Indian may spend the entire day just spending time with family, praying, singing, and eating. Another misconception is that Indian people need to get off welfare and that they don't deserve any more public assistance. This attitude ignorantly dismisses how devastating assimilation was to the tribes, and how much time is needed to rebuild when a vacuum is left from the destruction. Also, these people do not understand how contrary to the Indian way of life is the majority culture. They don't understand why Indians cannot save money. But Indians don't save money. They share it with family who need it, or they spend it on giveaways (a ceremony when they give things to people in honor of a member of their family).*

Another misconception is that all Indians are priests or medicine men. I have met very few Indian people who did not come with all the flaws that everyone comes with. In fact, several of the men whom I met who I thought were the most holy actually disappointed me the most. The books out there that describe an elder's life as being a medicine man of the Sioux, or some other tribe, usually mistakenly designate this man as a

216

spokesman for the tribe, when in actuality, no one man represents the entire tribe. This is a white person's notion, that we can find all the answers about Indians from one man, and that we can find extreme wisdom and mystical powers, or "answers to the world" from these medicine men.

AZB : You stated a misconception is that one Indian is like a leader, that "one man represents the entire tribe". May you explain it more? What about the Indian tribal chief or the other leaders?

DC : *Even in the old days, a chief did not represent the tribe. That is a misconception that the white soldiers never understood, and that is why negotiations were so complicated. It was assumed that a treaty signed by one chief was binding for the entire tribe, but this was not the case in the minds of the people. The chief was only a leader by example and virtue, not by forceful command. Since Indian governments now have been replaced with western style representative government, the chiefs are involved in ceremonies and tribal rituals. When an outside white attempts to write an all encompassing book about one certain tribe by interviewing one medicine man, he is only getting the stories and teachings of one family, not the entire tribe. Medicine men, not Indians, contain the magical secret to life. They do provide some great insight on how to live though, and one must sift through the good from the bad. Indian people are wonderful, funny, unselfish, and generous people. They can also be petty, vindictive, and immoral.*

AZB : You have a unique profession as a teacher of Indians and you like teaching; it is a special gift for someone who can do what he loves the most. Do you agree?

DC : *When I first came to St. Labre, the director of schools at that time told me that it takes four years to become a good teacher at St. Labre. His words were very true. Teaching at St. Labre is challenging, as is, I imagine, at all reservation schools. None of the teaching techniques I learned in teaching school worked. If anyone asked if I liked teaching during my first four years, I would say it's ok. It wasn't until my fifth year that I could say that I liked it, that I loved it. It wasn't until my fifth year that I felt I was really getting good at it. Each night I would go home and assess how I had done and plan ways to improve. It took this type of commitment. And during the day in the classroom, it took patience. There are many tremendous teachers like this at St. Labre. The ones that do not have these skills only last a year or two. The ones that stay are truly committed. Recently I ran into a student I had during my first year of teaching, in 1990. He was very glad to see me. I felt that I wasn't a good teacher back then. He didn't say whether he learned anything or not, but he did tell me that he knew that I cared, that I got involved. This is very*

217

important to the kids and their parents. I may have not been good at my craft when I first started, but the fact that they knew I cared was enough for them to appreciate me and trust me. I do feel blessed to have been a teacher on the reservation for 16 years. I have no regrets at all.

AZB : How do you spend the holidays?

DC : *I go back to Minnesota for Christmas. My parents are proud of me. They support St. Labre Indian School as well as other Indian schools. They come to visit me every year.*

AZB : Please, tell me more about your interest and love for poetry. Who is your favorite poet?

DC : *I love poetry and read it all the time. My favorite poets include many American contemporary poets, such as Billy Collins, Ted Kooser, and Mary Oliver. I also love Yedua Amicahai, Pablo Neruda, and Rumi. I have been accepted into an MFA creative writing program in Goddard, Vermont. I plan on working on my poetry as well as creative non-fiction. I have a lot of success teaching poetry at St. Labre. The students enjoy the poetry of Native writers such as Joy Harjo, Linda Hogan, Sherman Alexie, and Simon Ortiz. Native students love to write poetry, and their poetry is sparse, subtle, and beautiful, like the prairie landscape of their reservation.*

AZB : Having such unique experiences, you should write about them. I have learned that you started to write a book. What is it about?

DC : *I am trying to write a book about my friendship with one of the kids I met in the village. The book is called "The Boy Who Promised Me Horses" because when I asked him what he would do if he caught a wild horse, he told me that his grandma said that if he caught two, he had to give me one. He was killed in a train crash when he was 17. I met him when he was eight.*

An Interview with Bruce E. Johansen
A Professor, Writer[117]

Native American friends have taught me to value my own ancestry, and those of other peoples, too

Aleksandra Ziolkowska-Boehm (AZB) : In April 2007 you participated in a symposium held by the Jagiellonian University of Krakow as an expert and author of many books dedicated to the American Indians. The symposium was named: "Aboriginal People of North America and European Colonization-400th hundredth Anniversary of the Founding of Jamestown". You gave a speech: "Becoming Who We Are: American Indians, Europe and America During the Enlightenment's "Conversation" About Freedom".

What was your impression of that symposium?

Bruce E. Johansen (BEJ) : *Many of my friends in the US – native people and others –- were very impressed that serious study of their history takes place in Poland. The conference was enjoyable, and I met many interesting people, including you Aleksandra, and my host Bartek Hlebowicz, whom I knew from the pages of "Tawacin". I enjoyed seeing the old architecture of Krakow. Nothing in Omaha is much more than a century old.*

AZB : You participated in writing for "Tawacin", a magazine published in Polish in Poland and dedicated to American Indians. I have a very high opinion of that magazine. What is your opinion of a country not having Native Americans who are so interested/involved in that subject? Do other countries have similar studies and magazines similarly dedicated to American Indians?

BEJ : *Great Britain had such a magazine until a few years ago, when George Georgson, its editor and publisher, died. Italy has one*

---

[117] Bruce E.Johansen, Frederick W. Kayser Professor, Communication and Native American Studies, University of Nebraska at Omaha. Author of many books, like: "Enduring Legacies: Native American Treaties and Today's Issues", "The Native Peoples of North America: A History", "Global Warming in the 21st Century", "Encyclopedia of American Indian History", "Forgotten Founders: Benjamin Franklin, the Iroquois, and the Rationale for the American Revolution", "The Dirty Dozen: Toxic Chemicals and the Earth's Future", "Indigenous Peoples and Environmental Issues: An Encyclopedia".

called Hako. Marek Maciolek, editor of "Tawacin", tells me that Belarus has a magazine of this kind, and I have heard that Russia does, as well. (Russia did a symposium on the three hundredth anniversary of Benjamin Franklin's birth in 2006, and noted in its printed record the Iroquois influence on his political thinking). Japan manifests considerable interest (I have two books in translation there), and there is a European journal of Native American studies edited by Christian Feest in Austria. This is just an off-the-top-of-my-head quick survey. There may be others. "Tawacin" is distinguished for its focus on serious issues and its sensitivity to Native points of view. Many Native people have published there, and in fact, I was directed to Marek by the Mohawk artist, teacher and culture bearer John Kahionhes Fadden several years ago.

AZB : In your book: "The Native Peoples of North America: A History" you explore the new wave of Indians' activism that started in the late 1960s, but actually is more visible in recent years. One subject not so widely known is the repatriation of artifacts. I read that many scientists complain that it was done too much – because most of the artifacts were displayed to the public and the people could see them. The Smithsonian Museum gave back to the Native Americans so many items that their collection is ruined. So do you think it is lost for future generations?

BEJ : *Please understand the value that many Native peoples place on returning their ancestors' remains to the earth, to proper burial and also please consider the need of a people to control what happens to their ancestors' remains. While I understand the need for scientific inquiry, this kind of thing should be carried out with respect for Native peoples, living and deceased. Many back hallways in the Smithsonian's offices are still lined with boxes of Native remains that have not been returned and have never been studied by anyone. There is, in the US, a macabre market in the sale of Native remains among non-Indians, and this is a source of much Native resentment. This is a very personal issue for many Native peoples. There must be ways found to carry out necessary scientific study of remains, then procedures in place to return them to their people. Science should not be used as an excuse to control remains forever. The new Smithsonian Native museum, the National Museum of the American Indian, should play a role in this.*

AZB : I understand return of remains, but I think about the items for example like Indian art....Do you also think they should be removed from the museums?

BEJ : *This would depend on whether a given piece of art was manufactured for sale, or whether it was seized from a people without* *their permission. Art that was seized should be returned, in my opinion. The Iroquois' wampum belts, for example, were returned because they belong to them as a people, not to individuals. Artwork that was freely sold should stay with the museums, which are their rightful owners. Some things, such as "False Face" masks (The Haudensaunee call them "Grandfather Masks") should not be displayed, bought, or sold. These are religious objects, and their status as such should be respected.*

AZB : In your Encyclopedia of Native American Biography: Six Hundred Life Stories of Important People, from Powhatan to Wilma Mankiller, there are about seven hundred stories of Native Americans. Who is your favorite Indian person?

BEJ : *I do not have a single favorite. It would be unfair to choose one person above all others.*

AZB : I am intrigued by a modern Indian woman - Wilma Mankiller since she was chosen to be chief of the Cherokee Nation. It was not so common in the past to have Indian tribes represented by women. What is your opinion about it?

BEJ : *Wilma Mankiller is an extraordinary person, and a natural leader. Understand that many Native cultures highly value women's political role. The Haudenosaunee (Iroquois) are one prominent example. In their political culture, women (clan mothers) appoint the leaders, who are male. Thus, while the men have the public role, the women appraise their every move. Early US feminists (Elizabeth Cady Stanton being one example) were much influenced by the role of Iroquois women in the nineteenth century. Thus,*

Wilma Mankiller's position is an extension of some very valuable precedents mixed with society-wide emphasis today on reducing gender inequity. The Cherokees' traditional society has many parallels to the Iroquois.

AZB : In your very known book: Debating Democracy: Native American Legacy of Freedom" you wrote a very strong statement: "For those who are attached to the notion that our intellectual history is exclusively European -- and that European culture is superior to that of the rest of the world, the introduction of Native America into this discourse poses some fundamental problems of historical interpretation and even -- or especially -- self-definition concerning who we believe ourselves to be as Americans."

I learned that your book had a strong response from the critics.

BEJ : *This statement was being made in the context of how American history was presented years ago. In school, for example, I was taught the "history of the westward movement," as if Native peoples had no role or influence other than as obstructions to "progress." This is*

221

simplistic. My own ancestors are European, and I do not mean to denigrate them, or anything European. There is still a reasonable amount of ethnocentric thinking, but less perhaps than before (although I have found some very multi-ethnic thought even in the nineteenth century – read Walt Whitman, for one).

AZB : I believe it is common knowledge that the Iroquois played a strong role in founding of the American Constitution. You compare that role to the Greeks, Romans, the Magna Carta and the Swiss Cantons.

May you give more examples of such influence by the Iroquois?

BEJ : *Two books, "Forgotten Founders" and "Exemplar of Liberty" give examples that run to many pages. Anything I can do here would be only a sample. Take a look, for example, with regards to how the law of libel in the US differs from the British law. The Iroquois law says that leaders' skins must be "seven spans thick" to withstand the people's opinions. Our libel law (the principal case is New York Times versus Sullivan, decided during the 1960s) makes a successful suit by a public person virtually impossible.*

There are many similarities in the Iroquois practice of federalism and that of the United States federal government; the use of "conference committees" is similar to the Iroquois council's practice of throwing a proposal "across the fire". The idea of "sleeping on" an important subject comes to us from the Iroquois Law. The council was instructed not to decide an important issue until at least one night had passed, to allow passions to cool. To "bury the hatchet," another American idiom, stems from the instruction in the Iroquois law to bury all weapons of war under the roots of the Great Tree of Peace. Many of these influences are so much a part of our general culture that many people have forgotten their origins. For much more, please see the two books, which are available on the Internet in full text, free access.

AZB : I learned that the "Influence Theory" had many opponents among academic circles. Can you tell me more?

BEJ : *The subject has been very controversial, of course. The idea has sparked so much controversy that I have more than thirteen hundred items in my annotated bibliographies on it (the first 1,000 are in print) from wildly positive to condemningly negative. A lot of this is covered in Debating Democracy. I had no idea it would evoke so much controversy. It just seemed like an interesting idea worth pursuing to me. It should be part of our history. Please understand, however, that our European heritage is important, too. Complete history includes all influences.*

AZB : Which of your American Indian subjects has been the most popular with your students?

BEJ : *I do not generally teach in this area, although I did during the 1990s. I teach non-fiction writing in the communication department, from newspaper stories to magazine articles and non-fiction books. When I did teach this, I did an introductory course with a broad range of subject matter, so I can't really tell which parts were most popular.*

AZB : As a teacher, have you had any American Indian students who participated in your classes?

BEJ : *Yes. We have a significant number of Native students at our university, and a Native American studies program that soon may be expanded to a major. Some of my most fulfilling relationships have been with Native students.*

AZB : Which American president did the most for the Native Americans?

BEJ : *I have never really thought in those terms, because the United States president, the "great white father," leads the political juggernaut that was dispossessing the Native peoples. It might be like asking "Which Russian or Soviet leader was best for Poland?" It's much easier to talk about the worst ones, and in that field I would nominate Andrew Jackson, architect of removal policies, including the Trail of Tears, mainly during the 1830s. Regarding the best one, I have a surprise: in recent decades, it may have been Richard Nixon, who signed a number of laws that fostered Native revival and self-determination during the early 1970s. He also was president, however, during a time that the Federal Bureau of Investigation destroyed the American Indian Movement (AIM) with "dirty tricks," such as the "snitch jacket," by which agents caused AIM people to kill some of their own people by convincing them they had become informers for the government. This history is still unfolding, somewhat like the Polish controversies regarding collaboration with the Soviets before 1989.*

Before Nixon, Franklin Delano Roosevelt had a good record, in large part because he appointed John Collier to administer Indian Affairs, and signed laws that revived Native cultures and land bases in the 1930s. Even so, some Native people and scholars assert that these laws (such as the Indian Reorganization Act) were merely a refinement of colonialism.

AZB : Your present focus is on global warming, through books such as the three-volume Global Warming in the twenty-first Century (2006). What connection does this have with Native Americans?

BEJ : *I have been attentive to the weather from a very young age; concern over global warming also grew out of a Native American belief that all actions should be taken with the welfare of future generations in mind. Global warming is a very serious issue because it will feed upon*

Aleksandra Ziolkowska-Boehm

itself, and speed up, in coming decades, As ice melts in the Arctic, for example, darker ocean water absorbs more heat, speeding the whole process. The melting of permafrost injects more carbon dioxide and methane into the atmosphere, accelerating warming. In many ways, human burning of fossil fuels is acting as a trigger for natural processes that will make the problem worse. James Hansen, director of NASA's Goddard Institute for Space Studies, who has engaged the Bush White House on warming issues (and defied its censorship) says we have ten years to reduce emissions substantially before the feedbacks take over and deny humanity any role in solving this problem.

One must study the science – how the natural world works – to realize why so many scientists are making this issue such an urgent priority. Many people who debate the issue on a political basis do not understand the impact that global warming will have in years to come, most notably on the hundreds of millions of people world-wide who live on or near coastlines that will be inundated by rising seas. It takes time for the fossil fuels we burn today to express themselves in the atmosphere (about 50 years), and especially in the oceans, which have greater "thermal inertia." By the end of this century, we will have enough warming "in the pipeline," says Hansen, to raise sea levels 25 meters within two centuries after that. Take a look at a world map, note the number of large cities on or near the coasts, and "do the math".

June 2007

An Interview with Father Randolph Graczyk, OFM Cap.

Pastor of St. Charles Parish on the Crow Reservation in Pryor, Montana
Author of the "Grammar of Crow", University of Nebraska Press, 2007

Learn the language for understanding people

Aleksandra Ziolkowska-Boehm (AZB) : What is your recollection of Polish traditions growing up in a Polish family in Milwaukee? Did your parents speak Polish at home?

Fr. Randolph Graczyk (Fr.R.G.) : *My father is of Polish descent, however he is a third-generation American and there was nothing of Polish culture or traditions in our home. My father didn't speak Polish, although, according to my father's sister, my grandparents did, although apparently they never spoke it to their children. I grew up on the south side of Milwaukee, which was—and still is—a heavily Polish area. Lots of my grade school classmates had Polish surnames. My ancestors apparently came from the German-controlled part of Poland, probably in the mid-1800's.*

AZB : Where did you enter seminary in 1965? Tell me about those times. How did you start making summer work trips to Northern Cheyenne and Crow Indian Reservations? How much did you know about American Indian culture in your youth?

Fr.R.G. : *I went to high school at St. Lawrence Seminary, a boarding school at Mt. Calvary, Wisconsin, north of Milwaukee. After high school I entered the Capuchin Order, and after a year of novitiate at Huntington, Indiana, I went to our college seminary at Crown Point, Indiana. Then four years of theology at St. Anthony Seminary, Marathon, Wisconsin. Beginning in 1965, I spent summers (or parts of summers) on the Cheyenne and Crow reservations in Montana, which were Capuchin missions. Our ministry involved mainly religion classes and other activities with the children of the reservation. This was my first exposure to Native Americans, and I was fascinated by their culture and lifestyle, and also was made aware of their poverty. I had the opportunity to observe Cheyenne and Crow dances and other cultural and religious ceremonies. I also starting reading everything I could about Native Americans.*

AZB : When graduating in 1970, you asked for an assignment to the Lodge Grass Parish on the Crow reservation. What is your recollection of that time? Please tell me about your interest in the Crow language and how the plan to learn the language developed?

Fr.R.G. : *After ordination I asked to minister on the reservation, and in 1970 was appointed pastor of Our Lady of Loretto Parish, Lodge Grass, on the Crow Reservation. After a short time I came to realize that Crow was the dominant language on the reservation—everyone spoke Crow, even the smallest children. I constantly found myself in situations where everyone was speaking Crow and I didn't know what was going on. So I began to learn the language. At first I would ask teenagers for the words for body parts, colors, and other common vocabulary items. I got to know Ray Gordon, who was working on translating the New Testament into Crow for the Wycliffe Bible Translators, and he introduced me to the writing system that had been developed and helped me out with Crow grammar. I began working with other Crow adults who helped me out with learning Crow.*

AZB : In 1982, you entered the University of Chicago Linguistic Department and you earned a master's degree in linguistics. Later, you completed a PhD in the same field. How much did it help with your interest in the Crow language?

Fr.R.G. : *In 1982 I decided to take a sabbatical and I was admitted to the University of Chicago linguistics program, although at that point I had no formal training in linguistics. I had always been interested in languages, even as a high school student. (I studied Spanish in high school, taught myself to read French in college, and had a good background in Latin and Greek). I was fortunate to have some brilliant professors at Chicago, which had one of the top linguistics programs in the United States. They were able to help me with my analysis of Crow, even though they did not know the language themselves. After some years back and forth between Chicago and the reservation, I finally received my Ph.D. in 1991. Since then I have continued working on linguistics as my time permits. I try to get to one or two linguistics conferences a year, often giving a paper, and have had a few articles on the Crow published.*

AZB : You returned as pastor of the St. Charles Parish in Pryor, Montana and continued to study the language. The result is your book "Grammar of Crow", a reference book for Crow speakers. How many similar books dedicated to other Native American languages exist?

Fr.R.G. : *I continued working on a revision of my Ph.D. dissertation, which was finally published this past fall as A Grammar of Crow by the University of Nebraska Press, which regularly publishes books on Native Americans. The grammar is primarily a reference book most useful to people with some linguistic background. Hopefully down* the road we can publish some lessons for beginners. *Many Native American languages have published grammars, texts, and dictionaries of varying quality, although there is still a lot of work to be done, particularly with the languages that are on the verge of extinction.*

AZB : Share with me your thoughts about your life experiences as a pastor in Indian country. What is your hope for the future of your parish people? What is your dream?

Fr.R.G. : *Being a pastor on the Crow Reservation has been a ministry that is both challenging and rewarding. I feel that in many respects I have received as much from the people as I have been able to give them. My knowledge of the language has opened a window into understanding the culture and life of the people in a way that I could not have done if I did not know the language. I have tried to let the people know in various ways that the Church respects them and their culture, in contrast to the Church in previous eras, which actively worked at suppressing the culture and language. My goal is to have the people feel comfortable being Crow and being Catholic. The future is in God's hands.*

April 2008

Aleksandra Ziolkowska-Boehm

An Interview with Rod Trahan
Previously: Chief Planned Giving Officer for St.Labre Indian School in
Montana. Now an entrepreneur providing financial planning services.

You are an Indian too.

Aleksandra Ziolkowska-Boehm (AZB) :
You are Northern Cheyenne and Salish
Kootenai origin. You were born (in October
1967) and raised on the Northern Cheyenne
Reservation. Tell me please what do you know
about Salish Kootenai Indians?

Rod Trahan (RT) : *Unfortunately, I do
not know much about the Salish and Kootenai
confederated tribes. My father is Salish
Kootenai (SK) and is from Northwestern Montana where the SK
reservation is located. My parents split up when I was a baby. My
mother being Northern Cheyenne, missed her friends, family, and
familiar surroundings, so she moved us back to the Northern Cheyenne
Reservation in Southeastern Montana. My parents met in the 1960's
while attending Busby School. At that time, Busby had a huge boarding
school run by the Bureau of Indian Affairs (BIA). Hundreds of Indian
children from all seven of the state's Indian reservations boarded and
attended school there.*

AZB : How much do you identify with your Northern Cheyenne
heritage?

RT : *Over the years I have always strongly identified with my
Northern Cheyenne heritage, although I am also Salish Kootenai and
have a very small amount of Mexican blood (my grandfather's mother
was from Mexico). Throughout that time, being a minority has opened
and shut many doors ahead of me. So you might say, the door has swung
both ways for me; sometimes I probably didn't even realize it had been
otherwise.*

*As I have learned about the Northern Cheyenne people of years
gone by, I think about the wonderful, caring, generous, and trusting
people that they were. When I think about some of the things they had to
endure, it makes me realize how good I have it, and that if it were not for
my ancestors' strength of character, things might be a lot different. My
ancestors fought so hard for what they believed in and for their way of
life and the life of future generations. It would be a shame to see it go to
waste.*

AZB : How would you describe your Northern Cheyenne traditions and what are characteristics of that tribe?

RT : *I do not consider myself to be an authority on issues relating to my tribe. However, as I have come to understand, the Northern Cheyenne tribe is considered to be a plains tribe that once inhabited the Great Lakes region, and was pushed out onto the plains by pressure of encroaching Eastern tribes and Canadian tribes. These tribes were being displaced by settlers and trappers moving in and inhabiting the eastern seaboard. Unfortunately, many of the old traditions are slowly ebbing out of existence. There are a select few within our tribe that are keeping the traditions alive and understand their beginnings and relevance.*

AZB : What is your father like? Have you had contact with him over the years?

RT : *My father is a man with great principles. He dedicates much energy to his pursuits. Currently he is on the tribal council for the SK tribe. I think his most admirable trait is his blunt truthfulness. You know where you stand with him, and there is no question as to his view on any issue.*

Although he is somewhat outspoken, he is also a good judge of what's right and what's wrong, not just for himself, but also for the whole tribe. I think people see that, otherwise he would not have been elected to the tribal council.

I had relatively little contact with my father until I went to college. I attended college just an hour's drive from my father and his family, or should I say, the other half of my family. I have two half brothers and two half sisters from my father's side. My stepmother is a kind and wonderful woman as well. Together, my father and stepmother raised a wonderful family that has been very supportive of my endeavors over the years. It is comforting to know they are only a phone call away.

AZB : What are your recollections of your childhood?

RT : *I grew up at the edge of a small community called Busby, which is located on the Western edge of the Northern Cheyenne reservation. My maternal grandparents had a ranch a couple of miles from our house, so when I was young, I spent a lot of time on the ranch. I can remember each spring we branded cattle at the branding grounds, which were out in the hills. It was this time each year that my resolve not to become a rancher was renewed. Although I loved the evening meals, and playing with the other kids, as we got older we had to help brand cattle, give vaccinations, castrate the bull calves, and a myriad of other undesirable activities that usually gave the calves good reason to kick, scrape and bruise us when they could.*

Other things that come to mind as I think of my childhood are the days of summer that I looked forward to each spring with great anticipation. Each spring upon hearing the warble of the Western Meadowlark I would get excited at knowing the start of summer was not far behind.

I also remember playing on the "sandrocks" up on the north end of my grandfather's ranch. We played hide and seek, chased lizards, and slid down the sandstone outcroppings. Most days upon returning from the sandrocks, the pants of all the kids in attendance would have holes in the knees and in the seat.

AZB : What were your school years like?

RT : *I lived a half mile from the bus stop, but had a 25-mile (40 kilometers) ride to school. It took one and one-half hours depending on the number of stops. Some Indian children are bussed up to 50 miles (80 kilometers) each way to/from school. The roads are not crowded so distances can be traveled more quickly than in populated areas. In the old days, traveling by horse, the best you could travel would be 40-45 miles per day. I have been told that is why most towns in Montana are located roughly 40 to 50 miles apart. (64-72 kilometers)*

After school activities, I needed some way to travel home. Parents would car pool to accommodate travel requirements for children who participated in after school activities such as sports, etc. By the time I reached the halfway mark of my first year of high school, after school bus transportation became available for students. My school day started about 7:15 AM when I would leave home; my return home was usually a little past 9:00 PM.

Now I don't want you to get the wrong idea about my grandfather, but this reminds me of a funny little tidbit of information about him. As my grandfather was a rancher, he pretty much created his own time schedule. So toward the end of the week he would call my mother and tell her that he would go to town and pick me up after practice for whatever sport I happened to be playing at the time. Now keep in mind that this is during my seventh and eighth grade years, and I was actually a year younger than my classmates. But in any case, my grandfather would arrive in town around three p.m. and plant himself on a stool at his favorite watering hole (bar). There he would sit and visit everyone and anyone who walked through the doors. He was quite a storyteller and conversationalist. Long about seven p.m. after practice was over, I would run downtown and let him know that I was ready to go. Then the routine was for him to give me enough money to buy dinner at the diner next door. Upon finishing, he would say his good-byes to all the patrons, and newly found best friends, this usually took another half hour or so.

Afterwards, we would hop into his pickup truck, and I would drive us home, all the while listening to his funny stories of days gone by. My parents knew this occurred and they weren't particularly excited about it, but they had faith in my driving as I learned to drive a truck, tractor, and other farm vehicles the summer following my sixth grade year.

AZB : When did you have time for homework?

RT : *I always did it at school. I never had trouble keeping up with studies... like a lot of kids did. I guess I was lucky to have school come relatively easy for me.*

AZB : Tell me more about your grandfather.

RT : *My maternal grandfather (who passed away in February 2005) was a very interesting man. He was very well liked, many people visited him...he would have been a good person for you to interview...he told stories and jokes. He knew lots of stories that he could "rattle off the top of his head". Most stories he told were funny and some were amazing, but usually they were funny. He was a cattle rancher.*

AZB : I understand that it was not usual, nor common among the Indians to be ranchers or to have a ranch. Is my understanding correct?

RT : *Yes, you are correct. Not many Native Americans were ranchers. It is almost "funny" for a Native American to be a rancher because of the nomadic culture of the Natives, growing roots on a piece of land was enjoyed by a mere handful of tribal members. As a boy, I had six horses. My family background is really "something". I grew up with horses.*

AZB : And you always have had a very special relationship with horses?

RT : *Yes and no, in my younger days my parents came across a "good deal" on a kid's horse, or so they thought; it was a Welch mare pony. This is a horse larger than a Shetland pony, but smaller than a typical quarter horse. What that equated to was the mean and ornery temperament of a Shetland, with the size and strength of a midsize horse to back it up. I got "bucked off" numerous times, and it always seemed like it occurred when I was a long way from the home or the ranch. Over time I accumulated five horses out of that mare. I had 6 horses because I was looking for one that I could actually ride and enjoy. I owned Welch ponies and Shetlands that were very stubborn. They had their own minds, and they wouldn't go where I wanted them to go. One horse named Dirty Sally would only obey a grown adult, not me. She was about a foot (three-tenths of a meter) in height shorter than an average "quarter horse", but was extremely headstrong. On one occasion, I was galloping her across a field, and began to approach a stray bale of hay in the field. Dirty Sally saw the bale, and without skipping a beat, at about forty*

232

miles per hour[118], she made an immediate ninety-degree turn to the right. I, however, kept going straight! If not for my feet being in the stirrups, I might well have launched into the next county, but one of my feet stuck in the stirrup momentarily. That jerked me back into the general region of her head and neck. I held on for dear life, as Dirty Sally seemed to pick up the pace. There I was, blasting through the field hanging from the neck of my horse, dreading the inevitable. I am not sure if it was because my hands became too tired, or my legs, which were being pounded by Dirty Sally's legs, became sore too, but I hung on for about fifty yards[119] and finally fell from her neck. I was trampled a bit and was slightly bruised, but I limped home on foot to the corral about a mile[120] away. I saw that she was already home in the corral, and she looked at me as if to say, "What took you so long?"

My grandfather had a horse named Brown Jugs, she was a bit "pot bellied" and resembled one of the old whiskey jugs made out of brown clay; they say she was a racing horse in her younger days. She was very calm and even-tempered. One could use a halter on her, and she didn't need a bridle. She was very easy to control, and I hunted with her a lot, camping in the hills. After making camp, you didn't even have to tie her down.

My mother once told me that as soon as I was old enough, I could make my own decisions about my horses, like which ones to keep and which ones to sell. When that day came, I told my grandfather to take all of them to the horse sale and get rid of them. I bought a Honda trail bike with the proceeds. No more feeding and watering, no more trips to the veterinarian to address a horse's ailments and especially no more getting "bucked off" or "rubbed off" at an unsuspecting moments notice. Actually, now that I think about it, my parents bought that bike for me from my uncle. I seem to recall coming to an agreement with them that if I would put the money in the bank, they would buy the motorcycle for me. They always encouraged me to save my money and not to spend it hastily.

AZB : Rod, do you now miss horses a lot?

RT : *Not really. Horses take a lot of work to care for, you have to feed them, brush them, give them shots, clean hooves, etc. However, I was lucky because my grandfather was a rancher and did most of the work for me. I didn't have the full responsibility of caring for the horses. Most days I only had to return the horse to the corral, and my*

---

[118] Sixty kilometers per hour.

[119] 46 meters.

[120] 1.6 kilometers.

grandfather did the rest. He even moved them from pasture to pasture along with his other horses.

In the winter, to feed cattle, my grandfather would stack bales of hay on back of his truck, and drive out into the fields. He always liked to have someone with him. I was just a little guy, in first or second grade, and I was a willing hand because I liked to steer the truck. He would put the truck in low gear and let it idle along at about three miles per hour, and then he would tell me to keep her straight until he told me to turn. I would steer while my grandfather and uncles, would cut the baling twine and throw the hay off for the cattle. My uncles would yell: "Turn left, and I would make a big circle until all the hay was thrown to the cattle." Later, when I grew older, I didn't enjoy feeding the cattle so much, because I also had to cut the baling twine and throw the hay. The chore was difficult on the cold, brutal winter days. This is another reason I decided; no way was I going to be a rancher.

Now, I am probably the only member of my family who is not still ranching.

AZB : Your great passion was and still is hunting. Do you hunt for pleasure and for food? And what do you most hunt for?

RT : *I grew up hunting and learning to hunt. I can remember spending hours walking along the Rosebud Creek, pushing my way through some of the thickest, thorniest, sticker bush ever known to man, all in the hopes of flushing a rooster pheasant. I often carried a .410 caliber shotgun that my grandfather used to loan me, and that he eventually gave me when I got older. My uncle gave me my first .22 caliber rifle, and I think I wore out the barrel on that one.*

I like game meat, and my venison is stored in a cold storage locker. I use a cold storage facility to process the venison, clean it, and package it. Use of a cold storage facility for processing meat is dependent upon the animal carcass not having too many holes (from bullets) in it. The hunter has to skin the animal before submitting it to the cold storage facility. I do give a lot of venison to church missions.

My wife Nicole doesn't like venison. I think she didn't understand for a long time the difference between beef and venison ... it has to be understood that they are different animals and appreciate each for what they are. Each has its own taste, and not everything should taste like beef or chicken. Elk meat is very, very good! They are also a great challenge to hunt. I think I favor hunting elk the most, although I also like hunting deer.

I recently had an accident with my van and family returning from a funeral out of town; I hit a deer on the highway. The deer crossed in front of my van at the last second. I had to rent a car for our return, and

*there was four thousand dollars damage to my van ("A good smack")!
As I did not get a white-tail deer during hunting season this year, my
friends teased me by saying that I would go to great lengths to bag a
white-tail deer.*

*I usually hunt for deer and elk. I need a permit and a special license
to hunt big cats, like mountain lions. The State of Montana closely
follows big cats that are hunted, and when a certain quota is reached,
the permits to hunt are usually cut off. Big cats primarily are hunted in
Western Montana. Sometimes cats will come into the eastern area of the
state. One had come into the Ashland area and killed a colt and a mare.
The ranchers say that if you see a mountain lion, it is either old or sickly.
People don't realize that in Montana, mountain lions are around, they
are just very stealthy. The one in Ashland had probably been kicked out
of its area by a stronger younger lion, so it moved into the Ashland area
to prey upon the easier to kill farm stock.*

*My Great Uncle once saved his daughter's life... both were on
horseback, and as she rounded a cliff about seventy feet[121] in height,
there was a mountain lion on a top of the cliff crouching and ready to
attack the girl as she rode beneath it. My Great Uncle managed to see all
that was about to happen, pulled his rifle, and yelled at the girl to stop.
He shot the lion before it was able to attack.*

AZB : Rod, do you have pets? Do Indians have pets?

RT : *Yes, I do have a dog, our family dog that my children love very
much.*

*Do the Indians have pets? It varies by tribe...if you go to the
Northern Cheyenne Reservation, you will see a lot of stray dogs running
everywhere. The Cheyenne don't have feelings about dogs. It sounds
strange, but dogs are pretty much on their own. In fact, they are free to
leave a home just about any time. A lot of natives will not go searching
for their dog if it leaves. If it comes back, that is great, if not, well that's
the way things go.*

*This seemingly strange relationship with dogs is partly cultural, and
partly financial.*

*But you will not see too many cats around the reservation. My
family doesn't have cats as our grandfathers did. He had a few barn cats
around to eat the mice. My mother has cats too, and they all stay outside.
She feeds them, but they have to hunt mice for food as well.*

AZB : In the movie "The White Buffalo" (made in 1977) with
Charles Bronson, Kim Novak, Jack Warden and Will Sampson acting as
a Sioux chief (he was actually of the Creek tribe), there is a scene that

---

[121] 21 meters.

made me think. Would a full-blooded Indian, portrayed as a Sioux, slay a white buffalo that is considered so sacred to Native Americans, as was portrayed in the movie?

RT : *No, I don't think a native would slay a white buffalo. The white buffalo is a special thing; it is a mystical sign or a powerful omen. I typically look at the older movies with Native Americans in them and know that many of the things portrayed there are only Hollywood's view on things. Sometimes it's accurate and truthful, and other times its just nonsense.*

AZB : How do you remember your grandmother?

RT : *My grandmother was a quiet, dignified woman that I love and miss very much. She was very traditional yet accepted the constant changes to her people throughout her lifetime. She made a conscious decision not to teach her children the Cheyenne language, as she did not want them to be coupled with the stigma that many Northern Cheyenne Indians suffered who spoke English as a second language. They often spoke in broken English, therefore, people assumed they were dumb. Since my mother did not speak the Cheyenne language, she could not teach it to me. At some point, my grandmother changed her way of thinking and decided she wanted to teach her grandchildren how to speak Northern Cheyenne. So many times when I would visit my grandparents, she would only speak Northern Cheyenne to me. Often I found it tiring to decode her sentences and then answer her in Northern Cheyenne. Despite this effort, I still do not speak my native language. After graduating from high school and going on to college, my contact with tribal elders and other Northern Cheyenne speakers was less and less. I am now relegated to only being able to pick out a few recognizable words in a sentence spoken in Northern Cheyenne.*

AZB : What is your recollection about growing up on the reservation?

RT : *Growing up on the reservation is quite unique. Although I wouldn't change a thing, I now realize that there were many hardships that reservation inhabitants endured that most people in the United States do not endure. I can also remember as a small child, traveling to Lame Deer with my parents to see my great grandparents. They lived in a small one-room log cabin heated by a wood stove. The bathroom was an outhouse behind the cabin. The cabin was very dark and always smelled like dried meat inside. I disliked the smell, but didn't understand what it was at the time. As my great grandparents were somewhat poor, relatively speaking, a large part of their diet consisted of dried meat and potatoes. Whenever someone brought them a deer, my great grandmother would slice up the meat into large thin pieces and hang* *them over sticks hung from the rafters inside the cabin. She did this to keep the meat out of the direct sunlight and to minimize contact with flies.*

I can also remember going to the 4th of July "pow-wow" every year. It was a wonderful time, because I knew most of my friends, cousins, and other relatives would be there, and we would get to play together. We ran around the pow-wow grounds and the surrounding campgrounds playing child games without fear of harm whatsoever. Whether those days are gone now, or it was a false sense of security, I am not sure. I would not allow my children to run and play unattended at the present day 4th of July pow-wows.

AZB : Do you think the children presently on the reservations have experiences similar to yours?

RT : *Unfortunately, I don't think the present children on the reservation will enjoy such an innocent childhood. The drug problems on the reservation have ripped right through the age-old family traditions and values. The kids today are growing up fast and learning the hardships of life at a much younger age than kids of my generation did. We did not have gang problems growing up on the reservation. We did not have cable television, satellite television, or even satellite radio back then. The influence of the outside world affected life on the reservation much less thirty years ago. Today's children are bombarded by advertising and American pop culture to the extent that they are evermore identifying with that culture and society; and in the process, are losing contact with their own cultural uniqueness.*

AZB : How did you feel about being Indian - pride, confusion, and curiosity…?

RT : *I have gone through many phases as it relates to how I feel about my heritage. When I was very young, I thought all people were the same. I thought everybody felt as good about Indian people as I did. It wasn't until my mother sent me to third grade in Hardin, which is off the reservation, that I learned about cultural differences. Most of the kids in my class were good to me, but somehow, they acted different than my friends back home. Whether consciously or by nature, I became a student of the rules of my new environment. One thing I noticed right away was that the teachers seemed to be much stricter.*

I never lost pride in my heritage, but I did realize around the fourth grade or so, that not everybody shared my view. And yes, quite honestly, there have been times in my life that I had wished the color of my skin was lighter. Something that I have always found quite humorous happened to me in high school. I dated a number of Caucasian girls, many of them were afraid to bring me home to meet their parents.

Usually one or both of the parents was prejudiced against Indians. In one instance, the girl had a father that was much older than the typical parent of a high school kid. He had poor vision and could not see across the living room without his glasses. The girl's mother was not prejudiced and wanted very much to meet me. So my girlfriend, her older sister, and the mother concocted a scheme to have me over for dinner at their house without the father finding out that I was Northern Cheyenne. When I arrived in town that evening, I was to call her house from a nearby payphone, and then wait for her to call me back. This would give her older sister time to distract her father while my girlfriend swiped his glasses and hid them. So, when I arrived, he was in the living room sitting in his recliner smoking his pipe. My girlfriend and her mother met me at the door, and we exchanged greetings. Then they whisked me into the opposite end of the living room and my girlfriend cordially introduced me to her dad with a sunny smile and didn't forget to tell him that I was a "Dark German", whatever that was. He instinctively reached for his glasses, and fumbled around looking for them before he even said a word. I guess he might have thought it rude if he were to continue on with a full-scale search before saying hello, so he finally acknowledged my presence and said hello. The ladies then scurried me into the kitchen and sat me down at the exact opposite end of the table from where the father would be sitting. The mother had added every table extension in her closet to make the table long, and then she piled all kinds of wonderful foods on it to take up the space. After at least fifteen minutes of searching, the father came hobbling into the kitchen with a perplexed look on his face. He asked his wife if she had seen his glasses and she told him no. He must have asked her that ten times during the meal. Being aware of his extreme dislike of Indians, every one of my senses was operating at peak efficiency. I was prepared for anything and everything. It was quite amusing to see him look across the table at me and try to bring his eyes into focus. Throughout the whole supper, he tried numerous times to bring me into focus, all to no avail. Whenever he asked a question, I answered. At times my girlfriend or her older sister jumped in and answered his question for me, just to be sure it fit with whatever else they had told him before I arrived. At the end of the meal, the mother hugged me as my girlfriend and I left for the movies. The father said goodbye, and as far as I know, never fully suspected a thing.

AZB : Is there still a lot of (some?) prejudice about Indians in your state?

RT : *Unfortunately, a "red-neck" attitude exists in Montana. The closer you are to a reservation, the higher the instance of prejudice.*

Growing up on a reservation and going to school off the reservation, I can tell you that a lot of the non-Native kids are very prejudice towards Natives. Since I lived on the western edge of the Northern Cheyenne Reservation, I rode the bus forty-five miles[122] across the Crow Indian Reservation to go to school there. People there were very prejudiced against Crow Indians, somehow, they were not as prejudiced against Cheyenne Indians. They were not accepted as an equal, but one was more accepted if he was not a Crow. It's unfortunate that kids pick up the baggage that their parents carry with them. Most times there is no particular reason for their attitude, it is just picked up and reinforced in certain circles. At times I could feel prejudice and I could hear it when I was in a group that didn't include any other Crow Indians. But then again, I also heard derogatory jokes and such about non-natives when I was in native only groups.

I seemed to be more accepted, perhaps because I excelled in athletics and academics. Many students often said, "you are different". "We are not putting you down, but you are different". I used to think, "Different than what?"

AZB : Do you think, you are different?

RT : *Yes, I am different. Perhaps because I excel in both worlds.*

AZB : What image of Indians do you find that people have as you travel away from the reservation?

RT : *I will tell you a funny story. When I moved to Houston, I was attending table tennis clubs. There were a lot of people I met from outside of the United States. When I told them I was from Montana, they would respond,*

"Oh, Montana, is it cold there!" – "Yes, it's cold", I answered.

"You are a Native American?" – "Yes", I replied.

"Do you still live in tepee?"

"Why aren't you wearing your Indian clothes with feathers or a breech cloth?" – Because the Indian clothes you think I should be wearing are typically only worn during pow-wows or other cultural celebrations.

"Do they still ride in covered wagons up there?

I had to laugh, but only in my mind of course. The guy who asked me those questions was a manager in one of the "Popeye's Chicken" restaurants. He was educated, and smart enough to run a business, but he had no clue about Montana or Native Americans. Although, in his defense, I must say he was from China, and would probably have been limited in his exposure to Native Americans.

---

[122] 76 kilometers.

239

Aleksandra Ziolkowska-Boehm

AZB : Tell me about your college years, and what did you study?

RT : *I went to college in Missoula (western part of state), and studied at the University of Montana ...then, after graduation, I worked for a while in Billings with a company who had awarded me a scholarship. Later, I worked in Houston for about a year, but then went back to eastern Montana to work in an area that I could help my people, which eventually led to working at St.Labre Indian School in Ashland.[123]*

AZB : It seems that many of the Native Americans who have gained a university education desire to return to reservations (or close thereto) to help their people. How was it with you?

RT : *Yes, that is true for me. I realize that I am very lucky to have been able to complete high school and go on to college. By simply graduating from high school that puts me in a group enjoyed by few natives; by graduating from college, I am in an even smaller group of natives. A friend recently read somewhere that less than 1% of Native Americans have college degrees. That is a sad statistic.*

By telling about my success in school, it is not meant to brag or be boastful, but to lead into my next point. In many native cultures including mine, it is not acceptable to brag about oneself. My point: If only 1% of native people are receiving college degrees that is relatively few people going back to help their people, although most of those with an education want to help their people in some way.

AZB : Rod, are you the only one of your siblings who did so well?

RT : *My younger brother (on Dad's side) is pursuing his doctorate of Psychology at the University of Montana in Missoula. Growing up, I did not know that side of my family, as they lived at the opposite end of the state.*

For a long time, I thought I was the oldest child, but later I learned I had an older sister who was put up for adoption. She grew up in a loving family but not a Native American family. She feels it was the best for her, as she received many things she would not have had on the reservation. She does not feel any ill will towards my mother, as she would never have been able to provide many things for her daughter, including college. My sister lives in California now; she is married and has three children.

AZB : Now there is a legislative act, that a non-Native American family cannot easily adopt a Native American child. Is this correct?

RT : *Yes, in the old days, for example, an older sister would take a child for adoption and raise it as her own, with no difficulty. In my*

---

[123] This is elaborated more in a later question.

240

mother's case, there were no older sisters. My great uncle's children were all girls, and he and his wife always wanted a boy. When my mother was pregnant with me, they pressed my mother hard to allow them to adopt me. My great uncle offered a stable home, he was, a rancher too. Mom felt she could raise me right without all the luxuries offered by my great uncle. So... she and eventually my stepfather raised me as best they could.

AZB : Do you have other siblings?

RT : *On my mother's side, I have two younger sisters and the older one I talked about earlier. The youngest sister on my mother's side was born when I was in my junior (third year) in high school and she is much younger. After college, I saw more of my younger sister.*

She went to Missoula, also to the University of Montana. She completed three-fourths of her studies and then dropped out of college. She still lives in Missoula and is planning to finish her last year in the near future.

My middle sister, who is two years younger than I am, has four girls with three different fathers. She has had a rough life, and suffers from a drug problem. She can't seem to get her life together. Believe it or not, she has a college degree, and I admire her for pursing that while she was raising her family. But the year she graduated from college she fell prey to her weakness for partying and doing drugs.

AZB : Drugs are a big problem on the reservations. Who brings the drugs to the reservations?

RT : *It is a huge problem. Drug sellers do it because they can earn a lot of money. On the reservations, there is significant unemployment. People seem to live for the moment and not for the future. The biggest concept people have trouble in grasping is an appreciation for retirement. They don't save for the future, since they feel they may not be around in the future. Historically, Indians lived that way for years. They did not have the feeling they might be still around tomorrow. Because of alcohol and now drugs, people die young on the reservation. It is difficult for them to have the concept of a future when they are primarily concerned about how to get their basic needs met today. The average life span of a male on the reservations is over thirty years younger than that reached by an average American male. Reduced life span on reservations is primarily due to alcohol and drug abuse and the accidents that accompany that way of life.*

I'll tell you one of my family stories:

One day, my uncle was outside a bar drinking and socializing with friends. Another character was drunk and brandishing a rifle, and he began firing it over the heads of the customers. My uncle told the guy to get lost to no avail, and finally took the rifle away from him. He then removed the ammo, and took the rifle outside the bar and threw it into a ditch. Later, talking outside the bar, the gun owner came up behind my uncle, pulled my uncle's coat over his head and proceeded to stab him several times with a knife. It was after dark, the light was poor, my uncle's friends thought that only punches were being inflicted ...my uncle died of knife wounds. The next part is not because I am racist, but nonetheless it is another sobering reality of native people. In a day and age where people who write bad checks can go to prison for three to five years, the killer, who was not native, received a seven year sentence with three or four years of the sentence suspended.

AZB : Rod, what tradition do you offer to your children?

RT : *I have two boys, and they know they are Native American although they don't look Native. I am not sure if they identify yet with their ancestry... I told my eldest boy, who was six years old at the time, that he and his younger brother were going to come with us to a "pow-wow."*

He asked: "What's that?"

I responded, "That's where the Indian people get together, dance, meet and talk, eat, and have a good time, etc...."

"We're going to see those Indians?" he asked.

"Yes, you are an Indian too".

I am not sure they identified yet with ancestry.

I am teaching them about where they came from and where their family comes from. I will take them periodically to the reservation to see their grandmother and family.

AZB : Does your family have bad feelings that you married a non-Native American?

RT : *No, not my family. My mother likes my wife very much. But not all Native people have open acceptance as my mother does. There is some resentment of non-Natives by Indians on the reservation for those who are not full-blooded.*

AZB : Resentment happens in all societies...

RT : *Natives who are full-blooded particularly exhibit resentment. There are traditional natives and there are non-traditional natives...non-traditional characterized by not following tribal customs...those trying to learn to excel in non-native ways as well.*

Many have taken on the non-traditional ways, or do not follow the traditional ways as closely...when this happens there is a "disjunction" between the two types of people. As non-traditional people become older, many seek to find out where they came from, more about their culture, so they become re-acquainted with the traditional ways.

In my family, I am going to leave that choice up to my boys as well. I will teach them what I know about their culture, and if they want to learn more, it is up to them to ask for help in seeking the information.

There is so much that I don't know...it's sacred, you respect it, and there are some very literally powerful sacred beliefs Native-Americans have that are unexplainable. They are unexplainable because they are of the supernatural. Some say it's just God with Native American interpretation...there are some amazing things that I've experienced, things I never thought were possible.

Stories of experiences when related to others brought their reaction: "Yeah, right!"

I guess I would have had the same reaction if I had not been the person experiencing the event.

AZB : It is your openness, neutrality and vulnerability that make you special in comprehending "an amazing experience"?

RT : *It could very well be that it is my openness...certain cultural things Natives are not supposed to talk about...particularly if you don't know enough about it.*

There is a story. My close friend and I hunted regularly together in our youth. I considered him a brother as we were together all the time. He has since passed away.

We were out hunting one day with my friend's father. We saw absolutely nothing...it was one of those rare days when we saw no game at all. A couple of weeks earlier, we saw all kinds of deer in the same area. We hunted all morning, walked and walked. We stopped for lunch, joking about what happened to all the animals. My friend's father said:

"Let's start heading back home as it gets dark earlier".

He took out his medicine bag, opened it, took a pinch of the medicine from the bag and performed a particular ritual, which I cannot elaborate on. (Sorry) When we were finished, he said,

"Now you're going to get the biggest buck you could ever shoot. It's going to be so big, you may not want to shoot it".

My friend and I just laughed. We started driving home...and neared a spot where more than likely we would not see game as it was close to a main road. We came around a turn in the road, and there were three elk standing there...standing there as if they were waiting for us to shoot them. We ended up shooting two elk, the biggest we could have ever imagined. We did not shoot bucks (deer), but we did bull elk...and purposely, we did not shot the third elk as we only really needed two.

Normally, on the worst day of hunting, you might only see a "doe" (female deer), but there were no deer that day.

243

The elk were normally scarce in that area we hunted, and back then, to shoot elk on the reservation was pretty much unheard of. So you can see that the sudden reversal in our luck was quite extraordinary.

What did my friend's father do with his medicine?

I am not supposed to tell what he did with it...but it was a spiritual thing.

AZB : You told me about your grandfather, who was a rancher that is not so common among the Native Americans. What happened to the land after he passed away?

RT : *The debt on it was higher than the ranch was worth. He bequeathed the ranch to my mother, and unfortunately, although it is nice to have the property, there is so much of a financial load on it.*

AZB : Did your mother join the Native Americans, ranchers who fought the predatory lending system that since the beginning was working against them?

RT : *Class action lawsuits by farmers and ranchers were taken against banks guilty of predatory lending practices. Banks made loans to Native ranchers knowing full well they would have trouble repaying the loans. They were supposed to be trying to help them but really were not...Indians got in over their heads. The Farm Service Agency (FSA) is supposed to offer assistance to farmers and ranchers, to best utilize their property so that farmers and ranchers don't fail. The FSA were bad about doing their duty on the reservations... they would lend Natives money, give them more and more loans at such high interest rates, and ultimately the ranchers collapsed financially. The FSA was very quick to foreclose on ranchers in trouble. They would turn around and sometimes auction the property to other ranchers. Many of the ultimate purchasers were non-native, or were acquaintances of the FSA bankers. I am not aware of those purchasers ever having to pay the debt burden off. A whole lawsuit will come to bear. Claimers on class action lawsuits are not intending to make millions of dollars but to get the land back from the predatory lenders.*

My grandfather's ranch had debt far more than the land was worth...I stated that nowhere else in the country would lenders offer loans under such circumstances (inadequate asset value).

Reservation lands were sold, in many cases, to non-Natives such that reservation land was eroded (alienated from its rightful owners). The Northern Cheyenne have tried very hard to keep their reservation land intact. They endeavor to hold the land collectively rather then individually to lessen the chance of an individual losing the land to a non-Native.

The Farmers Home Administration (FHA) also made loans at horrendous rates. They also were quick to foreclose on unpaid loans to Natives. They too were forcing people into foreclosure, taking their land and reselling it. Relatives and friends of the bankers were able to acquire land at auctions. My suspicion: lots of land, not only Cheyenne, but lands in North Dakota, South Dakota, Montana, Wyoming has been taken over thereby reducing the size of reservations. My grandfather willed his ranch to my mother, so she will have to carry on the battle with the federal agencies. Lawyers in New York have taken on the class action lawsuits. In order to pay for the lawsuits, the Natives will have to acquire money for lawyers to get paid. They are expensive, big name firms with known reputations for handling similar lawsuits, and they command high prices for their reputation. I will see how it turns out... it is discrimination against a minority...pretty much a clear case in my opinion. I admit, Natives have made some bad choices but they should not be subject or liable for such discriminatory treatment. A lot of people lost their land and were kicked off of it. How are you going to make reparations there? Natives who wanted to go into ranching on their own were not given the opportunity to receive the assistance and training the government agency was set up to provide for all farmers and ranchers, natives included. Although they knew ranching from working on non-Native owned ranches, at times they faced problems in which they did not have the right solution. Meanwhile the government agencies stood by and waited for the native ranch to fail even while they may have been providing a non-native rancher advice and assistance on solving the very same problem that the native rancher was battling. When the native rancher came to ask for help or advice, they seemed to be pushed aside by the government agency. But of course, once the native rancher began experiencing trouble making loan payments, the lending agencies were quick to foreclose. The suit has been in litigation for five to six years now. ... For example the lenders claim the outstanding debt on my grandfathers property is more than a quarter of a million dollars and the property is only worth perhaps fifty thousand dollars as strictly ranchland. Furthermore, their records show no payment activity from my grandfather over many years, despite the fact that he was making payments to them. Now what bank in the world would keep lending someone money if they had not made a single payment on their current five or six outstanding loans?

AZB : How would you describe that ranch land?

RT : *There is farmland there, and very desirable property on my Mother's land. General Custer and his forces actually camped on the* land, *(obviously before my family owned it) on the north side of her ranch before the Battle of the Little Big Horn (the day before the battle).*

AZB : What would your mother like to do with the ranch land?

RT : *My mother wants to start a business using her ranch land. As I mentioned, the ranch is the last place that Custer and his men camped before they fought the next day at the Battle of the Little Big Horn. It is an "historic site", one of the fields my grandfather herded his cattle on turns out to be where Custer camped. The ranch has 640 acres (259 hectares). I want my mother to carry out some business planning to see how feasible it is to possibly operate it as an historic site, with campsites, tours to different locations etc. The Big Horn area is open land.*

AZB : Norman told me, that he recalls from history class how Indians were able to lay a trap for Custer when it was such open land.

RT : *General Custer made a big blunder when he ignored the advice of his Indian scouts not to attack, as the Native forces were much greater than his. The scouts warned Custer that he would be overpowered.*

"You don't want to go down there... way too many people... you'll be overpowered... wait for reinforcements to arrive".

He said: -"No... we are going".

Now they tell the story of the Battle of the Little Big Horn in a more neutral fashion. I went there when I was a kid. I heard a different story than they tell nowadays. Native stories are incorporated now telling how it happened from their viewpoint. Previously, these stories (not written down) were discredited as hearsay. If not written down it's not for sure.

Overall the story is told now with a version the Natives tell that can be corroborated with evidence found subsequently. There has always been a question where Custer actually died. An untrue replication shows a high point with Custer and his dying men surrounded by Indians. They say he actually was killed down closer to the river. He was actually shot at a low level...finishing skirmishes were on higher ground as his forces retreated. When Custer attacked, he ordered a regiment to come in on the south side of the village... the village was so long, it had so many Native tribes, and their actual encampment was more than a mile long. A few Native riders were able to hold Custer's forces locally where he first attacked...the word got back to the other end of the Indian's encampment by runners that soldiers were attacking... as Custer himself and his detachment of troops circled around and crossed the river on the north side of the encampment, the Indians were able to get back to meet Custer at the river. Native Americans say Custer was shot from the opposite side of the river where he and his soldiers were. I read a book called something like "Cheyenne Memories", with a lot of material in it that was corroborated by the "Moon of Popping Trees" version of the battle. I know a lot of tales told that were not true based upon my trips to the battle site as a boy.

AZB : Do you like the book by Rex Alan Smith "Moon of Popping Trees"?

RT : *Yes! I really enjoyed it! Rex Alan Smith had the unique ability to identify the many different events that were taking place in Native country as well as in the United States in general. Then he put them together like pieces of a puzzle to show how they played a part in the final outcome. This would then reveal, what I believe to be, a much more accurate and plausible story of historical events than what has been written in the past. Rex Alan Smith, as he mentions in the introductory chapter, maintains a neutral view as it relates to the many historical struggles between the "White Man" and the Indian. I find it very interesting to see how seemingly irrelevant and tangential events in history came to affect the outcome of other events. We may think we live in a microcosm of our own little environment, and we are unaffected by strangers hundreds and thousands of miles away, but we are affected by so many things, near and far, going on around us, we just don't recognize it. I read the book by Rex Alan Smith, and I gave it to my mother and told her: -" You have to read it".*

AZB : The Black Hills are sacred for Indians… There are so many misunderstandings, so many mistakes were made. Rex Alan Smith wrote about some of them.

RT : *About the Black Hills…Natives had no concept of finances the way the non-Natives did … they knew their dependence was on their culture and their relationship with the land… so they would overlook the more practical and personal traps that could be encountered… As they say, "Hindsight is twenty-twenty, but I think I understand the thinking of the white man and what motivated their thinking.*

On individual levels, Natives experienced a virtual "land grab". On a state level, the Natives did not have the organization and the authority to keep the trespassers off their land, and this ultimately was one of many factors that played a part in the Indians loss of the Black Hills.

An unfortunate thing, as far as Native Americans are concerned, is that the battles of the past were finished, but not so. The government is not willing to abide by terms that were agreed to years ago. Therefore, Natives are still being stripped of their rights and benefits.

Treaty rights are continuously being eroded away by politically slanted courts as they give way to the demands and justifications made by non-Natives.

Eastern and far-western tribes, by opening casinos, have actually gotten funds necessary to have some voice in standing up for their treaty rights.

AZB : A media article claimed that Indian casinos did not employ that many Natives. Norman and I believe it is not true as Casino revenues are doing a lot of good things. The classic one is the El Paso Casino owned by the Tigua tribe in Texas. We were there in 1997 and saw a beautiful community built up around the casino for Indian families. People had livable and attractive homes that were not pretentious, and they were living well. Then still Governor George Bush put the "kibosh" on the casino operation and closed it. He apparently succumbed to the lobbying influence of non-reservation casinos.

This is typical of what is going on in California too. Natives there have casinos, and there is a big lobbying campaign by gambling casinos not to allow gambling in Indian casinos on reservations...these casinos became popular with Californians resulting in a large inflow of funds for reservation infrastructure and a better life for those Indians employed in the casinos.

RT : *St.Labre approached a California Indian casino to request some of their charitable funds be used for a student dormitory project back at St.Labre in Montana. The Tribe was impressed by the school and its proposal project, but countered that they were restricted by political pressure from the State to utilize its funds for projects that would benefit residents of their state. The Tribe felt that if they did not comply with state pressures, the state would "hammer away" and take away what they do have and achieved. The Tribe was sympathetic to St.Labre and Native people, but they have to restrict contributions to state charities.*

AZB : Maybe my question is naïve, but why can't the Indian casino owners use their excess funds to help Natives around the country (versus giving to non-preferred recipients)?

RT : *California tribes had to comply with political pressures or were threatened with higher taxation levels. "They were making too much money" according to state politicians.*

"They give us with one hand and take away with the other". When the Federal Government gave states responsibility to determine if Indian reservations could have gambling on them, ours has never been a question in the state of Montana.

It was almost without question that "Vegas style" gambling would not be allowed on Montana reservations. I have heard say that some opponents of the idea to allow this type of gambling on reservations couched their vote to reject in statements indicating the desire to protect natives from this immoral activity. Actually, I have heard talk that it was pressure by the Bar & Tavern Association, who exercised its strong lobbying strength in Montana, to defeat Vegas style gambling on Montana reservations.

They don't want any revenues from gambling that off-reservation casinos are earning to be diverted to casinos on the reservations. There is limited gambling allowed in bars and casinos throughout Montana including casinos on the reservations. However, tribes should have the authority to determine the levels of gaming they would like to allow within the bound of their own reservations, they in fact do not have that authority, and furthermore, they are restricted to allowing the level of gambling that the State of Montana determines. Currently, they are allowed to offer only what off-reservation casinos offer, which is limited to a specific number of keno and poker machines within each establishment.

With all that said, I am not necessarily a proponent for allowing gambling on reservations. However, I believe each tribe should have the right to decide that for themselves. Unfortunately, revenues from casinos in tourist areas only benefit those areas. On reservations such as the Northern Cheyenne, where we are somewhat remote, the majority of revenue that our casino earns is derived from within the reservation itself. This is a reservation where there is tremendous unemployment and the average income is below the United States standard set for poverty level. Thus, I tend to think that the casino on our reservation merely extracts money from those on the reservation who cannot afford it, or who will eventually not be able to afford it.

AZB : Is alcohol available, or sold in the casinos?

RT : *On the reservations it depend upon whether or not alcohol is allowed on the reservation. We refer to this as whether the reservation is wet or dry. My reservation is dry, therefore alcohol is not allowed in the casino.*

AZB : Outwardly, it seems as if Congressman from your area (Montana, North and South Dakota) have little interest and/or success in improving the lives of their constituents on the reservations. Is this impression correct? If it is correct, what would you hope could be done (and how) to correct the situation?

RT : *I would like to offer some authoritative statement on that subject, but unfortunately, I cannot. In my young and foolish life to date, I have been guilty of paying little attention to politics at the national level and how our congressmen have represented their Native constituents. I suspect your observation is probably accurate.*

AZB : Is your grandmother still alive?

RT : *She passed away in 1996. I remember her funeral. She was dressed as she liked, her face was painted with particular colors in accordance with tradition, and her favorite jewelry was on her.*

During the wake the family would place things within her casket, to be buried with her at her funeral the next day. There were knick-knacks; things she thought as special were buried with her. At the actual burial things like clothes etc were placed in a suitcase and buried next to her casket. Pendleton wool blankets were placed over her body; another was placed over the casket.

AZB : Shouldn't her possessions be shared with the family instead of being buried?

RT : *Not many possessions are shared with family members, but in the old days all material possessions of a person who died were burned. The whole house was cleaned of the possessions of the person who died and was to be burned. Still today, a lot of clothing, shoes, etc. are burned, including family jewelry that was not passed on. Although, when my friend from boyhood died, as we hunted and fished together a lot, all his guns were buried with him. But the horns (antlers) of deer he had shot were given to me and others who hunted with him ...I still have the antlers he was most proud of.*

AZB : Are you supposed to bury someone who dies in one, two or three days or in a week?

RT : *The body cannot be left unattended when people are buried. There is no rule for the number of days that a Native must be buried within as far as I know. Historically, my understanding of why the deceased belongings were burned is that it was considered bad luck for those that possessed an item of the deceased. Lots of things that the deceased touched, or what he had, clothing and so on were wanted to be rid of so that no bad luck would come. Years ago, they would practice, not voodoo, but bad luck would come – say, if you had a lock of hair of the deceased. Indians tried to get rid of such things, so the deceased would leave with a clean passage to the other world. Beadwork is one material that is now passed on by relatives. I know that "buckskin" (deerskin) is passed on in many families.*

AZB : Before Christianity came to Indian tribes, did Natives have any feeling for what would happen to them after death?

RT : *They never talked about this directly...my understanding is that they believed in an afterlife, but the person came to that life in the same condition as he left this one. They were not supposed to look back so to speak. Warriors, when they died, didn't believe that was the end, but believed they would move to the next life as warriors again. When you went into the next world, you would keep your warrior status.*

That is why they did things culturally to their enemies when they killed them in fight or battle...they figured (this is second hand to me, but it makes perfect sense to me), they might cut off the dead enemies hand or arm, so that in the next world, the enemy would not have the upper hand on them. How you left one world is how you moved into the next one. For example, if you were an NBA basketball star in this world, you'd come back as an NBA basketball star in the next world. In other words, you didn't lose your talent, knowledge, or skills as you moved into the next life. But if you were maimed in this life, you carried that with you into the next.

As I understand, in afterlife, there was no jury or judging you of what you did in life.

The Supreme Being did not judge you, history was a judging of yourself or your personal life...even of animals.

Wind, rain, fire, etc. were not necessarily inanimate, but all carried a spirit... everything had a spirit. So there was a spirit for a man, a rock, a mountain, everything was dealt with as if it were a being. You did not disrespect something...if you did, something bad would happen to you. You should never have done something to that being.

Everything was in a big circle and affected by everything. What you did to one thing would come back around to affect you once again ("What goes around comes around" is the famous saying).

One did not kill just for the sake of killing, or wasting it, as other animals were affected. The Northern Cheyenne consider the "magpie" bird as a brother. The magpie actually helped the Northern Cheyenne to win "The Race". If it were not for the Magpie, the Northern Cheyenne would not be at the top of the food chain, or master of the other animals. A magpie was helpful because in the race, the magpie was on the side of the Cheyenne versus on the side of the buffalo and other animals. To make a long story short, the magpie won the race, and since he was on the Cheyenne's side, he won it for the Cheyenne too. Thus the buffalo and other animals became food for the Cheyenne; not the other way around. The magpie can be said to be a loud and obnoxious bird, but Northern Cheyenne do not shoot or kill them.

Eagles are also considered very spiritual, very powerful...they are respected. However, "Magpies are much higher in the order of importance than a dog is to Northern Cheyenne people".

Magpies are not held is such high stature by other tribes. The eagle is considered like a brother. Eagle feathers are considered very powerful and are used in ceremonies, whereas magpie feathers... nothing taken from a magpie would give benefit.

251

We know a lot of "superstitions". For example, those owls contribute to the bad times...if you see a sign of owls; anticipate a bad omen has occurred.

AZB : Do you pass on any Indian superstitious to your family, your children?

RT : *No, I do not pass any on to my family. I do things now that were my grandmother alive, I would not be allowed, nor would I do them.*

Example: One that is amazing... "Don't eat greasy foods after dark. Result is, you will have nightmares." Dreams are very powerful in Native culture, so you don't mix the supernatural with the physical world. Visions come from dreams, so something so powerful should not to be taken lightly.

Example: We were at my home, back from hunting, my buddy and I, and we were in the kitchen eating, and it was after dark. We had fried up some meat, and were enjoying our meal because we were very hungry. All of a sudden my buddy looked at me with a worried look and asked if it was dark outside. I looked toward the window and saw that it was dark outside, so I told him it was. He immediately flung the piece of meat he was eating at the trash can and wiped his hands and lips of any grease.

AZB : Rod, when you have a dream, do you think about it?

RT : *Yes, I think about it, but I was never told by my ancestors how to interpret dreams.*

Based on their world, historically and my understanding of it, they didn't want to do certain things because of it; they didn't want to do certain things that would make trouble.

AZB : How did you learn about the St.Labre School?

RT : *I had always known about St.Labre. I knew many graduates, relatives as well. My mother, grandmother, grandfather, all went there...all did not graduate, but one time or another went there.*

When I graduated from the University of Montana, I went to work in Billings, as the only place jobs were available. I had a scholarship from a company that had an office there, and that is also where I met my wife to be, Nicole. After graduation, she was looking for a job but nothing of interest was in the Billings area. She decided to take a job at St.Labre. But at that time, neither she nor I were interested in a long distance relationship. As part of my job, I was transferred to work in Colstrip, which is near St.Labre. Then later that fall, Nicole started working at St.Labre. I knew about the school but wasn't aware of a fund-raising position there. The school suggested that I would be better suited for a financial function rather than accounting. When I started to work at St.Labre, it just turned out that all my work experience from my previous jobs and my study at college came together to fit well in the area of Planned Gift Fundraising.

AZB : You work as Chief Planned Giving Officer. What are the most difficult and the most rewarding experiences about your work at St.Labre Indian School?

RT : *I can't say one experience was more rewarding than another, except that I want to help St.Labre ...I want to help Natives to achieve goals in their lives.*

I appreciate stories of those who turn to St.Labre and how they have overcome difficulties in their lives...the stories are amazing. Everyone thinks they've had "the short end of the stick", but others have had it worse. The stories of Indians are often tragic and how they have overcome tragedies without becoming "basket cases" themselves is a success for them and even to make a living will be a success for them.

Indian people don't often realize how bad they have it, or how dysfunctional their living situation is for themselves and their family; but since that is the only way they know how to live at that point in their lives, it all seems normal to them. The kids grow up in that environment and eventually repeat the mistakes their parents made. Many don't see anything outside of the reservation, not knowing they don't have to live the life they do.

St.Labre, through the education offered, enables its students to make a choice...with an education they can live life on the reservation, and if they need to, they can also live and function productively off the reservation.

AZB : Your uncle was a Vietnam Veteran who received a high award for valor, the Silver Star and for being wounded, the Purple Heart award. Tell me please more about him.

RT : *My uncle, Eddie Small was my mother's brother. He was the second oldest of five children, and grew up in Busby, MT. He was an avid outdoorsman and was very adventurous. He was only about five foot nine inches tall, but Eddie kept himself in great physical shape, which added to his handsome looks and charismatic personality.*

Although Eddie grew up on my grandfather's ranch, he didn't quite fit the standard cowboy mold; I saw him straddled atop more snorting bulls than ranch horses. While his other brothers competed in horse racing and calf roping at area rodeos, Eddie could be found readying himself for an eight-second ride on mad bulls seemingly as large as cars.

Eddie always seemed to have a patient nature and big smile for me whenever I spent time with him as a child. He taught me a lot about many things including hunting, fishing, and competing in sports.

AZB : You wrote a beautiful poem[124] about him...

RT : *I wrote the poem because I have always looked up to my Uncle Eddie. I know he wasn't perfect, but he had an influence on my life that only now, as I think about my days growing up, I have begun to*

---

[124] The poem goes as follows:

My First Hero

I always wanted to be like you, even though I knew I never would
No matter how hard I tried, I just never could.
Speed strength and endurance, you were second to none
You were my uncle, but I felt like your son.
The way you treated people, you certainly were not a faker
How you approached life, you were definitely a risk taker. One day we hunted for pheasants, another day, you gave me my first gun.
Your first trip to Vietnam, you brought back a Purple Heart and a brand new scar
Your second trip revealed bravery, a lifelong friend, and a hard earned Silver Star.
Aunt Norma says you had bad dreams, and woke with nightmares
But you never talked or complained, of your war terrors.
On the Reservation, where everybody earns a nickname, yours was Dirty Ed
Whether it was fighting or poker, you always used your head.
Some thought you were bound for a place of no good
But the right path was your choice, and I always knew you would.
You took it upon yourself one day, to protect all your friends
Who would have thought, it would lead to the end of all ends.
I know you're in Heaven now, and I know your okay
But I want to turn back time, and erase that bizarre day.
You were definitely my hero, and my first hero fallen
When I realized you were gone, I just started bawling.
You were only twenty-eight then, and I was just in the seventh grade
I am much older now, but grateful for the impression you made.
So in remembrance of you, this Memorial Day
I want to honor you in some special way.
Of you and the great man you were, I want them to know
That you planted a seed, and helped it to grow.
The good times we shared are too numerous to mention
But the lessons I learned would grab anyone's attention.
My success in life, is in part due to you
To say I did it myself is simply untrue.
Of my success and accomplishments; some say its drive
To me its honor, taking up where you left off, and keeping your memory alive.
I think it's fitting to say, you were my first hero Uncle Eddie
So when we meet once again, have your strong handshake, hug and smile ready!

realize this. My regret is that he died at a young age, and that I didn't get to spend more time with him, as I got older.

I think the poem gives the reader a little insight into a very unique man, one that I will always remember as being my first hero.

Many times we went hunting and fishing, I had so much fun.

AZB : How do some people acquire Tribal Trust land, while others acquire Trust Land and Allotted land? Did they decide what kind of ownership they would have?

What kind of changes could be enacted so that the land would be worth more?

RT : *Regarding how people acquire trust land versus allotted land is simple. The allotted land was allotted years ago to each enrolled member of the tribe at that particular time. This was a result of a specific congressional act called the Allotment Act, I believe. I am not sure about the date, but it occurred just prior to my grandmother's birth, so this might have been around 1932, but I am not sure about it so, don't quote me on this date. In any case, once land was allotted, it was no longer trust land, thus the allottee owned it without restriction, aside from the fact that he or she still had to let any rent or royalty payments go to their trust account at the Bureau of Indian Affairs. They were free to sell the land as they pleased, and many in the west did because they couldn't run a functional farm and ranch on land due to poor growing conditions and small acreage etc. So, today land that was once allotted may be owned by anyone.*

Land that is still held by the tribe would still be considered trust land, thus it cannot be owned by an individual, it is simply leased to them. If the land is a homestead, then the person gets a longer lease term, given the fact that their home is on the land. Thus they never really own the land, although they can use it as their own.

There is a process that I am told a person can go through to get land that was once a part of the reservation, say allotted land but at one time sold to a non-Native thereby losing its Native affiliation, back into trust status if it is now owned by an enrolled individual again. I am not familiar with this process, but I have heard that it is easier for an individual to get this done than it is for a tribal entity to do this. Again, I am not familiar with this arrangement, so I don't know if it is even a viable option for the average Native.

Why would a Native want to do this? Because the land then is released from the tax base of that state, thereby making it non-taxable by the state.

AZB : What kinds of changes can be done to make land worth more on the reservation?

RT : *I am not convinced that having land able to be worth more on the reservation is necessarily the best thing for native people as a whole. For the most part, land is only worth more if it is in high demand. If it is in high demand by non-Natives, there will always be someone rich enough to buy the land from the Natives, and eventually all the land would be sold off. The Southern Cheyenne Reservation is a prime example of this. Although the land is not aesthetically pleasing it was in high demand by non-Natives because they discovered oil on the reservation. Today, there is little if any land that would be considered reservation. There are a few wealthy natives because they steadfastly held onto their land, but I would venture to say that the tribe as a whole suffered.*

A current issue that is somewhat unsettling to me is the fact that oil is so high in price that there is now more of an effort in the United States to convert coal into a substitute. That in itself is not unsettling so much as the fact that the Northern Cheyenne Reservation contains a lot of coal. Historically the Northern Cheyenne have objected to strip mining of coal on their reservation. Lately, as more and more younger people come of age with less ties to the traditional ways of thinking, that objection is weakening. What worries me is that given the right circumstances and if the tribe had keen negotiators on their side, they might be able to tap into this resource without destroying the fragile cultural setting it now has. However, as history proves itself, this is unlikely, and more than likely the tribe will sell its soul for the short-term benefit of a few because of poor negotiations and uninformed tribal member participation. Thus, the possibility exists that the Northern Cheyenne reservation could suffer irreparable damage to its water table (and who knows what else) if the proper reclamation clauses are not put in place or not enforced in the future.

Finally, if the tribe did somehow opt not to sell or lease their coal, which is to say that the United States government as the trustee of that land wouldn't at some point in the future, force the Northern Cheyenne people to allow coal companies to harvest the coal, what would the bargaining strength of the Northern Cheyenne people be then? Probably next to none.

In a worst-case scenario, I can see the reservation being dismantled as a means to get to the coal.

I try not to be an alarmist, but I think these are real possibilities as this country begins to face greater demand for the limited supplies of natural resources.

AZB : Rod, the last and final million dollar question...

What would you do if you were the President of the United States concerning Indians so their lives would be better?

RT : *If I were the President of the Unites States, or even if I had a sympathetic ear from the President, I would work to clear up two areas of contention and injustice to Native Americans as a whole in the United States: First, work out a fair and just settlement for the native people regarding the Bureau of Indian Affairs' mishandling of individual and tribal trust accounts; second, I would work hard to correct past treaty violations and enforce native rights under current treaties that although old, are still in effect.*

I see the Bureau of Indian Affairs blunders could cost the United States Government billions of dollars; well so what, the United States currently sends many billions of dollars to third world countries all over the world rather than to its own people.

As far as treaties go, the Federal Government has done a poor job of enforcing treaty rights when there is economic benefit for a state or itself. Over the years, states and other government agencies have slowly eroded native treaty rights away, or in some instances ignored and/or exempted themselves from honoring them.

Lastly, I would look into ways to ensure Native tribes had more of an input and representation on legislation and issues affecting tribes within each of their respective states.

As the great Forrest Gump would say, " ... and that's all I have to say about that."

Good questions, thanks for asking.

Aleksandra Ziolkowska-Boehm

An Interview with Linwood Tall Bull
A Northern Cheyenne, the teacher, the healer

Come Back To Your Senses

Aleksandra Ziolkowska-Boehm (AZB) : You are Northern Cheyenne. Were you born and raised on the Northern Cheyenne reservation? How would you describe your Northern Cheyenne traditions and what are characteristics of your tribe?
Linwood Tall Bull (LTB) : *Yes, I was born on the Northern Cheyenne Reservation and am fifty-nine years of age.*

I am Northern Cheyenne, and also I am part Sioux. My paternal grandparents were Northern Cheyenne. I have Irish and French blood by my maternal grandfather, and Sioux by my maternal grandmother.

For Northern Cheyenne, the traditions and our language are sacred. We were very strict with ceremonies and language, and now we try to preserve them. We are characteristically very patriotic...as an example, uncles on both my parents' sides were in the military as I was.

AZB : You are a Headman of the Dog Soldier Society of the Northern Cheyenne Tribe. In earlier times, the Dog Soldiers were a military society, but now their sole role is to hand down the Northern Cheyenne traditions. May you tell more about it?

LTB : *I am a Headman of the Dog Soldier Society of the Northern Cheyenne Tribe. In earlier times, the Dog Soldiers were a military society, but now their sole role is to hand down the Northern Cheyenne traditions. We try to preserve the customs, the language and the traditions. Some of our effort is by formal lessons, but mostly, the responsibility rests with the family.*

AZB : What are your recollections of your childhood?

LTB : *I had a good childhood. I was raised on the southwestern part of the Reservation that was primarily farming land belonging to my grandmother. My father pushed us to speak the English language, but my Cheyenne grandmother didn't speak any English. She spoke to us only in her Native language, so I learned Cheyenne, and I am very happy now that I did.*

In those days, kids were kids. I was exposed in my early days to hunting, and all kinds of traditions. I am still a hunter. My grandmother knew how to preserve food for winter, and she dried berries, meat, etc.

AZB : What was your education like?

Aleksandra Ziolkowska-Boehm

LTB : *I went to school in Busby, Montana with a 5-mile bus ride after a 1-mile walk to the bus stop. So, I walked a lot, and it was a good for me.*

My father was a good example for me. He ran the school bus; he never took a sick day, and was always very dedicated to his work. My mother also worked at the school, and she never took a sick day. They both had to walk cross-country five miles to their work. They were excellent role models for my sister and me. After school, my 4 years older sister would come home and prepare our supper. My father listened a lot to the radio, and later, when the day was almost over, he read English books to us.

AZB : What kind of books did he read to you?

LTB : *He read good books to us such as "Moby Dick" by Herman Melville, "David Copperfield" by Charles Dickens. He liked John Steinbeck's books. It was all high-class literature. He read Christmas carols to us at Christmastime. He taught us to read a lot saying: "Discipline your body with reading, and always read from the first line to the end" or "Go to the library, pick out the biggest book you can find, and read it from cover to cover". That is how I chose "David Copperfield".*

AZB : What did you do after grammar school?

LTB : *I went to high school, also in Busby, Montana, and after three years, I joined the United States Army. I received training as a radio operator. I was in Germany for eleven months, where I volunteered to go to Vietnam, and was there for fifteen months. I was discharged November 23, 1967. I was in the 121st Signal Battalion of the 1st Infantry Division as a radio operator.*

AZB : Did you meet some prejudice being an Indian?

LTB : *As a little boy, I recall riding the bus with my father who was driving the basketball team to a game. He stopped in front of a small café, and showed me a sign posted on the screen door. The sign said: "We do not serve Mexicans, Indians or dogs".*

It made a great impact on me.

AZB : Sir, what year was it?

LTB : *It was in the late 1950's.*

AZB : What image of Indians do you find that people have as you travel away from the reservation? Does that image change in different areas of the country?

LTB : *Aleksandra, not a long time ago, a person from the East Coast asked me, if we Indians still lived in tepees... it is not easy to talk about or to explain that we too are in the twenty-fist century.*

AZB : You are known as one who takes care of the elderly in your tribe. You give lectures teaching that all caregivers of the elderly need to have respect for their patients, however, Sir, in the public knowledge, if I may say so, the Indians always take care of their elderly. How is the situation of the elderly now?

LTB : *Elderly people now are living longer. For 16 years I served with my Tribe's health outreach program. I always stress in my meetings the respect that all caregivers need to have for their patients so that the whole person may be healed. I stress that you don't understand how important the older people are until they are gone. One should give them time and patience and attention. They can give you a blessing. It is critical that we listen to the elderly, to their stories, even if we have heard them a hundred times. We need to show them respect.*

AZB : At the same time there is an image that the elderly, when they became a burden to their tribe, were left on their own in solitude to die. Is this image only from the movies?

LTB : *It was portrayed in a movie "Little Big Man".*
There are stories of times in the Alaskan Natives histories of leaving old ones. The circumstances and life are very hard in their country. I have no knowledge of any Cheyenne Elder ever being left on the prairie to starve. They are too precious to us for even the thought of this.

AZB : I have heard that the verification of your role for the elderly came to you as a vision …It is true?

LTB : *Yes, it is true. Verification did come to me in a vision. During the vision, I was led by an old woman to the dwelling place of old men where I was asked to care for their feet as I have done for other elders on the reservation. After taking care of their feet, I was told that we should always respect our elders, as they are very holy people.*

AZB : In the speeches you give in different places all over the country, you reflect on the Gospel of John and the Passion story of Jesus washing the feet of his followers. You stated that each part of the body plays a different role in wellness and that the feet are the foundation. Please, describe it more.

LTB : *When I think about care for the elderly of my tribe, sometimes I reflect on the Gospel of John and the Passion story of Jesus washing the feet of his disciples during the feast of Passover. I think of why Jesus chose this time to wash the disciples' feet; I believe it was done so that they would never forget him and remember his teachings.*
Most people are embarrassed of their feet, but feet represent "foundation". Look at the family: "good feet...good family". If people have smelly feet or heavy calluses, they won't hear what you say. But, by

Aleksandra Ziolkowska-Boehm

washing their feet and showing them respect, you've got them. They will listen to what you say. Jesus did it before the Last Supper to make them comfortable. Jesus knew if the disciples were comfortable, it would be a better time to counsel them.

AZB : Linwood, you told me, that you find many similarities between the Bible's New Testament and the Indian's religion. Please, tell me more about it.

LTB : *Our Indian Prophet Sweet Medicine, who lived for four hundred and forty-five years among us, was born to a virgin, like Jesus. And like Moses, who led people from Egypt and parted the waters of the Red Sea, a holy man made a hoop of willow, told his followers not to look up or down, and parted the waters of the Bering Straight so it could be traversed. Our oldest legend talks of the period of history when the Indian tamed a large animal and twenty warriors could ride it. There is also a legend about feeding the people. Like the Bible and the young boy, who fed his people from a bowl of fish and loaves of bread. A Prophet named Erect Horns was taking two young men into our sacred mountain, and they met with an old woman who gave them each a wooden bowl. One held buffalo meat cut up in small pieces and the other was filled with corn. She said your people will live a long time and will be without sickness if they eat buffalo meat and corn. The two warriors took the bowls to the people and they fed all who were encouraged to take as much as they wanted for future use. The bowls never were emptied until the two warriors and Erect Horns ate their fill.*

AZB : What is you opinion about religion? Do you find religion in people's life helpful or not in achieving an emotional stability?

LTB : *You must honor all religions.*

One should be sensitive, understanding, and forgiving. Go to the person you hurt and apologize. You will get rid of the bad feelings from your own body; those bad feelings are a poison. Don't stay angry, don't bury anger inside you, it works against you.

AZB : Sir, can you be considered as a modern medicine man?

LTB : *No, not in the traditional old meaning. I observe people. I know everyone on the reservation, and I can tell what is good and what is bad going on with their life. I am helping people to heal. I remind them to think about the circle of life.*

Life is a circle and is divided in four parts. The top left is the Spiritual part, the next is the Mind, then the Body and the last is Environment. None should be separated from the others because all of the parts are connected. Traditional medicine works with the whole, and each part in the circle need to be considered at all time to maintain balance.

AZB : You have a very interesting overview of the healing practices you have learned from the Comanche medicine man, Edger Monetathchi, Jr. Please, tell me about him.

LTB : *Yes, I did learn the healing practices of the medicine man, Edger Monetathchi, Jr. I spent seven days and seven nights in his company. Monetathchi taught traditional Indian Medicine at the conference I attended years ago. He inspired me a lot. He focused on how emotions, buried inside the person, are a cause for disease.*

AZB : You stated that the emotions buried inside a person are a cause for disease. How is one to live in a modern world showing freely his emotions? Doesn't modern civilization require a person to hide his emotions and keep them within, or just share them with very close trustful people?

LTB : *More than once I have emphasized the need to rid oneself of anger, because it poisons the body as well as the spirit. Like I said before, there are four parts of a person - spiritual, physical, mental and environmental or family - that must be considered for good health. As life is a circle, balance between the parts becomes important. If one of the parts is giving us trouble, our bodies become weakened and susceptible to illness or disease. People need to laugh, relax and enjoy their lives, to use their senses, to experience the gifts of smell, touch, hearing, taste and sight.*

These are all needed for our healing, and we need to take time to smell things, to see the beauty of things, to feel mother earth as you walk on her back.

The "quiet ones," the meek and humble people who do not like to attract attention, they are the ones who hold all their emotions within themselves. The quiet ones are usually the people who get the most terrible diseases such as cancer, renal failure, blindness and amputations. People having situations with their skin, that is your nervous system...so, why are you nervous?

The Medicine People say that when you keep all your emotions inside you, they will come out as a bad disease.

AZB : You emphasize the need to "rid oneself of anger, because it is a poison for the body and spirit". You warned that the power of herbal medicine is diminished if the patient is angry. How can we get rid of anger...being born with different personalities, in different cultures and different abilities to deal with our emotions? Is there one lesson for everyone? Do you mean that the real Indian characteristic is being stoic?

LTB : *Stress is a leading cause of illness; it kills people. Everyone should get rid of his or her emotions. There are many ways to do it, and they are peculiar to every individual. Everyone should know his or her* *own body and reaction and how to work with it. For example, I go on bike rides, and also talking to the plants and trees calms me down.*

AZB : Do you believe that we are born with such abilities, or that we have to work to control ourselves? Can we learn to laugh, relax and enjoy our life?

LTB : *You create your own reality, and it is up to you how you are living. The life style you choose is your choice.*

Listen to your body, the left side – woman's side, when it is in pain, means that a woman hurt you and you should be aware of it. The right side – the male in the family did impact you. Look for the cause that gives you illness. Indian Medicine and healing works from the inside out. Look for the root cause.

AZB : How far is the West's "New Age" popular trend from the lessons you give?

LTB : *I don't know much about "New Age", but I would like to say, that I have many non-Indians as students and as friends.*

AZB : You stress that the "quiet ones", the meek and humble people who do not like attention, hold their emotions within themselves. Do you really think that they are more prone to diseases? Or is the theory too simple?

LTB : *Aleksandra. Remember, nobody can heal us, only we can heal ourselves. Awareness is a key. The negative emotions are a waste of time and "you can get rid of them anytime you want". I relate how the Apache people put their unhealthy feelings in a rock and then throw it away. This is why you never pick up a rock when you are in Apache country, for it is said that you might pick up some one else's problems.*

AZB : Should we – not living in Apache country – collect, or not pick up any rocks? Sir, do you believe in taboos? What lesson do you have for the "regular people"?

LTB : *The Plains Indian people have many taboos that are observed in their daily lives. I can provide a list of more than 70. Many of those taboos are hard to understand, but they all should be respected without asking why they are observed.*

AZB : Being invited by the University of Alaska in Anchorage (in September 2004), you stated that fifty percent of the healing has already happened when a person makes the effort to seek help. Tell me more about it. How does it interfere with regular modern medicine?

LTB : *Western medicine works from the outside, while Indian medicine works from the inside. Modern medicine only reacts to the results; it doesn't look for causes. I also stress: Enjoy life. Come back to your senses. Learn again to smell, to taste, to touch. If you lose your senses, you lose it. I teach that one should use the smell, for example, of* the cedar. When you burn it at home, the children will always remember you whenever they smell it. All of your senses trigger memories, and it is important as they also start the healing.

I have tried to teach the ways of the medicine man to modern hospitals and was not even allowed to enter them. What would you say to a person who has cancer? The medicine man would say, "Tell them to enjoy it" because it took them a long time to make it.

AZB : You consider trees to have significant healing power. Trees surround many people. Please, tell me more about the special connection between the tree and the human being?

LTB : *One should talk to the tree. Touch the tree. There are different types of trees; a very healing tree is the maple. There are also nervous trees, like the aspen. I am able to touch a tree and feel its heart beat. If a child is angry, why do they climb a tree, because it takes away their hurt.*

AZB : What role do animals play in healing?

LTB : *As living creatures, animals play big roles in everyone's life. Their medicine is spiritual. It is not necessary to kill them for medicine. Everything is alive. Touching the plants is like touching the Creator. I talk to my plants. They make me feel safe. They take my anger away. Touch animals for their comforting feel. "Touch every living thing as if it were your Creator". To the Indian everything had life, and if it has life you must talk with it. If you believe this then you ask it for help, but you ask with your heart and your head.*

AZB : What is your dream about the future world – for Indians, and for others?

What legacy would you like to leave?

LTB : *I wish there would be less jealousy of each other among my fellow Indians.*

I like teaching people, explaining things.

I would like to leave as my legacy: Come back to your senses.

Aleksandra Ziolkowska-Boehm

An Interview with Billy Evans Horse
Kiowa

Now I have to turn white

Aleksandra Ziolkowska-Boehm (AZB) : You are Kiowa. According to the author Virginia Haase, the Kiowa are a tribe of the southern plains. Historically, they are known to have lived in the Kootenai Region of British Columbia, Canada, to have migrated to Western Montana, and then continued to move until they inhabited present day Nebraska, Kansas, Oklahoma and Texas. I have also learned that the Kiowa were nomadic buffalo hunters who lived in portable skin-covered lodges. They owned many horses and were expert horsemen. The Kiowa were fierce warriors who vigorously opposed the white settlement on the southern plains. They, along with their Comanche allies, made daring raids far into Mexico, capturing large numbers of horses and captives.

Billy, do you love horses? Your name is Billy Evans Horse.

Billy Evans Horse (BEH) : *Yes, I truly love horses, as all my ancestors did. I could not consider myself a true Kiowa if I did not.*

AZB : According to Wikipedia, after 1840 the Kiowa joined forces with their former enemies, the Cheyenne, as well as the Comanche and the Apache, to fight and raid the Eastern natives then moving into the Indian Territory. The United States military intervened, and in the Treaty of Medicine Lodge of 1867, the Kiowa agreed to settle on a reservation in southwestern Oklahoma. On August 6, 1901 Kiowa land in Oklahoma was opened for white settlement, effectively dissolving the contiguous reservation. While each Kiowa head of household was allotted eighty acres[125], the only land remaining in Kiowa tribal ownership today is what were the scattered parcels of "grass land" which had been leased to the white settlers for grazing before the reservation was opened for settlement.

Billy – what is your opinion about those allotments?

BEH : *The allotments were a perfect example of the intention of the Federal Government…give the Indian something with one hand and take it back later, or at the least take something back (usually of greater or more important value) with the other hand.*

---

[125] 320,000 square meters.

267

Aleksandra Ziolkowska-Boehm

AZB : I understand that today there are more than twelve thousand Kiowa, many of whom live like you in Oklahoma. The tribe is governed by the Kiowa Indian Council, which consists of all members who are at least eighteen years old. And you are a member of that Council? Tell me more about its function etc.

BEH : *Yes, I am a member of the Kiowa Indian Council as are all tribal members of eighteen years or older. The Council governs the activities of its people in dealing with the Federal, State and local governments, and is also responsible for maintaining law and order, protecting the rights and privileges of the Kiowa people, insuring adherence to democratic principles in its activities and executing budgetary controls for the reservation's order of business.*

AZB : The Kiowa were part of the Medicine Lodge Treaty of 1867 and were assigned a reservation in Oklahoma one year later. They never really confined their activities to the reservation, however, and resumed warfare with the white settlers in the vicinity. It wasn't until about 1875, when large numbers of their horses were captured and destroyed, and several of their leaders were captured that the Kiowa were defeated.

Please, tell me more about the Medicine Lodge Treaty and its consequences until now.

BEH : *I could sit here and cry on your shoulder all day long about the treaties, and I can cite each one and what the terms were.*

The Medicine Lodge Treaty effectively continued the Federal Government's intent at reduction in the size of reservations. There were actually three treaties...one with the Kiowa-Comanche tribes, one with the Kiowa-Apache tribes and the third with the Cheyenne-Arapaho tribes. These treaties assigned the tribes reservations, which were in close contact with the Sioux, Shoshones, Bannocks and Navajos setting the scene for more conflict for dwindling resources. The treaty was immediately controversial and was contested by most of the involved tribes. Because the tribes were all democratic societies, acceptance of the treaty was contingent upon ratification of three-fourths of the adult members of each tribe. This ratification was never obtained, and thus, the treaty was never valid or legal. The conflict continued for years until the Kiowa Chief Lone Wolf sued the United States Secretary of the Interior on behalf of the entirety of all the tribes, all of whom had been defrauded by the government. The case was decided by the Supreme Court in 1903, and their decision conceded that the tribes had never agreed to the treaty, but concluded that it did not matter because American Indians did not merit protection of the Bill of Rights, claiming they were "wards of the nation...dependent on the United States for their daily food". With this same legal status as the institutionalized, such as

268

the criminally insane and mentally retarded, they did not have the same rights as full persons of other races who were considered able to make decisions for themselves.

This legal precedent has never been overturned and still influences the position of the Government towards all aboriginal American tribes. Need I say more? What better evidence of the "putting down" (subrogation) of Indian people.

AZB : What was the basic effect of the treaties on the Indian tribes?

BEH : *One of the things that is really amazing, I call it the restoration process. When the United States filed a treaty with our people, and if you can study it as long as I have, you will begin to understand what happened because of the treaty. Essentially, it dominates, it takes away and all that kind of stuff. But what have you changed for us? If they ever let us lead, it is going to be interesting. We are not prepared, not by a long shot. Because they kept us down to the point where you see the enemy but you don't kill him. He gets up, you see him again, but you don't kill him. It gives you something to do but nothing else. If America had done well, they'd have done like they did in other countries, after a time of war. They spent billions of dollars in restoration, but not in middle America, because they sent us to school. I am a product of it.*

AZB : But talking to each other, to your children, writing about it, talking openly can make a difference, because knowledge is a first step for understanding, and for wanting to change.

BEH : *I lost my eye; I was attacked by whites, beaten up, and I survived. When I am thinking about that, and other things, the question becomes "why". The simple answer would be: ignorance, lack of knowledge, lack of understanding, and so forth. I've been in communities to try to eliminate prejudice, ignorance and whatever else. I can tell you a number of things.*

When I sit at council with my own people, they listen for awhile, but we don't talk about the problems. Who cares? You know it, I know it. Who cares? Until somebody stands up, and says this is what I am going to do...people are still not going to listen until something happens like an earthquake and or bombing of a building in Oklahoma City.

Knowledge is important, it will open a lot of doors and on and on and on. In all my life, I have a very bad habit of studying. I am always studying.

I never quit, because I was reared by my grandfather. I always have to say: my grandfather. I had a father, I had a mother, but I like my grandfather the most. He was like Moses to me. He talked Kiowa, he knew nothing else. He lived to be about ninety years old.

AZB : Tell me about your grandfather and grandmother and about your childhood.

BEH : *They were Kiowa and only spoke Kiowa. My grandmother was the same age as my grandfather, and ninety years old, when she died.*

AZB : How have you been able to live as an Indian in a white man's world?

BEH : *I have taken it upon myself to live as an Indian in a white man's world.*

Of the two worlds I was raised in, I went back to the one I came from, and I have no problem living today as an Indian.

AZB : Do you think there are feelings of distrust among the Indian tribes? Is it based on a history, as they were often enemies?

BEH : *We are made that way. We don't trust each other. You have to understand how you are made.*

God says this: "Be kind to one another". What does that mean? I have got to watch out for what is called distrust.

If we were all to sleep in the same room tonight, we would be like the jack-rabbit with one eye open. This is where we are at. This is why we have so many things we have to try and face.

I distrust myself because I have rights and wrongs...which one am I going to do?

AZB : Should you accept it and just live with it?

BEH : *You have got to understand yourself first. Some day, if you feel good, someone will come around. But if you are like a banker, you are going to be distrusted.*

If you distrust people, you are not going to trust anybody. What I am trying to demonstrate here is this...we are all make alike, we have two eyes, two arms, two legs. Only thing that is different is in here (BEH pointed to his brain). This thing is very powerful, you could move mountains, you could conquer the world and then you'd be nowhere, but when you begin to move and act, that's the dangerous part. When you think, you are going to become dangerous.

The point I am making is this... My peers have said to me: "You are what you are and you will do that until you go back to where you came from".

That means to me, I was a spirit before I got here and what you are hearing today is a human being that has both the faith and the spirit. When I go back, I am going back to the spirit and my way of doing things. I don't want to face hell. I don't want to know.

Because if I do that, what is going to happen? I am going to teach my children and my grandchildren all the things I think they should be taught. The positive part of my life is what I am going to teach them. They are going to learn faster than I can teach them.

AZB : What do you wish for your grandchildren as a life and understanding?

BEH : *What I wish for them is not going to happen because you have to bring them up like my grandparents did me.*

I tell you, when the children get out of school this evening, they are going to do the same things I do...watch TV, the most corruptive device ever invented.

When the sun goes down, I have nothing but "commandos" running around. And I say what is the world coming to?

AZB : Different time, different values...How was it when you were going to school?

BEH : *When I went to school... I was a non-Indian here (at home) and an Indian there (in the white community). I liked being an Indian more than I liked being a non-Indian.*

As Indians, we constantly faced the philosophy: If you do what I want you to do, you're civilized. If then you don't do what I want you to do, I'll give you a bat on the nose.

AZB : Billy, you know your Kiowa language. How much does it make you special among your people and among others tribes?

BEH : *This mind that I have here is Kiowa and uses "Indian words". I am a Kiowa in my mind, and I still speak the language. When I think, even before I talk, I still think as a Kiowa, and I am going to die that way. I don't want to be anything else.*

AZB : Are your children and grandchildren bilingual?

BEH : *This morning before meeting with you, I was talking to my granddaughter, she is in her mid-twentieth, and I asked her this question because I had just read up on it last night. I said,*

"What does bilingual mean to you"?

She said, "Well that's hard".

"What do you mean it is hard?"

She said, "Well, Grandpa, you know I can't speak Kiowa, just English.

And you ought to have heard what I told her I thought of the English language.

You need to speak your own language.

But I know it is almost impossible because of all other things that impact their life everyday. She can't talk Kiowa, because she works at the gas station or because she works somewhere else. It is not a Kiowa environment, so that prohibits us from practicing the language.

271

AZB : Your granddaughter wants to mix into the surrounding world, it is natural. Isn't it up to you to give her feelings of pride from her past, her heritage?

BEH : *Let me get back to the "click" on my mind. We Kiowa are right brained. Everyone else outside is left brained. And you try to cross over. I don't care how you do it. American Indians, the whole nation of the tribes, and there aren't going to be any Indians period. So, vice versa.*

Let me give you an experience I had one time. I was really upset. Went to high school, was the football quarterback, and all the girls were around...But I wanted a white girl, that's what I wanted.

In my Kiowa teachings, that is "no-no". So, to myself I went home and showed my grandfather myself in my football uniform. He shook all over when he saw me.

Now I have got to turn white. I got a bar of soap and I washed all over me. Grandpa watched me because he always knew what I was doing. He didn't say anything.

Every evening, I used everything that kills germs, a "colored boy" they called us... "Jackson". I am just trying to turn white, tried to talk the language they talked. And it got to where I wanted to change. That girl ain't gonna like that. I went and bought some sandpaper and tried to sand my skin off and I bled all over. I was trying to really change. That's how bad I was for a year or two.

I needed someone to talk to about it. Well, I didn't give up. Grandad put his hand on my shoulder and said:

"Grandson, I have got to talk to you a minute. You are going to kill yourself". So my point is this. I've got a lot of good news for Americans if they'll listen to me. Be what you are!

AZB : Billy you married a Kiowa girl and settled down and have lived as a noble Indian family.

BEH : *Aleksandra, I have led a good life, and the bad part I don't want to talk about because I am a human like you and everyone else, and I have done my share (of bad things). When you get down to the thinking process, I have to convince you that you look at us in terms like Columbus did yesterday and 500 years back: Oh those are Indians and he mislabeled us.*

But when they began to find out we were humans, they gave us another name...savages.

AZB : There were so many negative stereotypes, there are now too, and there are all over the world, not only here, in the US.

BEH : *The only thing that was negative was the lack of knowledge and ignorance. Hey Aleksandra, you know we were the kind of guys who* *said: "Brother, sister...come let's have a Thanksgiving, and that was all they wanted...the turkey, and then they left.*

AZB : Thanksgiving is one of the most cherished holidays in the US. There was a lot bad incidents, events, a lot of bad history… but then in 1787, the Constitution was written, and enacted three years later, the first in the world (by the way, the Polish constitution in May 3, 1791 was the first in Europe, and the second in the world). The good and bad past is now all history, but the Constitution stays and says that we are all equal.

BEH : *The history of the United States is written by non-Indians in terms of the Constitution. And they will reflect and see that the last Constitution was taken from that of the Iroquois Confederacy to the others and all that kind of good stuff.*

And tell me where you see anything outside of the comments clauses in the Constitution dealing with the Indians. Where does it say that a person has to be more than 1/4th Indian ancestry to be an American?

In order to understand who I am, and I know who I am, because I gave my name to begin with. In order for me to cash a check or do anything, I have to produce this ID card to tell them I am an Indian.

AZB : Can't you just use a driving license?

BEH : *I would like to if one were given to me. You are listening to a sixty-nine year old Indian.*

AZB : I don't fully understand the idea about the Indian ID card.

BEH : *There is lot to be understood, and the best part of it is going to be in attacking the so-called communications, and it has to be done right. You have to allow one percent for things not being done right. And that's been the story of my life...listen and all that kind of stuff. Those are the kinds of things I talk about to my own people when I sit in council.*

And if I ask them the same questions, they would ask me: "Why do you have to be 1/4th Kiowa to be a Kiowa?"

Let me tell you something. I have got a row of counsel members sitting over there. You don't let them hear words that they don't qualify. But in Grandpa's house, they were Kiowa. Even though their father may have been white or maybe Mexican or an Indian of national origin, he is still a Kiowa in that house. He is still my grandfather, and when I grab him around the neck and hug him, he knows it.

AZB : I don't understand a lot concerning the current life of American Indians. I try to read about the subject, and I have subscribed for over ten years to two Native American magazines. I have several American Indian friends...I only know that Norman and I have

273

compassion for Indians and the will to understand; but we are many times surprised learning new things, like you just are telling me now.

BEH : *Don't worry about it. Even we Indians don't understand everything about us. It is what you have to live with. Can you imagine in America where American children are going to? That's the story you should tell. I danced and sang in the first government school I went to, and they threw me out and made me do work. You don't do that in here, I was told. And that's the reason I am here.*

And I remember the teacher who taught me...see this is the true world you live in, she said. If I believe in the flag of the United States, and as a little kid I sit there and think "ok that's the one that killed a lot of people". How am I going to stand up and salute it? So, I stayed down. She called me by name and said: "You have to pledge allegiance to the flag of the United States of America.". I did not, so I was sent out and got hard labor. The "kicker" was that she said you children have got to know this. The father of your country was George Washington. I went home and knocked on the door, my grandfather answered it and I said to him: "Grandfather, you know I found out who my Daddy is finally". He said, "Who is he?"

"His name is George Washington."

You never hear of such damnable words to come out?

AZB : Are you a religious person? And what does it mean, if you are?

BEH : *My pickup on this area of religion is that here awhile back, my wife likes to go to church. She likes to read the daily Methodist reading (you don't have to read it). I sit there and listen. I am the sounding board. Sometimes I listen and don't say anything. She says, "I know you are thinking". She brought an issue home, and it caught my attention. According to the Scriptures, Moses was going to be picked as a prophet for his people. I am reading the same thing that happened to us. Here's how I picked up on it. The Egyptians had put the Israelis into "bondage". The Pharaoh was doing everything to make the Israelis' life miserable. At that point in time and before then, God had made a covenant with his people. He had to keep it. It came to pass, God said: "I am going to talk to you Moses. I am going to make you the leader of your people because of my covenant with your people. This is what we are going to do". One of the objectives was to take the Israelis out of bondage, and it seemed comical to me, because I have a different way of looking at things. When God spoke to Moses, Moses could hardly talk. He was like a misfit. The first time he got God's attention was when Moses burned the bush and the voice spoke out from behind. How are going to do that God?...so he gave Moses a stick which became a staff.*

274

Pick it up, hold it. Moses said, "What am I going to do with this thing? I have no power. So, he threw it down, and it became a serpent. Moses said "Wow".

I have got to tell the world about this stick being turned into a serpent. They're going to listen to Moses... to make it a rod and pick it up by the serpent's tail. So that's the reason he carried it because he was going to use it. Moses said, "You picked the wrong guy. I still can't talk right. They are not going to do what I say". God said, "Well, I am going to give you more power. Oh, by the way, you have a friend, and I am going to talk to him so he can help you out. So, you can talk to Aaron your friend". So Moses and Aaron became a team with Aaron the spokesman. God chose him.

So every time Moses did something, he would say, "Aaron, look at the fine mess you got me into".

I have to go back and do research on the Old Testament. Now I know, Moses became a prophet when he was eighty some years old and Aaron three years older. They were two old men becoming wise and prophets. That's the reason when you grow old, you get more knowledge. They did their work, and Moses got the Israelis to the Red Sea. And God parted it and then the Israelis went to the land of milk and honey and all that stuff.

It brought to my mind after reading that, the part of the Covenant was the Ten Commandments. Moses was asked to come to Mount Sinai to receive the Commandments. The Commandments show the people how they should live. He put them in a box... what caught my eye was when Moses took that and built a tabernacle. They put the Arc of the Covenant in the most holy place, and they had a curtain. Below it they burned incense and so on.

When I read that, and I closed my eyes thinking of the old people and all my teachings... that's where we lost it...Bringing it into focus here.

AZB : I have read that Native American don't like to celebrate Columbus Day (officially October 12th), because they don't consider Columbus a hero at all.

BEH : *Aleksandra, Columbus came, they don't talk about the people who came before him... and the people who came before him were Spaniards. And they came all around here and they wanted the gold, silver and all the riches. And they went back. The point I am trying to make is: the Spaniards brought their missionaries in the name of Christianity, they tried to fool the Native Americans and they did in some cases.*

And they didn't proclaim a certain language. At that point, when all that was brought here...the most high covenants with God, and believe it or not, today the Covenants are still with us. I talk to him like I am talking here. And really what I am saying, I am really talking to God because he gave us the right to do so. And when you hear of a "medicine babble", what are you talking about? That's all it is... the covenants between God and those people. I feel very fortunate that we still have them among us, and for my people it really gives them something to think about.

The basic premise of that is... if God makes you, gives you a way to work or believe or whatever you want to call it, and he gave you the language, we should be able to use it ... but when someone came and shoved our language aside and put his over ours, we have got nothing but problems here.

I am not anti-denominational or anti-Bible. I am just only quoting something that happened over there...and so here we are. So, what am I seeing...if Native Americans have anything that they can identify with, then you can get back to us.

And that's what makes us a great people.

Why doesn't the Constitution recognize us? I am a human being, but I am under the Department of the Interior (DOI). The DOI is for land and water, and animals. I am not an animal. But I am still under the DOI.

What happens if I want to build a gas station? I'd like to have the money to do it. Okay? My name is up there, and I am standing there... but I am told I can't do it, and it is because I am not equally protected by the Constitution.

I found that treatment everywhere I went. I sat there in Washington D.C. I can't tell you what happened to me up there.

AZB : What happened?

BEH : *I said – to hell with a guy by the name of Washington. He was a hero for the whites...*

They remembered my name. I talked about the United States Government for a couple of years. The point I am making is all the anti-Indian mentality...it makes it very difficult to think of becoming an entrepreneur in terms of business. I can do the same things anyone else can do, but I know what you are up against because of always having a fight in Oklahoma. I can go anywhere else, and it would be no problem. I'm sure. But if I try to do something in Oklahoma, you have the anti-Indian mentality there to deal with.

I am sorry to say that when I put my foot on the ground, I am ready to roll. All you have to do is get out of my way or whatever else. Today, I am not fully defeated, but I am not excited because of the opposition I have to go through to accomplish anything.

AZB : Hasn't the education available to Indians improved their outlook and their ability to take advantage of opportunities to further themselves?

BEH : *It depends on whose slant of education.*

We graduate. If we could do the things we were trained to do, they'd find a way to chop us out and hold us down. And that's what we're trying to break out of... it is very difficult. I don't care what they say, let me go and I am born... instead they tie me up, put me in a jail, or execute me. That's what they have done to all our leaders. I am no different. What I am trying to stress is that if America wanted to...whatever number of years it took, to restore us to the same capacity, so that we are all equal, (then Indians could compete in any field of endeavor). If I go over to the State Legislature here in Oklahoma, and I try to introduce a bill, I'll get no one to listen to me. If I go to Washington, they are not going to listen to me, because we are still "fair game". The Federal Government hasn't yet gotten all that they want.

AZB : Is there hope in having Indian representatives in the Legislatures (state and federal)?

BEH : *Let me ask you a question. Imagine, on the reservation that an election was being held and you had a voting booth and you were selecting a Senator and you were voting on the candidates. You tell the people that at 9:00 AM, the liquor store is going to open and the voting both is going to open. Will your voters come? ...but at the same time they've got enough money to go to the liquor store to get what they like. This is the hardest challenge in motivating Indians. Where will they be? Would they be in line to vote or in line to get the liquor?*

AZB : That's how they generated votes in the old days, in the industrial areas. Get a guy drunk and then get him to vote.

I think it is a very important to have a good representative to express your point of view in the legislatures. The other thing is the education for children, so they can choose the profession they want.

BEH : *You know Aleksandra, the other day, I use prayer a lot of ways. I have got a lot of grandchildren, and I am talking to God. I have got one and I raised him, as his parents are divorced. He is going to high school. He is kind of like a class clown to a certain degree. But that's only to get attention. This morning I asked him..."Grandson, what would you like to do when you grow up?" I thought he was going to say things that would get him into trouble and then having to be punished for that.*

He said, "Grandpa, what I would really like to do is get into computers. That's what I am interested in". I am going to work on him to

277

reinforce that ambition. I have another one (eighteen to nineteen years old) interested in the health field and laboratory work. She said when I get out of high school, I want to start my career in those ...so I've got to work on that.

My point is this: My family and I are going to have to make an effort to reinforce their ambitions. We, as a family, and the community are going to look out for them very seriously, because the young people are the future. For the future, it is up to my family to do our part and keep them on the track.

AZB : Billy, I wish your grandchildren all the best. Being with Norman on the Pine Ridge Reservation, we saw some very depressing scenes. The second biggest reservation has nothing to offer its young people.

BEH : *On the Pine Ridge Reservation, it's pathetic, I have been there on a weekend. I went to an Indian school to talk to them because I am one of their kind. They wanted to know my tribe...they asked me a million questions.*

Whether it is Pine Ridge, or my reservation, we must focus in on the needs of the young ones. We can't keep raising them in our environment of hate, greed and all that kind of stuff and that's exactly what we are doing and I don't like it. I don't like to talk a whole lot about money when I have my little ones around me, because that's when they get the disease. So, what I am focusing on with these young ones...what is essential in terms of needs, and they should try to figure out how to get a committee to respond to that. I have a problem right now with some people working for me at a university in Indiana. One contractor that I know wanted to give them my idea. Will you guys help me? This is what I want you to do. I want you to see how we can get a computer...and when we have enough of them, we can use them in Carnegie, OK. After we find out how many Indian children we have and after we figure it all out, we need to bring in a computer that will simplify the business if you will. Teaching them how to do that, we help them and ourselves. They're working on it... the last I know of, we may get a group of computers. That's one of the projects I am working on right now. I am looking for good things for those kids.

AZB : The school should help not only with the schooling but also with building self-esteem and instill the will to work for the better.

BEH : *We have to figure out how to attack these problems and how to make these changes at our schools. Somebody asked me the other day, as we drove by my rural country house and said, "You have a football team down there". I responded, "Oh, you mean you have seen my kids playing "touch football". You want to know why they like to play touch* *football. I'll tell you why...they are bored to death. They have got nothing else to do. But at least I've got them out in the country. Can you imagine them in the city?" You just drive around this city (Oklahoma City) ... I don't know this town. You have the children come in from school. You look at the neighborhoods, broken down, the poverty...put them to work and see what goes on. I'll bet two to one, if he goes to work and collects his money, he will go to school with a damn pistol or a blade and gold chains and radios. I don't think we are blind...I don't think that law enforcement is the problem...my point is the reason you have all the problems you can deal with is because you are letting them do it. You are hurting them by trying to help all of them.*

AZB : Tell me about the Kiowa tribe's migrations.

BEH : *Down there about ten miles there is a mountain. There is a pass, and that's where the Polish settlements are. From where I live in the corner of Oklahoma all the way down to El Paso, they've got rocks over there and they've got Indians. There was a siege by enemies of the Kiowa there for about ten days. They said the Kiowa will not get out of there alive. After a certain number of days, the Kiowa found an opening, they went through the opening, and they stayed in the area for a great number of days. A lot of history is there. There is a hundred mile long desert in there, a long way from where the rocky mountain opening is. They came through that, and there are a lot of landmarks there, all the way to El Paso. There were songs written about this, and the songs are still with us. Everyone was amazed. We have a lot of history, back and forth the Kiowa traveled all the way to Mexico City. They traveled as far as they could, and there were descriptions of what they saw. For the first time, they saw "little men" running on top of trees. They made trips as far as the West Coast and the East Coast, and to Alaska. My great-great grandfather was named "White Bear", and his name comes from the Kiowa having seen polar bears on their travels. There are a lot of landmarks in the United States that I know.*

There is a lot of history and no one wrote it.

AZB : Does Indian history recognize the visits by the Vikings to North America?

BEH : *What I know of the Norse people, I took from those people. In our whole history, we came direct from heaven to here. We have proof...we have a separate language, and no one can write our language. We are trying to, but with no success.*

AZB : You don't have any dictionaries?

BEH : *The old men tried. Not a long time ago, I worked in community college classes. I was going to teach them to talk Kiowa, but a lot of the professor's students already could talk Kiowa. With an effort*

279

you can make a dictionary. We decided that you can teach it orally, and what we taught was conversational Kiowa. The students follow me wherever I go.

AZB : Some universities have special programs to save the different Indian tribal languages, the stories. There are so many publications every year.

Billy, I have heard that Indians give the people a special name, not during the birth, but later in life.

BEH : *There were a bunch of Italian visitors on a second trip here who flew in from Chicago. They wanted to learn to speak Kiowa. But the names that we give have to be with some kind of consent. And I told them, listen closely. When I give you a name, you remember it. Then I wait for something to happen. We are in a "sweat-box", it is totally dark, and I said I am going to talk in my language for a little while and you listen. When I got through talking, and I sprinkled the water over the hot rocks, the rocks started singing. "You hear that? What do you say? He said, "thank you". I responded, "I could tell you some more, but we are going to stop, so, come out the door". Then, I told him his name: "Rocks That Are Singing."*

His wife, when we were up on top of the mountain looked around. I told her, "You can see as far as the eye can see. You are on top of the world. These trees that are growing up here are Cedar trees. In our history, God saw fit to take this Cedar tree and have it bloom all year round, and we are going to take a little bit of this and we are going to eat here, sleep here and think here". And I prayed, and God said to me, the lady's name is the Little Blooms on the Cedar Tree.

When a Kiowa gives a name, it means something.

AZB : What do you think my name might be? And why?

BEH : *He smiled and said: "Woman Who Asks Many Questions"...because you do, but they were good ones.*

AZB : You yourself have some other name besides Billy, what is your name?

BEH : *"Mediator" or "One Who Sits in the Middle".*

In our tabernacle, we build an alter from the earth in the form of the moon. In the middle, we put the sage on it and then this medicine we call Pindi and that's my name. We have this bush/flower called Indians' Red Rose and that's our altar.

When we name names, we have a meaning to it. Abraham Lincoln? Maybe Abraham's the one who brought the Lincoln. That's how our names are derived.

AZB : What is the most important thing to be done for Native Americans? What would you do if you could have the opportunity and the power?

BEH : *I would strive to have the Constitution amended such that the Indian's second class citizenship was eliminated and to abolish the law that says an Indian must carry an ID card to prove he is an Indian. Furthermore, I would promote the concept of outsourcing of industry to Indian Reservations (rather than to other countries) with priority given to those reservations that are the most remote and in the most need of work such that their people can escape from the "poverty line".*

Oklahoma City, Oklahoma 2006

An Interview with Homer Flute

A member of the Apache Tribe of Oklahoma, Chief Executive
Officer/Trustee of the SCMD Trust, a Native American nonprofit
organization.[126]

We have become beggars in our own land

Alekasandra Ziolkowska-Boehm (AZB) :
Homer, what is your tribe: Cheyenne?
Arapaho?

Homer Flute (HF) : *I am an enrolled
Apache tribal member, and also descendent
from the Cheyenne/Arapaho/Cherokee tribes.
My mother's name is Cleo Antelope Flute and
her father's name is Hugh Antelope who was
4/4 full-blooded Cheyenne, and her mother's*
name is Mary May Paisbizzy who was half Arapaho and half Apache. My
Mother and Grandmother were both enrolled in the Apache tribe, and
my siblings and I are enrolled in the Apache Tribe and raised in the
Apache culture. My father's name is Thompson Flute, and he was a 4/4
enrolled Cherokee.*

AZB : You consider yourself as Apache?

HF : *Although I am enrolled and raised in the Apache culture, I
have connected with my Cheyenne and Arapaho ancestry and heritage
and can function very well in those cultures.*

AZB : Please tell me about your ancestry on both parents side.

HF : *Because of my position with the Sand Creek Massacre
Descendants Trust, I have learned a great deal about my Cheyenne and
Arapaho ancestry. Through my Mother, I am a descendant of Cheyenne
Chief White Antelope (1789 - 1864) whose camp was located at Sand
Creek, Colorado on November 29, 1864 where his band was attacked
during the 1864 Sand Creek Massacre. Chief White Antelope was the
first killed while trying to stop the attack. White Antelope was among the
first Cheyenne to travel to Washington, visiting President Millard
Fillmore in September of 1852. In 1861 White Antelope joined Black
Kettle, Tall Bear, Lean Bear and Old Little Wolf in signing the Treaty of
Fort Wise. A striped blanket, reportedly taken from Chief White
Antelope's body at Sand Creek, is currently housed at the School of
American Research, in Santa Fe, New Mexico. This is my Cheyenne*

---

[126] An activist involved in seeking reparations for ancestors of the descendents
of Sand Creek, Colorado massacre by the US militia

ancestry and legacy as a descendant of Chief White Antelope and descendant of the 1864 Sand Creek Massacre; also, I am a descendant of the Trail of Tears through my Father, whose mother's name was Rachael Christie and whose parents and grandparents were labeled as immigrants from East of the Mississippi because they were brought to Oklahoma in the Trail of Tears.

AZB : What tribe of the Apache? I have learned that there are many different nations of Apache people with differences in language, history, and culture. For example, The White Mountain Apache Tribe, Mescalero, Jicarilla, Lipan, Western Apache, Kiowa-Apache, Chiricahua Apache ... I also learned that in all the history of the Federal Government-Native American relations, the situation which confronted the Chiricahua–Apache represents the most unprecedented case of injustice. There is also the Plains Apache tribe of Oklahoma.

HF : *I am enrolled in the Apache Tribe of Oklahoma, also known as the Plains Apache. The Plains Apache came from the north and because they were a small tribe in number, they were sometimes affiliated with or camped near either the Cheyenne/Arapaho tribes or Kiowa/Comanche tribes for protection and sometimes were known as the Kiowa-Apache.*

AZB : The Apache nations have very famous heroes, like Geronimo, a great leader and warrior, who fought against ever-increasing numbers of both Mexican and United States military. Is it true, that when finally released from prison, he was moved to Fort Sill, Oklahoma, and in his old age, Geronimo became something of a celebrity? That he appeared at fairs, including the 1904 World's Fair in St. Louis, and that he sold souvenirs and photographs of himself? He rode in the United States President Theodore Roosevelt's 1905 inaugural parade. I have read that, but at the same time, I have learned he was not allowed to return to the land of his birth.

HF : *As far as I know, Geronimo and his people were held as prisoners of war at Fort Sill, Oklahoma and upon release, the people that returned back to their homeland in New Mexico are known as Mescalero Apache and those that stayed in Oklahoma are known as Fort Sill Apache and received allotments within the Kiowa, Comanche and Apache reservation.*

AZB : Geronimo died of pneumonia at Fort Sill, and he is now buried at the Apache Indian Prisoner of War cemetery. Is his grave a special sacred place for the Apache?

HF : *Geronimo's grave is more of a special or sacred place to the non-Indian than it is to the Indians. There was a story about several young men from some type of non-Indian secret society trying to rob Geronimo's grave.*

AZB : Another very well known Apache is Cochise, also a great leader and warrior, who died at the Arizona reservation in 1874. The famous movie "Broken Arrow" features a fictionalized Cochise as its main character, and I bet many people all over the world know his name. Those two legendary warriors have to be a great pride for all Indians, not only Apache. Were you as a boy, and now as an adult, proud of Geronimo and Cochise?

HF : *Cochise and Geronimo are recognized as great chiefs and warriors, but other tribes have their own legendary warriors and chiefs that they have great pride and respect for. For instance, I admire White Antelope because of the moral principles that he believed in and practiced during his life. White Antelope had been in Washington in 1863 and favored peace and friendship with the Whites. He could not believe that the soldiers were attacking his camp in what is known as the 1864 Sand Creek Massacre, after he had been telling his people for months that the Whites were good and peace was going to be made. He told many of his people that his camp was under the protection of the United States government and no harm would come to them. When the attack on his camp came by United States soldiers and after trying and failing to stop the attack, he did not wish to live any longer, he stood with his arms folded and began singing his death song and was shot dead by the soldiers.*

AZB : The Native Americans children should be taught their culture, history, language. They can be so proud of their heritage.

HF : *The US government established the Bureau of Indian Affairs (BIA) to shepherd the Indians through a forced assimilation into the white culture. One of the first things that the BIA did was to establish the Indian Boarding Schools run by Christian Missionaries. The missionary's task was to change the Indians and in order to change the Indian they had to take away their pride in their culture, heritage, songs and language. Most people who went to these schools came back and didn't speak their native language. Many of the people remember the punishment that they faced at school for speaking their language or practicing their culture and didn't want their children to have the same experience, so they didn't stress maintaining their culture and heritage and didn't teach their children their tribal language or songs.*

AZB : There should be an apology at a very high level... not only from a church but the church at its national level. The same apology is expected by the African American people as well. Honestly, I don't understand why the American President doesn't do it? It is all in the past, and why not to clear the past for the present good? It takes a man to issue an apology. Pope John the II apologized in the name of the Catholic

Church to Jews and showed how great a person and Church leader he was. (President Bush apologized to the Polish nation for its betrayal at Yalta by the Allied leaders Roosevelt and Churchill).

HF : *What good is an apology, if it is only meaningless words. An apology by itself is like faith without works, or works without faith. The US and State governments through the BIA, Courts, and federal and state government agencies need to respect the sovereignty of each tribal government and help the tribes to truly attain tribal self-government and self-sufficiency. Practicing paternalism and bureaucracy to usurp the authority of tribal governments rather than giving tribes the technical support they need is detrimental to the tribes.*

AZB : I would like to stress that Catholics now do a lot of good things. The schools Norman and I visited were all Catholic. It looks like Catholics were the only missionaries that went up to the Dakotas. Norman was surprised when he didn't find schools run by Protestants.

HF : *There were not only Catholic missionaries but also Quakers, Mennonite, Baptist, Methodist and Dutch Reformed missionaries. The Christian missionaries' only interest was to change the Indians to be like the white man, not to have Christ like attributes. The missionaries failed in teaching the Indians about Jesus Christ, who he was and what his mission was.*

AZB : Everything happened because of the white people who in those days came straight from Europe, countries like England, Denmark, Germany, etc. They overcame the Native Americans, and in so doing, killed and destroyed them. It happened to aboriginal people in Australia as well.

HF : *The Indian were never really defeated on the battlefield. The Indian was defeated because of ignorance. The white man used treaties and falsehoods as the mechanism to defeat the Indian. It was all the bureaucracy and trickery by the government, which still exists today.*

AZB : I recall that it cost the lives of six thousand federal troops trying to move the Seminoles out of the Everglades in Florida.

HF : *After the Sand Creek Massacre in 1864, the Cheyenne, Arapaho and many other plains tribes united and went to war against the United States. After the government realized that fighting the Indians was too expensive because to kill fifteen or twenty Indians, it cost a "million dollars" each. And recognizing the cause of the war with the Indians was dishonorable and disgraceful, look at how the government treated the Indians at Sand Creek in 1864. War was useless and expensive, and the government finally decided to resort to peace treaties.*

AZB : There are so many misconceptions of and labels for the Native Americans.

HF : *Ignorant and insensitive people put labels on everybody and everything that they don't understand to cover up their own insecurities.*

AZB : Have Indian tribes become more self-reliant with efforts to learn farming while still practicing protection of the environment?

HF : *Most Indians don't farm their land because the land is so fractionated and ownership is held by numerous owners, thus the land is leased out to white farmers.*

AZB : How do Indians feel about the significance of the Pledge of Allegiance?

HF : *Indian people are by nature very patriotic and will fight to protect their country.*

AZB : My impression of the Bureau of Indian Affairs (BIA) is very negative from what I have learned about it...a rather inept and unfair bureaucracy. What have they done?

HF : *Basically, the BIA practice of paternalism and bureaucracy deprives the individual Indians and tribal government of tribal self-government and self-sufficiency and creates an un-level playing field for the Indians. You can choose almost any year since the BIA's predecessor, the Indian Department, was created in 1824 and find the government's reports describing poor management, no accounting system, missing money, no attempt to fulfill the fiduciary duty to the Indians as promised and required by law.*

AZB : How to prevent the alcoholism? It is such a big problem on the reservations.

HF : *Most Indians have used alcohol at some time in their life, and it is most often because they don't have a direction and are not ready to accept responsibility.*

AZB : How were you able to overcome your alcohol problem?

HF : *Accepting Jesus Christ in my life was the greatest event of my life; it gave me a direction and helped me to accept responsibility for myself and others.*

AZB : Homer - do you have children?

HF : *I have three children and nine grandchildren.*

AZB : Are they all doing fine?

HF : *They are all doing great. My grandchildren are all in school, and my children are all working.*

AZB : Are there good work opportunities?

HF : *Yes, if you have sufficient education, work experience or training, there is work. If you don't have any of these, you may have a problem.*

AZB : The young people return to the reservations because they can't find work, and they don't know what to do with themselves.

HF : *There's been so much down-sizing in the industries, because a lot of technology has taken over for the human. Those people who don't have the ability to move on with the technology are left out.*

AZB : That problem is almost all over the states (country?)

HF : *It is a time of change all over.*

AZB : What is your dream?

HF : *I think a lot about my tribe attaining tribal self-government, accountability and self-sufficiency that they can look after the education, health and welfare of all tribal members and not just the few.*

AZB : What kind of life would you like for your children?

HF : *I would like to see all my children accept Jesus Christ as their Lord and Savior, and live a long peaceful and prosperous life.*

AZB : Homer, what good would you like to see happen to Indians?

HF : *I would like to see Indians regain their culture and heritage and attain self-sufficiency.*

AZB : What is the most important thing to be done for Native Americans?

What would you do if you could have such an opportunity and power?

HF : *I would build a sovereign government that has its foundation built on accountability and is self-sufficient and responsible for the education, health and welfare of all tribal members.*

AZB : Do you attend the pow-wows?

HF : *Yes, I do. We are having a pow-wow; the next one may be in December. We are still in the planning stage. You are welcome to attend.*

AZB : We will be happy to.

Does "Dago Te" means "hello" in Apache? How can I say: "See you soon"?

HF : *I don't know that word.*

Oklahoma City, Oklahoma 2006

An Interview with James A. Humes[127]

A Chickasaw and an Oklahoma businessman and entrepreneur working
to benefit the people of his tribe.

One acre at a time

Aleksandra Ziolkowska- Boehm (AZB) : I
think that being Indian, or part Indian, was
considered for years very cool not only in the
United States (my husband Norman always
dreamed of being an Indian), but in many
countries all over the world…

James A. Humes (JAH) : *Really? Look
at the movies, or at children playing. You will
see, for example, non-Indian children dancing*
around in cowboy outfits, shooting their cap pistols. Who is going to be
Indian? Obviously, no one wants to be "an Indian". No one, because all
of the children want to play cowboys, not Indians. In the movies the
cowboys always won, the Indians never won.*

AZB : In the old "Indian movies" the plot was usually that "savage"
Indians killed the peaceful pioneer settlers…

JAH : *And our children have to face those movies, where there is a
battle. It always upsets me. The Indians are shown as evil savages, and
when we did win a battle, it was portrayed as a massacre or a surprise
attack.*

*When the dominant society always portrayed the soldiers as
winners, it was shown as a great victory in the progress of taming the
savage Indians and a step in civilizing them.*

AZB : But in recent years, many different movies have been made,
with scenarios written by people more aware of Indian history and Indian
people, and many were based on real events. Like the beautiful movie by
Kevin Costner "Dances With Wolves" (1990), or "Thunder Heart"(1992)
with Val Kilmer and Graham Greene. In "Dances With Wolves", the
Indians were beautifully portrayed as caring, family oriented, and
honorable.

JAH : *For good or bad, the Indian was usually portrayed as a
"sidekick" to the white man. He was never portrayed as his life really*

---

[127] Jim Humes passed away in the Spring of 2008. In regular contact with the
author, Jim anxiously awaited the final publication of this book in the United
States.

Aleksandra Ziolkowska-Boehm

was. Also, the movies treated Indians generally rather than concentrating on one tribe in particular.

AZB : Does Indian history recognize the visits by the Vikings to North America?

JAH : *There are quite a few stories about that. There were blonde-headed, blue-eyed, light skinned pilgrims, even in Oklahoma, with evidence dating back to the 1400's. There were routes used by Scandinavians or some people that were carved in the sandstone. Over the years, parts of the sandstone cracked off, but there is one-preserved part that was compared/extrapolated...the conclusion being that they knew their ancestors had come to this new land.*

AZB : Jim, what led the Government to initiate so many treaties?

JAH : *Their main intent was to take Indian land or resources. The Military made the decisions on what action to take without the sanction of Congress. The Military were responsible. The policy makers were not out in the West where the action occurred. And the Military do not make peace...they make war.*

The only thing that led to the treaties was that fighting Indians wars became a very unpopular thing. It kept costing more money and the Military had to keep asking the Treasury for more money. The government was struggling to pay for civil and prior wars back East (French Indian etc). Indians won playing the White Man's rules. They won a Supreme Court decision that the relocation act of the "Five Civilized Tribes" was unconstitutional. President Jackson, who had already signed the orders to relocate the tribes said: "The Supreme Court has made their decision, now let them enforce it".

The Indians probably could have gone to the Supreme Court to obtain a "restraining order" against President Jackson's action. They probably believed that it would be easier to let them try to enforce the orders rather than having to stomp out their attempt or to derail or supersede the society. Obviously, there was a lack of governmental controls.

AZB : You need the land; you need money to buy the land. Are your people doing that?

JAH : *One acre at a time. Our reservations are like "chessboards" because over the years, the Indians were subjected to unfair lending practices where the lender knew full well that the borrower would never be able to repay the loan. Hence, when the borrower defaulted, the land would then be sold to a friend or family of the lender at attractive rates. All of the reservations are Indian land, but through the years there have been non-Indians taking bits and pieces in this manner.*

290

AZB : What are the problems in enforcing local municipal laws versus reservation laws?

JAH : *The problem is that people who reside on a reservation are subject to Indian laws, and it's only been in recent years that tribes have exercised their sovereignty saying our laws apply. Non-Indians have objected to it tremendously. In a lot of cases, there have been misunderstandings. People have gotten away with automobile incidents such as "running over" somebody on the reservations. In my own tribe, a guy killed someone, he was kidnapped by municipal police, taken to jail, tried and sentenced for killing until a lawyer said: -"Wait a minute, he didn't kill somebody in the U.S., he is under the jurisdiction of the tribe and reservation law". The tribe doesn't have a pure set of rules that says it is against the law to kill anybody. The Supreme Court said that the only laws that apply in Indian country are those passed by the tribes and the tribal governments themselves. Therefore, the case had to be retried under Indian law. There is no differentiation between the various types of crimes (minor to violent) being subject to law other than tribal.*

Federal law prohibits all other law when the crime is committed on reservation land; laws favor vets in these kinds of incidents.

Historically, federal law was enforced by the Military who tended to usually be violent or near violent. Over time, with the recognition of tribal law as having jurisdiction on the reservations, the problems have tended to be who had jurisdiction, tribal or local municipal or state police. This was due to the questions of: "who committed the crime", "where was the crime committed" and thus, "who had jurisdiction"? Cross-jurisdictional agreements between tribes and local police units have been enacted to alleviate this problem.

AZB : The situation on the reservations where majorities of the people do not have a job and live on welfare is sad and not widely known to the rest of the country.

JAH : *In the "Oklahoma Gazette" an article was published regarding taking people off welfare. The status of the Indians is the result of bad federal policy, lost dignity and the ineptness and unfairness of the Bureau of Indian Affairs (BIA) who acted as masters of the Indian people and who were instrumental in the loss of their sovereign rights. Historically, the BIA has failed in its responsibilities to support and ensure the rights of Indian people.*

Oklahoma was the repository for the Eastern tribes, and thirty-nine tribes were subject to relocation. Their assigned lands were held in "severalty", i.e. the property was owned as an individual right and not shared with any other. To acquire Indian land, unscrupulous white men would marry Indian women and then kill them to obtain their property.

291

Unassigned land (including what became Oklahoma City) were acquired by white men. The Federal Government promised each man forty acres (16.2 hectares) and a team of mules to settle these lands.

AZB : There is a big awareness about names. Is it true that you do not want to be called Indians or Native Americans?

JAH : *Yes, it is true. We don't want to be called Native Americans similar to Asian-Americans, Scottish-Americans, Italian-Americans, etc. We want to be called Apache, Kiowa, Chickasaw, whatever, not Indians.*

AZB : I understand. I don't want to be called Slavish. I am Polish.

JAH : *Like Asian-Americans want to be called Chinese, Taiwanese, or whatever.*

AZB : Sometimes it is a result of lack of knowledge. How do I know what tribe you belong to so that I can call you Cherokee, Cheyenne, Kiowa or Apache. Should I always ask? ...By the way, JAH, what tribe are you from?

JAH : *Chickasaw. Also, I am a member of the only minority in the United States such that I have to carry a card to prove I am a member of that minority.*

AZB : Please tell me more about those identity cards... who issues them... on what form of a document, and when do you use them? How long have they existed and whose idea were they? Do you need them only to have some privilege in buying or opening a business? I understand that in every day life for example, you have a driving license, credit card, social security card, etc.

JAH : *The Dawes Commission was founded only to take away land held in "severalty" by Indians. It only recognized those tribal members who were on their original rolls (those who were actually issued land). The original identity card holders would be quantified as a hundred percent Chickasaw or Choctaw ancestry for example. The identity card was needed to obtain Government contracts, participate in state programs etc. The current day identity card carriers through dilution may only have an ancestry of 1.5 percent or less. The identity card does not replace a social security card, a driver's license, etc.*

AZB : Jim, please tell me how the lineage of your ancestry developed, that is for both parents.

JAH : *On my father's side, all were Chickasaw Indians. My grandfather was Jesse James Humes. My father was Galloway Humes. My mother whose maiden name was Ida Delphine Robb was Scots-Irish ancestry, and her father was a Methodist minister. They were married in 1936. I was born in 1938 at the Indian Hospital in Lawton, Oklahoma. The Indian Removal Act resulted in my family being forced from the rural area to Oklahoma City. Growing up and attending public schools, I* *was subjected to white antipathy of Indians in white territory being called such names as "wagon burner" and "blanket ass'. My father worked construction jobs, was a taxi driver, a "roughneck" on oil drilling rigs, and became an oil-field drilling superintendent. He also had a very fine baritone singing voice and was a member of the "stump" (?) quartets who entertained at festivals. At one festival, he met my mother. My mother was a nurse who worked in the Veterans Hospital in Sulfur, OK.*

AZB : In what way was your childhood different from others since you finished college and are representing the smaller group of the Native Americans who are educated and doing well, if I may say so.

JAH : *I attended high school in Oklahoma City, obtained an associate degree from Central State University in Edmond, a bachelors degree from the University of Oklahoma while working for the Veteran's Administration and a masters degree in hospital administration from Trinity University in San Antonio, Texas.*

AZB : Do you have siblings and what are they doing?

JAH : *Yes, I have a brother William Barry Humes who recently died. He was a Vietnam veteran and suffered exposure to Agent Orange. Prior to Vietnam, he married and had one son and was later divorced. After Vietnam, he experienced bad times as a result of the Agent Orange and suffering from diabetes and got into drinking and carousing. My mother then directed me to take responsibility to straighten him out which I did. After a period of time, William overcame the alcohol and cleaned up his life. I arranged a job for him with the Veteran's Administration Hospital as a nurse's aid where eventually he met my future sister-in-law who was Chief of Nursing Services there. They married, William went on to obtain a high school degree and a degree from George Mason University.*

AZB : The average income on the Indians reservations is much lower than the rest of the country. (source …Almanac). Do you think there is an awareness of this among the reservation people? Do they know how the other people live? Do you think there is such knowledge among the people in the rest of the country?

JAH : *Oklahoma has many natural resources and a better climate than many tribes faced in other parts of the country. So, the tribes were better able to thrive there than elsewhere.*

However, during the droughts and dust bowls of the 1930's, there was an exodus from Oklahoma to California. In California, they were able to buy homes for six thousand to ten thousand dollars that appreciated in value over the years into the millions. Many of these people returned to their roots in Oklahoma and bought farms, ranches, etc. with their wealth.

During 1975-1980, I worked for the Chickasaw Nation and was involved in efforts to increase the population. At least five thousand people from my area returned.

AZB : In recent years, American businesses are outsourcing to China, India etc.

You wrote on the Tribune of Chickasaw Nation about the article published in the Oklahoman by Phil Busey entitled "Outsource to "Indian Country". The author calls attention to the fact that, instead of "outsourcing jobs overseas", there are five hundred and fifty-seven federally recognized Tribes in the US which are recognized as being sovereign "nations" with sovereign lands. He reminds us, that if tribal members are hired, there are recognized federal tax credits for the business.

Jim, Lou Dobbs, the anchor and managing editor of the CNN 6 PM news program is particularly critical of outsourcing and offshoring in light of the increasingly massive United States trade deficit, particularly with China. Why move American business overseas, why not invest here and help our first and fellow American people by moving business to their reservations or their land? This move would also alleviate the chronic unemployment of Indian people, which reaches as high as 80% for some tribes. Why not utilize this land and the people? Why don't the big companies move some of their business to Indian reservations and take advantage of an inexpensive labor pool. It would be a patriotic thing to do something for our "first Americans" after the years of neglecting them.

Why don't companies build factories on Indian land, reduce unemployment there and slowly allow Indians to become self-sufficient and regain their pride?

JAH : *The Chickasaw Nation has been purchasing large amounts of land, which are minimally utilized, and it would be a great idea to attract companies to locate their business there and to create a true economy for all. I would think that this would serve to attract both Chickasaw business owners and the employees that they would hire to create a vibrant economy within our Nation.*

AZB : Maybe the current and possibly a similar future status for the Indian people should be more stressed to the American general public to make them aware and allow for more public consciousness?

I found that people have a lot of compassion and even love for American Indians, the only thing is how to reach them? Those

Americans who are aware financially support Indian schools, relief centers, etc

JAH : *We as Indians have not done a good job of selling ourselves. Not explaining, not defining ourselves.*

AZB : Do you have any access to the media? Mexicans have their own TV channels with programs every day all over the country. There are papers published by Indians, like "The Lakota Country Times", also "Indian Country Today" (I have subscribed to them for the last few years).

JAH : *We have a radio station with country music.*
My tribe owns a radio station. They have a thirty-minute show on Saturday mornings, but that is about all.

AZB : How would you describe being an Indian in the United States? What does it mean for you?

JAH : *Be what you are. Take pleasure in it, and be proud of it.*

AZB : What are your feelings about diminishing rights of all Americans in today's legal atmosphere?

JAH : *By law you cannot have the Ten Commandments displayed in our courts, by law you cannot have silent prayers, you can do a lot of things that everybody takes for granted, and as Indians, we learned them by heart. My favorite saying is "If the only tool you have in your tool kit is a sledgehammer...look at every problem as if it were a spike".*

AZB : As far as keeping your language, we were in the Dakotas and Montana where we visited three Indian schools that we help support. We are very happy that we are doing it. One of the things we heard was, that one of the schools on a Crow Reservation taught Crow as the first language and English as the second. While at the other two schools, English was taught first and the native language wasn't even emphasized. So, the teaching of the original language is difficult, but for a couple of the people we spoke with...it didn't seem to bother them.

JAH : *I feel badly about that too. My grandmother was forced to go to a BIA school, and at that school, she could not speak her own language (Chickasaw). She had to learn and only speak English. She would speak her language, but was punished, put in solitary confinement, had her mouth washed out with soap, laughed at in class. She always promised herself that when she got away from there, she would never speak English again. I never knew her to speak a word of English.*

AZB : That's nice... she had character. Do you speak Chickasaw? You have to do it when you are young, because you can't do it when you are older. Language comes easy and naturally when you are young.

295

Aleksandra Ziolkowska-Boehm

JAH : *The bad thing about language is, one's capability diminishes unless you are using it everyday. I think that it is great to use Chickasaw at home. Unless you have that daily experience you don't learn. Well, I can understand it, I can piece it out, but as far as translating it back, I am at a loss.*

AZB : Those schools we visited were all Catholic. They were the only missionaries that went up to the Dakotas. Norman was surprised, being Protestant.

The first Catholic missions were an example of cruelty forced on children by not allowing them to use their own language, like you mentioned your grandmother's experience. Besides that, they did a lot of good things, but it is blemish on them (I am Catholic). Do you think the Catholic Church should do something about those years?

JAH : *The Catholic Church finally issued an apology to California tribes for their mission building era in California. The church issued a written apology, and it came from the Vatican. It was John Paul II.*

AZB : Tell me about the religion among the Indians...

JAH : *We brought religion with us when we came to Oklahoma. Prior to that, the Caddos and all the Plains tribes would travel though here, Oklahoma. The Caddos and a few other tribes which were subsequently decimated and lost to history were the only ones who established themselves here permanently. Most of the tribes just passed through Oklahoma.*

AZB : Have the so-called religious rights, freedom and independence guaranteed by the Constitution been available to American Indians?

JAH : *That is the ironic thing ...without exception; immigrants come to the United States for two reasons – first and foremost to escape religious persecution and after that to escape from poverty. And then, rid of these oppressions, they tried to develop the Constitution that guarantees freedom. They patterned this after the Iroquois Confederacy constitution, which included freedom, not constriction, not stereotyping, and not everyone having to abide by the same marching orders (independence?). Then, they turned around and brought their missionaries, who were not allowed to practice while they were ahead, but who brought us the same problems here in Oklahoma. You have to be a recognized as a Christian to be anybody.*

The Creator, who's that? The way that they taught us was to make us do menial work. They would say...let us white people adopt your Indian children. And that is what they were able to do because they had ownership of the oil lands and the power that went with that ownership. They'd adopt the Indian children and promptly neglect them... in some

296

cases, they would have them murdered because they were court-appointed guardians. As court appointed guardians, they could do anything they wanted to with the children or the land the Indian children had. They would adopt children and kill them so they could inherit their land.

AZB : Those horrible things are not known by the average American. Is there historical documentation of any kind verifying such stories? How is the average Indian state of mind with such knowledge of the past?

JAH : *The whites murdered adopted Indian children, and even murdered their own children by Indian wives in order to acquire their land and the oil rights thereto. All this is common knowledge in Oklahoma oil land. One interesting story is about three brothers who each married Chickasaw women to acquire their land that amounted to some five thousand square miles[128]. One of the brothers even murdered his wife. The acquired ranch on the Red River is now owned by an oil man in Colorado. The Chickasaw are trying to buy the land back.*

AZB : Have non-Indians wasted Indian natural resources without compensation therefor?

JAH : *A good example: Down south in the Chickasaw Nation there is a place in Chickasaw National Park near Sulfur where there are sulfur springs and mineral springs throughout the area. It used to be known as the treaty grounds. Indians would come there for the potential health and restorative benefits that the springs afforded. At the turn of the century, it became a tourist attraction for the people from back East. In Dougherty, Oklahoma, people who owned private railroad cars would come down from Sulfur, park their railroad car conveniently on a siding, to consume the spring waters, take baths in the mud etc. I should be trying to bottle the water for the Indians have a saying: "If you drink this water, it will add a year to your life for every bottle you drink".*

AZB : I've heard of the Sand Creek massacre (1864) when the Indians tribe (Cheyenne and Arapaho) were encamped and flying an American flag as well as a "white" flag of peace. The Indians had been taught that the flags would protect them from harm, and they were expecting to be safe. The protection was not forthcoming. What happened at Sand Creek?

JAH : *An interesting thing. The reason for the massacre is that the Colorado militia was commanded by a member named Colonel John Chivington out of Denver who, when not on militia duty, was a Methodist minister. Although a minister of a Christian denomination, he hated the*

---

[128] 1,295,040 hectares

Indian people. The militia committed the massacre which included cutting off women's breasts, noses and making necklaces from them. While this horror was going on, the regular Army higher-ranking personnel did nothing to keep him from carrying out the massacre. It was only last year or the year before that the Methodist Church finally apologized. My friend Homer Flute is presently lobbying Congress for reparations to families of the Sand Creek massacre.

AZB : It seems that for one piece of good news for Indian tribes, there always follows two or three pieces of bad news for them. Have I over dramatized this conception?

JAH : *Let me tell you a story: One day God appeared to Moses and said, "Moses, I am going to cause a plague in Egypt, and it will make the Egyptians very uncomfortable to the point that the Pharaoh is going to say, " Moses, I will let you take your people to the land of opportunity. That's the good news. More good news is that whenever you come to the Red Sea, the Pharaoh will have changed his mind and will still want your people kept in bondage. So after you are gone, he is going to come after you. But, I am going to cause the Red Sea to part, so your people can cross into the land of opportunity. Moses said: "That's great God, that's the best news I have heard in my lifetime".*

God responded, "The bad news is you have to prepare the Environmental Impact Report".

AZB : Why in America do some groups have such powerful lobbies. The Indians have a lobby and maybe it should be more powerful?

JAH : *That's very true.*

The treaties guaranteed these things to us. They give us this and so on. But they haven't, and they are not going to.

In modern times, we really have not learned the sins of our parents. In certain places, we can control elections like here in Oklahoma. I will give you an example of that: Carl Albert was Speaker of the Oklahoma House for 16 terms; he was from a town in Central Oklahoma. When he stood for the first time for election to the United States Congress, he was running against a very strong opponent. He went out into the field and wound up in a runoff election with his opponent. He pulled a small political maneuver... he went to the Choctaws and the Chickasaws who were primarily in the congressional district he was running for. He talked them into registering to vote in the runoff election. His opponent had more strength in voting numbers because of the fact the Indians prior to that had not exercised their right to vote. But this time with the influence and efforts of my grandfather who was a Methodist minister, they did register to vote. Carl Albert promised him for his efforts that he would help the Indians if elected. They were instrumental in electing Carl B. Albert. He was of the old school of politicians who paid off their political debts. Carl B. Albert helped Native Oklahomans build the Indian Health Facility. That was one of the debts he owed the people from there.

AZB : We all know how important it is to be involved in local politics, to vote, and that politicians should care about you knowing that every voice is important. Is this evident in Oklahoma?

JAH : *That's the power in Oklahoma in particular. If the Indian voting rights were exercised, they could control any election from the Senate down to local levels. I can't understand why it isn't done...why the tribes do not exercise their right to vote.*

AZB : Is there any evidence of Indians becoming more involved in politics, at least at the local levels?

JAH : *Yes, of all the states, Oklahoma has the largest number of Native Americans (fourteen) elected to its state Congress.*

AZB : You yourself are involved in business, please, tell us more about it. Do you care about/encourage other Indian entrepreneurs?

JAH : *Yes, I care. I have been involved in business and I can remember talking to some of my Indian tribal associates. I tell them I want to put together a business venture. They always put me off or don't want to do anything. But they turn right around when a white guy comes in and says I want to do something (and he is the most crooked guy in the world); they will give their support to him. They'll put a business in. Indians don't make moves; white people do.*

I can build anything; I can create anything that anyone else can. But I can't do it by myself. We can do a better job on this... we can embellish it. We can make this "cup" (example) better than if it is mass-produced.

AZB : What is the most difficult obstacle you have to overcome?

JAH : *The hardest thing for me to do, even in dealing with my own Chickasaw tribe unfortunately, is to have them consider what we are working towards and for their benefit, but not other dominant tribes. I don't know what the answer is... you try your best; you educate people, but without any immediate positive outlook being formed. Gathering interest for a common activity is difficult to achieve...to find someone with the right frame of mind and deal with him on a person-to-person basis. To deal with people and get them working at spreading the word that Indians can take charge and control their own destiny is not an easy task.*

AZB : That's what we were saying about awareness. What you can achieve if you are united and aware of it. You can do everything if you are together and vote.

For example, up in South Dakota at the Pine Ridge (which is huge a reservation, as you know), participation in voting could have a dramatic impact on the state and the Sioux natives.

I don't think they vote. Apparently, there isn't anyone to lead them to vote. Their Congressmen should come and talk to them and try to do something.

The other problem is these bright Indian students male or female, graduate from the Indian school, go off to college and earn a degree. When they return to their reservation, their own people resent them because they have gotten an education. They are not helping themselves.

JAH : *Education is very difficult to sell ... future versus "immediate satisfaction". If you are going into something you say, "Together we can win, together we can make a difference, we can create something...which is the future." But let them see something, touch it, smell it, handle it... the immediate bottle of booze or a car or whatever turns them on that's immediate, and they'll follow anybody to get that immediate satisfaction rather to plan and work for a future benefit.*

AZB : Jim, education is a key, isn't it?

JAH : *We need to have more schools up North and West. We need to have more schools right now.*

AZB : The Indian schools Norman and I visited were very impressive. You know Billy Mills. He is a Lakota Sioux. We are supporting three Indians schools, two Sioux schools and one Cheyenne, and also the organizations "Running Strong for American Indian Youth", "American Indian Relief Council" and "Native American Heritage Association". So, we actually came to one of the schools, and saw a video of his Olympic victory when his final sprint left the field behind. His message in the video was very clear – "Stay away from alcohol". That was the essence of his speech to the young Indian people. He was very eloquent and his speech very impressive.

JAH : *Alcohol is something Indians are coming out of with the help of Alcoholics Anonymous. There are very few Indian drunkards in Oklahoma. My father, who owned an oil drilling services company, especially hired Indian drunks and would then lead them into rehabilitation.*

AZB : How much can you count on people's understanding of the benefit of education to help Indian people?

JAH : *There is a volunteer group here in Oklahoma City that take donations of... they don't buy new computers, but they take old*

300

computers, refinish them. Add memory on and then donate them to Indian schools.

AZB : Education is a big step, but don't schools have logistical obstacles to reach Indian children who live long distances from the schools?

JAH : *A "USA Today" front-page article says there is a shortage of school bus drivers. Children are missing classes because they can't get around to them, they are trying to stagger the classes, one starts early, and one starts late. This has gone far enough. Why not have... with the economy as it is, not one wants to be a part-time bus driver... why not have different hours as parents have different working hours? Late evening class, mid morning class, etc. the teachers won't put up with it. They don't want to work.*

Everyone complains about the results... not one of us is willing to tackle the problem. We need to do whatever it takes to improve the education of all the children. Education will do away with prejudice...do away with anti-social acts.

My college first-degree education was psychology. We talked about what would be the next evolution of mankind? We had seen a lot of diseases cured, improvement in diagnostic and treatment work, but the mind is a terrible thing to waste. That's where we need to transcend the things we've gotten caught up in...improve and evolve into the best we can do. But we can't do it if we keep doing as we are.

As I say ... "It is hard to fly like an eagle when you have to run around with all these 'turkeys'".

AZB : But unemployment is a big problem in many remote areas and others as well.

JAH : *That's one of the problems in Tulsa. There is nothing to do there. Boy, talk about severe conditions.*

AZB : The people return to the reservations because they can't find work, and they don't know what to do with themselves.

JAH : *In Oklahoma, telemarketing firms still have to use computer screens to type the information in and now with automatic dialing and voices that come on "hold, we have an important message for you".*

They say a button can replace every man in the world, except at any church where he has to be replaced by a burden.

AZB : What is the most important thing to be done for Native Americans? What would you do if you could have such an opportunity and power?

JAH : *Create more jobs with incorporation acts. A great deal of Indian land has not been probated. Only the Five Civilized Tribes are subject to probated laws. For example, my grandmother has been dead* *twenty years, yet her will has not been probated yet so ownership validity is "up in the air". Oil royalty checks (some in the amount of ten thousand to fifteen thousand dollars) paid into Indian Money Accounts are not shown as deposited and therefore money is not accessible to the owner. The present Bush Administration is not the only one at fault...previous administrations are at fault as well. They've all allowed the BIA to be irresponsible...do you know what BIA stands for? "Boss Indians Around".*

AZB : You are involved in working on behalf of the "Lost Cherokee Tribe" (L.C.T.) of Arkansas to obtain their Federal recognition. Tell me about your endeavors, their inception, current status and future outlook.

JAH : *Making contracts with other tribes. The L.C.T. has a package with me to represent them. We are seeking to buy harbor property on the Arkansas River and building a waste processing facility.*

AZB : You have also embarked on a exciting business opportunity with the State of Arkansas. Is the Lost Cherokee Tribe involved? Tell me more about your project.

JAH : *I consult for the L.C.T. I write articles for Indian Country today. I work to make the tribal governments more responsive to ideas and opportunities. The Chickasaw constitution was ratified in 1987, however, because of a weak governor, the casino operators are driven by gambling influence and not working for their people. As we say, "they are not dancing to tribal drums".*

AZB : You promised your Grandfather to work on behalf of the Chickasaw Nation. In what capacities have you done so?

JAH : *I worked for the Chickasaw Nation from 1985 to 1990. I was the Director for several programs including the Food Distribution Program, Women Infants and Children Program (WIC). I was then the Director of our Tishomingo Health Clinic, and I started the construction of the Ardmore Health Clinic.*

I then helped our current Governor get elected to his first term of office; he had been Lieutenant Governor before that time. Once elected, I served as his Chief of Staff for three years. During that time, I got us involved in our start in Gaming Casinos at Goldsby and Marietta, Oklahoma.

I also started the concept for Chickasaw Nation Industries (CNI) as the business arm of the Nation. Chickasaw Nation Industries was the Gaming and Tobacco sales operation.

I left CNI and have started my own business ventures.

AZB : I understand your name is "Aka illa pila Nashoba (LONEWOLF). Who gave you this name?

JAH : *Friends.*

Oklahoma City, Oklahoma, September 2006

Aleksandra Ziolkowska-Boehm

Appendix 1

NATIVE-AMERICAN POPULATION DATA
and
STATE NAME SOURCE
Prepared by Norman Boehm
Data Source: TIME ALMANAC 2006
(resident census population 2000)

State	Total Population of State	Native-American		State Name Word Source
		Population	% of Total	
Alabama	4,447,100	22,430	0.5%	Choctaw: "thicket clearers" or "vegetation gatherers"
Alaska	626,932	98,043	15.6%	Aleut: "great land" or "that which the sea breaks against"
Arizona	5,130,632	255,879	5.0%	Arizonac: "little spring" or "young spring"
Arkansas	2,673,400	17,808	0.7%	From Quapaw Indians
California	33,871,648	333,346	1.0%	
Colorado	4,301,261	44,241	1.0%	
Connecticut	3,405,565	9,639	0.3%	Quinnehtukqut: "beside the long tidal river"
Delaware	783,600	2,731	0.3%	
Florida	15,982,378	53,541	0.3%	
Georgia	8,186,453	21,737	0.3%	
Hawaii	1,211,537	3,535	0.3%	
Idaho	1,293,953	17,645	1.4%	
Illinois	12,419,293	31,006	0.2%	Algonquin: "tribe of superior men"
Indiana	6,080,485	15,815	0.3%	From Indian: "land of Indians"
Iowa	2,926,324	8,989	0.3%	From Indian: "this is the place" or the Beautiful Land"
Kansas	2,688,418	24,936	0.9%	Sioux: "people of the south wind"
Kentucky	4,041,769	8,616	0.2%	Iroquoian: "Ken-tah-ten" or "land of tomorrow:
Louisiana	4,468,976	25,477	0.6%	
Maine	1,274,923	7,098	0.6%	
Maryland	5,296,486	15,423	0.3%	
Massachusetts	6,349,097	15,015	0.2%	Massachusetts: "at or about the great hill"
Michigan	9,938,444	58,479	0.6%	"Michigana" or "great or large lake"
Minnesota	4,919,479	54,967	1.1%	Dakota: "sky-tinted water"
Mississippi	2,844,658	11,652	0.4%	From Indian: "Father of Waters"
Missouri	5,595,211	25,076	0.4%	Missouri: "town of the large canoes"
Montana	902,195	56,068	6.2%	
Nebraska	1,711,263	14,896	0.9%	Oto: "flat water"
Nevada	1,998,257	26,420	1.3%	

New Hampshire	1,236,786	2,964	0.2%	
New Jersey	8,414,350	19,492	0.2%	
New Mexico	1,819,046	173,483	9.5%	Aztec: "place of Mexitli" (Aztec god or leader)
New York	18,976,457	82,461	0.4%	
North Carolina	8,049,313	99,551	1.2%	
North Dakota	642,200	31,329	4.9%	Sioux: "allies"
Ohio	11,353,140	24,486	0.2%	Iroquoian: "great river"
Oklahoma	3,450,654	273,230	7.9%	Choctaw: two words meaning" red people"
Oregon	3,421,399	45,211	1.3%	
Pennsylvania	12,281,054	18,348	0.1%	
Rhode Island	1,048,319	5,121	0.5%	
South Carolina	4,012,012	13,718	0.3%	
South Dakota	754,844	62,283	8.3%	Sioux: "allies"
Tennessee	5,689,283	15,152	0.3%	Cherokee: exact meaning unknown
Texas	20,851,820	118,362	0.6%	From Indian word meaning "friends"
Utah	2,233,169	29,684	1.3%	Ute: "people of the mountains"
Vermont	608,827	2,420	0.4%	
Virginia	7,078,515	21,172	0.3%	
Washington	5,894,121	93,301	1.6%	
West Virginia	1,808,344	3,606	0.2%	
Wisconsin	5,363,675	47,228	0.9%	French corruption of Indian word: "is disputed"
Wyoming	493,782	11,133	2.3%	Delaware: "mountains and valleys alternating", same as Wyoming Valley in Pennsylvania

306

Appendix 2

Addresses of schools and organizations in the United States that need some help.

St. Labre Indian School
P.O. Box 216
Ashland, Montana 59003-0216
Tel. 1-866-753-5496
www.stlabre.org

St.Joseph's Indian School
P.O. Box 100
Chamberlain, South Dakota 57325-100
Tel. 1-605-234-3300
www.stjo.org

Red Cloud Indian School
100 Mission Drive
Pine Ridge, South Dakota 57770-2100
www.redcloudschool.org

American Indian Relief Council
P.O. Box 6200
Rapid City, South Dakota 5777091-6200
Tel. 1-800-370-0872

Crazy Horse Memorial Foundation
Avenue of the Chiefs
Crazy Horse, South Dakota 57730-9506
Tel. 1-605-673-4681

LAKOTA COUNTRY TIMES
Box 386
Martin, South Dakota 57551
Tel. 1-605-685-1868

INDIAN COUNTRY TODAY
1920 Lombardy Drive
Rapid City, South Dakota 57703
Tel. 1-605-341-6940

Native American Heritage Association
410 Sheridan Lake Road
Rapid City, South Dakota 57702-2495

Running Strong for American Indian Youth
Christian Relief Services
P.O.Box 670
Raton, New Mexico 87740-9970

Red Feathers Development Group
P.O.Box 52652
Bellevue, Washington 98015-2652
www.redfeather.org.

Indian Law Resource Center
601 E St. SE ,
Washington, District of Columbia. 20003,

Indian Law Resource Center
602 North Ewing Street
Helena, Montana 59601
Tel. 1-401-449-2006

International Indian Treaty Council,
710 Clayton St.
San Francisco, California 94117

Bibliography

A History of the Northern Cheyennes told to Sister Sacred Heart by George Yoakum, ex-Soldier – [W:] The Bird Tail, by Sister Genevieve McBride, Ohio State University, Vantage, New York, 1974.

Aaseng Nathan, Navajo Code Talkers. America's Secret Weapon in World War II, Walker and Company, New York, 1992.

Bernstein Alison R., American Indians and World War II .Toward a New Era in Indian Affairs, University of Oklahoma Press, Norman, OK, 1991.

Bison Book, University of Nebraska, 1982.

Bordewich Fergus: M., Killing the White Man's Indian, Doubleday, New York, 1996.

Bordewich Fergus M., Revolution in Indian Country, AMERICAN HERITAGE, July/September, 1995.

Connell Evan S., Son of the Morning Star, Promontory Press, New York, 1993.

Curtis, Edward S., Sacred Legacy and the North American Indian, Barnes &Noble, New York, 2005.

Daily Robert, The Code Talkers. American Indians in World War II, Franklin Watts, New York, 1995.

Deloria Vine, Jr., Custer died for your sins, Univerasity of Oklahoma Press, 1988.

DeWall Robb, Crazy Horse and Korczak. Korczak Heritage, Crazy Horse, South Dakota, 1982.

DeWall Robb, Korczak. Storyteller in Stone, Korczak Heritage, Crazy Horse, South Dakota,1984.

DeWall, Robb, Carving a Dream. Korczak's Heritage, Inc., Crazy Horse, South Dakota, 1997 50th Anniversary Edition.

Gagern Friedrich von, Prawdziwe życie Skórzanej Pończochy. Historia Pogranicza w latach 1807--1813. Translation Lidia Zacharska, Iskry, Warszawa, 1966.

Gerstenzang James, Clinton visits Indian reservation, LOS ANGELES TIMES, reprint: PHILADELPHIA INQUIRER, July 8, 1999.

Hayden Thomas, Carpenter Betsy, The Modern Life of American Indians, U.S.NEWS and WORLD REPORT, October, 2004.

Ian Frazier, On the Rez, Farrar, Straus and Giroux, New York, 2000.

Iwanski Len, Indian ritual revived to stop bison killing, SUNDAY NEWS JOURNAL, February

Joe Haines, Code Talker, OKLAHOMA TODAY, May-June 2000, pgs. 57-59.

Johansen Bruce E., Debating Democracy: Native American Legacy of Freedom, Clear Light Books, 1998.

Johansen Bruce E., Enduring Legacies. Native American Treaties and Contemporary Controversies, Praeger Publishers, 2004

Johansen Bruce E., Grinde Donald A., The Encyclopedia of Native American Biography, Six Hundred Life Stories of Important People, from Powhatan to Wilma Mankiller, Da Capo Press; 1st Da Capo Press Ed edition, 1998.

Aleksandra Ziolkowska-Boehm

Johansen Bruce E., Grinde Donald A., Exemplar of Liberty. Native America and the Evolution of Democracy (Native American Politics Series No 3), University of California, American Indian Studies, 1991.

Johansen Bruce E., Life and Death in Mohawk Country, Fulcrum Publishing Inc., 2006.

Johansen Bruce E., The Native Peoples of North America. A History, Rutgers, 2006.

Johansen Bruce E., The Praeger Handbook on Contemporary Issues in Native America (2 volumes) (Native America: Yesterday and Today), Praeger Publishers, 2007.

Levy Bernard-Henry, American Vertigo, Random House Publishing Group, New York, 2006.

Lipowicz Zenon, Zbyszewski Jerzy, The Arabian Horses, Waseca Minnesota, 2007.

Lowie, Robert H., Indians of the Plains, introduction Raymond J. DeMallie,

Mankiller, Wilma and Michael Wallis, Mankiller., A Chief and Her People, St. Martin Griffin, New York 1994

McBride Genevieve, A History of the Northern Cheyennes told to Sister Sacred Heart by George Yoakum, ex-Soldier [w:]The Bird Tall, Ohio State University, Vantage, New York, 1974

McMurtry Larry, Crazy Horse, A Lipper/Viking Book, 1999.

Tradycyjne życie i rezerwatowa rzeczywistość. Materials, Śródmiejski Ośrodek Kultury – TIPI, Kraków–Wielichowa, 2006.

Pióropusze i krawaty. TIPI, Wielichowo, 2007

Sajna Mike, Crazy Horse. The Life Behind the Legend, Castle Books, New Jersey, 2005.

Sandoz Mari, Crazy Horse. The Stranger Man of the Oglalas, New York, 1942.

Smith, Rex Alan, TRhe Carvinbg of Mount Rushmore, Abbeville Press Publishers, New York 1985

Svingen Orlan J., The Northern Cheyennes Reservation 1877–90, University of Colorado Press, 1993.

TAWACIN, Pismo Przyjaciół Indian, Nr 3 (175) fall 2006, Wielichowo

THE INDIAN COUNTRY TODAY, Canastota, New York, years 1996–2006.

THE LAKOTA COUNTRY TIMES, Martin, South Dakota, years 1996-2006.

Thornton Russell, American Indian Holocaust and Survival, A Population History since 1492 (Civilization of the American Indian Series), University of Oklahoma Press, 1987.

Waldo Arthur L., True Heroes of Jamestown, American Institute of Polish Culture, Miami, Florida, 1977).

Townsend Kenneth William, World War II and the American Indian. University of New Mexico Press, Albuquerque, 2000.

Korczak Ziolkowski – Bibliography

200,000 Tons Blasted Off Crazy Horse Mt. Carving, GWIAZDA POLARNA, December 10, 1983.

A rough, wild, wonderful land, CHICAGO TRIBUNE, June 17, 1990.
Assignment. Crazy Horse, Dreams of chief, sculptor stay alive in Black Hills, CHICAGO TRIBUNE, November 21, 1990.
Budrewicz Olgierd, Orzel na gwiazdzistym sztandarze, Warszawa, 1979, pg. 14-28.
Carving a Dream In the Black Hills, NEWSWEEK, May 31, 1982
Crazy Horse eyes, THE RAPID CITY JOURNAL, December 6, 1990.
Crazy Horse rides once more as world's biggest work of art, THE TORONTO STAR, July 11, 1981.
Crazy Horse sculptor's wife Ruth Ziolkowski in charge at 80, THE LAKOTA COUNTRY TIMES, Martin, SD, July 4, 2006.
Crazy Horse. Dignity carved on a mountain, USA TODAY, July 19, 1990.
Crazy Horse's journey back to Black Hills is inspiring, STAR TRIBUNE, August 28, 1990.
DeWall Robb, Crazy Horse, Korczak Ziolkowski, Sculptor-Carving a Dream, Crazy Horse edition, July 3, 1990.
Dewline John, Little Big Horn Battle, DEADWOOD MAGAZINE, May/June, 1995.
Face it: There is more to the Black Hills, DALLAS MORNING NEWS, October 10, 1993.
Heads above the West, THE PHILADELPHIA INQUIRER, July 28, 1991.
Judycki Zbigniew, Kronika polonijna, GŁOS KATOLICKI, Paris 36/1994, pg. 11.
Korczak would have been pleased. 5 Polish dignitaries climb to summit of Crazy Horse, THE RAPID CITY JOURNAL, October 30, 1990.
Kwartalnik Biograficzny Polonii (Paris), Nr 6, 1995.
Monumental Hoopla, TIME, July 15, 1991.
Mother Nature Speeds Progress On Emerging Face of Crazy Horse, POLISH DIGEST, Stevens Point, VI, June, 1992.
Muszyńska Lidia, Historia wykuta w kamieniu, RELAKS, February 13, 1988.
Neuharth visits Crazy Horse toasts efforts, CUSTER COUNTY CHRONICLE, August 29, 1990.
New 13 Cent Issue Pays Tribute to Crazy Horse, THE NEW YORK TIMES, January 10, 1982 .
Pelc Ryszarda, Nie zapominaj o swoich marzeniach, PRZEGLĄD POLSKI (New York), June 10, 1993.
Polish writer-journalist tours Hills as part of month-long visit to U.S., THE RAPID CITY JOURNAL, October 24, 1995.
Pomnik Crazy Horse, NOWY DZIENNIK (New York), June 25, 1992.
*Progress-News from Crazy Horse Memorial Foundation, South Dakota – 50 editions.
Seidler Wiesław, Niezłomny Indianin, szalony Polak, NOWY DZIENNIK (New York), October 17, 1996.
Seigel Jessica, A Head Above the Others, CHICAGO TRIBUNE MAGAZINE, October 5, 1997.
Spirit Nation, TRAVEL, Decatur, Illinois, September 8, 1991.

Aleksandra Ziolkowska-Boehm

Spotkanie, Mieszanka Firmowa, PRZEKRÓJ, March 23, 1986.
The Big Picture, Nose Job, LIFE, December, 1993.
Ziółkowska Aleksandra, Nie tylko Ameryka, Warszawa 1992, pg. 97–102.
Ziółkowska Aleksandra, Rzeźbiarz gór, AMERYKA, Wydawnictwo Rządu
Stanów Zjednoczonych, Fall, 1990.
Ziółkowska Aleksandra, Rzeźbiarz gór, NOWY DZIENNIK (Nowy Jork), June
1–2, 1991.
Ziółkowska-Boehm Aleksandra, Korczak Ziolkowski, A Storyteller in Stone,
NEW HORIZON (New York), October, 1998.
Ziolkowski honored at Polish convention. THE RAPID CITY JOURNAL, July
15, 1990.

Other Articles

Armatys Jaroslaw, Zemsta Manitou, NOWY DZIENNIK (New York),
November 14, 1998.
Armatys Jarosław, Szkielet w indiańskiej szafie, NOWY DZIENNIK (New
York), November 13, 1988.
Balz Dan, Sioux warrior's remains begin long journey home, WASHINGTON
POST, reprint: Houston Chronicle, September 26, 1997.
Berger Thomas, Little Big Man's Man, An Interview by Andrew Ward,
AMERICAN HERITAGE, May-June, 1999.
Brooke James, Use of Devil's in names of sites sparks spirited arguments, NEW
YORK TIMES, reprint: Houston Chronicle, November 17, 1996.
Couturier Lisa, Speaking in Silence. Native American Spirituality, NEW
WOMAN, March, 1992.
Crary David, Canada apologizes to native peoples for injustices, HOUSTON
CHRONICLE, August 1, 1998.
Delaware Nanticoke work to preserve their heritage, THE NEWS JOURNAL,
December 4, 2005, pg. 1,8.
Dobrowolska Anna, Indianie w Delaware, Indianie dzisiaj, TERAZ
(Philadelphia), October-November, 2003.
Dobrzynski Judith H., A Monumental Achievement. Mount Rushmore owes its
power to Gutzon Borglum, timing and budgets, THE WALL STREET
JOURNAL, July 15, 2006.
Dobrzynski Judith H., Casino profits help tribe reclaim its history, NEW YOK
TIMES, October 7, 1997.
Ferrara Peter J., Choctaw Uprising, NATIONAL REVIEW, March 11, 1996,
pgs. 30–31.
Freemantle Tony, No home on the range, HOUSTON CHRONICLE, April 14,
1997.
Gerstenzang James, Clinton visits Indian reservation, LOS ANGELES TIMES,
reprint: PHILADELPHIA INQUIRER, July 8, 1999.
Hayden Thomas, Carpenter Betsy, The Modern Life of American Indians,
U.S.NEWS and WORLD REPORT, October, 2004.
Iwanski Len, Indian ritual revived to stop bison killing, SUNDAY NEWS
JOURNAL, February 28, 1999.

Karaim Reef, 7 Native-American standouts, USA WEEKEND, September 17, 2004.

Kirn Walter, Jones Landon Y., Roosvelt Margot, Leading Men, Lewis and Clark, Faces of the Trail, TIME, July 8, 2002.

Lamb David, Once destitute Maine Indians now a financial power, SUNDAY NEWS JOURNAL, reprint: LOS ANGELES TIMES, Dec 13, 1992, ps A17

Lemonick Michael D., Dorfman Andrea, Who Were the First Americans? , TIME, March 13, 2006.

Lowe Karem, Warrior ends long journey, HOUSTON CHRONICLE, September 29, 1992.

Miller John J., Honest Injun, NATIONAL REVIEW, March 28, 2005.

Miller John J., Off the Rez, NATIONAL REVIEW, December 30, 2002.

Miller John J., Roots-Deep Ones. The perils of looking into American prehistory, NATIONAL REVIEW, June 25, 2001.

Mulrooney Rick, Learn about those who gave us Appoquinimink, Naamans and others, THE NEWS JOURNAL, November 18, 2005, pg. E4-E5

NEW YORK TIMES, reprint, Houston Chronice, October 20, 1992.

Nickerson Colin, Despair deepens for Canada's indigenous people, BOSTON GLOBE, reprint: HOUSTON CHRONICLE, March 23, 1997.

Peter T.Kilborn, Poverty runs deepest on desolate Sioux reservation.

Reid Jan, The Forgotten people (Kickapoo), TEXAS MONTHLY, February, 1997.

Richard Lacayo, A Place to Bring the Tribe, TIME, September 20, 2004.

Roosvelt Margot, Utah's Toxic Opportunity, TIME, Inside Business, April, 2006.

Shen Fern, The Past and present collide on a Washington mural, THE WASHINGTON POST, November 24, 2006.

Smith Gene, Lost Bird, AMERICAN HERITAGE, April, 1996.

Smith Mark, Challenging the law: Two lenghty battles over cultural patrimony, HOUSTON CHRONICLE, February 22, 1998.

Sopylak Grażyna, Pasażerowie "Mayflower", NOWY DZIENNIK (New York), November 23, 1993.

Stockel H. Henrietta, Farewell. Mildred Imach Cleghorn, OKLAHOMA TODAY, 1997, Year in Review, pgs. 72-74.

Susan Montoya, Pueblo Indians reburied, THE NEWS JOURNAL, March 23, 1999.

To Native Americans, the bison is a sacred beast, HOUSTON CHRONICLE, April 14, 1997.

Wallace Terry, Success Isn't What You Have. It's What You've Given Away, PARADE MAGAZINE, June 2, 1996.

Zalewski Tomasz, W sądzie, a nie tomahawkiem, NOWY DZIENNIK (New York), May 11–12, 2002.

Chapters and Articles
by
Aleksandra Ziołkowska-Boehm

In Books

"A Storyteller in Stone", Aleksandra Ziółkowska-Boehm,The Roots Are Polish, Toronto, 2004, pgs. 225–231.
„Dzikie gęsi i zachody słońca w Kenorze", Aleksandra Ziółkowska-Boehm, Kanada, Kanada... , Warszawa, 1986, pgs.119–131.
"Sunsets and Wild Geese in Kenora", Aleksandra Ziółkowska-Boehm, Dreams and Reality, Toronto 1984, pgs.149–162.
*Rzeźbiarz gór, chapter : Nie tylko Ameryka, Warszawa, 1992, pgs. 97-102
*Pueblos w Nowym Meksyku, rozdział : Nie tylko Ameryka , Warszawa, 1992, pgs. 65-68
*Wsłuchiwanie się w ciszę. Indiańskie prawdy wiary, : Nie tylko Ameryka, Warszawa, 1992, pgs. 74-78
*Gorzkie wspomnienia z indiańskich szkół, rozdział: Nie tylko Ameryka, Warszawa, 1992, pgs. 69-73

In Articles

Ziółkowska-Boehm Aleksandra, Indianie – dinozaury Ameryki? NOWY DZIENNIK, PRZEGLĄD POLSKI, (New York), November 19, 1999.
Ziółkowska-Boehm Aleksandra, Indianie – rana Ameryki? NOWY KURIER (Toronto) Nr 791/2001, 792/2001, 832/2003.
Ziółkowska-Boehm Aleksandra, Indianie Lenape z rzeki Brandywine, TERAZ (Philadephia), March, 2003.
Ziółkowska-Boehm Aleksandra, Indianska szkoła Saint Labre w Montanie, part 1, TERAZ (Philadelphia), October 2005, part 2, November, 2005.
Ziółkowska-Boehm Aleksandra, Indiańskie prawdy wiary, TWÓJ STYL, October, 1994.
Ziółkowska-Boehm Aleksandra, Nadciągają Indianie, POLITYKA, Na własne oczy, July 22, 2000.
Ziółkowska-Boehm Aleksandra, O indiańskiej edukacji. Z Montany. ODRA Nr 12, 2005.
Ziółkowska-Boehm Aleksandra, Posiadanie ziemi, part 1, TERAZ (Philadephia), December, 2000; Sprzeczności, part 2, TERAZ (Philadelphia), January, 2001.
Ziółkowska-Boehm Aleksandra, Prawdziwych Indian prosimy o powstanie, PRZEGLĄD POWSZECHNY Nr 11, 2004.
Ziółkowska-Boehm Aleksandra, Przemieszczanie się Indian Szejenów i Lenape, BORUSSIA 24/25 2001.
Ziółkowska-Boehm Aleksandra, Rozmowa z Rexem Allanem Smithem, NOWY DZIENNIK–WEEKEND, (New York), April 22, 2006.

Ziółkowska-Boehm Aleksandra, Smutek rezerwatów, RZECZPOSPOLITA, July 28–29, 2007.
Ziółkowska-Boehm Aleksandra, Szejeni- rasa smutku, TERAZ (Philadelphia), April, 2003.

Aleksandra Ziolkowska-Boehm

Index

317

Aleksandra Ziolkowska-Boehm

322

ABOUT THE AUTHOR

Aleksandra Ziolkowska-Boehm, Ph.D. in Humanities from Warsaw University, was born and educated in Poland, began her writing career as an assistant to Melchior Wankowicz, a prominent Polish writer. His status in Poland might be compared to that of Ernest Hemingway in the English-speaking world. For her help and research with his latest book Wankowicz not only dedicated his last book to her but also bequeathed her his archives.

Aleksandra is the author of many books, some of them bestsellers in Poland, five of her books had two or three editions. One was chosen as the book of the week, the other was awarded the best book of 2006 by the Polish Writers Union Abroad in London. Aleksandra is recipient of numerous literary awards, scholarships or fellowships. Awarded a fellowship in Literature – Creative Nonfiction discipline by the Delaware Division of the Arts in 2006, a Fulbright scholar in 2006-2007. She is a member of the Society of Polish Writers, Warsaw, the PEN American Center, New York, the Kosciuszko Foundation and PIASA Institute– New York, the Union of Polish Writers Abroad, London and the Fulbright Association, Washington DC. Her works have included historical biographies and autobiographical stories of her peripatetic life.

Since April 1990, she has lived permanently in Delaware. In 2010, her non-fiction book about travels with her cat is scheduled to be published by a mid-western university press and also her history book about a Polish partisan by Military History Press.

The great niece of Korczak Ziolkowski, sculptor of the Crazy Horse mountain carving in the Black Hills of South Dakota, the author was inspired by him in this writing project.